FLYING
AMERICAN
COMBAT AIRCRAFT

FLYING AMERICAN COMBAT AIRCRAFT

COMBAT AIRCRAFT

The Cold War

Edited by Robin Higham

STACKPOLE
BOOKS

Published in 2005 by
STACKPOLE BOOKS
5067 Ritter Road
Mechanicsburg, PA 17055
www.stackpolebooks.com

Printed in the United States of America

10 9 8 7 6 5 4 3 2 1

FIRST EDITION

Library of Congress Cataloging-in-Publication Data

Flying American combat aircraft : the Cold War / edited by Robin Higham.— 1st ed.
    p. cm. — (Stackpole Military history series)
  "This book contains articles selected from the three volumes of Flying combat air-
craft of the USAAF-USAF".
  Includes index.
  ISBN-13: 978-0-8117-3238-3
  ISBN-10: 0-8117-3238-X
  1. Airplanes, Military—United States—History—20th century. 2. Air pilots, Military—
United States—Biography. 3. Airplanes—Handling characteristics—United States. 4.
Cold War. I. Higham, Robin D. S. II. Flying combat aircraft of the USAAF-USAF. III.
Series.
  UG1243.F5 2005
  358.4'183'097309045—dc22
                       2005006976

Table of Contents

Introduction

In this second volume of *Flying American Combat Aircraft*, the reader is taken from the pioneer piston-engined era of 1903-1953 into the subsequent jet age, from speeds measured in miles an hour to those indicated by Mach numbers related to the speed of sound.

The transitional period from 1944 when jets first flew on operations to 1965, when the United States Air Force became predominantly a jet force, saw both useful piston-engined machines—such as the A-1 Skyraider and the C-47 "Gooney Bird"—still operational, but also hybrids such as the B-36 Peacemaker with both piston-engines and jets.

Pilots had to learn that the jet required more forethought and planning and needed a longer take-off run, but once airborne and cleaned up, its climb was spectacular, its altitude greater, and the distance covered much more than in a piston-engined machine. On the other hand, its fuel consumption at lower altitudes was voracious, and the decision to land had to be more carefully planned, as the options were more limited. On the whole, jets compelled a greater situational awareness.

However, as dog-fighting speeds are relative, the basic principles remained the same although turned circles increased considerably.

Also to be taken into account were the growth and sophistication of electronics—notably radar—and missiles, as well as combat-closing speeds. Decisions have to be automatic or automated and can involve targets literally over the horizon.

Moreover, because of the cost of jet operations, much training is now carried out in simulators on the ground which can replicate almost all flight situations including combat.

As the twentieth century passed, the cost of airframes, engines, and equipment rose dramatically, while speeds and ranges were part of an equation that included economics. One result has been the gradual evolution and improvement of aircraft such as the F-16 so that the newer twenty-first-century models are twice as powerful as the original 1970s version. Another option has been to gut the airframe and then to re-engine it and fit a complete new suite of electronics for navigation, detection, defense, and offense.

Such work means that on the one hand pilots accumulate many more hours on type than they did in piston-engined aircraft, but that they have also continually to be trained up to newer standards not so much to fly the machine, but to be capable of operating it to its fullest.

The transition from piston-engined to jet aircraft can also be seen in the growth of weights and abilities, as well as in labor-saving. For instance, the F-105 of the 1960s traveled at nine times the speed of the B-17, carried three times the bomb load (which it delivered far more accurately), and weighed 10,000 pounds less—but used only one or two crew versus the World War II heavy bomber's crew of thirteen.

The aircraft featured here fought in the Korean War (1950–1953), the Vietnam War (1962–1972), the First Gulf War (1991), and the Iraq War (2003)—as well as being employed in such lesser conflicts as Afghanistan (2001) and elsewhere around the globe, sometimes vicariously.

The aircraft described here by the pilots who flew them represent the continuity and change of the Cold War half of the twentieth century. Many of them are likely to be operating well into the twenty-first century, when airframes may well become twice as old as the pilots who fly them.

Robin Higham
Manhattan, Kansas
January 2005

Flying the F-15 Eagle

George W. Hawks, Jr.

My first impression of the F-15 Eagle, as it sat on the ramp at Luke AFB, Arizona, was the large size of the fighter. All of my previous fighter experience had been in the F-4, another McDonnell Douglas aircraft, which seemed to be dwarfed by the Eagle. But the F-15 is only 5 feet 6 inches longer and has a wingspan that is 4 feet, 5 inches wider than the F-4C so this impression of large size is far out of proportion to the actual statistics. I attribute this massive appearance to the high mounted wing, the large fuselage required to hold the two Pratt and Whitney F-100 Turbofan engines, the two vertical tails that tower 18 feet, 8 inches above the ground, and the long landing gear upon which the Eagle perches.

The first flights in the F-15, as in any fighter check-out program, are to familiarize the pilot with the handling idiosyncrasies, and to develop a feeling for the aircraft before flying intercept and air-to-air combat rides. Therefore, the first few rides I flew were to "learn how to fly the bird." Later, I would learn how to use it effectively.

The first step in any ride is to preflight the aircraft. The walk-around of the F-15 starts at the nose gear and proceeds clockwise around the machine. The inspection is divided into four areas: nose, center fuselage and wing, aft fuselage, and underside of the fuselage. There is quite a difference in the preflight of the F-15 compared to the F-4. Unlike the F-4, there is no need to bend and crawl to check all of the required items, since the F-15 is not a low-wing aircraft like the F-4. The F-4 always seemed to leak oil and hydraulic fluid. Invariably, a pilot would emerge from the preflight covered with grease and hydraulic fluid. You don't get as greasy preflighting the F-15. On the walk-

---

Opposite page: An F-15 in flight.

1

around, the aircraft is checked to insure that all panels are secure, tires in good shape, the tail hook is locked full up, no leaks are evident, and the exterior of the airplane appears ready for flight.

Entry to the cockpit is via a special ladder which hooks over the canopy rail or by the integral retractable stepladder which can be extended from the fuselage. The special ladder is always used when at home station, because it is more stable. The integral ladder is used when at a base that does not have the special over the canopy-rail ladder. The integral ladder was quite flimsy in some of the early aircraft and offered little security when mounting up. A recent beefing up of the integral ladder has helped.

The preflight continues after climbing the ladder. Before entering the cockpit, a check is made of the IC-7 ejection seat. This is a fully automatic rocket system which will jettison the canopy followed shortly by firing of the rocket catapult which ejects the pilot. This seat is capable of safely ejecting the pilot at zero altitude with zero airspeed. To preflight the seat, the mechanical ejection seat ground safety handle is checked in the down and locked position. This handle is called the "head knocker" as it extends from the head rest of the seat. With the pilot strapped into the seat, it will hit him in the head, notifying him in the usual manner for attracting fighter pilots' attention, that the seat is in a safe condition.

Continuing the preflight, the firing control cable is checked for proper attachment to the initiator and all external safety pins are checked removed. The seat survival kit control is set in the automatic mode to deploy the life raft and survival kit four seconds after the main parachute deploys. The emergency harness release handle, used to manually separate from the ejection seat if it fails to function automatically, is checked to insure that its initiation cable is properly installed.

The entire F-15 fleet at Luke AFB is equipped with the IC-7 ejection seat, the same one installed in the A-7 aircraft. Newer F-15 aircraft are equipped with the ACES II seat, and soon all F-15s will be retrofitted with the ACES II. The ACES II ejection seat is also a fully automatic catapult rocket system but it has three ejection modes which are automatically selected, opposed to the single mode for the IC-7 seat. The first mode is low-speed, in which the parachute is deployed almost immediately after the seat departs the aircraft. The second mode is high-speed, in which a drogue chute is deployed to slow the seat followed by deployment of the personal parachute. Mode three is a high-altitude mode in which the sequence of events is the same as in mode two, except that man-seat separation and deployment of the pilot's parachute is delayed until the man and seat reach a safe altitude. The ACES II seat incorporates two side handles to initiate ejection as opposed to the between-the-legs handle on the IC-7 seat.

Once the seat has been inspected, an easy step down is made to stand on the ejection seat cushion and look over the top of the aircraft. I survey the top of the aircraft for missing panels or wrinkled skin. The impression of large size is reinforced while looking back over the top of the F-15, down on the two huge humps that house the engines and afterburners and up at the twin tails that rise well above the raised canopy. The top of the F-15 appears to be all lift-generating surface.

F-15 strap-in procedures are faster than in the F-4, as there are no leg restraint straps to route and buckle to each leg. The harness worn by the pilot is identical to that worn by F-4, A-7, A-10, and F-16 pilots. Like those aircraft, the F-15 has the survival seat kit and parachute as an integral part of the ejection seat. The pilot attaches these items to his harness and straps the lap belt snug to complete strap-in. The anti-G suit is hooked into the aircraft connector and then cockpit pre-start checks are begun. These follow the usual Air Force procedure of left to right around the cockpit. After checking that all cockpit switches are set, the cockpit pressurization control is set to insure that the cockpit will be air conditioned and pressurized after engine start. All personal maps and equipment are stowed in the cavernous map case located on the right console, and then the major items in the cockpit are rechecked using the VERIFY checklist:

1. Emergency air-refuel handle—DOWN
2. Throttles—OFF
3. Formation lights—OFF
4. Emergency landing-gear handle—IN
5. Hook—UP
6. Landing-gear handle—DOWN
7. Master arm switch—SAFE
8. Emergency brake/steering handle—IN
9. Emergency vent handle—IN & VERTICAL (this is the cockpit pressurization dump valve handle)
10. Electronic Engine Control (EEC) switches—ON
11. Anti-ice switches—OFF
12. Avionics—OFF

The engine start introduces the new Eagle pilot to the convenience and combat practicality of a self-contained start capability. This is done by using the F-15's Jet Fuel Starter or JFS, a small self-contained turbine engine which burns aircraft fuel. It is started by placing the JFS switch ON and pulling the

JFS handle, on the right front panel, causing one of two hydraulic accumulator bottles to discharge and spin the JFS up to speed while the JFS generator provides ignition. Once the JFS is started and stabilized in idle, a green light on the engine control panel illuminates. This indicates that the JFS is running and ready to be engaged to the main aircraft engines. The entire starting procedure is monitored on the cockpit gauges; but, once familiar with the sounds of the start, the aural indications provide a good cross check that the start is progressing normally. The finger lift on the right throttle is raised to engage the JFS to the right engine. There is a decrease in the whine of the JFS, the airframe vibrates and rumbles, and then the whine of the JFS increases as the F-100 engine begins to rotate.

At about 14 to 17 percent rpm the emergency generator comes on line, and for the first time powers the rpm and Fan Turbine Inlet Temperature (FTIT) gauges. (All other instruments are unpowered until the first main generator comes on line.) At 18 percent rpm the right throttle is placed in idle and fuel is provided for start. At about 25 to 27 percent rpm, a deep muffled "whump" is heard as the fuel ignites and the rpm rises at a faster rate. At 42 to 45 percent rpm the right main generator comes on line and energizes all aircraft electrical busses (circuits). At this point, the right engine intake ramp bangs to its full down position. The JFS disengages from the engine around 50 to 53 percent rpm after rising to an ear-piercing whine. The engine rpm accelerates to 64 to 70 percent in idle.

The right engine is started first so that the right utility hydraulic pump can be checked for proper operation. As in the F-4, the utility hydraulic system is pressurized to 3,000 ±250 psi by a hydraulic pump on each engine. To prevent the utility hydraulic pumps from resonating, check valves with different operating pressures are installed on the pump output lines. This causes the right engine utility hydraulic pump to operate at a pressure of 2,775 psi while the left pump puts out 3,000 psi. Once the right engine is running, the utility hydraulic pressure gauge is checked to insure that it reads 2,775 psi plus-or-minus 225 psi. After the left engine is running, this gauge will read 3,000 plus-or-minus 250 psi. If the left engine were started first, there would be no way to tell if the right utility hydraulic pump was putting out the proper pressure.

The left engine is started using the same procedure as that used to start the right. Once the left engine reaches 50 to 53 percent rpm, the JFS automatically shuts down. All systems are then turned on and checked for proper operation. To test them there is a comprehensive built-in tester or BITS system. The Built In Test (BIT) panel is located on the left console. A particular system

---

Opposite page: An F-15 performing maneuvers.

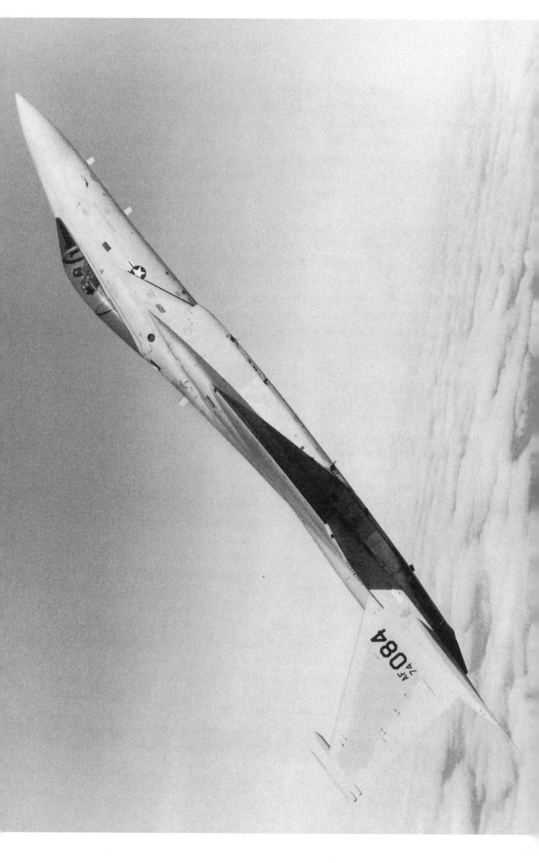

is selected by rotating the BIT knob to that system. The BIT test button is then depressed and an automatic check of the selected system is conducted. If the system is OK, the respective BIT system light on the BIT test panel will flash as the test is carried out and then will extinguish at test completion. If the system is defective, the BIT light will remain illuminated after the test is finished. This allows the pilot to determine his weapons system capability prior to takeoff. If a system is defective, many problems can be corrected by having the ground crew change a defective Line Replaceable Unit (LRU or black box). This is done by shutting down the engine on the side of the aircraft containing that LRU. The other engine remains running and powers all other systems. The easy access panels in the nose of the aircraft can be opened and the defective LRU removed and replaced. The system can be turned on and checked with just the one engine running. If the problem is cured, as it often is, the easy access panels are closed and the engine is restarted using the JFS. This capability has saved many ground aborts or cancelled missions and enhances the combat capability of the F-15.

The F-15 is equipped with an Inertial Navigation System (INS) which has the capability to store twelve destinations. This provides the capability to aid in navigating to targets and in returning to base. As in all fighters though, the old faithful dead-reckoning navigation and a route map is still relied upon to make sure you get to the proper place at the proper time. Before the INS can be used as a navigation aid, it must be "aligned" prior to flight.

An INS has been described as a "system that will tell you where you are if you tell it where it is!" The alignment procedure is done before each flight and is the point at which the pilot tells "the INS where it is." The system is turned on, local magnetic variation and present position are entered into the INS, and it automatically aligns itself with the local magnetic field.

There are three types of alignment used on the F-15. The full gyro-compass alignment takes about 9 1/2 minutes and provides greatest system accuracy. The Best Available True Heading (BATH) alignment takes about 3 1/2 minutes, but is less accurate. The Stored (STOR) alignment is accomplished by obtaining a full gyro-compass alignment, then turning off the INS. After removing electrical power from the aircraft, the INS mode knob is placed in the STOR position. When the aircraft is started and the first main generator comes on line, the INS begins to align itself. In 3 1/2 minutes the STOR alignment will be complete and provide accuracy near that of a full gyro-compass alignment. The full gyro-compass alignment is used on the majority of missions when plenty of time is available and accuracy is needed. The BATH alignment is used when time is short or excellent accuracy is not required.

The STOR alignment is used when the aircraft is on alert and when both time and accuracy constraints must be met. Alert aircraft must be airborne in minimum time from the time the "SCRAMBLE" order is received, and the INS must be accurate to perform the Air Defense mission. No matter which alignment is used, once the INS mode selector knob is placed in the INS position, the Eagle is ready to taxi.

Taxiing requires a different turn lead point from that used on the FA because of the nosewheel location behind the pilot. With the aircraft heavily loaded, a slight addition of power is required to get rolling. Heavily laden, the aircraft must be slowed well below 10 knots ground speed before turning or the main gear tires can be damaged. Using the normal training configuration at Luke AFB the throttles only have to be moved a little above idle to get rolling. Care must be exercised to monitor taxi speed and not allow it to get too high.

The idle thrust of the two F-100 engines is substantially higher than that of the F-4 engines. This high residual thrust will push the aircraft along the ground at well above 50 knots unless wheel braking is used to maintain a more moderate speed of 20 to 25 knots. The aircraft does not wallow along, as did the F-4. It just rolls smoothly out of parking to the end of the runway. The taxi checks are the standard: brakes, nosegear steering, and flight instruments.

At the end of the runway, our maintenance troops quickly check for cut tires or leaks to complete the before-takeoff checks. The radar is turned to the operate mode, parachute harness checked, ejection seat checked armed, flight controls checked, trim and flaps set, canopy checked down and locked, and the aircraft taxied onto the runway for engine runup.

The engines are individually run up to military (MIL) power which gives an rpm of about 90 to 92 percent. The Fan Turbine Inlet Temperature (FTIT) is checked and is normally around 900° or slightly higher. Oil pressure, fuel flow, and nozzle position are checked for proper indications. Once the runup is complete, the Eagle is ready to enter its element—flight.

Takeoff speed and distance will vary, depending on the configuration and gross weight of the aircraft, as in any fighter. The normal configuration at Luke AFB is two wing pylons, 1 centerline external fuel tank, 1 AIM 9 Sidewinder missile, full fuel of about 15,000 lbs., and 900 rounds of 20 mm ammunition. This gives a takeoff gross weight of around 44,000 1bs., allowing use of one of two types of takeoff—the normal takeoff, on MIL power without the afterburner (AB), or the AB takeoff.

The MIL power takeoff is accomplished by running the engines up to 80 percent rpm, then releasing the brakes and smoothly advancing the throttles to MIL power (90–92 percent). There is a firm pressure in your back, and the aircraft quickly accelerates to normal rotation speed of about 120 Knots Calibrated Airspeed (KCAS). Liftoff comes about 2,500 to 3,500 feet down the runway, depending on runway temperature and altitude. This is about the same distance I used in the F-4 with two external fuel tanks and full AB at a gross weight of about 46,000 lbs. It is not necessary to compute takeoff roll unless it will exceed one-half of the usable runway, and, consequently, it is seldom figured. If a MIL power takeoff will give a long takeoff roll, due to high temperature or a short runway, then an AB takeoff can be made to get the machine into the air quickly. I do calculate a takeoff distance at bases other than home station, just to be conservative. However, in only one case did I ever get a takeoff roll of one-half the usable runway length for a MIL power takeoff, and that was at a base with a 7,000-foot-long strip on a warm day. By using the AB I was comfortably airborne well before half the runway was used.

The MIL power takeoff is a comfortable acceleration and liftoff, but that experienced during a full AB takeoff is eyewatering. The only difference in procedure is after brake release, the throttles are placed in the AB range and pushed smoothly to full AB. The F-15 has a soft AB light, but each of the five AB stages can be felt as they light, providing a solid kick in the rear. Acceleration is tremendous, and nosewheel liftoff speed is reached in a matter of seconds, followed by takeoff speed. The ground run is half that used in the MIL power takeoff, or about 1,500 feet. Quick reaction is required to get the gear and flaps up before the gear limit speed of 250 knots (external tank onboard) is exceeded. Before the end of the 10,000-foot runway at Luke AFB, the F-15 has 350 KCAS and pitch is increased to 40–45° for the climb. This pitch attitude is required to maintain climb airspeed of 350 KCAS until .95 Mach can be intercepted. If a lower pitch attitude is held, the F-15 will quickly accelerate to supersonic speeds.

This climb profile will have the F-15 at 30,000 feet in 1 minute, 15 seconds. For comparison, an F-4C would take about 3 minutes, 20 seconds to reach the same altitude at a similar gross weight.

Once in flight, the F-15 enters a large operating envelope. It can fly up to 800 KCAS or 2.33 Mach. One minute transients up to 2.5 Mach are allowed. Although this is the limit for the basic aircraft, these areas are seldom explored, for with external stores attached a lower limit is normally placed on that store. Furthermore, it is not necessary to go this fast to perform the air-to-air combat mission effectively.

Once airborne, for the first time in the F-15 I noticed, with a great deal of satisfaction, that a fighter aircraft again had been built with that most valuable

Opposite page: The 185 maintenance access doors and panels of the F-15 stand open for inspection.

of characteristics, visibility out of the cockpit. You can look back over your shoulder and actually check the six o'clock position by looking between the twin tails. In a 60° bank turn it is possible to look over the canopy rail and check the belly area for bandits. This was one of the first of many pleasant surprises for me during my checkout.

Another surprise was the effective cockpit pressurization and air conditioning system, called the Environmental Control System (ECS) in the F-15. This system provides conditioned engine bleed air to the cockpit and avionics for pressurization and cooling. It also runs the windshield anti-fog and anti-ice, the anti-G suit pressure, canopy seal, and fuel pressurization systems. The ECS system is controlled by the emergency vent control handle (emergency dump valve), the air source knob, and the temperature control switch (both located on the temperature control panel). With the vent control handle full in, the temperature control switch in auto or manual, and the air source knob in the position to supply bleed air from the engines, the system operates automatically. During climbout, passing 8,000 ft. MSL, the cockpit is pressurized. It maintains a cabin altitude of 8,000 ft. until the aircraft reaches an altitude of about 24,000 ft. MSL. Then the cabin altitude increases as the ECS system maintains a 5 psi pressure differential between cockpit pressure and ambient air pressure. The beauty of this system is that it keeps the pilot more comfortable than any previous fighter aircraft pressurization and cooling system. The F-4 air conditioning system was useless during hot weather until airborne. The F-15 ECS system keeps you comfortable at all times, even on the ground.

Most modern fighters are pressurized to keep the pilot in an environment that will minimize hypoxia and evolved gas problems (such as the bends). Air Force regulations, based on sound medical rationale, prohibit unpressurized aircraft from exceeding 25,000 ft. MSL. The alternative to pressurizing fighter aircraft is that the pilot would have to wear a pressure suit (very cumbersome and restrictive) or be unable to use the full operational envelope of modern fighters. The F-15 system continues to improve the state of the art in fighter pressurization and cooling.

On early flights in the F-15 a series of maneuvers is carried out to familiarize the pilot with the handling characteristics of the aircraft, with little time devoted to using the weapons systems. During these early rides I found the F-15 easy to fly and very forgiving. The maneuvers flown to show these points varied from slow flight, to high G turns and aerobatics.

During the slow flight demonstration I learned to appreciate the forgiving nature of the F-15 and its handling ability. Slow flight is entered by decreasing airspeed and allowing the Angle of Attack (AOA) to increase. Angle of Attack is shown on a round dial on the instrument panel. This gauge is calibrated in arbitrary units from 0 to 45 units. For comparison, the F-4 AOA gauge was calibrated from 0 to 30 units. While decreasing airspeed, the AOA increases. Around 20 units AOA there is some buffet, which grows slightly in intensity as AOA increases.

The F-15 can be flown easily at 30 units AOA using aileron and rudder. This is quite different from the F-4. Above 23 to 25 units in the F-4 the nose would rise slightly, slice or yaw across the horizon, and then abruptly depart controlled flight by rolling opposite the stick input. If controls were not neutralized, a spin would ensue. The F-15 does not have this problem. I have flown it at 45 units AOA with the aircraft under total control. Above 35 units the aileron is not very effective for banking or rolling the aircraft, but rudder rolls can be done with little effort. In the early F-15s there was a warning tone that came on at 30 units AOA to warn of high AOA, with the gear up and locked. On later aircraft, and via a retrofit modification, this feature has been removed. This tone still comes on around 30 units if the gear is down to indicate a high AOA situation in the landing pattern. The 30 unit AOA tone, with the gear up, has been replaced by a yaw rate warning tone. This tone comes on if the aircraft yaw rate exceeds 30 degrees per second. It increases in frequency until a yaw rate of 60 degrees per second is reached, at which point it stabilizes. This feature is to warn the pilot of out of control/spin conditions. But though this feature is available, due to the spin resistant nature of the F-15, it is not often heard.

While doing the slow flight exercises I first noticed the two intake ramps constantly move up and down in my peripheral vision. This movement is controlled by separate air inlet controllers for each intake so that air is provided to the face of the fan at optimum subsonic flow. As pitch and roll inputs are made to the flight controls, the ramps reposition smoothly and quickly. Though a bit distracting initially, I soon learned not to notice these movements. After the slow flight demonstration, a series of aerobatic maneuvers were flown.

Two of the more impressive of these maneuvers were the AB loop and the idle power loop. The AB loop is initiated at 250 KCAS using a 20 to 25 unit AOA pullup. This pull is maintained until the aircraft is flat on its back with the nose coming back through the horizon at about 100 KCAS. Total control is still available in this attitude and at this airspeed. Accelerating out of the bottom of this loop, airspeed is allowed to build to 500 KCAS and the throttles are placed in idle. At this point a second loop is performed with the throttles in idle for the entire maneuver. This is possible due to the clean aerodynamic profile of the aircraft and the high-lift wing with no artificial lift-inducing devices, such as slats or maneuvering flaps. For an ex-F-4 pilot, these two maneuvers are unbelievable.

The speedbrake on the F-15 rises from the center of the wing, on top of the fuselage, and is huge. I was shown how effective it is to slow the aircraft by establishing 500 to 550 KCAS, placing the throttles in idle, and extending the speedbrake. I was abruptly thrown forward in my shoulder harness and the airspeed decreased rapidly. When fully extended, the speedbrake sticks up at a 45-degree angle and disrupts the airflow over the twin tails so that you can see the tails vibrate back and forth in the rearview mirrors mounted on the canopy. Later I found this effective speedbrake useful in air-to-air engagements to slow down from very high speed to make a turn. By slowing from supersonic speed to subsonic, the turn radius can be decreased and you can be back into a fight quicker or outturn an adversary. The turning ability of the F-15 is phenomenal and is explored in the early rides.

The ability to turn while sustaining or gaining energy is demonstrated by a series of high G turns performed at various airspeeds and altitudes. Entering a turn in the 350 to 450 KCAS range in MIL power and again in AB, various G loadings are tried. This is to discover the power, airspeed, and G conditions that the aircraft can sustain. With 450 KCAS, in full AB, I quickly found I could hold 6 Gs and accelerate. The added airspeed could be traded for altitude or more G could be pulled, up to the airframe limit of 7.33 Gs at a gross weight of 37,400 lbs. This exercise is flown to develop a "seat of the pants" feel for the various G loadings and to develop a data bank to be used in air-to-air combat. As airspeed increases, more Gs can be pulled, but turn radius increases. As airspeed decreases, turn radius decreases, but the aircraft can get behind the power curve and will dissipate airspeed if the G loading is maintained.

The F-15 has the advantage of being able to sustain Gs at airspeeds other aircraft cannot. This is possible because of the two F-100 engines producing so much thrust (25,000 lbs. each in AB, static sea level thrust), which gives the Eagle a thrust-to-weight ratio superior to most fighters in the world. The high G turning demonstration was my first clue that the aircraft now entering the fighter inventory can surpass the physical limits of the fighter pilot, and it increased my respect for the F-15. The F-15 can literally pull 6 to 7 Gs until it runs out of gas. These maneuvers comprised the familiarization of handling characteristics on the initial few rides.

I discovered that loops, Cuban eights, Immelman turns, and cloverleafs can be accomplished in half the airspace used by the F-4, with a feeling of total

Opposite page: A formation of F-15s.

control. Later I would discover that if the nose is allowed to remain straight up and the airspeed goes to zero, not to worry! The aircraft will slide backward on its tail for a moment, then swap ends. Once the nose is down, airspeed quickly increases and the machine is flying. This is a comforting characteristic, when compared to the departures and spins experienced in the F-4, induced by an overeager student. If the F-15 ever feels like it doesn't want to do what is requested by the flight controls, merely neutralizing controls for a moment brings immediate recovery. Then, the maneuver can be continued.

Departing the aerobatic area for recovery and landing, I had time to study the cockpit instruments and the Heads Up Display (HUD). The cockpit flight instruments are the more or less standard flight director grouping: Attitude Director Indicator (ADI), Horizontal Situation Indicator (HSI or compass card with TACAN course deviation indicator), Altimeter with a drumand-counter readout (as opposed to the old three-pointer altimeters), and an instantaneous Vertical Velocity Indicator (VVI). All of the engine instruments are the round gauge type as opposed to the vertical tape instruments used in the F-105. The HUD provides navigation, airspeed, altitude, heading, and attitude information. With the gear and flaps down, the HUD also presents AOA. Though initially confused by all of the displays on the HUD, I soon found that I could use the information provided to advantage. I now use the HUD as another instrument and cross-check it with the round gauges in the cockpit.

The F-15 has the capability to fly Instrument Landing System (ILS), TACAN, Automatic Direction Finding (ADF), or Ground Controlled Radar Approaches (GCA). The standard approach for the first ride at Luke is a TACAN penetration to a visual initial for a 360° overhead traffic pattern. The F-15 is flown down initial at 325 KCAS and the 180° break turn to the downwind leg is made using 3 to 4 Gs, with airspeed decreasing throughout the turn. Care is required that too tight a pitchout to downwind not be made. At 325 KCAS and the normal gross weight, at recovery the F-15 can pull its airframe G limit of 7.33. If this amount of G was used, the turn to downwind would have such a small radius that the aircraft could be rolled out over the outside edge of the runway. From this position, a safe base to final turn cannot be made. On the normal downwind leg, about a quarter to a half of a mile from the edge of the runway, the aircraft is rolled out wings level, with the airspeed around 220 KCAS. The gear and flaps are placed down, hydraulic pressures checked, gear down and locked lights checked, and the tower radioed that the gear is down and checked. The base to final turn is made beginning at 180 KCAS with airspeed decreasing throughout the turn to onspeed AOA of 20 to 22 units. This is about 142 KCAS for a 35,000-lb. gross weight airplane and decreases as gross weight decreases. I do not use the speedbrake during the base to final turn or on final, as many do, as it causes the airframe to buffet and mask the normal nibble of a buffet at 20 units AOA. This nibble gives a good seat of the pants feeling for how the pattern is going.

The F-15 must be flown down to the runway and flared to make a smooth landing with touchdown coming around 110 to 120 KCAS. This is quite a departure from the controlled crash landings of F-4 days when onspeed AOA of 19.2 units was established and held until the aircraft impacted the runway. Once on the runway, the pitch attitude is increased to 12–13 degrees nose up on the HUD pitch scale (also called the pitch ladder) to aerobrake. Care must be taken not to rotate to greater than 15 degrees of pitch or the tail cones and exhaust nozzles will scrape the runway. At 80 KCAS the nose is lowered to the runway and the wheel brakes are used to stop. The F-15 does not have a drag chute nor reverse thrust like some European fighters, but the aerobraking maneuver and wheel brakes are more than adequate.

Post-flight checks consist of turning off equipment, running BIT checks on the radar, and checking the accuracy of the INS. Once complete, the engines are shut down. After dismounting, a quick postflight walk-around is made to be sure all parts onboard the aircraft at takeoff are still attached.

That is how the F-15 is flown on the first few flights to learn how the aircraft handles. However, the Eagle has claws, and employing them is the sole reason pilots are trained to fly this fighter.

I soon learned that the F-15 is an easy aircraft to fly but requires hard work to employ properly the radar and weapons systems to their fullest. This is so because of the vast amount of information available to the pilot to intercept and kill an airborne target. The avionics provides this information, and its capability surpasses the wildest dreams of any F-4 pilot.

The F-15 radar can be operated in a manual mode, with switches on the radar control panel designating radar scope range, azimuth sweep, and elevation bar scan. This requires that the pilot remove his left hand from the throttle to change a switch for a changing situation. The more convenient automatic mode lets the pilot use the controls on the two throttles and the flight control stick grip to change all parameters. This is invaluable in a dynamic air-to-air combat situation.

During close-in visual dogfights there are three automatic acquisition modes for the radar which can be selected by manipulating the auto-acquisition switch on the stick grip. This allows the pilot to maintain visual contact with the bandit and get a radar lock-on. A radar lock-on is desirable as it optimizes all weapons employment.

The human engineering designed into the F-15 cockpit and weapons systems makes employment of all weapons possible by a single pilot. Use of the cockpit switches requires practice, but once proficiency is gained, it is second nature. This is a must in air combat.

During air-to-air engagements, the turning ability and acceleration of the F-15 has proved invaluable. It has a tighter turn radius and can generate a greater turn rate (more degrees of rotation per second) than most aircraft in the world. This lets an F-15 pilot stay and fight with a bandit, if the tactical situation will allow, or accelerate away quickly. The acceleration and turning ability are far more important to an air superiority fighter than its maximum speed in a straight line. This designed-in capability for maneuverability allows F-15 pilots to out-turn, out-climb, and out-accelerate almost all adversaries. Those with comparable maneuverability can be disposed of using the all-aspect radar-missile capability or by properly employing tactics to hit, kill, and run.

The weapons available to the pilot are the AIM 7 Sparrow radar guided missile, the AIM 9 Sidewinder Infra-red guided missile, and the M-6120 mm Gatling Gun. The pilot selects the desired armament with a weapons select switch mounted upon the right throttle. This convenient location allows quick ordnance selection under all maneuvering conditions and is a vast improvement over the F-4 switch requirements of a few years ago.

Because of the foresight of some of our past and present leaders in the Tactical Air Forces, we, today, are able to exercise the full potential of our fighting machines during training. The F-15 is routinely employed in multi-bogey engagements, using many scenarios which have been experienced in previous conflicts and those anticipated in any future conflict. This environment, though tightly controlled with specific Rules of Engagement (ROE), lets the fighter pilot fully explore the full potential of his aircraft. It does little good to have the best air-to-air combat aircraft in the world unless the training is rigorous and demanding enough to allow the fighter pilots to learn how to fight with it.

A routine part of these missions is air-to-air refueling. The F-15 is extremely easy to air refuel as it has the air refueling receptacle mounted on the left forward shoulder, within sight of the pilot via the rear view mirror. The automatic trim feature on the flight controls negates the need to trim while fuel is onloaded. The large amount of thrust produced by the engines allows refueling above 30,000 ft. MSL, at high gross weights, without using afterburner. Although I always thought the F-4 was easy to refuel, I find the F-15 far surpasses it.

Opposite page: The armed underside of an F-15.

Without air refueling the F-15 still has long legs. The F-100 Turbofan engines burn very little fuel at higher altitudes. With three external fuel tanks installed, I have easily flown from Luke AFB, Arizona, to Langley AFB, Virginia, a distance of approximately 2,000 miles. Fuel flows are well under the F-4's old standard of 6,000 pounds per hour I used. Cruise speed is between .85 and .9 Mach, with a true airspeed of approximately 510 KTAS. Flying at altitudes above 40,000 feet, with ease, in the F-15 you are well above the majority of the bad weather, which gives smooth rides out of airline traffic.

The F-100 Turbofan engine has one quirk that can nip a pilot—it can stagnate. This is a condition in which a compressor stall, normally induced by selecting AB at very high altitude, high AOA, and low airspeed, can occur. This compressor stall then degrades to a stagnation. The stagnation has been described as a bubble of air inside the engine which continuously stalls out the internal blades of the engine. The stagnation is normally noted by a loud bang (compressor stall) followed by decreasing rpm and increasing FTIT. The engine must be shut down once a stagnation has developed and then be restarted. Airstarts of the engine are easy as there is continuous ignition to the engine with the throttle in idle or above. Although the stagnation problem has cropped up with this engine, I have never had one in over 700 hours of flying the F-15. If throttles are modulated carefully when in the high altitude-low airspeed regime, and AB is selected without throttle bursting, the stagnation can usually be avoided. Pratt and Whitney has made great strides at investigating and curing the conditions that cause this problem. These efforts have put us on the road to the stagnation being a problem of the past.

The F-15 is the ultimate fighter for a fighter pilot. It has excellent visibility, acceleration, maneuverability, and the most usable set of systems and weapons controls yet put in a fighter. I have never failed to get a thrill from flying the Eagle. It allows a pilot to have total confidence in its ability to jump into any fight and win. It has no hidden handling characteristics that can nip an unwary pilot at an inopportune moment. The recent Israeli air combat victories with the F-15 underscore the lethal ability of the aircraft in actual combat situations. I know of no pilot who has flown the F-15 that did not immediately love all of its features. If I go to combat again, I want it to be in the F-15—the finest fighter to ever fly.

Maj. George W. Hawks, Jr., began his fighter aviation career as an F-4E aircraft commander. He flew 299 combat missions over all areas of Southeast Asia. He has been a Flight Test Maintenance Officer and a Replacement Training Unit Instructor Pilot in the F-4E. He has flown the F-4C, D, E, and slatted E. He has over 700 hours in the F-15 and has spent three years as an Instructor Pilot at Luke AFB, AZ. He is presently attending Air Command and Staff College at Maxwell AFB, AL.

The B-52 Stratofortress

Col. Robert E. Vickers, USAF (Ret.)

On that cold and wintry day of December 17, 1903, it is vaguely wondered if Orville and Wilbur Wright could have even fantasized or much less ever imagined that their first powered flight in a dare-devil type heavier-than-air machine from Kill Devil Hills, North Carolina would usher in the dawn of quantum leaps in razor's edge aviation technologies which—a scant 50 years later—would give this Nation's military an incredibly complex, multi mission, intercontinental jet bomber weapon system such as the Boeing B-52, and its later variants? Or, could the U.S. Army Signal Corps some 4 years later on December 23, 1907—when it issued the first specification for a Wright Brother's military airplane—have ever dreamed that the later accelerated evolution in aviation advancements would justify this decision times-over by the mid-century's era wherein a high altitude military air combat vehicle, as the B-52, could fly non-stop, point-to-point, around the globe with air-to-air refuelings? And, that all of this state-of-the-art, which in ridiculous comparison, would vastly over-shadow the scant 120 feet distance at an altitude of 10 feet and 12 seconds flying time which Orville first achieved on aviation's hallmark date that blustery day at Kitty Hawk in 1903? Hardly conceivable as reality then.

Arguably, the many pilots and crews who literally have walked in the footprints of the Wright brothers over these many decades later, and those specifically who have flown and maintained the B-52 airplanes since the post-50 era through present day could readily describe this remarkably reliable jet bomber as perhaps the most indomitable and trustworthy "air warrior" of modern times for all heavy bomber combat operations—both strategic and tactical. Not only this exceptional aircraft be readily categorized as a 'legend

---

Opposite page: The Stratofortress in flight.

21

in its own time' and a true combat work horse, its longevity of being in the USAF's jet bomber force structure since the mid-50s doing its assigned tasks as well as its recurring adaptability in continuing to meet many hi-tech, global combat mission requirements currently and into the foreseeable future out to a forecasted airframe service lifetime to around the year 2025—collectively, represents an incredible endorsement of this great bomber's versatility an reliable performance factors in the modern ascendancy of Boeing aircraft products from the World War II B-17 "Flying Fortress" onward.

The latest "H" model of the B-52 series now is much older than most all present day pilots and aircrews who fly it. And, as big and formidable looking as this giant plane might appear, its docile and dependable flight characteristics, if flown professionally "by the book", are undoubtedly the most forgiving in ease across-the-board to fly and operate than any heavy bomber, ever. Since early inception it has been tabbed in wide aviation circles with the moniker— the BUFF, or the "Big Ugly Fat Fellow". And while there have been other nonprintable connotations of this nickname bantered about over the years as well, the B-52—for those who have flown it extensively in many mission situations—will always be held in highest regard and respect for its combat capability and accomplishments whatever it may be called—this author certainly included.

My first impression of flying in the early B-52 program, which began in mid-1957, would have to be mirrored in a flash back of time some 5 years prior beginning in 1952. It was on April 15th of this earlier year which marked the maiden flight test of Boeing's YB-52 Stratofortress bomber prototype from Seattle—and also my entry that Summer into flying Boeing's first operational multi-engine jet bomber aircraft, the six engine B-47 Stratojet. Essentially, the B-47 would become basically the predecessor to its later 'Big Brother'—the B-52. Then, I had just completed SAC's "triple headed monster" training requirement wherein at least one of the two pilots who were selected to fly any B-47 aircraft in any operational unit had to be dual rated also as a 'Aerial Observer Bombardier" (AOB), or simply, to have earned a Radar Navigator's (RN) flight rating. Ostensibly, the early thinking behind this SAC-levied requirement stemmed from the fact that since the B-47 had only a three-man crew, i.e., two pilots and one Radar Navigator, an emergency "backup" to the RN was needed in a worst-case setting, especially during a strategic weapons delivery scenario, should the latter become incapacitated and unable to perform navigation and bombing duties.

As an aside, it required one year's training to obtain this added RN rating, 6 months Navigation training at (then) Edington Field, Texas followed by another 6 months training in Radar Navigation and Bombing techniques at (then) Mather Air Force Base, California—and graduating with fully rated Radar Navigator wings. This required training early on to pilot a B-47, undoubtedly, cost untold USAF dollars for each individual to acquire this additional aircrew member rating. It was a proud achievement for the individual's involved—and the powers-that-be at the time felt it was an essential criterion. However, in latter assessment the "payoff" merits of this requirement in actual practice in terms of across-the-board B-47 aircrew operations over the years which followed appears to be a matter of conjecture. No such Pilot/RN requirement to fly the B-52 later was ever known to be levied in that program simply because: the B-52 crew complement had both a Navigator and a Radar Navigator). Following pilot transition in the B-47 at McConnell Air Force Base, Wichita, Kansas, my crew and I were assigned to a Strategic Reconnaissance Wing and stationed (then) at Lockbourne Air Force Base near Columbus, Ohio. My Wing, the 26th SRW, was equipped with the new reconnaissance (Recce) model of the Stratojet, the RB-47E. The Stratojet aircraft represented SAC's new generation of high performance, high altitude, swept-back wing jet Bomber and Recce airplanes. (The first prototype model of this plane was Boeing's YB-47 test flight on December 17, 1947 from Seattle).

Characteristically in first seeing and then later flying the B-47, one easily had to regard it as one of the most truly sleek, clean, trim and graceful aircraft of any USAF/USAAF bomber-type models ever built before. In piloting it, I always felt it was a "bomber pilot's—fighter plane" due to its speed and handling properties! One had to learn quickly the B-47's hi-tech, aerodynamic intricacies and these, while not 'tricky' or unsafe by any means—demanded detailed knowledge and full mastery about such matters as: wing flex and wing "warp" which at high indicated airspeed (IAS) near 425 knots resulted in an aerodynamic control situation called "aileron reversal"; flight "optimum" cruise altitudes for best fuel range and endurance at given gross weights; and (in pilot parlance) avoiding the "purple heart corner"—a possible in-flight situation wherein the high speed 'buffet' and the low speed 'stall' airspeed curve boundaries would virtually coincide at the apex of the flight envelope should the plane be flown considerably above charted altitudes for a given weight and recommended "optimum" flight level. These newly learned high altitude jet aircraft operation's flight parameters were diametrically different from any of those ever experienced before in reciprocating, non-jet, lower operating altitude aircraft of earlier times.

Flying the B-47 airplane was a challenge, but one easily mastered—provided the aircraft's operating instructions (the Dash One directive) and stated limitations were followed closely at all times by its crews. These latter criteria were essential to the backbone and core of the "professionalism" ingrained in

SAC's post-war training and operational programs for all crews and individuals. You, as a SAC aircrew member, acquired this level of performance; you lived by it day-by-day as you were expected to do; you took individual pride in being part of it; and if you could not perform, you would quickly become 'history' in a Cold War SAC unit, rightly and quickly. There was no room or place for a poor individual performer—it was unsafe for the person, their unit, and the high performance aircraft they were now being entrusted to fly. General Curtis LeMay, the early SAC Commander, in these times demanded this individual commitment of strict aircrew and aircraft disciplines in every organization for without such—the heralded SAC Motto/Shield, "Peace Is Our Profession" would have never been attainable during the troubling times faced during the early years of the Cold War challenges from the 50s and onward. The 'esprit de corps' generated within these early Strategic Air Command units as a result, and the pride of having belonged, still lingers even to this day in the feelings and hearts of those still about who can re-join once again at reunion times with former comrades.

The broad experience gained in flying the B-47 over a five-year span before entering the B-52 program in mid-1957 proved to be of incredible value later. In those five years, I was able to amass nearly 2,000 hours as a Pilot and Standardization Board Instructor Pilot in my RB-47 operational unit—thus gaining a treasure-trove of never-to-be-forgotten knowledge and capabilities in this new era of high altitude (and later, very low altitude as well), heavy jet, strategic bomber operations. Singularly significant among these newly experienced areas over these years which boded well in preparation for later B-52 flying was: exposures to maximum aircraft performance parameters, both at altitude, cruise and in take-off and landing techniques; high altitude weather phenomena such as "jet streams," CAT (Clear Air Turbulence); individual aircraft mid-air, and in-mass formation, refuelings (the latter often referred to as 'Mass Gas Gaggles' which some were during poor in-flight visibilities and air tanker maneuverings!); and, most important, learning and following the newly developed SAC Tactical Doctrine of standardized ground and in-flight procedures fitting all air operational circumstances and conditions to meet the ever serious challenges of the Cold War. This Tactical Doctrine was the "professional bible" of every unit, aircrew, and individual operating these new SAC weapons systems. Mission capability, combat readiness and assured success in mission performance demanded its strict adherence—and it worked.

In early 1957, my RB-47 aircrew and I were selected for an assignment to a newly forming B-52 "D" model unit in South Dakota which was converting over from the large, peacetime bomber, the Convair B-36 "Peacemaker". The unit we would go to was the 28th Bomb Wing stationed at Ellsworth Air Force Base near Rapid City after completing crew transition program training in the B-52 at Castle Air Force Base near Merced, California which was the "home" of the 93rd Bomb Wing, equipped also with the early B-52s, and possessing the on-station SAC training group, the 4017th CCTS (Combat Crew Training School). All pilots, aircrews and other individual crew members slated for B-52 units were required to complete this 4017th program. Accordingly, having 'cut our teeth' figuratively speaking during the prior five years in the RB-47, my crew and I looked forward with great anticipation to this assignment and being accorded an opportunity finally of "we can't wait to get in this big fellow".

The B-47's behemoth, new Big Brother, created an exciting impression for all of us! In the years following, we would never have any disappointments or misgivings whatsoever for this first impression. In a close up look-see of this great giant of a bomber, we readily noticed some interesting and most favorable aircraft configurations from an aircrew standpoint, as compared to the B-47 crew stations especially. On the aircraft's interior, some of these new arrangements included: a much larger and certainly more spacious upper flight deck area, which among other 'crew friendly niceties,' accommodated a wide, side-by-side pilot and co-pilot seating in the forward section (not an in-tandem arrangement as in the B-47 models where both pilots were not in direct visual contact with each other); an easy-to-interpret array of engine, flight instruments and fuel system controls across the pilots' wide front panel with the throttle control, etc., pedestal located between the seats and easily accessible to both pilots; a somewhat 'roomy' lower deck as one came up the forward entry hatch ladder into the Navigation station which provided for the Radar Navigator and (new crew member addition) Navigator seating side by side with all their respective scopes, dials, meters and controls directly before them including a celestial observation port above; the rear portion of the upper flight deck which now accommodated another new crew member station, the ECM (Electronic Countermeasures) Officer and his assorted switches and dials related to the aircraft's installed jamming equipment; another new crew member provision in the addition of a senior enlisted man Gunner who would take up his station encapsulated in the plane's pressurized tail cone compartment complete with a gun-laying radar tracking system tied into the 20-millimeter cannon, rear firing armament equipment (B-52 "D" models only). Other crew station arrangements observed were: 'jump seat' slightly to the rear and between the pilot seats to provide for an extra observer or pilot instructor; two bunk-type canvas beds on the mid-upper deck for brief crew member rest periods on extremely long flights; an in-flight oven where prepared in-flight TV type dinners could be served hot; and an extra observer's seating arrangement just behind the Navigation station on the lower deck—which seat of all ironies was the top of the chemical toilet should Mother Nature seriously call while airborne! Such were some the readily observed features of this new plane and the pleasant expectations of now having a total of three new crew members added which would bring the total to a crew of six persons for these early B-52 equipped units having models "A" through "D", the latter series which we would now fly.

Turning to the exterior of this new bird, a number of differences and innovative changes over the Stratojet were to be noted. First, the main landing gear setup was interesting. While the larger "Tip" gear on each wing tip section of the B-52 had a similar configuration and operation as that of the B-47, the main gear featured two sets of "trucks" for both fore and aft gear assemblies—i.e., two separate oleo compression struts with two dual wheels on each, both trucks running side-by-side, front and rear 'underneath the wider fuselage. The much heavier gross weights associated with this far larger bomber models (up to a possible 450,000 pounds maximum in the "D" and earlier) dictated this wider, dual gear arrangement. And not to be overlooked was the cleverly designed and certainly ingenious method of this main gear's retraction/extension system into/from the fuselage gear wells, fore and aft. For example, the electrically actuated- hydraulically operated individual gear trucks on retraction would turn and "curl" neatly up into the respective fore and aft wheel wells and stow, tucked away side-by-side, conserving fuselage space, as well as aerodynamic qualities in not having these massive, but necessary 'appendages' hang out and down for longer than possible in creating unwanted "drag", especially during take-offs where "cleaning up" the aircraft quickly with gear (and flap) retraction was an important flight factor. The Boeing engineers had come up with this unique and brilliant solution in the B-52, as opposed to that of the much smaller B-47's gear arrangement where one fore and one aft main gear truck retracted straightway up and into the fuselage wheel well. Aside from these newly configured features, there were others about this gigantic bomber which were readily seen. To name but few, these on close inspection were: the massive wing span of 185 feet with a 3000 gallon (18,500 pounds of fuel) tank, fully jettisonable, attached beneath each wing tip ("D" models on); the outer wing section 'flex' of some 19 feet upward once airborne such that the running lights mounted on the tip of the wing could then be seen from the cockpit—a factor not possible when the plane was sitting static on the ground; the extremely tall vertical tail section which appeared easily to exceed that of a two to three story building; and the new and innovative, movable (from cockpit trim control) horizontal stabilizer which looked much larger than the side of any barn, much less that of a barn door! This stabilizer comprised 'the major aspect of this big bomber's pitch control, as opposed to a primary 'elevator' control system customarily found on all previous large aircraft. While the B-52 had a small elevator involved with this large horizontal stabilizer arrangement, it played little part in pitch control of the plane if the stabilizer was not "trimmed" properly for the flight regime being flown. Stabilizer operation was a critical part of the B-52's flying behavior and was directly associated with the aircraft's "trim" in all flight modes. More elaboration on this feature will be covered later.

Finally, the eight (8) large Pratt & Whitney J-57 turbo-jet engine power plants, arranged in four separate pods, two on either wing, rounded out the key features surrounding this new bomber we were about to fly. The advertised total of 96,000 pounds of thrust (roughly equal to total 'horsepower') which these engines developed at take-off, military rated thrust (MRT) settings held an awesome capability. And the four (4) big alternators, which powered the ship's entire electrical system, reportedly, had the output sufficient to power up a city of 30,000–35,000 population on an average day's usage! These units were driven by another unique design feature—the engine's hot 'bleed air' system which literally took 12th stage jet engine compressor air and piped it into the fuselage through a manifold arrangement running down each inside portion of the plane. Each side was protected by an 'interconnect' shut-off valve in the cockpit and manually controlled in order to 'isolate' each manifold one from the other, except during ground operation where air bleed air ran throughout the plane until all engines were started, and the four alternators were 'on the line'. This interconnect feature provided emergency protection for the plane's electrical system during all other operations in case one side of this pneumatic air piping arrangement became damaged causing possible alternator failures on one side. Two alternators could handle the ship's essential, emergency conservation needs in the latter case, if need be.

One other new technical feature on this plane we were about to fly was also most unique in design as no other aircraft had before. It was the wing mounted "spoiler system" which served two primary purposes: to 'roll' the ship into turns, right or left, based on control column inputs; and to function as 'air brakes' when the manually operated air brake lever on the throttle quadrant was placed in various detents in order to create degrees of drag—thus aiding in slowing the airplane down and avoid a high build up of airspeeds, especially during high rates of descent. For turning the plane, the spoilers were like 'fingers' which rose up on the inner section of each wing when demanded by the pilot's deflection of the control column to begin a turn, left or right—thus, spoiling the lift on the respective wing resulting in a

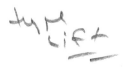

controlled, corresponding 'roll' in one direction or the other. This feature can be seen in today's commercial air fleets as one looks out on the wings, particularly during turns and during descents from higher altitudes. These new so-called 'wrinkles' for controlling the aircraft, both in pitch up/down and for turning, were somewhat radical departures from prior bomber designs—the latter having ailerons on the wings for turning, and elevators on the horizontal stabilizer(s) for climb and descent.

Notwithstanding, the B-52 featured both ailerons and elevators; however, both played smaller parts in actual lateral and vertical control of the plane's axis. In the instance of the elevator which was mounted on the after portion of the big slab and moveable horizontal stabilizer, proper "trim" of this stabilizer for the mode of flight was absolutely essential in order for this elevator to be effective in making all required corrections desired in pitch and roll of the plane. The stabilizer was a massive "trim tab" in itself as all pilots would appreciate. The small ailerons approximately in the middle of each wing section played the same, but small role in the roll/turn axis of the B-52, as compared to the instantaneous effects of the finger-like spoiler system in executing turns. The ailerons were most effective in making minute corrections to headings and such (about 2 degrees of control column displacement in either direction without getting into the 'spoiler range') and were especially useful during air refueling operations where very small lateral axis corrections were needed to stay in the tanker-bomber refueling "envelope". On first glance, one might feel that the reduced roles of ailerons and an elevator on these B-52 aircraft could have had them designed out of the plane altogether—but by doing so, pilots used to flying planes with these features would not understand this arrangement at all! However, such was not the case in design of the B52's control features inasmuch these standard controls common to most all planes of the past did play an important role, albeit somewhat smaller in this new plane's versions.

Of course the weapon delivery capability of this huge bomber was easily appreciated when we looked up into the massive bomb bay area. Designed as a high altitude nuclear delivery vehicle at the outset, it was readily apparent in comparison with all other earlier bomber-type aircraft, that the B-52 models could carry any kind of munitions, nuclear, conventional, or otherwise depending on desired configurations with minimal modifications to do so. The latter has proven to be the exact case-in-fact in the roles and incredible versatility this great bomber has displayed from the Cold War, Vietnam conflict and present day operations in the Middle East and Asia. As we looked over this amazing and new 'Big Brother' of the earlier B-47 bomber and finally completed our 'transition phase' in the plane consisting of about 40 hours of ground school and 25 hours of flight instruction at Castle, we then looked forward with earnest anticipation to flying it—once settled down in our new assignment with the 28th Bomb Wing in South Dakota.

The Wing was being equipped with brand new B-52 " model planes and at the outset was slated as a "45UE" (Unit Equipped with 45 aircraft) unit having 3 major Bomb Squadrons, and an aircrew personnel complement which would bring the Wing up to a total of 72 "combat ready" crew status ultimately—a status in SAC which no other similarly equipped B-52 Wing ever achieved, before or since, and for which the unit was awarded a Unit Citation. As an aside on this subject in passing: Since the SAC units went to a smaller, aircraft equipage status later under the dispersed, Strategic Bomb Wing plan with each having around 15–18 bombers assigned—the 45UE Wings were broken up as a result to provide for this strategic re-alignment and dispersal concept in view of the mounting Cold War missile threats in order to assure greater protection and far more execution flexibility for the long range SAC bomber strike forces in EWO (Emergency War Order) operations, should a National Emergency situation ever dictate.

Once our crew was "field checked" with a Wing Standardization crew's certification, we were delighted to be turned loose, as it were, to begin flights in the Wing's concentrated and most professionally administered aircrew training program. The latter upgrade program would serve all 28th Bomb Wing aircrews extremely well as the Wing was given many detailed operational missions later, placing heavy demands on both aircraft, aircrews, maintenance support and many other essential unit agencies. It was a distinct pleasure to know that one's crew could play a vital part in these accomplishments with this new aircraft as the 28th excelled in every mission operational challenge it was ordered to perform. To this day, the 'record' will reflect this unit's professional effectiveness of those early times then. Performance in SAC airborne alert first operations in "Head Start I" and "Head Start II", flying with a full complement of nuclear weapons aboard each sortie, in the late 50s with no aborts and successful air refuelings on every mission resulted in top-notch professional achievements on behalf of all participating aircrews. And later, the Wing's outstanding performance in Airborne Alert operations during the Cuban Missile Crisis was equally well executed throughout.

In every instance, the high reliability of this B-52 bomber and its systems contributed immeasurably to these marked successes. Down to a single individual, no one ever doubted this giant plane's versatility and ruggedness to do the tasks required of it—and certainly those persons of our newly expanded bomber aircrew. To frame an overview of what it was like to fly a combat crew training mission in a B-52, explanation might be served well if a step-by-step, chronological portrayal of each phase involving typical aircrew mission plan preparation; briefings and then actual ground and air operations was given, as the following brief paragraphs are trusted to provide.

Aircrew Mission Planning and Briefings. For day-to-day training flights, all mission planning, i.e., map layouts, plotting, crew specialized briefings, radar bomb plot and air refueling schedules; communication's and ECM briefs and every possible facet concerning the crew's next training (or operational) sortie was laid out in special sessions with the appropriate Wing Staff representatives to ensure precise mission accomplishment in every phase of flight. These sessions and crew preparation would generally require least 4–6 hours of detailed work with briefings as a minimum and take place on the day prior to the flight. If the crew happened to be "on SAC Alert" status in the Wing's alert facility (sometimes called the 'barbed wire hotel'), mission preps as described would be accomplished in the alert facility the day prior, provided the crew was scheduled to 'fly off alert' the following day, taking their R&R time afterward which was acceptable standard procedure in many units. Many times the 'mission paper work' and volumes of aircraft operations manuals which the crew members had to take with them on a mission was felt to be—overwhelming each time. In fact, a popular pun among crews was: 'When the gross weight of our mission paper work with these crew manuals equals the gross weight of the airplane—then and only then can we take off on our mission!". A humorous exaggeration of course, but typified the magnitude and complexity of "readiness" reference materials required to successfully perform any mission. There were never any haphazardly and half planned missions on behalf of any SAC aircrew who was ever worthy or capable of being called "professional." SAC Wings never tolerated any lesser performance across-the-board for as General LeMay once reportedly remarked "We do not have the time or patience to determine the difference between the incompetent and the unfortunate in building this force". It was a creed lived by.

Crew Station Time and Aircraft Pre-Flight. On the day of the flight, crew "station" time at the airplane would normally be about two V2 hours prior to scheduled take-off time. The latest weather briefings for the mission route, and required airborne clearance paper work would have been completed just prior to the crew assembly at the plane. Before commencing pre-flight checks, crew members would line up with their personal equipment laid out in orderly fashion—and, on comment from the Aircraft Commander (First Pilot), each would cover their emergency procedures for their respective crew positions having to do with ground emergencies; egress (bailout or ground exit) procedures; and other required "red border" emergency actions of each's crew check list which had to be recalled exactly in order by rote memory. Once completed with these preparations, the aircrew would proceed with an external aircraft 'walk-around' visual inspection of the entire plane, most normally with the ship's maintenance Crew Chief accompanying the pilots. A "checklist" for these walk-around inspections was to be followed always such that no small piece of equipment, or required external checks of the aircraft would be missed. This close attention to detail paid off many times for the crew over the years. Following the external inspection the crew went aboard the ship to their respective positions in order to accomplish other essential equipment and systems checkouts, using again the prescribed "check lists".

The B-52's assigned ground crew would have all required ground support equipment (GSE) in place for this routine preflight operation—including MD-3 electric power supply cart hook up, and the 'pneumatic air cart' equipment plugged into #3 engine pod for the starter initiation come 'engines start' time. During preflight, every system possible was given a thorough run-up and checkout at every crew member's station including radars, radios, power packs, and related system operations. Particular attention and visual check was made on the operation of the big, horizontal stabilizer's movement in response to the pilot's trim button inputs, up and down, with both the Tail Gunner and Crew Chief assisting in this procedure by intercom reporting to the cockpit. Finally, time would come for engine start, which as a normal procedure would be 40 minutes prior to scheduled take-off time. With a re-check of the large fuel control panel's proper settings, and all switches ready, the pneumatically operated starter on #5 engine would be energized for starting and this engine's throttle advanced to increase the "bled air" going through the manifold system in order to start the remaining engines on both wings. Once all aircraft systems were placed 'on the line' with the ship's power now providing all electrical needs, final 'taxi' check lists were completed preparatory to begin taxiing operations which normally was set at twenty minutes before take-off tithe. After the landing gear wheel chocks were pulled by the ground personnel, the pull away from the parking stub immediately called for a firm check of the ship's brakes before moving onto the taxi strip. Once on the taxi strip's painted center guideline, the 'taxiing' checklist was completed by the pilot, and the oxygen regulators were once again checked throughout and reported on. During taxi operation, another interesting feature in the B-52s engineering design was the crosswind crab system installed, and its checks prior to take-off. This unique system provided the aircraft with a capacity of taking off with a prevailing crosswind at a maximum of 25 knots velocity and 45 degrees off the nose of the plane! Ostensibly, this system was designed to give the B-52 great flexibility in operating from remote airfield locations where little or no provision was ever made to line up a major runway with the locale's predominant strongest wind direction under worst conditions. In actual practice, the crosswind crab feature rarely ever had to be used during operations from SAC designated airfields. If needed, the pilots would radio for the local runway wind condition; then consult the plane's operating manual regarding crosswind settings to be used which was then 'dialed' into the system (dial control was located between the pilots on the lower part of the throttle pedestal) just as the plane was turning onto the active runway for take-off. What happened with a crosswind feature set in? Actually, the main landing gear trucks would be lined up with the runway centerline during take-off, but the fuselage from the cockpit perspective would be 'crabbed off' in the direction of the prevailing cross Wind—a rather weird feeling for the pilots, but it would work. (This author had to use this feature on one occasion taking off in a 'Texas Northern' from Carswell. The take-off with about 12 degrees of 'crab' set in went splendidly but when the flight line hangars suddenly tended to block out the strong cross-wind effect late in the take-off roll—it was like trying to control an unruly, wild whale until we finally broke ground!). As standard procedure, this system was normally checked out during taxi operation with small dialed-in settings, left and right, and then centering out these inputs as taxiing continued. Viewing a taxiway with several B-52 moving along in line and each checking crosswind gear features reminded one of 'the waltz of an elephant herd' as the tail sections weaved side to side.

Take-Off and Climb Out. Taxiing into #1 take-off position short of the active runway saw pre-take off checklists run by all crew stations and air traffic control flight clearances received for departure procedures, climb out altitude instructions and cruise-level route matters. With Tower clearance obtained, usual procedures involved a 'rolling take-off' from the pre-take off spot following the guide-in lines to the active runway. Within 15 degrees or less from intersecting the runway center-line, the Taxi/Take and Land steering mechanism was placed into the "Take-Off & Land" setting which effectively reduced the front gear trucks' steering parameters over that required for Taxi operations. Once full throttles were set, the next important phase was checking for proper acceleration of the plane through line speed checks as the take-off roll progressed. Charted minimum airspeed specs were carefully computed in ground pre-flight computations beforehand based on aircraft cruise weight, ambient temperature, etc., and thus the crew could readily determine if the engine thrust was providing required acceleration early on in order to continue a safe take-off run. The procedure would call for the pilot (usually the copilot) announcing over intercom "coming up on 70 knots, ready now". On this 'hack' one of the Navigators would click a stop-watch and be ready to call out a pre-determined number in "seconds" elapsed (generally around 15–17 seconds) at which moment an indicated air speed (IAS), also pre-computed, should have been reached or exceeded by the plane's acceleration. (Usually at training sortie take-off weights, this minimum speed would compute out in the range of 118–122 knots, as best recalled.) Failing to reach the minimum speed in the elapsed seconds dictated an immediate take-off roll "abort" by the Pilot for safety due to inadequate aircraft acceleration—it was a 'sick' bird for some reason or other, usually poor engine outputs. Once this acceleration speed check passed safely and the take-off committed, the next key IAS point coming up was the "Unstick" or take-off speed, also pre-computed beforehand with gross weight, airfield elevation and temperature being the parameters in determination. Generally, these take-off speeds would fall in a range of 152–164 knots (175–188 mph), from training sortie weights to maximum heavy ones. Take-off distance was another major consideration, especially if operating off shorter than usual runways. SAC airfields (and most commercial ones now in use) have around 12,000 feet of take-off concrete or more in some cases, thus making take-off length a somewhat moot factor, at least for average training sortie plane gross weights (in the order of 6000–7000 feet for the B-52 "D"s), but considerably longer on a maximum weight EWO take-off which would run out to 11,000 plus feet based on a higher-than-standard day temperature. The latest model of the B-52, the "H" series and now the only model in the heavy bomber inventory, enjoys far shorter heavy weight take-off distances in its performance with the highly efficient (new), Pratt & Whitney TF-33-P-3 Turbo-Fan engines which can generate 17,000 pounds for each engine. In fact, a 'thrust gate stop' setting is computed for each take-off [amounting to a lock-stop position arrangement or guard-on the throttle quadrant such that the engines will not be "over-boosted" inadvertently on take-off. On approaching take-off speed, the wing (tip) would literally 'begin to fly' and flex upward as the Pilot used small aileron inputs (and little rudder steering ones) to keep the giant plane's wings level on the run to going airborne. Once safely off the ground, landing gear retraction was called for by the Pilot and acceleration to initial climb out speed of 180 knots initiated with full flaps still down until reaching 1,000 feet altitude. At this height, flap retraction began as the climb out continued and a flap retraction speed schedule followed to ensure max speed retraction/flap position parameters were not exceeded and no more than 225–230 knots airspeed reached before flaps were fully retracted. As the flaps came up, the aircraft would tend to pitch downward somewhat due to aerodynamics of lift and drag, which required some up-nose "trim" inputs on the huge horizontal stabilizer, all very manageable and safe. Following flaps up, airspeed would be increased to a climb out speed of around 270 knots for most operations. This speed was held constant

until reaching higher altitude, usually until the Mach .77 (around 440 knots True Air Speed [TAS]) performance chart point was intersected which was the normal cruise condition Mach/TAS relationship generally followed thereafter at high altitude cruise flight levels—usually between 30,000–42,000 feet depending on gross weight and air traffic control clearances thereafter. Thus, after appropriate after-climb and level off checklists were read by each crew member at his station, the mission would continue, 'as briefed' and as cleared by traffic control agencies. Range, endurance, and speed for the B-52 aircraft across-the-board varied for a number of factors depending how the plane was operated; all flight parameters including gross weights and altitudes to name but a few major considerations. However, the 'advertised' and generally accepted performance capabilities in these areas were/are: at maximum gross weight (450,000 pounds for the B-52 "D" and 488,000 pounds for the "H" model), the approximate maximum flight level speed is listed at 449 MPH (IAS) with a range of 10,000 miles un-refueled; and a maximum 'ceiling' of 50,000 feet altitude. The significant variable here is, as concerns maximum air-speed and altitude: the B-52 is a sub-sonic aircraft and therefore has to be flown under any condition at less than Mach One. Most probably around a max Mach of .97 would be the upper limit under most airspeed, altitude and temperature limitations, all which would have a bearing on fuel consumption which again would dictate maximum range and endurance as interacting, determining factors as well. Finally, the B-52's handling characteristics at cruise altitudes, including refueling, were excellent for such a giant aircraft. (Refueling techniques will be covered briefly—subsequently). Except for combat practice maneuvers including simulated nuclear weapon delivery and 'escape' procedures at low and high level altitudes, and normally flown manually—most all other cruise modes and conditions (except refuelings) employed the use of the autopilot. This latter system in B-52 aircraft was exceptionally reliable as well as that of the B-47 aircraft prior—both far superior than those found in most all previous World War II type planes flown. The B-52 was a marvelously stable bombing 'platform' aircraft in all respects.

Mission Termination and Landing Procedures. Normally, stateside combat crew training missions, most every one planned and flown with a combat mission "profile" in mind (and without actual weapons of any type aboard) consisted of navigation by both radar and celestial means (later, astro-tracking, GPS, and other far more sophisticated systems have vastly outdistanced these early airborne "fixing" capabilities); simulated radar bombing runs employing many RBS (Radar Bomb Scoring) sites established initially by SAC all around the country; and scheduled air refuelings in prescribed airspace

---

Opposite page: A B-52 on the runway at Guam, from which it bombed targets in North Vietnam.

areas. Average duration of these flights would be between 8-11 hours flight time in most instances though some could go longer under special training situations. Conclusion of a mission would most always end up in the crew's home station area, terminal landing weather considered. Most usually an 'en route' descent from cruising altitude would be requested through air traffic control by the Pilots in order to bring the aircraft down to the terminal navigation fix (VOR, TACAN, etc.) where a standard handbook published 'jet penetration' from a prescribed altitude (generally around 20,000 feet) could then be executed to the final approach course for landing. Often times as an alternative, clearance could be given for a ground radar controlled descent wherein the local base area Approach Control would pick up the aircraft and vector the pilot to the final approach course where a Ground Controlled Approach (GCA) by radio with ground controllers, or an ILS (Instrument Landing System) instrument approach could be completed to the landing runway. With a jet penetration off of an established 'fix' from 20,000 feet altitude, the procedure would go generally as follows in the B-52. The jet penetration pattern would usually be a 'tear drop' one off the fix and having prescribed turn altitude during the descent where a 180 degree turn would be made in-bound to the runway's final approach course—a wrap around, opposite heading change required for the maneuver down to a set minimum altitude once the turn and descent was completed going inbound. Once over the fix, the landing gear extension was made as the nose was lowered somewhat for descent; the throttles pulled back to idle; and air brakes position #6 (all spoilers fully extended) selected. The corresponding rate of descent would then (as a standard) settle down right at 4,000 foot-per-minute as the ship was flown down the jet penetration pattern 'chute' with the IAS reaching about 230–240 knots maximum with the added drag of the extended air brakes and gear fully extended. As experienced, the B-52 seemed always to want to 'settle down' comfortably at the above rate of descent and speed range such that the Pilots' main functions were to closely monitor all flight instruments throughout the penetration. Roughly one-third of the starting altitude was completed (most letdown plans) during the descent until the prescribed and published inbound 180-degree turn was begun. About 2,000 feet above the minimum inbound (published) altitude, a sound procedure was to decrease the rate of descent to one-half (or 2,000 FPM) and allowing the IAS to begin bleeding off below 230 knots preparatory to calling for flap extension (that speed was a max placard one for flap operation). At 1,000 above the published level off altitude, rate of decent was cut in half again, and again at 500 feet above with the same small adjustments such that level off maneuver was a gentle 'slide-in' to the minimum inbound heading with IAS still coming down as the flaps reached e fully extended position. The throttles were gently brought up to higher settings during the latter phase, and set to stabilize the plane at the computed final approach speed plus 30 knots initially out on final inbound until intercepting the final glide path. (Best Approach Speed for the final approach to landing was computed as a function of landing gross weight extracted from the aircraft performance charts and this reference, plus 10 knots, was always the recommend final approach speed down to the landing flare out. At this time, the air brakes had been gradually and earlier reduced to position #2 for the approach. A customary procedural technique for most pilots was to use the master Fuel Flow meter readings, which were very sensitive to throttle settings, to set and adjust the engines' power for an easily controlled rate-of-descent (and approach speed) once on the glide path—which rounded out generally to about 550–600 FPM. In this manner, 'throttle jockeying' became unnecessary for a smoothly executed instrument approach and landing in this big, easy-to-handle bomber. It was always a pleasure to fly this B-52 in these situations, as it never failed to 'behave' admirably as large as it was—a true performer. On landing touch-down with the main gear trucks firmly on the runway surface, the Air Brakes once again were extended to full #6 position to create maximum drag and as the speed fell below 160 knots, the massive 32-foot ribbon 'drag chute' was called for by the aircraft commander. (This speed was the maximum deployment placard one to preclude shear pin failure and cause the chute possibly to disengage if exceeded). This 'chute was packed in a compartment on the bottom side of aft fuselage near the tail and was manually deployed from a cockpit lever on the copilot's side of the throttle pedestal. The feature of an ABS (anti-skid, anti-lock) braking system also on the plane permitted the Pilot to use maximum brake pedal pressure without inducing any tire skid or scuffing during the roll out as the system would compensate for this protection. On runway turn off, the drag 'chute would be kept inflated and billowing by advancing power on the inboard engines, as needed, until reaching a safe 'chute jettison area on the taxiway where it would be retrieved by ground personnel. After final after-landing checklists were completed, the pilot would be directed to a final parking stub and most generally one where an underground refueling pit 'receptacle' was readily available for immediate single-point refueling of the aircraft using a Bowser refueling GSE unit. (No practical provision for an 'over-the-wing' refueling capability existed for this aircraft as in many World War II and later planes. All such was accomplished employing the single-point hose connection process to fill all fuel cells—a much faster, safer and efficient method as most aviation refueling tanker trucks had far insufficient capacities to fill up a B-52 having a maximum load potential of roughly 37,000 or so gallons). In concluding these sorties, the entire aircrew would be picked up and transported to their debriefing sessions, usually held within their assigned Bomb Squadrons—all requiring roughly two more hours of duty time with completion of mission 'paperwork' being a major requirement. And with that—a "typical" aircrew training mission day was completed—probably one perhaps of 17-18 hours duration, portal-to-portal from their respective quarters.

Air Refueling Procedures and Techniques. Not dwelled on above, a brief run-down of a typical B-52 air tanker refueling operation would go generally as the following notes. In early B-52 Wing operations, the later KC-135 jet tanker was not yet available for most all crew air refueling training. Thus, the much slower (but capable) KC-97 (former Boeing Stratocruiser, and once a commercial airliner) was reconfigured as an aerial tanker in the early training of SAC crews, mostly in the early B-47 era. The KC-97 was a reciprocating engine plane, and at best was "strained" to near limits in speed requirements to refuel the new jet bombers of the B-47 and B-52 categories, both of which had to slow down considerably, and drop down to much lower altitudes to 'get the gas' off-loads scheduled for the mission. In many instances, the amount of the off-load barely offset the fuel poundage lost for the bombers to descend to the KC-97's max refueling altitude, and then climb back again to their optimum, high altitude cruise levels. And that is precisely why big jet tanker aircraft were sorely needed, as today, for both bombers and fighters in deployment and area combat operations. Flying refueling sorties against a KC-97 will not be elaborated upon as it was a tremendous challenge for the B-52 bomber Pilots to slow this behemoth down to below 200 knots in most cases and take on a max internal load of JP-4 fuel with the bomber totaling out to over 400,000 pounds gross weight after refueling in order for the crew to receive credit for a "max gross weight refueling" requirement. The big bird could often encounter a sloshing of the fuel at these low speeds and flight attitude while on the refueling boom, which, to say the very least, was somewhat a discomfort to the bomber crew, especially the Pilots. Also, to see the heat flames passing out of the KC-97 engines, particularly at night, as the its crew 'strained' to give the maximum speed possible during this interesting encounter, tended to heighten all such experiences.

But, the case of refueling against the new KC-135 jet tanker was a pleasant change, both in training operations, and later in Airborne Alert missions. With this new capability, having to descent below 30,000 feet to take on fuel, and fly greatly reduced airspeeds below normal cruise ones as before with the KC-97 was eliminated—not to mention the fuel savings economy which resulted. A typical refueling operation against the KC-135 tanker would be orchestrated by following standard SAC Tactical Doctrine refueling procedures along the following principles. Training refueling areas were designated in the jet high altitude structure as MARSA (in ATC parlance, "Military Assumes Responsibility for Separation of Aircraft"—both altitude-wise and laterally) controlled and operationally reserved for these ops—generally between the heights of 29,000 to 35,000 feet. On a high altitude IN Navigation map these specific areas (by nickname) when plotted appeared as a rectangularly shaped area, some 30 miles in width and approximately 100–120 miles long with a 'briefed' refueling course (track) down the middle. The KC-135 for a pre-briefed operation and bomber/tanker "rendezvous" time and altitude would be on station in the designated refueling area at least 30 minutes prior to rendezvous—flying a 'racetrack', elliptical pattern around the briefed refueling track (heading). Both bomber and tanker would have their radar refueling "beacons" on such that each could identify each other by briefed coded 'blips' on their respective navigation radar scopes. The B-52 (receiver) could normally pick up the tanker's code about 125–175 miles away, or vice-versa, should one plane's system be having a malfunction. With tanker identified in its orbit pattern and the bomber now driving on towards the area, the "pre-contact" air refueling checklists were run at both the pilot's and navigation team's crew stations.

Prior air route traffic control acknowledgements and clearance would have been completed by both aircraft preparatory to these operations (except in very remote areas where such was not practicable, applicable or required). At these altitudes, the bomber-receiver would be flying generally higher than, or perhaps lower than the briefed refueling altitude (normally set between 29,000–35,000 feet), and during the latter approach phase would adjust accordingly in cruise flight level. Most generally, refuelings took place with no inter-communications made between aircraft in order to complete a successful, radio silent operation, as often practiced. (However, briefed air refueling inter-communication frequencies were always given to both aircraft in every operation in the interests of air safety). As the bomber approached the refueling track, altitude was adjusted to 1,000 feet below the briefed refueling level (at which the tanker was flying in its orbit) in order to ensure full separation until both planes got into closer up visual contact with each other (but on some occasions visual contact was not possible due to clouds until the receiver got up into the "observation" position, or about 50 feet below the tanker and around 75–100 feet back from the 'flying boom'). Final leg of the tanker's orbit would be that coming almost straight toward the bomber's heading (but slightly offset). Normally at altitude, their respective closure speeds would be in the order of 840 knots, or covering about 14 nautical miles-a-minute toward each other. The bomber could be driving along then at about 280–290 knots

IAS normally, preparatory to slowing down to fly the programmed Tactical Doctrine 'speed schedule' beginning at 4 miles away from the tanker. As the tanker approached nearly head-on it would commence a 180-degree turn back onto the briefed refueling track when separation between the two aircraft came down to 21–22 miles apart (with planes in prior radar and/or radio contact now). The receiver would then be lined up on the refueling course as well and commence flying a programmed speed schedule (maintaining 1,000 feet below the tanker) on into the so-called 'observation' position; i.e., 270 knots at 4 miles; 260 at 3 miles; 250 at 2 miles; 240 at 1 mile; and then gradually as closure continued, reducing IAS to 23 0–220 knots. The briefed refueling speed for both aircraft would be in this latter range normally and the final closure by the receiver was very carefully executed with the pilot now in visual contact. From the last one mile range, the receiver pilot would gradually have closed the vertical altitude separation from 1,000 feet to 500 feet, thence to around 100 feet with small increments of power now in order to close; very slowly and carefully on tanker, thus avoiding any chance of a dangerous overrun. The refueling "observation" position was reached following which placed the receiver 50 feet below the tanker and at an optimum distance of approximately 50 feet back. At this position, the bomber "stabilized" with refueling check lists completed, and refueling receptacle doors—open, and signaling "ready for contact, receiver". From this point on, very deliberate and smooth receiver pilot technique was demanded on every refueling operation, obviously. The bomber (for best approach results) would raise up the remaining 50 feet 'eyeballing' the end of the tanker boom nozzle exactly in the centerline of the aircraft's nose and in the middle of the windscreen. Speed closure would be no more than 1–2 knots as the bomber moved forward to the boom 'envelope' and eased through the 'down wash' shield coming off the tanker as the "contact" position was reached. About two feet or so in front of the windscreen, the tanker boom operator would raise up the 'flying' refueling boom, ready to insert the nozzle in the receiver's refueling receptacle (located overhead and to rear of the bomber cockpit on top of the fuselage). When "receiver contact, tanker contact" condition was made between the two (and it became readily evident to the receiver pilots as the boom 'plugged in' with a firm jolt). A 'contact' telltale light illuminated on the refueling panel confirmed the successful formatting. From that point on, the receiver pilot used the "Fore, Aft, Up and Down" director lights located on the under fuselage of the tanker to show what corrections needed to made to stay 'in the green' and in the middle of the boom's envelope. The flying boom would telescope, retract, or move side to side of center if the receiver was not squarely in this envelope, and its displacement would directly effect the director light signals in telling the receiver Pilot which correction to make to get 'back in the green'. It required very smooth techniques on behalf of the latter and required minute corrections to complete a successful refueling without a disconnect, but after a number of such operations, most every bomber crew 'mastered' the refueling technique regardless of conditions. (Indeed they did or their combat ready status and even their future in the SAC bomber business was over). It had to be mastered both day and night, all weather conditions! Typically, a 40,000 pound 'offload' of JP jet fuel would be made in these training operations; many times less than that amount, and just practice "dry contacts", intentionally going on and off the boom often would be the briefed program. The KC-135 could offload fuel at a maximum rate of around 6,000 pounds-per-minute, thus typical refueling encounters did not require much time for either aircraft. With the tanker aircraft flying on autopilot, seasoned bomber Pilots most always (and prided themselves) took the offload with 'one gulp", and with no disconnects. During the early Airborne Alert drills, "Head Start I and Head Start II" for example, while assigned to the 28th Bomb Wing, we flew a number of 18 hours and later 24 hour missions, configured with Mk-28 nuclear weapon loads, flying prescribed northern routes where typical air refuelings required briefed offloads from supporting KC-35 tankers (out of Loring and Ellison AFBs) of 100,000–110,000 pounds of fuel to successfully fly the plans. These on-loads would be taken in approximately 16–17 minutes on the boom in one continuous 'gulp' with little problems—all weather, all conditions regardless, being encountered. Briefed provisions were always in place between tanker and bomber crews to execute "emergency breakaway" procedures to separate these planes quickly should an unforeseen, near-collision situation suddenly arise. In recall crew-wise, no requirement ever resulted in having to execute such an emergency procedure because of an actual airborne situation of this type. With the trusted reliability of the B-52 and its systems, an aircrew's "professionalism" in executing every airborne task assigned was made a matter of prideful accomplishment—both in those early days—and certainly now with its crew personnel of today's B-52 "H" force.

Combat Training Readiness Maneuvers/Modes. The aircrew readiness procedures for operations which might be faced in actual combat missions situations were practiced and simulated continually and became a way of life in every SAC crew member's daily training routine—both when they were on "hard alert" status and isolated in the new and most comfortable Wing Alert Facility complexes with their 'cocked' B-52 nearby on the Christmas Tree parking stub or flying combat profile training missions. In addition to the detailed study of every facet of their Combat Mission Folders (CMFs) which laid out the individual crew's flight plan and directive for an actual mission and specifically designated target should the EWO ever be executed—there were a great number of other techniques, flight maneuvers, ground alert modes and such which the crew had to master as well. These are all too numerous to mention in one writing, thus a few major ones will be covered here.

The B-52 was initially designed through USAF specifications to be just a high altitude, nuclear weapon delivery aircraft: However, in the late 60s it was soon learne4 that successful weapon delivery tactics also had to depend on the airplane being able to survive at very low bombing altitudes by getting under the enemy's more sophisticated and new surface-to-air missile (SAM) protection batteries. The SAC Tactical Doctrine's thus dictated that the B-52 be taken low level in actual EWO planning. Structured aircrew training missions with navigation and RBS-scored bombing on simulated targets along many newly designated Low Level routes called "Oil Burner" corridors in the ATC Airman's Guide were laid out throughout the U.S. in major attempts to void all congested or heavy agricultural areas. The addition of low-level ops in-crew EWO/peacetime training also introduced a new problem with the early B-52's design. It was realized that the service lifetime of the airframe, due to turbulence, wind shear effects in low level flying as well as high speed maneuvers required, was effectively reducing the plane's life expectancy and some type modification to "beef up" the tail section aft of the bomb bay was needed. Effectively, the aircraft was being 'worn out' 5 times faster flown at low level than at high altitude, or simply every hour of flying in the low level regimes was equivalent to 5 hours up high. The ultimate "fix" or "mod" was to weld a long steel 'tie' down each side of the ship's fuselage, aft of the bomb bay back to the tail cone—thus, providing more rigidity to offset structural degrading 'twisting' moments encountered often in low level missions. This new addition can be seen readily on the early B-52 model "gate guards" planes now permanently standing today as silent sentinels of the past in a number of major air museums, designated air installations and air parks in the U.S. and Britain (Duxford). Simulated nuclear weapon delivery tactics at both and high and low altitude were an essential part of an aircrew' s training in order to minimize or 'escape' the devastating effects of a weapon. At high altitude, the "breakaway', high banked turn of between 90–110 degrees in the 55 seconds immediately after release maneuver was made and RBS scored pass or fail. At low altitude release, it was fast descents to lowest, minimum safe altitude to avoid the super-sonic, nuclear ground wave. On the "Short Look" low level bomb run with the B-52 driving in at 300-plus knots IAS, 300–500 above the terrain, a "pop up" maneuver during the last 30–40 seconds of 'time-to-go' was executed. This maneuver pitched the plane up into a climb during the last few seconds of the bomb run in order for the Radar Navigator to take a final short look of the 'cross-hairs' placement on the simulated target, and following the 'bombs away', the Pilot would take the plane immediately back down to the very minimum altitude possible, tail on to the weapon 'burst' (trusting in an actual combat situation to escape the weapon's Mach-Y stem nuclear burst ground wave, surely to come, with this maneuver). It was 'survival training' practice in an entirely different set of circumstances for both crew and plane during all these EWO training situations—all worthwhile and necessary in every respect. There were many "tests" both for aircrews and the B-52 at each and every turn, almost every day. Often, the unannounced 'exercise' practice of taxiing aircraft on alert into an MRP (Minimum Reaction Posture) position near the active runway for an instant "Go" within a 5–8 minute period after receiving an execution order (simulated) occurred frequently in honing everyone's reaction time. Since each SAC unit was always readily aware of the BMEWS (Ballistic Missile Early Warning System) time limit to get all their (normal), 'one-third alert' ships into the air before incoming weapons could be raining down on the U.S. and the base, all alert training exercises (and Operational Readiness Inspections) used a criteria of a max 15 minute 'warning time window' in which to launch their alert aircraft after a BMEWS alerting would be sounded out of NORAD's control center. These continuous training rigors served to train and perfect every aspect of a Wing's operational, maintenance and support structure, and this B-52 airplane was always ready to answer the demands required of it. One last and actual practice training procedure each aircrew had to accomplish semi-annually was the MITO (Minimum Interval Take-Off) operation. This periodic training maneuver consisted of a minimum of 3–4 B-52s (usual number) of taking off with only a 15 second interval between each plane. It would follow the pattern of an actual alert launch if the EWO "Go" Code execution order were ever received. Accordingly, these take-offs would see at least 3 of the B-52s in line going down the active runway, 15 seconds apart as this interval was proven to be the safest separation one possible between these giant planes, especially after breaking ground and getting into possible 'wake turbulence' of the preceding aircraft. It was a strenuous, exacting aircrew training operation but was the only assured way in which SAC's "secure retaliatory force' manifested in its one-third alert aircraft posture could survive in getting airborne within the BMEWS warning time. All alert actual combat launches were predicated on using the MITO procedure to ensure the latter could be accomplished, reliably and safely. And finally, these were just some of the many combat training practices in all SAC B-52 operations at the respective Bomb Wing level.

Aircrew Emergency Bailout Methods and Procedures. The egress systems of the early B-52 "D" aircraft (and not much has changed since except a crew member location) consisted of upward ejection seats for the two pilots and the ECM operator; two downward ejections chairs for the lower deck Navigator team, and an explosive bolt arrangement which would permit the Tail Gunner to disengage his tail gun cone from the entire aircraft, allowing him to bailout. (The Tail Gunner crew position was abolished much later in later aircraft, as today). While emergency bailout procedures were repeatedly rehearsed verbally by each crew member every mission, it was realized that egress from the aircraft by some members could be 'dicey' at best in low altitudes emergencies. Namely, the downward ejection of the Navigator positions at an altitude below 300 feet, as during a dire take-off emergency requiring a Pilot's bailout order to be given as a last resort. That minimum altitude was probably the very lowest which conceivably would permit a hoped-for, survivable situation for these two members. Fortunately, it seems no one ever had to experience this tragic possibility in the B-52, and most crew pilots would brief an emergency zoom up' maneuver on take-off should one such situation ever be encountered. All crew members before take-off in these low altitude operations and immediately prior would hook up their parachute rip cord to their ejection seat lanyard' in order to permit a "zero-delay" feature for the parachute's actuation once the individual left the seat after ejection. Reportedly, and in the case of the Pilot's upward ejections, if a minimum airspeed of 120 knots was reached while on the ground on take-off and an emergency situation arose, a survivable ejection was possible? Fortunately, once again, this stated capability was never known to have been demonstrated in an emergency with a B-52 crew.

In all other and higher altitude regimes of flight, ejection bailouts and the like were less problematical, even if the crew member had been rendered unconscious. Stowing of the "zero-delay" lanyard device shortly after take-off (a crew check list item) would then permit a high altitude bailout with the aneroid, altimeter feature of the parachute to actuate the chute release mechanism at any altitude of 14,000 feet or below. These were the aircrew safety provisions built into the crew's personal and aircraft equipment packages. Of course there were many other protective features for a combat situation and not the least of which was "flash curtains" installations should nuclear weapons delivery be necessary in forestalling crew member blindness, and a combat aircraft pressurization setting for this aircraft system to minimize effects of a possible crew compartment area puncture in actual combat situations.

The B-52 Aircraft in Today's USAF Operations. Many sophisticated upgrades exist. The state-of-the-art, cutting edge of new airplane technologies in making this aircraft and the crews who fly them in today's multi-mission environments are literally mind boggling, at least to those who flew the first operational models of this early "warrior". Today, the planes and their crews have so many, tried and true capabilities at their disposal in order to operate, and succeed in proven situations time and again in all tactical and strategic operational settings required of them, as their record continues to reflect. The B-52H, the only remaining plane of its ancestry, is truly a weapon system for "all seasons and all reasons" in mission dictates, both strategic and tactical, whenever needed. By report, some 94 of these planes remain active in the USAF inventory. The armaments in each are staggering in capabilities: 12 AGM-86B Air Launched Cruise Missiles (ALCMs), or AGM-129A Advanced Cruise Missiles (ACM5) externally with provision for 8 more ALCMs or gravity weapons internally; conventional weapons including AGM-86 CF/D Conventional ALCMs bombs up to 2,000 pounds, cluster munitions; GBU-30 IDAMs, and on some aircraft, 3–4 AGM-142As and NAP missiles or 8 AGMMO-84 Harpoons in under-wing clusters. In addition, there have been numerous upgrades in Avionics Midlife Improvement programs for the B-52H including Electronic Attack features as well as Electronic Countermeasure and aircraft protection systems. And finally, as a concluding comparison of aircrew-airplane capabilities past: where once upon a bygone time if a crew could repeatedly achieve a performance of placing a (simulated) weapon within a CEA (Circular Error Average) of 500 feet of a target, that achievement was regarded as a truly professional success. Today's B-52 crew can put a 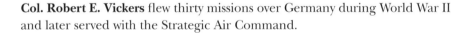 weapon within three (3) feet of the same target—an accolade for all time which speaks for the 'old air warrior' as well, undoubtedly placing it in the category of being the very best multi-engine bomber ever built, bar none.

Col. Robert E. Vickers flew thirty missions over Germany during World War II and later served with the Strategic Air Command.

F-84 Thunderjet

Charles D. Bright

For the pilot who was new to the straight-wing F-84 Thunderjet its appearance on the ground was no preparation for the labors of takeoff. Even with center-line tip tanks, which it carried for normal flights, it appeared to be sleek and speedy. Without any external fixtures it looked even racier with its small stubby wings. Takeoff would prove to be contrary to expectations, a fitting introduction to an airplane with unusual qualities. This was especially true for pilots who made the transition to the 84 from a piston fighter.

In contrast to the F-51's spirited takeoff—which gave a sense of impending flight shortly after the roll began—the F-84, though it was powerful, gained speed slowly and felt heavy even at liftoff. It did this under the best of conditions, using almost two miles of runway—a marked contrast to the F-51's half-mile.

Under the worst conditions, with full fuel and armament loads on a hot Korean summer day, the takeoff had no margin for safety. In this case the pilot was forewarned. Auxiliary fuel, bombs or napalm, and sometimes rockets or jet-assisted takeoff (JATO) bottles crowded onto the narrow undersurfaces of the F-84 gave it an overloaded appearance. The pilot could say to himself, "Well, the kitchen sink isn't there, but only because there is no place to hang it." Fully loaded, the gross weight of the E model was 10 tons.

The pilot used as much runway as possible, running up to full throttle with the brakes locked. This gave him 4,900 pounds of thrust. At the beginning of the roll, when there was little lift, the weight would cause the struts to hit bottom often. As the speed slowly built up, a careful reference was made between the airspeed indicator and points chosen by the pilot to mark

---

Opposite page: Two F-84s.

47

progress down the runway so as to measure performance by "feel." (This was before "tech orders" enabled a pilot to calculate progress speeds and check them against markers placed at the runway sides.) The progress was more critical than it would be today, for the Air Force did not use barriers (arresting cables for jet fighters) for many years of the F-84's service life. An estimate by the pilot that flying speed would not be attained meant releasing the externally mounted armament and fuel tanks and then trying to brake to a stop on the graded dirt overrun or, if desperate, to retract the landing gear and slide to a stop on the plane's belly. The F-84 had a robust landing gear, and more than one survived undamaged in the overrun or beyond where most other fighters would have come to grief with collapsed gear.

If all appeared to be going well, the externally mounted JATO bottles were fired. Later, and more accurately, these were called RATO, for rocket instead of jet. Although welcome, the added thrust from these engines always felt disappointingly small at a time when the pilot knew all the runway had to be used at best. The F-84 used two or four of these engines, each producing 1,000 pounds of thrust for fourteen seconds. But RATO was not all blessing. While the first pilots to take off had a clear view ahead, those following had to contend with a thick white smoke over the runway from earlier RATO firings. They not only had to strive for best takeoff performance but also had to include reference to the instruments for blind flying. Although smokeless RATO was later developed, newer fighters have a much better system for thrust augmentation in their afterburners.

When flying speed was reached, the 84 pilot did not fly his plane off the runway. Instead he mechanically placed the joystick in the full back position against the seat, making sure that no stray object, oxygen tube, or radio wires impeded complete travel. The F-84's nose would rise and the plane would unstick at about 160 mph when fully loaded. After a few moments, at slightly increased speed to make sure that the aircraft would not settle back to the runway in its near-stall state, the gear handle was moved up. As speed built up, the flaps could be "milked up" (brought up in steps). Over a designated area the rocket engines could be dropped. As drag reduced, there was a marked, rapid increase in speed. The nose could be lowered rapidly, and, no longer sluggish, the 84 moved forward in swift, pleasing flight.

The Thunderjet now presented a contrast to its behavior during takeoff. The basic airplane had low drag; even with its centerline tip fuel tanks, an F-84 kept at full throttle and low altitude would soon be pressing on its Mach limitation (Mach .82, which is about 620 mph at sea level on a standard day). Acceleration when not burdened with the drag of any external stores was both exhilarating and frustrating. The straight wing and conventional tail

---

Opposite page: An F-84 armed with eight high-velocity, five-inch serial rockets.

were relics of the piston era and imposed such low limits on performances as to make the F-84 a most unusual aircraft. Instead of almost always flying comfortably below its structural limits as do most aircraft, the 84 had the power and streamlining to reach those limits quickly. It was frustrating to have the power to go faster but be forced to observe the airframe limits.

Inattention to or deliberate violation of the F-84's speed limitations below 15,000 feet resulted in a pitch-up—a sudden, uncontrollable nose-up attitude—and the airframe normally could not withstand the radically changed airflow. The result was disintegration, with the wings failing. At high altitude the plane could be forced through this limit and still be controlled, but this resulted in a rough ride, for the airflow around the F-84 above Mach .82 was not smooth. The effect was like that of clear air turbulence. The battering on the airframe at 40 (indicated) mph past the Mach limit was so heavy as to raise fears of structural failure, even though the 84 was built in the Republic tradition of rugged airplanes.

Just as the pilot could drive through the limits above 15,000 feet, he could, with diligence, stay within the limits below it. By planning entry speed, with careful throttle handling and monitoring of the airspeed indicator, he could split-S into a vertical diving attack from 10,000 feet above the ground. The result was excellent ordnance accuracy together with low vulnerability to flak.

Pilots were generally most unhappy with the need for frequent attention to structural limits while in combat, the more so because the limits condemned the F-84 to inferiority in combat against the MIG-15—a more modern design. The 84 did not even have the usual shelter of the slower fighter—a smaller radius of turn. It simply could not turn with agility. Using both hands the pilot could force a hard turn at high speed. That is, he could enter it, for although he could achieve three Gs momentarily, the airspeed indicator would rapidly unwind. The result was a failure to turn effectively and a sacrifice of available speed.

The straight-winged F-84s, outclassed in air-to-air combat in Korea, are credited with eight MIG-15s destroyed in combat against a loss of eighteen. One F-84 pilot with credit for two MIGs on one sortie was asked how he did it. He answered something like this:

> Well, the first flew in front of me and I squeezed the trigger! I got him. Later two got on my tail and I couldn't shake them. I thought, "They'll never follow me through a pitch-up, and maybe the wings will stay on." So I dove and rammed the throttle full forward. As I approached the Mach, I tried to help the plane into pitch-up early in hopes of easing the load on the wings. The wings stayed on! And sure

enough, the MIG's couldn't turn that corner! One didn't pull out of his dive and he's my second victory.

The 84 in this double victory was inspected and found to be sound. But where it had been one of the nimblest planes in the wing, it became both lame and a hangar queen—a real "dog."

Air Force pilots never forgave the F-84 for its inferiority to the MIG-15. Thus, although the 84 did the same yeoman fighter-bomber service in Korea that Republic airplanes have done in all three of our modern wars, it never approached the popularity with pilots of the P-47 and the F-105, both of which had air superiority capabilities. This was unfortunate, for its qualities made it a superb fighter-bomber. The high speed increased the effective range of the F-84's ordnance and permitted operation at the extreme limits or outside the effective range of enemy flak. Its speed meant that the front lines could be reached quickly—in around 20 minutes from a ground-alert scramble. On none of my missions nor any I heard of did the 84s arrive too late to help the ground forces. There was fuel for loiter of around 30 minutes, and I never had to cut short a sortie because of lack of fuel. The F-84's sturdiness allowed it to operate under rough airfield conditions and to take battle damage. The lack of maneuverability produced a solid, steady gun platform. This was enhanced by an adjustable power boost system for the ailerons, with which one could select the ideal boost setting for his conditions of flight. There was no torque or need for rudder control. The gunsight computed for bombs and rockets as well as for the six .50-caliber machine guns; we could easily line up and smoothly track a target from two miles out, and the results could be impressive.

General Otto P. Weyland, Commander of the Far East Air Forces, said that the F-84 attacks on the Toksan and Chasan reservoirs in 1953 were "perhaps the most spectacular of the war." F-84s flew 86,408 sorties and dropped more bombs and napalm (55,987 tons) than any other Air Force fighter in the war; they fired only a small share of the rockets, however. Only 153 F-84s were lost to enemy action, and only 98 of their pilots were killed.

The qualities that produced a great gun platform made the F-84 a fine plane for instrument flying. It was smooth and easy to control at any instrument flying speed, so blind flying was easier than in many other planes. The same properties made it an easy plane to land. One type of pattern was circular out of a pitch (a turn with 90 degrees of bank). Speed brakes were extended and throttle brought back to almost idle. Wingmen pitched later for spacing and delayed dropping gear and flaps to avoid the need for power in the pattern. When the airspeed fell into the region where the gear could be extended

without damage, it was dropped and the flap handle put down. The flaps would extend themselves gradually as the airspeed slowed to the 160 mph used for a normal final approach (40 mph faster than the F-51s). If the pilot set up the appropriate glide to the runway, he would be nose low. Shortly before contact with the runway he could bring back the stick. The nose would respond and the plane would take up a landing attitude. But the flight path would not noticeably alter; there was no flare or float at normal airspeeds. Touchdown would be easy but noticeably one with finality out of the mushing descent. Crosswind or gusty landings were no problem-in sharp contrast to an F-51, which was sensitive and had to be handled with care through the whole landing sequence and landing roll. If a go-around was necessary, engine response time was comparable to that of the F-51: the 84 had slower engine acceleration, while the F-51's throttle shouldn't be rammed forward at low speeds because of the high torque.

The F-84's qualities enabled it to be in the vanguard for several modern fighter activities. It pioneered in the use of both flying boom and probe-and-drogue aerial refueling for Air Force fighters. Using aerial refueling the F-84s made notable ocean crossings en masse as early as 1952. The F-84 was the first single-seat fighter capable of delivering a nuclear weapon. Its stability and ease of maintenance contributed to its choice as the aircraft for the first Thunderbird demonstration team, formed in 1953.

For all the honors, a pilot will also appreciate the airplane that brings him home. I once had engine failure while 25 miles from base at 8,000 feet and 300 mph. After the automatic turn towards home and climb to the best glide speed, the distance was unchanged, but there was now 11,000 feet of clearance above runway elevation. Since the F-84 had a glide ratio of 14 miles forward progress for the sacrifice of one mile of altitude, it appeared feasible to try a dead-stick landing. (Had bailout been necessary, most F-84s had an explosive-driven ejection seat. The canopy was explosively released, before the seat was fired, by raising the hand grip on the right armrest. Then the pilot positioned himself, raised the left grip, and squeezed the grip's trigger. After ejection he would kick clear of the seat. If the pilot chose or was in a nonejection seat model, bailout was similar to that in piston fighters.) The choice on this flight was to take the plane home, yet it seemed unbelievable that the ground-loving F-84 would actually float all that distance when the glide of a powerless F-51 was like the legendary "streamlined brick." Course was set directly for a base leg, where the landing gear was pumped down by hand. The approach proved to be ideal with a deliberate slight overshoot. The dead-stick landing turned out to be a "piece of cake."

Opposite page: Newly delivered F-84s on the ramp at Fuerstenfeldbruck air base in Germany, 1950.

Watching the miles slip quietly and effortlessly by while the altimeter unwound with a casual slowness in engineless flight, it was hard to believe I was in the same ground-loving beast that had to be pried into the air for take-off. But this was only one of the contradictions and surprises of an airplane with many unique and unusual properties. Nearly 4,500 were built, and they were used by a large share of the Free World's air forces. Obscured by the great F-86, the Republic F-84 nevertheless figured large in the shaping of the jet age. General Weyland called it the workhorse of the Korean War. It deserves an important rank among America's combat aircraft.

Lt. Col. Charles D. Bright was a B-17 lead navigator in the strategic air offensive against Germany and an F-84 pilot in the Korean War. He is retired from the USAF.

Opposite page: The sleek, swept-wing F-84 was capable of high air speeds and long-range operations.

C-141 Starlifter

Alton P. H. Brewer, Jr.

The date was December 17, 1963, sixty years to the day after the first powered flight at Kitty Hawk. Leo Sullivan and three members of his test-flight crew boarded a sleek, new, swept-wing aircraft. Minutes later the graceful bird lifted off the runway at Dobbins AFB, Georgia, and the maiden flight of the C-141 Starlifter was under way.

This flight on #12775 was originally scheduled as a taxi test. Only a handful of people were aware that the test crew had a "green light" for flight if all systems appeared stable. Assembled photographers and reporters (an aircraft as well known and as large as the Starlifter attracted media representatives even for a taxi test) were treated to an unexpected and historic moment as the big bird accelerated, then rose into the air.

This flight generated a keen interest in all of us scattered throughout the Military Air Transport Service (MATS) worldwide airlift system. It meant we were one step closer to the day when we would get an aircraft designed explicitly for strategic airlift. Under the guiding pressure of airlift's number one congressional champion, L. Mendel Rivers, two modernized interim aircraft, the Boeing C-135 and the Lockheed C-130, had been purchased for MATS. The C-141 was destined to replace both of these as well as the C-118. On January 1, 1966, the MATS (operational since June 1, 1948, with a mission of cargo and personnel transport) became the Military Airlift Command (MAC) and was placed on a par with other major combat elements. The C-141 was to become the MAC workhorse.

An initial cadre was assembled to learn the operation of this magnificent new machine and then to train crews. Moving from a propeller-driven aircraft

---

Opposite page: A C-141 Starlifter.

into a fan jet requires some reorganization of one's thought processes, even if the transition is from the relatively fast and high-flying C-130. "Getting behind the airplane" is an anxious feeling and a common sensation for almost everyone who has made the transition from either a smaller or a slower aircraft. For this reason, MAC pilots do not spend their first hours at the controls of the aircraft. Instead, the pilots, along with the primary flight deck crew members and the engineers spend four weeks in a classroom learning the aircraft systems. This is followed by two weeks of simulator flying built around ten flights that involve learning normal and emergency procedures and the crew coordination required and getting "a feel for the bird." Only then is a pilot ready to step into the real thing.

Most pilots are introduced to the C-141 on the flight line at Altus AFB, Oklahoma, home of MAC'S Transport Training Unit (TTU). The crew bus stops a few feet from the nose of the aircraft and one can begin to visualize the true size of the machine. Huge, swept wings, attached to the very top of the fuselage, droop out and down until they are within eight feet of the ground. The engines, mounted beneath the wing, can be inspected from the ground without the aid of a ladder because the bottom of the outboard engine is only five feet from the ground. The wings betray their size: 3,228 square feet of wing surface housing 153,352 pounds of fuel (25,558 gallons). The fuselage, designed for loading direct from a flatbed truck, is usually about 18 inches from the ground. The aircraft fuselage curves gracefully up and in to form the horizontal stabilizer. Finally, forty feet above ground level, perched precisely on top of the vertical stabilizer, is the horizontal stabilizer housing the elevator trim motors and elevator actuators. The bullet-shaped leading edge of the stabilizer is the high-frequency antenna. At first sight, head on, I was anxious to be about the business of operating the real machine, yet a bit apprehensive about manipulating those huge wings and powerful engines.

Pilots arrive at the aircraft to find the engineers busy with their preflight chores. On training missions navigators and loadmasters are usually not assigned to the flight. On an operational mission with either cargo, passengers, or both, the minimum crew complement will be two pilots, two engineers, one navigator, and one or more loadmasters. Routinely this complement is augmented with instructors and students to meet the demands for operational mission training.

The Starlifter is a crew-served airplane, with each crew member an expert in his discipline. Operation of the airplane requires each crew member to work in his area virtually unsupervised. All efforts are coordinated by adhering to the copilot's checklist and are keyed to the pilot's commands. A new crew member, or one transferring from a much smaller aircraft, finds the crew coordination requirement one of the top challenges for qualification in the C-141.

Preflight inspection consumes approximately 45 minutes of predeparture time; when complete and the crew has settled into the cockpit, the checklist ritual begins. The pilot commands, "Before Starting Engines Checklist." With that the engineer sets up fuel, electrical, hydraulic, and environmental systems while the pilots tune radios, position flap controls, and select navigation systems displays. Outside, the alternate engineer, called the scanner, signals the launch crew to remove the landing-gear pins and main-gear chocks and to insert nose-gear chocks. The activities of all fuse as the copilot challenges each for his report—"Engineer's report, Scanner's report"—and then reports to the pilot, "Before Starting Engines Checklist complete."

To start the four 21,000-pound thrust engines, bring them to idle speed, and complete the usual hydraulic and electrical checks associated with engine start takes approximately four minutes. This time has been halved very easily in several special circumstances, specifically when the aircraft came under fire in Southeast Asia. The pilot starts the engines by pushing in a starter button, which is automatically held in until the pneumatic starter cuts out, and then moving the Fuel and Start Ignition switch to the run position when the high-pressure compressor section of the engine achieves 15%. The engineer's role in the engine-starting procedure is almost as simple. He positions pneumatic bleed air switches to route the air pressure for starting the engine and then, once it is idling, checks the performance of the engine-driven generator and hydraulic pump.

Taxiing is very easy with proper respect given to the big bird's 160-foot wingspan. A slight advance of power out of the idle range and the plane is under way. On a level ramp, at average weights, taxi seldom requires more than an idle power setting, idle being expressed as a percentage (54 percent rpm) of the high-speed compressor section. The engine at full power turns at 9,655 rpm. Nosewheel steering for the pilot renders the task virtually effortless. Conversely, for the other crew members the time spent taxiing for takeoff is one of the busier periods. The final checks are run and the copilot makes radio adjustment, copies the flight clearance, sets wing flaps, and arms the spoilers in case of an aborted takeoff. The navigator must program the computer and tune the radar. The engineer is occupied with the environmental systems operation and completes a checkout of the fuel system. The loadmaster, busy with passengers or cargo, is active up to the moment the Starlifter is eased onto the runway to start the takeoff roll.

A pilot's physical exertion in controlling the C-141 is minimal. All control surfaces are hydraulically powered. Trim is either electric or hydraulic motor driven. In addition to the nosewheel steering, a hydraulic-powered rudder pedal steering system allows the aircraft to be steered from either pilot's seat and the takeoff to be made without holding the nose-gear steering wheel.

Taxi in heavy crosswinds even up to fifty knots can be accomplished with ease on a dry surface, using only the nosewheel steering and holding in a little upwind aileron to keep the wing down. The natural droop of the wing helps considerably here.

Lift-off speeds run a gamut from the 110–115 knots used for a light training mission to the 139 knots at maximum gross weight of 323,000 pounds. As the computed speed is reached, a slight back pressure to establish a nose-up angle of 6 to 8 degrees will find the aircraft airborne and rapidly accelerating to the climb speed of 280 knots.

Stick pressures in the aircraft are surprisingly light: slightly more than the C-130, significantly less than the C-47 or C-54. On a typical mission, only the takeoff, the first several minutes of the climb, and the last hundred feet on approach and landing are hand flown. "George," the pilot's best friend, is put to work for the remainder of the flight. The Starlifter's "George," or Automatic Flight Control System (AFCS), is an immensely capable friend. Coupled to the navigator's computers or ground-navigation facilities, "George" deftly guides the lateral axis. Once cruise altitude is reached, altitude hold will maintain the level within a few feet—even at Flight Level 410 (41,000 feet). With control-wheel steering, the pilot can use the autopilot systems to trim the aircraft by zeroing out the forces he feels on the ailerons and elevators. With the addition of the Category II All Weather Landing System, in conjunction with the Instrument Landing System, the aircraft has been flown to many touchdowns in zero visibility by the autopilot at various airports throughout the world.

The C-141, with less wing sweep than most jet transports and a wing thickness that allows a slower takeoff and landing speed, pays for such features by surrendering cruise speed. We were indeed a curiosity when we first arrived in the high-altitude jet airspace structure! The C-141's optimum cruise regime is FL 350 through FL 410 at Mach .74 (495 mph). Other transport aircraft in this airspace cruise between FL 300 and FL 350 at Mach .82 (707 or KC-135) or even Mach .85 (747).

The C-141 handles like a real sweetheart in engine-out conditions. At 20,000 feet and full power on one outboard engine and all of the others at idle, it will trim out for hands-off flight at 210 knots. A single engine-out approach and landing is flown exactly like a full four-engine normal landing.

But with two engines out on one side, the asymmetrical thrust will make the pilots earn their money just as in any other multiengine machine. With fully redundant hydraulic and electrical systems, many problems plaguing earlier aircraft were engineered out of the Starlifter.

The versatility of the Starlifter is impressive. It can carry 154 troops or 123 paratroopers. Outfitted with airline-style seats, it can seat 120 passengers with the comfort pallet (removable lavatories and passenger galley). In its air ambulance dress, eighty litter patients can be accommodated with eight attendants. In strict cargo configuration it was designed to airlift a payload of 68,500 pounds.

The many missions performed by this workhorse during its first decade in operational service exemplify the theme of airlift.

The C-141 has positioned presidential limousines; carried Arabian horses, musk oxen, and panda bears; transported hundreds of thousands of American fighting men to and from combat zones and served as an "angel of mercy" in airlifting the wounded home; airdropped divisions complete with men and equipment; hosted astronauts and their space machines; trained several thousand crew members; and most dramatic of all flown several hundred Americans and Vietnamese out of Hanoi.

My long association with this magnificent machine has now spanned the years. It began when I was an initial cadre member from the 76th Military Airlift Squadron, based at Charleston, S.C.

The mission of an airlift squadron is to provide fully qualified aircrew members to operate their assigned type of aircraft throughout the MAC system on training, transport, or combat airlift missions. The airlift squadrons receive crew men initially trained in the aircraft from the TTU at Altus AFB. Instructors and examiners of the operating squadrons take the crew men arriving from the TTU and provide on-the-job training in the daily operation of the aircraft on actual missions. At present (1975), an airlift squadron is assigned 18 aircraft and 36 complete aircrews. At the height of the Southeast Asia conflict this ratio was doubled to 4 crews per airplane.

A second aspect of the operating squadron's mission is to provide continuation training in any special mission assigned the unit, such as the Combat Airdrop Mission (CAM). On the East Coast, Charleston AFB owns this mission and on the West Coast, Norton AFB is assigned the CAM crews.

Once a crew member becomes fully qualified in the normal airlift mission, he returns to Altus for the special CAM training. Once qualified in this mission, the squadron has the task of keeping him current by providing periodic training flights to practice the formation and airdrop maneuvers.

On its high-density routes, MAC has made extensive use of the "stage" system, whereby one crew arrives at a station to enter crew rest to the next station—a modern version of the pony express. At the height of the Southeast Asia conflict, Yokota Air Base often had forty crews staging at one time, each waiting its turn to pick up an incoming plane and press on. In those days, a crew was seldom on the ground at Yokota more than sixteen to eighteen hours. Such was the flow of Starlifters.

One of the more welcome side effects of the C-141 achieving operational status was the reduction in crew members' time away from home. A C-130 or C-124 assignment to a Pacific mission from the East Coast meant eighteen to twenty-one days to work around the system. Outbound stages were through Travis, Hickam, Wake, Guam, Clark, Kadena, and Tachikawa; inbound itinerary was Wake or Midway, Travis, and home. The C-141, with its extended flight capabilities, completes the Northern Pacific route (NOPAC) with a stage at Elmendorf, Yokota, Kadena, Elmendorf, then home—a total of six or seven days in all.

A typical mission begins with a phone call from the squadron duty officer, alerting the crew member. "Show" time is usually one hour later. A crew usually includes at least one newcomer. After introductions the aircraft commander briefs initial mission routing, altitude, fuel requirements, training objectives (if any), seat assignments, and special duties. Then with baggage in hand, the crew boards a bus for transport to the plane. Preflight duties quickly get under way. Loadmasters and engineers preflight the aircraft, and the copilot checks radios and life support equipment. The aircraft commander and navigator do flight planning at base operations and check through the Airlift Command Post. Upon their return to the aircraft, the loadmaster will be completing his loading duties and the engineers closing up the huge petal doors at the rear of the cargo compartment. The aircraft commander will glance through the cargo compartment to check the security of the load or, on passenger missions, the progress of preparations for their boarding.

As the flight-deck crew members take their seats and fasten in, the engineer delivers a TOLD card (takeoff and landing data) to the copilot. After a quick double-check, the copilot passes the data card on to the pilot where it is fixed into a clip holder on the instrument panel for display throughout the takeoff, approach, and landing. Most pilots will use the few moments prior to starting engines to brief the final departure details such as route and altitude assignments, navigation radio set-up, and emergency procedures for an aborted takeoff.

The loadmaster gives his briefing after the passengers are loaded, showing emergency exits, location and function of oxygen equipment, and the other life-support equipment. As soon as the loadmaster finishes, the pilot starts the engines and taxies for takeoff, calling for the succession of checklists that tightly control the activity of all of the primary crew members. Six checklists—Before Starting Engines, Starting Engines, Before Taxi, Taxi, Before Takeoff, and Line Up—will have been accomplished before the Starlifter becomes airborne.

The big aircraft fairly leaps into the air. With the huge flaps at approximately 75 percent, the climb immediately after liftoff is relatively flat, approximately 6 degrees nose-up, until gear retraction. I was always an advocate of engaging the autopilot as soon after takeoff as possible for two reasons: to relieve my inside-the-cockpit workload so I could watch outside more, and to allow me to broaden the span of my attention to the monitoring of navigation radios and to interphone coordination as inflight duties progressed. The copilot is the primary operator of the communications radios, traffic lookout, and altitude and heading monitor. The navigator closely monitors the flight path and his radar, alternately checking weather and terrain and updating his flight plan with ETAs based upon actual departure versus the filed anticipated departure time. A scanner, with primary traffic monitor duties is assigned to the jump seat between the two pilots whenever the aircraft is below 10,000 feet. Other crew members are generally seated on the flight deck, which has seat belts for ten. Seating is restricted to a maximum of nine, however, due to the structural inadequacy of the jump seat in the event of a crash landing or ditching. In addition to the regular crew, an instructor or examiner from one of the three aircrew disciplines manning the flight deck is usually on board.

The initial power reduction, to approximately 92 percent, follows gear retraction and just precedes flap retraction, according to the climb schedule being flown. When 10,000 feet is passed, the power is established at normal rated thrust (NRT), which is the maximum continuous power setting for the remainder of the climb.

As the climb profile is established, the loadmaster begins an initial beverage service for his passengers and the flight deck crew. This service is more than just a courtesy. Fluid intake is necessary to combat the dehydration experienced when working many hours in an environment with an extremely low humidity factor.

The scanner slips back to check the hydraulic service centers and the pressure door, returning to the flight deck to silently indicate all is well. The time required to achieve cruise altitude varies, of course, but usually averages about 25 minutes, or 2,000 feet per minute.

Although the crew refers to a "climb power setting," the power used is really normal rated thrust, the maximum continuous power setting. The parameters of thrust, rpm, and fuel flow change gradually throughout the climb as the engines gain maximum efficiency with altitude. Initially the power is reduced to approximately 90 percent of the N2 rpm or high-speed compressor at a fuel consumption of 40,000 pounds per hour, but as cruise flight is entered at altitude, the rpm will have increased to approximately 95 percent and the fuel flow decreased to 22,000 pounds per hour. In cruise flight the rpm is usually 87 percent at a fuel flow of 12,000 pounds per hour. The Starlifter will enter climb at about 3,000 feet per minute vertical velocity in all but the hottest climates. It will usually pass 20,000 feet at better than 1,000 feet per minute.

During the climb, the engineer has calculated a target power setting and indicated the airspeed necessary to obtain the desired Mach number for cruise. When this speed is reached, the power comes slowly back and cruise flight begins. As an old Gooney Bird pilot I had subscribed to the "step" theory and invariably climbed about 100 feet above the cruise altitude and descended into cruise to find a knot or so extra for the same power setting. However, the Starlifter with its altitude hold and broad power range, has defied application of this technique. In long-range cruise the airplane will traverse several different temperature environments, requiring power changes to maintain constant speed just as gradual power reductions are required as weight decreases. With the increased span of parameters such as weight, altitude, speed, and autopilot control, the phenomenon of the "step" has been lost.

However, another of the "old" techniques of C-47 days is applicable to the operation of the C-141 today. This technique—synchronizing the fans—has proved to be a valuable "carry-over." Prop aircraft developed after the C-47 were equipped with propsynchronization; thus automation took care of the job. The C-141's engine fans chew their way through fairly dense low-altitude air at high power settings and the resulting annoying vibrant harmonic is loud enough to be heard under the pilot's headset. This noise can be smoothed out by applying the technique used to achieve synchronized props in the C-47 or C-54-just a gentle nudge of the throttle to increase or decrease the engine's power. This procedure in the prop airplane involved moving the prop pitch lever. In the C-141 the only lever to move is the throttle. The results, however, are identical: the harmonic vibration blends into smoothness. The pilot is

Opposite page: A Lockheed C-141.

guided in this procedure by a crew man or a headset stationed to the rear of the aircraft so that he will know when the setting is correct.

The C-141 can cruise for what seems an eternity. The daily route structure features mission segments such as Hickam to Anderson (Honolulu to Guam), usually an eight-hour flight plan, or Yokota to Travis (Tokyo to San Francisco), seldom less than nine and a half hours. Longer legs are possible. I have flown as long as ten and a half hours, and others have done more than eleven. In-flight crew rest facilities for such missions are essential. On the flight deck proper, two people can bunk, one in an upper berth, which is used by the pilots, and one in the lower bunk, which is used by the off-duty engineer. Immediately aft of the flight deck and situated above the comfort pallet or number one pallet position, MAC has added a crew rest facility, containing two additional bunks. The loadmasters, navigators, and any extra crew members rotate through these bunks.

In the cruise flight regime two crew positions will always be manned: one of the two pilot positions and the engineer's panel. Depending on the route location, the navigator may not be required (flying air ways for example). During long-range cruise, a specific work-rest plan is used. Although exact duty times vary from one crew to the next, most crew members will work for two to three hours then break for two to three hours. MAC rules require the pilot in command to be in his seat until cruise altitude is reached, thirty minutes prior to descent, and when penetrating an Air Defense Identification Zone (ADIZ). For these reasons most aircraft commanders will take a sleep break at the midpoint in a long flight. During cruise, when beyond the range of VOR or TACAN stations, the navigator must keep the inertial computer programmed through celestial shots or LORAN. This computer output is displayed on the pilot's heading situation indicator (HSI) in place of ground navigation guidance. Coupling the autopilot into this mode reduces the pilot's duties to tending the communications radios, monitoring fuel-range plots prepared by the navigator and engineer, and passing the hourly position report.

MAC utilizes a somewhat unique system for its oceanic position reports. First of all the reports are passed directly to a USAF Global Communications network instead of directly to the controlling civilian air traffic control facility. The USAF Globcom station then relays the report to the civilian controller— an efficient way to reduce frequency congestion. Second, with each position report goes a computer-calculated wind speed and direction report which is forwarded directly to a central weather and flight-planning computer. Thus the flight plans for MAC's worldwide routes are continually updated.

In cruise flight, the C-141 reveals its true luxury to former fighter and bomber pilots: the space to stand and stretch, to go for a stroll, or to use a fairly spacious and comfortable lavatory!

Almost without exception pilots of the Starlifter prefer en route descents rather than the jet penetration. A penetration, easily accomplished by the C-141, requires spoiler deployment to the maximum in flight limit and thus produces a noisier ride with more vibration. It does provide for a descent rate of 4,000–5,000 feet per minute, allowing the aircraft to drop from 20,000 feet to ground level in 30 miles and about five minutes of elapsed time. The en route descent from FL 350 is begun ideally about 110–115 miles from the approach fix and generally about 35 minutes prior to block-in. A descent rate in the vicinity of 2,000 fpm is common. This requires a small amount of engine power, some of which is also necessary to maintain pneumatic pressure for the environmental systems pressurization of the aircraft. During the descent the checklist ritual begins anew with the Descent and Before Landing checklists to be accomplished prior to turning final. Below 10,000 feet the speed is limited by regulation to 250 knots. Above 10,000 feet a descent speed of 280–300 knots is used.

By far the preferred approach is radar vectors to an ILS final. The aircraft, equipped with the all-weather landing system, can be flown to touchdown by the autopilot on runways equipped with the landing system. The touchdown, flown by the autopilot, is slightly harsher than one flown by hand, and for this reason most C-141 pilots will uncouple the autopilot at decision height and hand-fly the remainder of the approach. My personal technique for the fully coupled all-weather approach has been to use automatic facilities available, including automatic throttles for power control and control wheel steering to provide priority guidance to the autopilot which was actually flying the approach. Using this technique I would establish a few degrees nose-high attitude just prior to touchdown instead of the rather flat touchdown attitude programmed into the all-weather landing system. The result is a very smooth touchdown. As the nose gear is lowered to the runway, the pilot calls for spoiler deployment to destroy the lift of the wings and simultaneously deploys the thrust reversers by bringing the four throttles behind idle into the reverse idle position. With full antiskid braking, spoilers and thrust reversers employed, deceleration of the Starlifter requires very little runway ground roll, often in the vicinity of 3,000 feet. Full use of brakes and thrust reversers on a 10,000-foot runway to achieve a 3,000-foot ground roll causes unnecessary wear and noise, and therefore most pilots deploy thrust reversers, check the brakes, then let the aircraft roll out to runway's end.

Arriving on the blocks at the destination begins another flurry of activity for the crew. As soon as the passengers are off-loaded, the crew baggage comes off to be loaded into the crew bus. Often the outbound and inbound crew's baggage pass on the ramp, separated by a concrete pathway between the bags.

The outbound crew's pilots, navigators, engineers, and loadmasters seek out their counterparts on the inbound crew to learn details of the aircraft's performance, load, and any mission peculiarities. A quick-service maintenance team, usually composed of three ground-crew men, receives a briefing by the engineers regarding any repairs necessary, then refueling begins as the inbound crew hustles off in the direction of the MAC command post.

With maintenance debriefed on the aircraft's status, the forecaster debriefed on en route weather conditions, the command post duty officer advises the crew when their alert call can be expected. This is followed by a short drive to the base billeting facility where once again the baggage comes off the crew bus and goes into quarters. Some MAC troops joke about the old-time crew members whose arms hung below their knees—a result of 10,000 and more baggage drills! A minimum crew rest period is 12 hours; however it usually averages 18 to 24 hours, depending upon the number of crews in stage, maintenance, or the nature of the mission.

The diversity of the big airplane's many missions is perhaps the most gratifying aspect of association with it. For example, between 1970 and 1972 I flew missions to all continents except the Arctic and Antarctic (Thule Air Base in Greenland should give almost Arctic credit). The many varied missions included a routine resupply at Learmouth on the far Australian coast and at tiny Diego Garcia in the Indian Ocean; the round-the-world Embassy run through Thailand, India, Saudi Arabia, and Spain; combat airlift missions; dropping paratroopers and equipment; initial reduced interval formation (on the wing formation); nuclear airlift; Minuteman missile airlift; an extremely exciting presidential support mission through Salzburg, Austria, Moscow, and Poland; and the Med-Evac missions, some of which were nearly overwhelming in pathos and challenged one's most professional capabilities to provide a smooth ride.

One of these missions stands above all others in terms of job satisfaction. Our crew was alerted at Yokota Air Base, Japan (near Tokyo) for a Med-Evac mission direct to Travis, nine and a half hours away. We breezed through the flight planning drill using Alameda Naval Air Station near San Francisco as our alternate. En route weather was good, averaging seventy-five knots tailwind following a mid-Pacific routing about equidistant from Midway Island to the Aleutian Islands. To take advantage of this jet stream our planned altitude was 35,000 feet, distance to run: 4333 nautical miles. Any difficulties encountered near the midpoint of our route which precluded returning to Yokota or proceeding on to Travis would require diversion to Wake or Midway Islands in the mid-Pacific, or to Shemya, Adah, or Cold Bay in the Aleutian chain.

With these details accomplished we proceeded to the aircraft to find the medical crew, composed of a Medical Crew Director (MCD)—Senior Nurse—a flight nurse, and three medical technicians busy checking their equipment and preparing for the patient on-load. Our flight crew, finished with their preflight checks, were tidying up loose equipment while the loadmaster supervised the fleet service personnel stocking the comfort pallet with the in-flight meals. The engineers reported full fuel tanks at 153,000 pounds and no significant mechanical discrepancies.

Prior to loading the patients, the pilot, loadmasters, and medical crew director had a conference to review aircraft emergency procedures, the route, weather, and any special patient requirements. Burn patients in Stryker frames are particularly uncomfortable and sensitive to any jostling, acceleration, and deceleration. Our flight nurse informed us that we had such a patient in our load of twenty litter and thirty ambulatory patients. A sparkling little lady in her midtwenties, but a veteran of a year's worth of these Med-Evac missions, our senior nurse asked that we be as smooth as possible. We promised that we would.

In the predeparture crew briefing I stressed our goal to be as gentle as possible in aircraft operation from the physical manipulation of the airframe to the management of the pressurization system. After the patients were loaded and while the nurse delivered her briefing to the patients and passengers, we copied our flight clearance to be ready to start engines as soon as she finished. With engines started, the checklists complete, and taxi clearance received, I slipped the parking brake off and inched the throttles out of idle to build up enough forward thrust to overcome 323,000 pounds of dead weight. As the wheels started to turn forward, the marshaller signaled for a right turn out of parking and we were off the blocks. Almost as soon as the roll was started, the throttles had to be returned to idle to prevent excessive taxi speed—such is the power of these engines, even at idle.

En route to the runway the copilot went through the checklist and configured the aircraft for takeoff. Once cleared, the takeoff roll began, using a rolling takeoff technique where power is gradually set as the air craft accelerates, sacrificing several hundred feet of runway for the extra smoothness.

Our initial climb altitude was 33,000 feet, which we reached about 25 minutes after takeoff. Several hours later, with about 30,000 pounds of fuel burned off, our weight was down sufficiently to permit a climb to 37,000 feet. We maintained 37,000 feet as our final altitude. Using the USAF high-frequency global communications network we phoned ahead to provide information about the aircraft's maintenance status and patient requirements. We learned that Travis had rain showers with cumulous buildups in the area. This meant our navigator with his radar would become a key figure in the descent for landing as we rely on him to thread our way around the buildups to avoid the fierce bumps as we maneuver for the landing runway.

We picked our way past gateway Redwood and established contact with Oakland center, which would guide our descent to 6,000 feet, at which time Travis AFB approach control would assume responsibility. At 135 miles out I eased the throttles back and nudged into a 3° nose-low attitude to find the 2,000 feet per minute rate of descent that I like.

An abrupt change of sound in flight causes anxiety among passengers and when the passengers are patients, the anxiety is intensified. For this reason, when I reduce power for the en route descent I take most of the power from the outboard engines and leave the inboard engines set well above idle to provide the bleed air required for pressurization, thus avoiding a significant sound-level change.

Throughout the descent the navigator double-checked each heading and altitude assignment for terrain clearance and suggested headings to avoid the areas of turbulent clouds. As we crossed the northern end of Napa Valley, Oakland center passed us off to Travis approach and suddenly we were busy configuring for our landing. The determination to be smooth, plus the wet runway, produced one of those few touchdowns heard but not felt. Taxi into the blocks was as cautious as the taxi out had been. The deep satisfaction of a long day's work done well was realized when the senior nurse came forward after the patients were offloaded and commented, "Colonel, that was the smoothest flight I have ever had!" I never flew with her medical crew again, but that praise had the same effect on my psyche that is produced by the superb golf shot that occurs when everything grooves perfectly—soul-satisfying contentment for today, keen challenge for tomorrow!

Col. Alton P. H. Brewer, Jr., graduated from Aviation Cadets in 1954 and began his USAF flying as a SAC fighter pilot. After a tour in USAFE flying support C-47s and a two-year stint as a Civil Air Patrol liaison officer, he was assigned to MAC in 1963. Since then he has served in five of MAC's Strategic Airlift Wings and has served a three-year tour in MAC's Aerospace Rescue and Recovery Service. He has been a line pilot, instructor pilot, flight examiner, squadron and wing chief of aircrew standardization (chief pilot), squadron operations officer, commander of the 15th Military Airlift Squadron, and presently serves as Assistant Deputy Commander of Operations for the 62nd MAW at McChord AFB. He has 10,000 hours, 7,000 of which have been in MAC, in approximately eighteen Air Force aircraft.

Transition from C-141s to Helicopters

Gary L. Stevens

Helicopter assignments in 1970 for C-141 Starlifter pilots were somewhat like accidents to be avoided, but nothing to lose sleep over because they always happened to the other guy.

As a twenty-four-year-old C-141 aircraft commander with the Military Airlift Command, I felt I had my career well on its way. I was responsible for a $7 million aircraft with a worldwide mission, was building flying time at a furious rate, and was supporting our nation's efforts in Southeast Asia. Certainly the Air Force would never take me away from such a crucial assignment and start me from scratch again learning to fly helicopters. I was wrong.

My assignment to Sheppard Air Force Base, Texas, for transition training in late 1970 looked like the beginning of professional disaster. I had accumulated over 1,300 flying hours in Starlifters in less than two years apparently for naught. I saw myself trading a safe, comfortable, tremendously powerful aircraft for something that, in my eyes, defied all natural laws by even leaving the ground.

As someone once observed, a helicopter is held aloft by a variety of forces and controls working in opposition to each other, and if there is any disturbance in this delicate balance, the craft stops flying, immediately and disastrously. I agreed wholeheartedly.

Such a negative attitude was not too unusual among my classmates as they arrived at Sheppard as experienced pilots in C-141s, B-52s, KC-135s, C-130s, and various other large fixed-wing machines. For me, the attitude never sur-

---

Opposite page: Among the C-141's functions was dropping paratroopers.

73

vived the first flight, and I think that, too, was widespread. One exposure to hovering, autorotations, sideward flight, and low-level operations dimmed forever the appeal of being a systems monitor on a flying robot like the Starlifter.

Coming out of a multijet heavy transport, preflight planning for a helicopter mission seemed a complete study in contrasts. From jet routes to low-level Visual Flight Rules, from cruising speeds computed in percent of Mach to those in tens of knots, from concerns over 200 knot jetstreams to concerns over 30 knot surface winds, almost every facet of the planning was essentially opposite from my previous strategic airlift experience.

Of course, the tremendous variety of missions possible with a helicopter directly affects the nature of the planning, but most missions require special emphasis on certain aspects peculiar to helicopter operations. These factors include landings and takeoffs from unprepared remote sites, low-altitude cruise, field operations away from normal maintenance and servicing support, and the necessity to compute hovering capability under widely varying and often unpredictable conditions.

Once out at the aircraft, the transition pilot finds the preflight procedure to be relatively conventional. After checking the maintenance forms, a walk-around inspection of the aircraft is in order. I found the H-1 Huey rather well suited for teaching a budding flingwinger what to look for on his preflight inspection. The systems are relatively simple and accessible, although inspection of the main rotor assembly requires a climb up the right side of the fuselage and a short walk across the cabin roof. In strong winds or on wet days, that portion of the preflight can become sporty.

Besides the usual checks of the engine compartment, fluid levels, and over-all airframe condition, a chopper pilot pays a great deal of attention to the rotors, both main and tail. There is little parallel in my fixed-wing experience, with the critical importance of bolts or other fasteners, to such vital components as the rotors. It would be almost like having the maintenance troops routinely remove and replace the Starlifter's wings if secured by several large bolts.

On the Huey, for example, the main blades each were fastened to the rotor head by one very large nut secured by one very large bolt which is very well safety-wired. Even though I had the utmost confidence in the professionalism of our maintenance troops, I also recognized that they, like me, were subject to human error, and it only took one mistake with that big nut and bolt to ruin my whole day in the air. That assembly was a high interest item in my preflight.

Once strapped into the seat, I found the cockpit environment similar to a fixed-wing bizjet in complexity and instrumentation. Below the panel were two sets of pedals resembling in appearance and function the rudder pedals of the

Starlifter. In front of each pilot's seat was a stick virtually identical to that found in many fighter aircraft. To the left of the pilot's seat, however, was a control that resembled little more than the parking brake handle in a Volkswagon. It was this shaft-like fixture called a collective that directed a helicopter through so many of its unique maneuvers. Movement of the collective once the rotors are up to speed will result in the vertical liftoff maneuver with which rotary wing craft made their name.

Engine start was a procedure somewhere midway on the spectrum of complexity between the Throttles—Idle, Starter Button—Depress routine of the C-141 and the artistic juggling of three toggle switches and two throttles on the prop-powered T-29/C-131s I flew for proficiency training after my return from Southeast Asia.

The throttle on the TH-1F operates almost like a motorcycle throttle, with a twist of the grip on the collective. Unlike the motorcycle, however, constant corrections of power need not be made with the twist grip. Once the approximate rotor rpm desired has been set, an internal governor in the fuel control system will increase or decrease fuel flow as necessary to maintain that rpm. Occasional throttle movements still may be necessary under certain conditions of rapid large power fluctuation, but for the most part, manual throttle operation is unnecessary.

Motorcycle enthusiasts have had their moments in Hueys because of that throttle similarity, though. They soon discover that the Huey throttle operates the opposite of cycle throttles. A twist of the wrist, then, that would send their cycle roaring off into the sunset brings the Huey engine coasting down to idle, sometimes with hair-raising results.

With engine start in the Huey, I experienced a critical difference between Starlifters and helicopters; a Starlifter doesn't begin to fly until it accelerates down the runway, but the Huey is flying as soon as the rotors start turning. Essentially, the only difference between resting in the chocks with the rpm up and flying at 3,000 feet is the pitch of the rotor blades. For obvious reasons, then, my instructor stressed the necessity of handling the controls from engine start until shutdown as if I were flying—because I was.

The Before-Taxi Checklist is not radically different in a Huey from that of a small fixed-wing aircraft. The instruments, the radios, and various systems are checked or activated as appropriate while the rotors are turning at flat pitch, keeping the aircraft firmly planted on the ramp.

As rotor rpm increased during that first engine start, I sat waiting for the instructor to initiate an emergency shutdown. I was firmly convinced that the aircraft was about to shake apart. When the instructor simply continued his patter as he went through the checklist, I finally asked him if it was normal for my innards to be jellified by all that shaking. He grinned. I thought he shook his head "yes," but I wasn't sure if the head-shaking was intentional or rotor-induced.

Taxiing is the next radical departure from my past experiences as a fixed winger. Instead of pulling the chocks, clearing the area, and advancing the throttle(s), the Huey pilot clears the area, adds collective, and starts flying. It is a basic characteristic of vehicles without wheels to resist movement across the ground, and the skid-equipped Huey is no exception.

Because of this design quirk, the beginning student does not get to taxi a Huey until after he has developed a feel for the aircraft in normal forward flight and in a hover at the practice areas far removed from other helicopters and equipment.

With the instructor on the controls, taxiing looks deceptively easy. He seems to simply increase the collective to increase the pitch of both main rotor blades simultaneously, lifts to about a three-foot hover, checks the engine instruments, eases the cyclic stick slightly forward, and begins to move slowly forward along the taxi lines just as if he were rolling along on extended landing gear. Not readily apparent to the new student is the tremendous amount of coordination required among collective, tail rotor pedal, and cyclic stick inputs to produce that smooth taxi maneuver. To the untrained eye, there seems to be little control movement required to lift off and to move forward along that taxi line, or even to make the gentle turns en route to the takeoff point. The student's first efforts on his own, however, are usually an enlightening and humbling experience.

I recall all too vividly my own first effort. The instructor had taxied out to the departure pad at Sheppard and departed along the route specified to avoid sharing airspace simultaneously with the Air Training Command's T-37s and T-38s using the nearby runways and adjacent airspace. Once away from the congestion of the pattern, the instructor turned the controls over to me and directed a few gentle turns and climbs and descents.

The Huey was remarkably similar to fixed-wing aircraft in its response to the cyclic in-cruise flight (90 knots) and was relatively simple to handle during climbs and descents with the collective.

To turn right, I simply moved the cyclic to the right and added enough right rotor pedal to keep the turn coordinated. As long as the bank angle remained less than about 10 degrees, I had to add a little collective to maintain a constant altitude.

Those first few turns introduced me to another quirk of helicopter control; if the cyclic was used like the stick in a fixed-wing aircraft, the aft movement to maintain altitude in a turn would simply bleed off airspeed, with no amount of throttle movement counteracting the loss. Instead of moving the stick into the direction of turn, coordinating with rudder, maintaining altitude with back pressure on the elevator, and adding throttle to hold airspeed, I discovered a whole new sequence was necessary.

The primary difference was that unlike maneuvering a Starlifter, a helicopter's throttle is not the primary control for airspeed. Instead, airspeed control requires a combination of cyclic and collective movement during a turn. The degree of movement for each depends upon whether the maneuver is a climb, a descent, a turn, or some combination of the three. For my level turn, then, I moved the cyclic in the direction of the turn until the desired bank angle was achieved. Then I centered the cyclic laterally while maintaining the same forward displacement as I had prior to the turn to maintain my 90 knots, increasing the collective slightly to maintain both altitude and airspeed which would otherwise decrease because of the bank angle. Meanwhile, I coordinated the turn with a little rudder pedal in the direction of the turn. Even with over 1,500 hours of fixed-wing time under my belt, I still found that I quit chewing my gum during the first few turns!

Like so many other aspects of flying, the initial intense concentration required soon diminished until the proper input of the proper control at the proper time became second nature. Before the end of the first flight I could make a 90-degree heading change and roll out on desired heading, airspeed, and altitude with hardly any interruption in my gum chewing. But during my first attempt at hovering, I swallowed my gum!

In today's vernacular, hovering for chopper pilots is "where it's at." That's how chopper pilots earn their keep. It didn't take me too long to feel reasonably comfortable with the Huey in normal cruise flight, but any overconfidence I developed in those first few minutes was completely devastated by the workout on the practice pads a few minutes later. Naturally, the instructor flew the first approach to the pad, terminating in a rock-solid three-foot hover.

After a short demonstration of hovering and sideward flight, he rolled the nose over and started another trip around the pattern. Traffic pattern altitude was 500 feet above ground level (AGL) at an airspeed of 80 knots indicated airspeed (KIAS), descending to 300 feet AGL during the turn to base while slowing to 60 KIAS. The Before-Landing Checklist was normally performed on downwind, consisting of a short crew and passenger briefing, a power check, a check of shoulder harnesses, and an extension of the landing light, if required.

I handled the downwind reasonably well, holding heading, airspeed, and altitude within the ball park. The approach began to go to pot a little as I tried to simultaneously turn 90 degrees, descend 200 feet, and lose about 20 knots of airspeed. But the turn to final went a little better as it involved only a heading change to line up with the approach course to the pad with a constant airspeed and altitude.

The traffic pattern procedures to this point, except for cyclic/collective gyrations in the turn to base, would look familiar to any light-plane pilot. Once on final, though, virtually all those sacred laws of fixed-wing aeronautics began to take a beating. For openers, the approach angle was ten times the familiar 3-degree slope I had come to know and love from my Starlifter days. Cardinal Rule number 2, "keep your airspeed up on final 'til the flare," converted instead to "gradually decrease your airspeed as you descend so as to achieve zero ground speed as you arrive over the pad, three feet in the air."

Contrasts between fixed-wing and rotary-wing procedures are probably most pronounced in the landing and takeoff phases of operations. Put simply, the fixed-winger is worried about accelerating on takeoff to gain sufficient lift for flight and must maintain certain minimum airspeeds for all phases of operation to keep flying. The chopper pilot, in contrast, has all the lift he needs (within limits, of course) at the lift of the collective. Thus airspeed to him becomes simply a measure of how long it will take to cover a given distance instead of being a controlling factor in staying airborne.

The other reason for the direct contrasts during the takeoff and landing phases for the two types of aircraft is the consolidation of functions in the helicopter rotor system. The main rotor on a Huey translates engine power into both lift and thrust, combining the functions of wings and power plants of fixed-wing planes. As a result, the transition pilot is faced with learning to do the reverse of what he's done in the past to perform a given maneuver. He pushes the stick forward and dips the nose to take off, stops in the air before touchdown, and worries about stalling the aircraft by going too fast.

That last quirk may seem strange at first, but makes sense when you stop and think about it. The rotating blades create lift equally only when there is no wind relative to the whole rotor system. As the rotor system (with helicopter attached) accelerates forward, the relative wind increases over the advancing blade(s) just as it would over a wing, with a similar effect. The retreating blade(s) on the other side, however, experience a decreasing relative wind velocity, eventually stalling just like a wing on a slow-flying conventional aircraft.

The high-speed helicopter stall is about as undesirable as the low-speed stall in conventional aircraft. Depending on the rate of acceleration, it will be anything from a burble accompanied by a tendency to bank left to a full-fledged snap roll in that direction. The secondary effects of a chopper stall are the real threat, though. A rapid roll as you cruise along can be unnerving, but the problem compounds as you end up inverted and slowing down. This places negative forces on the rotors far beyond design limits. Under such circumstances, rotors have been known to either fly apart immediately or tear themselves apart as they cut into the cockpit and tail boom. Either way, it's a tough way to end a flight. I learned during that first attempt to hover that a helicopter's airframe is exposed to about as much risk in hover training as it is during high-speed flight. My first approach to the pad deteriorated to the point that the instructor took the controls and salvaged it. Once stabilized in a hover, he turned the aircraft over to me again, one control at a time, and the maneuver became more like hover aerobatics as I gained more controls.

Hovering is the heart of helicopter operations. "To fly is heavenly, to hover, divine," is a popular saying in chopper circles, but "divine" in the phrase would seem more appropriate if it were changed to "impossible" for the transition student.

The key to good hovering is anticipation of required control inputs and the use of a series of very small inputs instead of a few large ones. No matter how many times the instructor stresses the latter point, only experience can drive it home. I thought I knew about small control inputs from flying formation at 500 knots in the T-38 Talon during pilot training or flying a good instrument approach in the C-141. I didn't.

No previous experience prepared me for that first crack at hovering a Huey. For about the first five seconds, I just held everything the way I took it from the instructor and we stayed at the same point in space. A gentle shift in the wind, though, was all it took to create chaos. I sensed the aircraft drifting slightly backward and applied forward pressure ever so lightly to the cyclic to counteract it. Nothing happened. I put more forward pressure on the cyclic. Simultaneously, the initial input took effect and before I could negate the second movement, the Huey started creeping forward. In trying to stop the forward movement, I repeated the sequence of overcontrol in the opposite direction with similar but amplified results.

Within 15 seconds, I was 30 feet in the air, 10 degrees nose high, 50 feet east of my original point, 20 degrees off my heading, and out of control. The instructor let me thrash around long enough to illustrate his point but not long enough to crash before he took over again. He stabilized the hover three feet over the center of the pad and began to explain to me what I had done wrong.

Two basic mistakes on my part brought me to grief in that first effort. One, of course, was the element of overcontrol. The second was failure to allow for the delayed control response inherent to most helicopters. This is where the anticipation element enters. A sharp pilot must anticipate the need for control input before it develops or else his hover position will wander a little. It sounds difficult because it is. The difference between a competent helicopter pilot and an expert helicopter pilot is largely the degree of development of this sixth sense of impending drift while hovering.

It was just a matter of a little repetition for me to fly a normal approach to that practice pad in gentle winds and come into a reasonable hover, but with

600 hours of helicopter time under my belt now, I still should not consider myself an expert.

During my year in Southeast Asia flying CH-53 Super Jolly Green Giants, I had occasion to hover over a small stream with my ramp over the bank while a live water buffalo was offloaded. Even with hundreds of hours of combat experience in the aircraft, I still had trouble holding a stable hover while my cargo walked to the rear of the cabin and stepped off the ramp. I just didn't have that sense of anticipation properly developed.

Learning to hover the Huey was an experience similar to that of learning to land the Starlifter. After repeated unsuccessful attempts, suddenly I could do it. I recall that my first few approaches on the Starlifter resulted in consistently high flares prior to touchdown until I finally adjusted to the size of the aircraft and made one proper flare. After that, it was simply a matter of polishing my technique because the proper flare picture was embedded in my mind.

In hovering, I discovered about 12 flying hours into the program how to stabilize that Huey over a given point, and from that day on, I worked at polishing technique and learning to cope with a greater spectrum of variables. At that point in training, I had just got the feel for hovering in a manner reminiscent of seeing the flare picture back in 1969 aboard a C-141.

Helicopter pilots also need to have a flare picture in their heads, although they may not need to use it quite as often as a fixed-wing pilot. It comes in handy during autorotations, the fling-wing version of dead-stick landings. To autorotate, the collective is lowered to the flat pitch setting for the main rotor blades. This establishes a descent which can then be adjusted with the cyclic to increase or decrease the rate of descent. The sensation during autorotation is very much like that of an engine-out glide in a light aircraft. Rather than simply falling out of the sky like a rock, a helicopter in autorotation comes down under virtually complete control of the pilot. The rotor rpm is maintained by the air passing through the rotor system with a pinwheel effect, providing lift and controllability.

The rate of descent is a function of airspeed the same as in a glide; lower the nose and the airspeed and rate of descent increase, raise it and they decrease. Instead of risking a stall, however, when airspeed and descent rate decrease below safe minimums, the problem is loss of rotor rpm. The end result is loss of lift, which is just as bad as a stall, as both require sufficient altitude to permit acceleration again.

The need for a good flare picture becomes evident as the helicopter approaches the ground, still maintaining airspeeds somewhere above 50 knots. Unlike the gliding fixed-wing plane, there is no need for the helicopter to maintain airspeed above stall speed until impact—only rotor rpm sufficient

Opposite page: Three C-141s protrude from hangars at a Lockheed facility in Georgia.

to provide lift. Therefore, chopper pilots learn to raise the nose at a predetermined height above the ground by pulling the cyclic aft, causing the relative ground speed to decrease and the rotor rpm to increase because of the increased angle of attack. This dual-purpose maneuver ideally results in a 0–15 knot relative ground speed and sufficient rotor rpm to permit a soft, controlled landing through judicious use of the collective to increase rotor blade pitch and to produce lift enough for a normal landing.

The ability to autorotate into a relatively small clearing is probably the single greatest morale builder going for new Huey pilots coming out of multi-engine jet bombers, tankers, and transports. I found considerable assurance in my ability to consistently put a Huey into a particular clearing in the practice area in good shape after the instructor called out "simulated engine failure" without warning in the course of a training flight. In a single-engine helicopter, that capability is pretty good life insurance.

Initially, a standard autorotation profile is used to teach the basic procedures, and as proficiency improves, variations to the profile are introduced. The practice maneuver begins at 500 feet AGL at 65–100 KIAS. After lowering the collective to begin descent, the throttle is decreased until the torque indicator reads zero, thereby simulating engine failure while retaining the ability to recover rapidly if the maneuver goes sour. A usable touchdown point is selected within gliding distance, preferably upwind or close enough to allow maneuvering for a touchdown into the wind. During descent, an airspeed of 70 KIAS is maintained, resulting in a rate of descent around 1,500 feet per minute. The approach is planned to permit a flare about 75 feet AGL to slow to 0-15 knots ground speed directly over the intended landing spot and break the rate of descent. The flare should terminate no lower than 25 feet AGL by leveling the helicopter with forward cyclic and descending vertically. At this point, the training maneuver begins to vary from the actual emergency procedure.

In training, the collective and throttle are increased in order to stop descent three feet above the ground. In an actual autorotation, the collective is used to break the rate of descent just prior to touchdown just like on a normal landing from a hover. The difference is that the rotor rpm is decreasing rapidly with the increased blade pitch, and if the cushioning effect is prolonged beyond a few seconds, the rpm will decrease below flying rpm and the chopper will literally fall out of the sky. If the collective is not pulled up soon enough or far enough, though, the touchdown will result in a crash landing. It is an example of seat-of-the-pants flying in its purest form.

Because engines seemingly never fail during flight over terrain of known elevation, the ability accurately to judge 75 feet AGL and 25 feet AGL is critical to safe autorotations. It's the helicopter pilot's flare picture and he learns it just as religiously as his fixed-wing counterparts memorize their own flare picture.

Once I had the basic practice profile down pat, the instructor began working on my response to simulated engine failures at high speed and low altitude, on takeoff at low altitude and low airspeed, in a hover, and in just about any other stage of the mission profile where loss of power could be a critical problem. With a little practice, I managed to walk away from anything he threw at me.

The transition course at Sheppard took 12 weeks to convert me from a jet transport aircraft commander to an H-3 Jolly Green Giant copilot with enough proficiency to fly operational missions with a more experienced pilot in command. The Huey phase took about six weeks, with the last half of the school devoted to preparing me specifically to fly the H-3. After eight months of H-3 experience with the Aerial Cartographic and Geodetic Service at Forbes Air Force Base, Kansas, I spent a year flying the CH-53C, Super Jolly Green Giant with the 21st Special Operations Squadron at Nakhon Phanom Royal Thai Air Base, Thailand.

These assignments exposed me to virtually every aspect of helicopter operations under a variety of conditions. I hauled everything from aerial photographers to water buffalo and flew over prairies and mountains in tropical heat and Colorado Rocky Mountain cold. I made instrument approaches to 11,000-foot concrete runways and visual approaches to ridge lines only large enough for one main landing gear at a time. Many of the missions were single-ship but most involved up to seven other CH-53s in formation. I called my assignments a lot of things from time to time, but I never called them dull.

My transition experience is about six years into my past now, and since my return from Thailand in 1972, I've had a desk job at Military Airlift Command headquarters at Scott Air Force Base, Illinois. I logged about 200 hours in transports at Scott during the proficiency training I mentioned earlier, but my heart has stayed with choppers.

In fact, as this is written, I have orders to return to the cockpit this spring (1976) to fly the CH-53 again, this time with the 601st Tactical Air Support Squadron in Germany. The mission and environment will be entirely different from my previous experience, but I'm confident that I'll like it.

After all, I'm still a firm believer that "to fly is heavenly, to hover, divine."

Capt. Gary L. Stevens was a 1967 AFROTC graduate from Mississippi State University. After pilot training at Craig AFB, AL, he was assigned to the 438th Military Airlift Wing at McGuire AFB, NJ, flying C-141s. He accumulated about 1,350 hours before transitioning into helicopters in 1971 at Sheppard AFB, TX. He has also flown the TH-1, T-29, and C-131.

B-58 Hustler

Robert E. Hinnant

At Carswell Air Force Base in 1960 we were afforded regular views of the B-58 supersonic bomber, then being tested at the General Dynamics (GD) plant, which was across the runway used jointly by GD and the Air Force. The delta-winged Coke bottle fuselage, perched on long mosquito-legged tricycle landing gear without elevators, looked weird for a four-jet-engine nuclear bomber. Having B-47 and K-135 experience and having been assigned B-52s on base, I found the B-58 a completely different bomber; it had a sleek aggressive look, even with its long large pod hung under the belly to carry fuel and nuclear weapons or equivalent ballast.

It was no secret when the afterburners of the J-79 engines cut in that a B-58 was being flown by GD. Windows rattled and nerves were jangled for the 7,000–9,000-foot run on takeoff. I never really got used to the noise—just accepted it with earplugs or insulated earmuffs for the next nine years at three bases.

Finally the first aircraft went to the Air Force Test Force Group, and phase testing was completed. Aircraft were assigned to the 43rd Bomb Wing, were eventually declared combat ready, and went on to win the Strategic Air Command bombing competition within three weeks—an outstanding performance considering the seasoned B-47 and B-52 crews and aircraft competing as well as the crews and planes of the British Royal Air Force that participated in the competition under the same rules.

The B-58 operations began in 1958. Eight aircraft were configured as trainer-bombers in which the student pilot occupied the front seat, the instructor pilot the second, and the defense system operator (DSO) the third station.

Opposite page: The Convair B-58.

85

(The instructor pilot's seat was installed off-center so he could peek around the pilot during takeoff and landing.) A few hours in the trainer was all the pilot got before he was strapped into a bomber and waved off the ramp on his own. Many times the instructor who signed him off as qualified would run his beads through as he sat and sweated out the return and landing. Since the crews were handpicked with high standards, qualification solo flights were not a problem; the weak were weeded out before this phase of training.

We entered the three individual crew compartments from a stand that was rolled alongside the forward left side of the aircraft. In the first station was the pilot, in the second an observer (radar, navigator, bombardier), and in the third another observer (electronic countermeasures, remote fire control, and assistant to the pilot). The seats were open-jawed escape capsules, extremely complicated but 100 percent dependable. After checking the proper insertion of safety pins, we took our seats in the capsules. The first amazing realization was that the B-58 had a flight control *stick*, not a control column with a wheel. Secondly, we became aware that the cockpit was completely full—engine instruments, flight instruments, buttons, switches, lights, levers, throttles, and even a rearview mirror.

After stowing lunch, briefcase, and related papers we completed the electrical "power off" checklist; then the ground crew connected the external power and air conditioner, and the "before start" portion of the checklist was completed by the three crew members. A ground crew member, stationed in front of the aircraft on interphone, worked with the crew during aircraft systems checkout. When the three crew members agreed that the aircraft was satisfactorily configured for the particular mission, the aircraft commander (pilot) told the ground crew that he was ready to start engines. The "start engine" sequence was arranged so that aircraft electrical power and hydraulic (orinite) pressure output could be checked and used. The crew chief on the ramp determined that the engine air starter had properly disengaged, and the flight controls were checked visually by the ground crew in coordination with the pilot's movements of the stick and rudder. The B-58 had no fly-by-wire flight control systems or elevators. The elevons acted as aileron and elevator— a sophisticated system that gave the pilot the same feel all the time although control surface movement varied greatly during various flight conditions. When the external electrical power, air-for-start, and air conditioner were disconnected and another lengthy checklist completed by all three crew members, clearance for taxi was received from the control tower.

The above procedures were followed for routine training flights but were altered drastically when the aircraft was "cocked" on alert. In such a case the

---

Opposite page: Coming in for a landing.

aircraft was configured for its specific wartime mission, normally with five atomic weapons, and a numbered crew assigned to a tail number aircraft. Under these conditions the complete alert force could be launched within five minutes from ground-alert posture. Practice "scrambles" from ground-alert posture were ordered by higher headquarters at random times and conditions, and the flight crews never knew whether or not it was the real thing until the appropriate code was given when ready for takeoff.

Taxi-out was simple and quick with nosewheel steering; the engines idled at about 72% rpm, gobbling fuel. Sharp turns were avoided when feasible, for the main landing gear had eight wheels each, small in size and inflated to approximately 265 psi with nitrogen (so a blown tire would not support combustion of any material). After aligning the aircraft on the runway and obtaining clearance from the control tower, the throttles were advanced, all instruments checked, then brakes released as power was advanced through afterburner cut-in.

The aircraft seemed to lunge forward as each engine contributed over 15,000 pounds of thrust. Computed takeoff data were used to check performance as the thousand-foot markers were passed; since takeoff air speed, stopping distance, and three-engine performance were known, rapid decisions had to be made until you passed the point on the runway where you were committed to go regardless. By then airspeed was around 190 knots; as the computed airspeed for takeoff was attained you rotated the aircraft positively, broke ground, and held attitude as a definite rate of climb was indicated and airspeed increased. At sea level the fully loaded B-58 climbed at a speed in excess of 17,000 feet per minute—a rate of climb that would have been creditable for a fighter of that day. When lightly loaded the Hustler shot upwards at 46,000 feet per minute, with afterburner! When the landing gear was retracted and "locked" indicated, airspeed was allowed to increase to climb speed; then you could listen to ground control or the bitch box and take a deep gulp of oxygen, check your flight plan, listen to the navigator or defense system operator (DSO), and become released from ground control.

Now it was simple if everything went according to plan. You put the autopilot in the mode desired and followed your flight plan. If things were not operating normally, a female voice told you so (voice warning); if more than one malfunction occurred, the "old bitch" would tell you the most important one and would keep on until you did something about it. Of course warning lights flashed indicating malfunctions; you could cover them up, but you couldn't stop the voice. The DSO was very helpful in reading various checklists, but the pilot took the actions or told the DSO to pull certain circuit breakers (he had hundreds in his compartment).

The B-58 responded to control stick and rudder movement very much as did the F-102, which was used for transition into the program because of its delta wing. When speed was increased through Mach 1 to Mach 2 or less, the center of gravity was shifted by either automatic or manual transfer of fuel into or out of the ballast tank located in the aft portion of the fuselage. This allowed the aircraft to ride on the downhill slope of the sonic air crest. Also, as speed increased the spikes or center cones in each engine inlet had to extend so that the sonic shock wave never entered the engine, now that the speed was limited by maximum allowable inlet air temperature and by structural factors. The aircraft was *not* power limited. Normal speed for cruise was over 525 knots (Mach .92), over 600 knots at sea level, and 1,147 knots above 40,000 feet. The B-58 has been flown above 85,000 feet with a payload.

The four engines were the J-79-5B General Electric axial type with afterburner. The sea level static ratings were: maximum power with afterburner—15,500 pounds thrust at 7,734 rpm maximum continuous for 120 minutes; military power—10,300 pounds thrust at 7,460 rpm continuous. Normal cruise was 9,700 pounds thrust continuous with a maximum allowable exhaust gas temperature of 1,105 degrees Fahrenheit under all conditions.

Air refueling from a KC-135 tanker was easy compared to other air-refueled receivers. The A/R receptacle was aft of the crew compartments atop the fuselage; when flying within the refueling "envelope" you were below the jet wash of the KC-135, with the directional lights on the belly of the tanker right in your face. On refueling to full tanks, it was best to put the two outboard engines in afterburner, then adjust power on the inboard engines to maintain position. The dependable KC-135 tanker with proficient crew was a welcome sight, for the rendezvous was accomplished many times over midocean or polar ice cap. Range with one refueling was 7,400 nautical miles; without refueling, 4,450 miles.

There were two types of pod carried under the belly. The MB-1 type was a single unit in which fuel and nuclear weapon/ballast were carried; some contained photo equipment. The two-component pod carried fuel in the lower section, which could be jettisoned after the fuel was used; the upper component contained the warhead. Four smaller nuclear weapons could be carried externally, two on each side, between the inboard engines and the fuselage, one behind the other. When the B-58 was configured for combat, it was loaded with five atomic weapons; thus five separate targets could be hit at either low or high level. Exit from the target area was made by a zoom to maximum altitude at Mach 2 or to low level at Mach .92. The electronic countermeasure (ECM) equipment was superior in all respects, and the bomb/navigation equipment provided accurate delivery of high-yield weapons.

After penetration, escape from defended areas was enhanced by the B-58's high speed, small size and minimum radar reflectivity, radar warning systems, defensive ECM systems, and tail turret. When all else failed, you could "punch out" in the capsule with a supply of oxygen, signal for directional finders, and dispense chaff for radar tracking. Parachutes opened automatically and let you down gently; if in water, the flotation gear inflated. You had with you a full survival kit including radio, flares, gun, food, water, clothing, and even sunburn lotion and fishing kit!

At the termination of a mission, a normal jet penetration was made from a known beacon to the airfield; usually the Aircraft Control ground unit would direct you for the approach to the runway, and Ground Control Approach would pick you up and complete the circuit to the runway. Both Instrument Landing System (ILS) and Tactical Air Navigation (TACAN) were installed in all aircraft and usually worked well. After computing the best approach speed, which varied with aircraft weight, you flew that speed until you bled off airspeed to computed best flare speed for touchdown. You could not add a few knots speed for your wife and one for each child and still stop on the runway, even though a brake chute was used. You flew the speed and rate of descent exactly, and your attitude was 16° nose high. Just adding power, nose high, would not hack a decrease in descent rate. The nose had to come down to streamline the aircraft before airspeed increased and rate of descent decreased. This may sound odd to some, but the delta wing has that trait. On the runway, on the proper heading, you pulled the brake chute at 160 knots or below and raised the nose high to get aerodynamic braking with the lower wing surface. The brake chute shear pin would shear at above 160 knots—a safety feature in case a go-around was attempted after deploying the chute. At normal landing, ground roll of 2,580 feet was required.

After turning off the runway, completing the after-landing checklists, parking, and shutting down, you unstrapped yourself from the aircraft, installed the three ground safety pins in the capsule, and were helped to unfold and climb out onto the entrance stand. You then walked around the aircraft before going to maintenance and operations debriefing. We were usually numb, so questions were answered with a shrug, a nod, or sometimes a recitation concerning the complete outfit with name-calling; after 45 minutes we were turned loose to make our way home to hear what really happened today—from our families.

Overall the B-58 handled and performed beautifully. The utmost skill was used in the application of miniaturized automatic solid-state components, exotic metals, plastics, rubber, grease, and orinite to make the aircraft exceed

---

Opposite page: A B-58 glistens on the runway.

its design specifications. It was expensive to fly (dollars per flying hour), but that's progress, I guess. The aircraft seemed to have their own personalities for some crews, especially some tail-numbered dogs or jewels. Most crew members were especially proud of the airplane. Even though those in the second and third stations only had a 4 X 6-inch window to look through, claustrophobia never seemed to cause a problem, for you were too busy to look. The tandem seating arrangement required close crew coordination and cooperation at all times, especially during malfunction and high-speed flight. Most crews were gung ho, like that of N. R. Smith (later killed in Vietnam on his second mission in an O-2): when he came out after weather briefing to board the aircraft, a panel was yet to be installed after a discrepancy had been discovered on preflight. He told the crew chief, "If you want that panel to have as much flight time as the airframe, you'd better screw it on quick—I'm going." Prior flight experience in B-47s was a real asset, as was delta-wing fighter time.

The B-58—fast, complicated, computerized, and not power limited—ranked above the B-47 and B-52. Detailed knowledge of the aircraft systems and thorough flight planning were necessary, and takeoff time was scheduled well in advance. The two observers in the B-58 had two or three aeronautical ratings, and the aircraft commander (pilot) was usually triple-rated. In the B-47 there was a copilot who could fly the aircraft, operate the tail guns, act as radio operator, and serve coffee or water when necessary. In the B-58 the crew members were on their own in separate stalls, and everyone had his separate duties. You could stand and stretch your legs in the B-47; the B-52—with its two pilots, two or three observers, and tail gunner—gave some freedom of movement and relief from duties at odd intervals; not so in the B-58.

Everything was not always smooth flying in the B-58. The bombing navigation system would act up (even though there were nine modes of bombing); and there were flight control malfunctions, engine problems, and wheel and tire explosions. During the cold weather test in Alaska an aircraft skidded sideways, and three of the four engines flamed out. The second-station operator asked on interphone what was going on and where they were; there was no answer, for the pilot was giving all his attention to keeping the aircraft in the air, straightening it out, and getting some engines running again. The navigator, second station, kept asking where they were but received no response. Since the airspeed and altitude were going to pot he decided to "punch out." By the time the pilot had started another engine and landed safely, a rescue helicopter had picked up the navigator and deposited him on the ramp. When the haggard pilot crawled out of the aircraft, the navigator rushed over, stuck his face within inches of the pilot's, and demanded, "Why didn't you tell me where we were? I am the navigator and have a right to know!"

Opposite page: A B-58 in flight.

To again illustrate the caliber of crew and aircraft, another incident is noteworthy. A "roll cloud" was in the vicinity of Bunker Hill Air Force Base, and the weather was bad. The pilot was cleared for an approach, but as he was descending on the glide path he entered the roll cloud and was forced down by the draft. He applied power but was not able to avoid a high commercial power line, which sheared the control cables to No. 3 and No. 4 engines. The landing gear snagged a chain link fence and dragged about 30 feet of it as they proceeded to the alternate and landed safely. This was a determined crew and a good airplane.

Many other interesting accomplishments are known, but none of the B-58s now stored at Tucson, Arizona, is likely ever to fly again. It was an extremely formidable deterrent weapons system; although it never had to perform its mission, it did its job by being ready for eight years.

Col. Robert E. Hinnant spent twenty-one years with Strategic Air Command, nine of those with B-58s, primarily in a support capacity—supply, maintenance, inspections, retrofit, and modifications of the weapons system. He retired after twenty-eight years of active duty.

Opposite page: Another B-58 in flight.

OV-10 Bronco

James A. Richmond

Long before I ever saw the OV-10 I had read several articles concerning its development as a triservice counterinsurgency aircraft; I had also seen artists' conceptions of the airplane as well as early pictures of it in *Aviation Week*. When I first actually saw the Bronco, on the ramp at McClellan Air Force Base during a stopover there while I was flying the C-141, it gave me the impression of being a prehistoric bird or a giant flying insect. The airplane sat high above the ramp on its spindly looking main gear, while its short wings and twin booms combined to give it the appearance of being ready to leap into the air. The oversize, unusual-shaped canopy was undoubtedly this thing's eye on the world. One approached the Bronco almost cautiously; unlike other forward air controller (FAC) aircraft, there was no doubt that the OV-10 was built to go to war, and its four sponson mounted machine guns gave it a certain air of authority.

Notification that it was my turn to go to Southeast Asia came soon after my first physical encounter with the OV-10, so with a favorable impression in my mind I asked for and was given the assignment to fly OV-10s during my tour of duty there. It was still another year before I was to fly the Bronco and fall in love with it. Training in the OV-10 and the fine art of being an FAC was conducted at Hurlburt Field, Florida. After a few hours of classroom instruction and study, a pilot was ready for his first flight. Right away the combination of the airplane and the mission stirred a "kick the tires, light the fires" image in me, and I quickly developed a habit of kicking the tires during the exterior inspection. There really wasn't that much to the exterior inspection anyway: the pilot had to check the level of the fuel in the drop tank, make

Opposite page: An OV-10 with two rocket launchers mounted under the fuselage.

sure the armament was installed properly, check the general condition of the aircraft, and—in Southeast Asia—make sure there were no bird nests in the exhaust stacks. He was then ready to get into the airplane.

After flying other ejection-seat aircraft that had required lugging an unwieldy parachute out to the aircraft and stowing it in the seat prior to getting in, it was a real pleasure to walk out to the OV-10 wearing only an ejection system harness. But there the pleasure stopped. Getting into the Bronco was almost impossible for the novice and never mastered gracefully by anyone. Perhaps North American planned it that way in order to get the pilot in the right frame of mind for the demanding mission. To enter the cockpit he unfolded a small step in the right side of the aircraft, mounted via the step, and climbed in through the right-side canopy, which folded upward like the gull-wing doors on a 1952 Mercedes 300SL coupe. After getting situated in the seat, the pilot then needed help attaching his shoulder harnesses, which were also his parachute risers. Attaching the shoulder harness solo wasn't impossible. but it required considerable contortions and took a lot of time.

Once in the cockpit he could get on with the business of getting the OV-10 airborne. The interior preflight was easy, followed a logic sequence, and could be completed in approximately one minute—providing the pilot didn't get hung up on cranking the rudder pedals in or out. Starting the engines was also easy; they had the smooth continuous windup that was typical of a turboprop. Since the OV-10 was intended for use at forward fields where ground power equipment might not be available, it was designed to start on its battery; but the Air Force soon found out that making routine battery starts on the Bronco was not really the way to go. A battery start was generally slower, was hard on the batteries and engines, and had to be accomplished without full engine instrumentation. The engines were started with the propellers "on the locks," which was in a flat pitch position. This required that the throttles be moved momentarily into the reverse range in order to get the props "off the locks" prior to taxiing.

Taxiing the OV-10 was easy but a little tricky, and it was an operation that was always closely scrutinized and invariably criticized by almost every instructor pilot. Turns could be accomplished by use of differential braking, differential power, the nosewheel steering system, or any combination of the three. Using differential braking was usually frowned upon unless it was necessary for a very tight turn; nosewheel steering was used only for turns requiring more turning power than was available from differential power; differential power was normally used for small turns and to keep the aircraft going straight. As can be seen, when to use which system was largely a judgment matter and easily open for instructor criticism.

Reaching the end of the runway, the OV-10 was almost ready for takeoff; but as with all aircraft with an external ordnance load, an end-of-the-runway inspection and weapons arming was required. In the daytime this was a quick operation; at night we had to shut down the engines, since an instance had occurred where an armorer had been seriously injured at night when he had accidentally moved into the invisible arc of the spinning propeller. After being armed and collecting the pins from the armorer, we were ready to go.

On the runway the power levers were advanced to the takeoff and land position, the throttles were advanced to 100% rpm, the engine instruments were given a quick check and we were under way. Originally designed as a short takeoff and landing (STOL) aircraft, the OV-10 could lift off at 73 knots in 700 feet on a standard day at sea level, clean, with full internal fuel. That was fairly impressive to most of us reading the Bronco flight manual for the first time. After all, most of us were transplanted transport, bomber, or fighter pilots used to much longer takeoff rolls and higher liftoff speeds. However, we were soon dismayed to find that the STOL liftoff was below the minimum safe single-engine speed and that at least one pilot had crashed after losing an engine on a STOL takeoff. We were, therefore, restricted to using a higher rotation speed—one that got us airborne after the minimum safe single-engine speed.

But we were in for yet another surprise, particularly those of us headed for Thailand. The fully loaded 300-gallon centerline fuel tank and its associated effects on takeoff performance gave extra drag and extra weight, increased liftoff speed, and lengthened takeoff roll; it also severely decreased climb performance. If an engine were lost immediately after takeoff, the airplane was too heavy to fly; it would be necessary to jettison the external stores or put the aircraft back on the runway. Despite all the problems the Bronco always seemed to get airborne with little difficulty. I don't recall ever aborting a takeoff for any serious problem. Low torque seemed to be the main cause of aborted takeoffs, but that was generally evident before the brakes were ever released.

Once in the air the OV-10 performed nicely with the training load we had at Hurlburt Field but more sluggishly with a full combat load in Southeast Asia. Nevertheless, for me and most of those I knew, flying the OV-10 was a welcome interlude between bomber, tanker, or transport assignments. Invariably the first things that impressed all pilots flying the Bronco were its turning performance and visibility. Old-timers would have said that it would turn on a dime and give you five cents change. I don't know about that, but the turning performance was spectacular and a particular plus for the FAC. He could stay over a target and observe the activity below very easily because of the turning

performance and visibility. In the area of speed most pilots were not impressed, but there were few grumbles about its fairly slow top speed either. After reading the flight manual and seeing 350 knots as the top speed, I had sort of expected to be able to attain 350 knots easily. That was not the case. The Bronco was power limited and could attain only about 210 knots clean and 170 knots with a combat load at 5,000 feet. Many Broncos would not even do that. I tried to get the OV-10 up to 350 knots a couple of times but found that it was a difficult task, requiring a steep dive angle and full power.

Nearly all Air Force pilots like an acrobatic airplane, and the Bronco was fully acrobatic. The two booms with twin rudders gave the airplane plenty of directional control, and the exceptionally large elevator was effective well below stall speed. The ailerons were assisted by a set of spoilers on the top of each wing which combined to give the OV-10 a good roll rate at all airspeeds. The flight controls were so effective that the OV-10 could literally be flown out of a spin. The engines were the only big limitation on its acrobatic perform-ance. After a few over-the-top maneuvers we would have to stop and climb to a good starting altitude again. In fact, when the airplane was heavy, a level 60° bank turn couldn't be maintained. Even with its problems, the Bronco was really a little fighter. There were those of us who occasionally couldn't resist the urge to try out some aerial combat on a willing friend, and then we saw just how maneuverable the OV-10 really was.

I have heard some pilots who flew the aircraft but never in combat say that the Air Force should not have bought the OV-10, but I doubt that these critics were considering the alternatives—the O-1 and the O-2. All the OV-10 pilots I knew in Southeast Asia thought the OV-10 did an excellent job. The superb visibility, short turn radius, relatively large ordnance load, and excel-lent loiter time (especially with the 300-gallon centerline drop tank) made the Bronco an unequaled FAC aircraft. The Navy and Marines also used it as a light attack aircraft.

The OV-10 could accept several different combat configurations on its five external stations. On the centerline station the Air Force birds usually car-ried a jettisonable fuel tank, and the four sponson stations carried the ord-nance. The sponsons were two small winglike protuberances on the bottom of the fuselage that appeared to be an afterthought. The normal ordnance loads carried by FAC aircraft were pods of seven 2.75-inch folding fin smoke rockets for daylight target marking or canisters of flares or ground marks for night target marking. In addition to the external ordnance the OV-10 carried four M-60 machine guns, two mounted in each sponson. The machine guns, how-ever, were normally used only on special missions. Starlight scopes were

---

Opposite page: A US Navy OV-10 takes off to provide air cover for a river patrol boat in the Mekong Delta area of Vietnam.

mounted in some airplanes for night work, and in 1971 a few Broncos were modified to accept a laser illuminating device to guide the recently developed smart bombs to their targets.

The FAC's job was to perform visual reconnaissance, direct air strikes, and assess the damage after an air strike. In Vietnam where the plane could work as low as 1,500 feet above the ground, reconnaissance was performed with the naked eye; along the Ho Chi Minh trail where the plane was driven up to a minimum altitude of 6,500 feet above the ground by antiaircraft fire, the FAC had to perform reconnaissance with the aid of binoculars. The large expanse of Plexiglas in the OV-10 made this an easy job whether working with the unaided eye or binoculars. Initially, trying to watch the ground below with binoculars and fly the airplane as well was not easy, but after a while the pilot got used to doing both jobs at once.

Once a target was located and the fighter/bombers were ready to work, the FAC had to mark the target accurately and direct the strike. Marking a target with the OV-10 required arming a rocket pod, setting the desired depression in the bomb sight, rolling into a dive on the target, and firing a smoke rocket. Firing or dropping ordnance from an OV-10 could be accomplished only from the front seat, but instructor pilots prided themselves on being able to line up on a target from the rear seat and direct the pilot in the front seat to fire with greater accuracy than the pilot in the front seat could achieve by using the bomb sight. Marking a target at night with flares or ground marks was done from level flight with the help of a navigator FAC in the back seat. After an air strike was completed, the FAC assessed the damage to the target and reported it to the strike flight and the airborne controller.

Radio coordination was a big job for the FAC, since it required listening to two or three radios simultaneously. He was constantly requesting air strikes, directing air strikes, or making reports. The OV-10 was well equipped for this portion of the FAC's job but poorly designed. It had at least one of each type of radio used by the Air Force or Army; but switching from one radio to another, talking on the radio, and flying the airplane really required three hands. Somehow we managed, but never with the greatest of ease.

Range was of little importance to the FAC aircraft, but endurance was. With the 300-gallon drop tank the pilots thought that, if anything, the Bronco had too much endurance! Normal missions were four and a half to five hours long—an awfully long time to be sitting immobile, strapped into an airplane. We put down five and a half hours as the endurance on our mission sign-out sheets, but I once flew a five-and-three-quarters-hour mission and still returned to the base before reaching the prescribed minimum fuel state.

Opposite page: Two low-flying OV-10s in search of enemy activity in Vietnam.

Returning from a mission the standard approach for an OV-10 was a 360-degree overhead pattern, and that was what the pilots liked best. However, at most bases we couldn't fly a 360-degree overhead pattern with any ordnance on board, and it was seldom that we returned without a few rockets left over from the day's mission. Therefore, our pattern usually had to be a large box pattern flown outside the base perimeter. At Nakhon Phanom most Bronco pilots liked to announce their return by making a high airspeed, steep bank turn onto the outside downwind leg of the traffic pattern, which was just opposite the quarters area and near the busiest section of the base. The doppler effect took care of the arrival announcement by sending the roar of the engines right into the quarters area. There was even a small competition, particularly among the lieutenants, to see who could arrive with the loudest roar. The controllable pitch of the propellers made a steep glide slope possible and spot landings easy. Once on the ground the combination of reverse thrust and wheel brakes gave the Bronco a short landing roll.

One of the ideas incorporated into the Bronco as a triservice counterinsurgency aircraft was its multimission capability. Provision had to be made for paratroops, but to the best of my knowledge troops never bailed out of the OV-10. That was something reserved exclusively for the pilot and extra crew member in the tandem seats. Fortunately the OV-10 had one of the best and most reliable ejection systems around. I am a particular fan of its ejection system because I had to use it on one occasion after my plane was hit by antiaircraft fire. The seat was rocket-launched right through the canopy of the aircraft. The ejection itself was rather soft by most standards. No one I knew who ejected from the OV-10 ever suffered any aftereffects more than a little soreness and some singed hair on the back of his calves from the rocket blast. The ejection sequence could be initiated at any speed or altitude within the envelope of the aircraft with an almost sure chance of success. One inexperienced back seater even punched out successfully while the aircraft was parked, when his arming pin streamer became tangled with the ejection D-ring and he initiated the ejection sequence accidentally. The seat worked just as advertised, and he walked away from his experience somewhat shaken by his sudden unplanned departure from the airplane but otherwise okay.

As in any flying organization, talking about our missions and the airplanes we flew occupied a great deal of our off-duty time. Using those discussions as an indicator of how the FAC pilots felt about the OV-10, I would say that there were few who didn't love the airplane. It wasn't fast, it wasn't very powerful, it wasn't aerodynamically beautiful, but it had a place all its own among Air Force aircraft.

Capt. James Richmond completed his flight and tactical training in the OV-10 at Hurlburt Field, Florida, in late 1969, after which he was assigned to the 23rd Tactical Air Support Squadron, Nakhon Phanom RTAFB, Thailand. He is presently assigned to the 4950th Test Wing, Wright-Patterson AFB, Ohio.

Slipping the Surly Bonds with a Zip—The F-104

Robert E. Messerli

When I first saw the F-104 Starfighter I knew in an instant why the press dubbed it "the missile with a man in it." With its sleek needle nose and long, slender fuselage it looked like it was doing Mach 2 just sitting still. Affectionately called the "Zipper" by those who flew it, the F-104 had razor-sharp leading edges and stubby wings which contributed to its lightning-quick appearance. It's horizontal stabilizer was set high on the tail fin and was shaped like a "T" for optimum stability from takeoff to plus Mach 2. This aft section, with the entire horizontal stabilizer moving as a "flying tail," was a unique feature. The success of the Starfighter's empennage proved to be one of the few times such a design performed satisfactorily.

The innovative canopy design was an aviator's dream. Pilots were on top of the world while comfortably poised on the nose of the aircraft, enjoying virtually unlimited visibility. It was akin to a motorist being seated on the hood of a car rather than confined behind the wheel. The excellent rear visibility was especially important to fighter pilots and had been unequaled until production of the F-15 and F-16.

The F-104 cockpit was entered via a metal stepladder placed alongside the canopy. From the top of the ladder, you stepped into the cockpit, placing the heels of your feet into the stirrup attachment. This fastened the spurs onto the end of a cable as you put foot pressure against the snap. The rest of the procedure consisted of a backpack-type parachute and conventional two-shoulder harnesses attached to the lap belt. Subsequent modifications to the

Opposite page: The F-104.

West German F-104G aircraft have included the Martin-Baker seat, which did away with wearing the backpack-type parachute.

The very first models of the F-104A had downward ejection. The aircraft was designed that way because when using upward ejection the seat would not clear the high vertical tail during high-speed ejections in excess of 1.8 Mach. However, a modification was made to change all the aircraft to upward ejection because the success rate of downward ejection was not very good and the probability of ejecting above 1.8 Mach was considered unlikely.

The intricate and detailed design which had gone into the layout of the F-104 Starfighter's cockpit was evident immediately upon entry. The 360-degree cockpit visibility was previously unmatched. In addition, the simplified instrument panel was one of the best ever constructed. Every switch was within easy reach, annuciators were grouped together for high visibility, and gauges were easy to read and interpret. The simple instrumentation, with emphasis on such features as the gunsights, made this "manned missile" a fighter pilot's best friend.

Pilots were required to wear spurs on the heel of each flying boot. These spurs were fastened to the end of cables extending from the stirrups of the ejection seat. This maneuver proved to be a bit tricky during my first few attempts to get hooked up properly, but once I got the hang of it, I was not even aware of the attached cables. This design was to prevent knee and leg injuries during ejection. The cable would retract and pull your feet safely back within the stirrups prior to the ejection sequence. There was no doubt that when you stepped into the cockpit of the F-104 you strapped the aircraft to yourself and became part of this awesome machine.

Once strapped in, it was one of the easiest aircraft to start. The starting procedure consisted of connecting external electrical power and air pressure. The procedure was rapid and included the following steps:

    a. Start-Stop Switch—place to Start.
    b. 10 percent rpm—throttle out of cutoff. (Fuel flow 400–800 lbs).
    c. 14 percent rpm—ignition.
    d. 40 percent rpm—Start-Stop Switch to Stop.
    e. 67 percent rpm, Idle Power—disconnect external power.

The entire procedure only took about one minute once electrics and air were connected. The pilot therefore could be taxiing in roughly one and a half minutes. The J-79 engine accelerated and responded to throttle movement immediately. Quick and simple pre-takeoff checks, coupled with rapid acceleration in rpm, made the aircraft ideal for scramble starts and takeoffs.

Opposite page: Another view of the F-104.

Even the taxiing was expedited because of the pilot's position high on the nose of the aircraft. The great visibility, together with the short wing span and nose-wheel steering, made you feel as if you wore the aircraft. Consequently, you could taxi in and out of tight areas that no fighter has been able to do as well since.

During its time, takeoff in the Starfighter was an experience like no other. After taking the runway for engine run-up on a cold day, it was impossible to hold the aircraft using brakes without skidding. Lineup was especially critical because the instantaneous acceleration could place you fifty feet off center-line if you were not initially centered on the runway.

One of my most memorable moments in aviation was the initial takeoff in a clean Starfighter on a cold day at Wright-Patterson AFB. As I advanced the throttle to military power, the engine began its familiar howling sound. Its force was so strong that the aircraft appeared to crouch while the brakes were being held. Upon brake release, the plane suddenly shot down the runway. The early afterburner on the J-79 had four distinct stages. As each one was lit on takeoff roll, it felt as though I had selected an additional afterburner. With the slightest movement, I rotated the nose and my plane leaped from the run-way—I was airborne!

These breathtaking accelerations were very impressive and regularly left the pilot behind the aircraft on his initial sorties. The subsequent climbout was no less spectacular than the takeoff roll. Within twenty seconds after brake release the aircraft was airborne at 186 to 210 knots depending upon load and ambient air temperatures and altitude. The ship passed through 350 knots indicated very rapidly thereafter and seconds later it had reached .9 Mach. At this speed you eased the stick back and began a constant Mach climb. The climb altitude was close to 45° and made you feel as if you were lying on your back with your feet pointed towards the sky. In looking aft, it was difficult to see the wings because they were positioned so far back on the fuselage. Looking off to the side, you could see the runway falling away and becoming a thin grey line, while inside the cockpit the VVI was pegged at 6,000 rpm. In this climb profile it was no surprise that the aircraft's perform-ance was well ahead of the cockpit instrumentation, such as the vertical veloc-ity indicator and lagging altimeter.

Below are the Lockheed F-104 Starfighter "world time-to-climb records":

9,842 feet—(3,000 meters)—41:85 seconds
19,684 feet—(6,000 meters)—58:41 seconds
29,527 feet—(9,000 meters)—1 minute 21:14 seconds
39,370 feet—(12,000 meters)—1 minute 39:30 seconds

49,212 feet—(15,000 meters)—2 minutes 11:1 seconds
65,616 feet—(20,000 meters)—3 minutes 42:99 seconds
82,020 feet—(25,000 meters)—4 minutes 26:03 seconds

Invariably, pilots would overshoot their level-off altitude until they became familiar with the F-104's tremendous climb speed and attained a feel for the aircraft which could not be substituted for by instrumentation. The Starfighter's level-flight capabilities continued to illustrate why the aircraft was a real performer in the air. Its in-flight acceleration was superior to any other aircraft. Deliveries began as early as 1957 and the aircraft, although not the smallest fighter in the inventory (the F-5 is smaller in length and weight), has the shortest wingspan ever introduced into the U.S. inventory. During the time when the USAF utilized the Starfighter in an operational role, it could virtually dictate at will when to engage or disengage Air Combat Maneuvering (ACM) with any other aircraft.

Accelerating from .9 Mach to Mach 2 in the F-104 took less than three minutes; however, the transition from subsonic to supersonic speed was hardly noticeable. While slipping through the sound barrier, the Mach needle jumped slightly, providing the only indication that you were traveling beyond the speed of sound. Between .96 to 1.4 Mach the aircraft hesitated slightly, but then the engine went into "T-2 reset." This allowed the engine to overspeed and increased the thrust. The turbines whined at 104 percent rpm, and the sudden increase in performance again reminded you that the Starfighter was truly a supersonic bird. The F-104 was the first operational jet aircraft to exceed Mach 2 in level flight. It also proved it could maneuver and fight at that speed. Throttle movement was unlimited, speed brakes could be extended, and all flight maneuvers could be attempted while flying within the supersonic speed range. When flying at this high speed, retarding the throttles out of afterburner was like applying brakes; as you felt the sudden deceleration, you again were reminded of just how fast your aircraft was traveling.

I have always felt that the F-104 was an honest airplane—if attention was paid to its operational limitations and warning systems. However, it was a terribly unforgiving aircraft for the ham-fisted jock who refused to handle and treat it gently, for those pilots who attempted to muscle the controls and were not smooth and deliberate with the aircraft. It was possible to pitch-up the aircraft if you ignored the angle of attack/airspeed relationships and built-in stick shaker. But even if you ignored these indications, it had a stick kicker built into the system which automatically positioned the horizontal stabilizer just below neutral to recover before pitch-up occurred. But the kicker *could* be rendered ineffective if the pitch rate inputs were fast enough to allow the controls to

pass through safe transient ranges too quickly. When these warning indications did occur the pilot needed only to release the pressure on the stick and fly out of the dangerous condition. The F-104 needed to be controlled in the vertical plane allowing for high-energy maneuvering. This resulted in maximum use of the aircraft's acceleration and power.

Another innovation designed for the F-104 was the boundary-layer control system which provided greater lift. High-velocity compressed air was piped from the engine into the wing, where it was ejected from a slotted tube over the upper surface of the trailing edge wing flap. These streams of air smoothed out the airflow over the wing flap and allowed pilots to land at lower airspeeds of 160–165 knots instead of hurling themselves towards the ground in excess of 200 knots.

Initially, formation flying was quite difficult for a pilot because of the short wings. While rocketing through the air at supersonic speeds, pilots were unable to detect the initial banking by the leader until he had already established a bank into or away from them. Night-formation flying was especially challenging; however, a modification of adding special wing-tip lights and formation-strip lighting alleviated this problem. Once pilots were no longer required to play catchup with their leader, F-104 flights became the most illustrative examples of close-formation flying.

The "Zipper" also had the distinction of being an extremely stable platform for weapons delivery. Again the Starfighter's phenomenal acceleration contributed to the aircraft's combat capability by providing the instantaneous overtake required for launching missiles so that they had an airspeed advantage needed for overtaking. Guns firing 4,400 rounds per minute earned this aircraft an awesome reputation. Other aircraft went to great lengths to avoid any air-to-air confrontation with the Zipper. When not armed with missiles, it often carried 2.75" RXs or Napalm on the pylons. This reduced some of the clean configuration capabilities; however, a Zip with any weapon was the meanest thing of its day.

Firing the weapons only can be described as effortless. The Lockheed designers built the entire aircraft with simplicity as their major objective. One only had to set a couple of distinctive switches, set the sights, and fire. And once engaged in combat, few aircraft could escape the wrath of the F-104. The simplicity and ease of interpretation allowed the pilot to concentrate on maneuvering for position in order to destroy his target.

Highly sophisticated radar for its day also aided the pilot in his quest for air superiority. The air-to-air radar was both accurate and reliable, but the real advantage of the Zipper's low-level system capability was the contour mapping and terrain avoidance. Today's terrain-following radar is the direct result of

Opposite page: An F-104 in flight.

the F-104 system's success. This system was greatly advanced for its time and provided the pilot the capability to navigate the aircraft for strikes into enemy territory.

I cannot talk about bailing out as I have never ejected nor have I witnessed anyone ejecting from an F-104 aircraft.

On a normal training mission, endurance for a clean aircraft is about 1.5 hours. Tip tanks increased the endurance to approximately 2.5 hours.

Back in the pattern, the F-104 was like a graceful falcon gliding in for an effortless landing. Rolling into the pitch, with flaps in the takeoff position, sets up a 4-G turn onto downwind. Once rolled level on downwind, it was immediately ready for gear down and full landing flaps. Within seconds it was time to roll into a smooth, final turn and begin the descent to the runway. At this point it was a power-on approach all the way, in order to keep the boundary layer control activated for the extra lift required while flying at slower airspeeds.

Simulated flameout patterns provided an extra measure of excitement. Hi-Key was set up at 10,000 feet over the runway, yet within moments you were starting the flare with a horrendous sink rate. With a 240 knot touchdown speed and the distinct feeling of literally falling out of the sky, it is no wonder that flameout procedures were only utilized for precautionary patterns.

The F-104 provided an extremely stable platform for instrument approaches. Paired with aircraft response, this made approaches relatively simple once the pilot became familiar with the accelerated sequence of events. Even the air traffic controllers had to be reminded of the F-104's high approach speeds. If not, they would be back at the final approach fix while the pilot was already in the flare! Of course, any good landing in any aircraft was always a challenge, and as the tires squeaked at touchdown and the drag chute burst open, pilots experienced the ultimate satisfaction of having slipped the surly bonds with a Zip.

The success of the F-104 was highlighted by the overwhelming foreign demand for this aircraft. Several versions were built and with the introduction of the F-104G, the aircraft was heralded as one of the greatest achievements in American aviation. Contracts were signed with West Germany, Canada, the Netherlands, Japan, Belgium, Norway, Denmark, Greece, Turkey, Spain, Nationalist China, and Pakistan. Furthermore, the largest international aircraft production resulted from factories such as Lockheed, Messerschmitt, Fiat, Dornier, Heinkel, Siebel, Fokker, Aviolanda, Mitsubishi, Sabca, and Calac. The use of special modifications for astronaut testing and short (zero length) launch testing along with the outstanding production record attested

---

Opposite page: Note the F-104s slender, sleek design.

to the 104's reliability and safety. In all, over 2,500 Starfighters have been produced, and over fifteen countries have utilized this aircraft.

Some impressive records established by the Zip include:

World Altitude Record
91,249 feet
Maj. H. C. Johnson, USAF
May 7, 1958

World Speed Record
1404.9 mph
Capt. W. W. Irwin, USAF
May 17, 1958

USAF Time-to-Intercept Record
TARGET: 35,000 feet
172 miles from base
Time-to-Intercept: 8 minutes, 59.9 seconds
Capt. M. Schaff, USAF
Capt. B. Jones, USAF
December 10, 1958

World Altitude Record
First aircraft to exceed 100,000 feet
103,395.5 feet
Added World Time-to-Climb Mark
98,424 feet (30,000 meters) in 15 minutes
Capt. Joe B. Jordan, USAF
December 14, 1959

The F-104 became the only aircraft ever to hold world records for speed, altitude, and time-to-climb, simultaneously.

The Starfighter was also always the first aircraft to deploy during any crisis. In September 1958, it was sent to Taiwan in defense of the Republic of China and was unofficially credited with being a major factor in preservation of peace at Quemoy. Later in 1961, several squadrons deployed to Europe in response to the Berlin crisis. Again, in the Cuban missile crisis, it was the F-104 that was called on first to be ready to defend our country. Even after the decision had been made to phase out the aircraft, squadrons were sent to Vietnam and

Opposite page: An F-104 coming in for a landing.

Thailand from 1965–1967. Clearly the Zip was our "Ace in the Hole" and in its heyday, wherever the Zips flew, there was nothing that could compete.

Brig. Gen. Robert E. Messerli is Commander of the 45th Air Division, Pease Air Force Base, New Hampshire, the largest Strategic Air Command flying division. General Messerli has command responsibility for SAC's two FB-111 wings and two B-52 wings. In addition he monitors the readiness status of four Air National Guard air refueling units.

Opposite page: A formation of F-104s.

An A-1 in flight over South Vietnam, 1970.

A-1 Skyraider

Donald E. Jones

I remember my feelings in August 1964 when notification came that I had been selected to fly A-1s in South Vietnam. As an F-100 pilot with more than 1,000 hours in the "Hun," I was mildly surprised that the Air Force should want to retrain me and send me into combat in an unfamiliar weapons system. The idea of going into combat wasn't bad, but the thought of not going in the F-100, with which I felt very confident, was disturbing.

In January 1965 I reported to Eglin Auxiliary Field #9 (better known as Hurlburt Field), Florida. There I was to receive approximately 100 hours training in the machine that would see me through my war experiences in Southeast Asia. What an airplane! A "tail dragger," of all things, in this modern day; I had never flown an aircraft with a conventional landing gear. Its reciprocating engine was so high off the ground that I had to chin myself on the cowling to inspect it, and each of its four huge prop blades was longer than my six-foot frame. And bomb racks: all across the bottom were the racks that would carry as much ordnance as a B-17—15 stations in all. With full fuel, oil, and pilot, the aircraft grossed out at approximately 16,000 pounds. Maximum gross weight for takeoff was 25,000 pounds. Climbing up the wing was like scaling a small mountain, and one misstep off the antiskid area during rainy weather could send a guy embarrassingly to the ground.

Preflight inspection of the Skyraider was simple and straightforward. Beginning in the cockpit to ensure that all switches were off (especially the magnetos), the pilot proceeded to the left side-engine upper exhaust pipes, left wing, lower engine, right wing, right side upper engine for oil quantity and exhaust pipes, and finally, around the tail section. We used a locally fabricated, external rudder lock that prevented the rudder from being slammed about by prop wash or wind gusts. One novice had the misfortune to attempt a scramble takeoff from Qui Nhon with the rudder lock in place, and engine torque pulled him off the left side of the runway into soft sand where the gear collapsed and a fire ensued. Luckily, he got out of it with his life, but the accident board nailed him with pilot error.

Preflight became a graceful ballet of putting on and taking off gloves. You could always identify the A-1 pilots by the oil on their flight suits and gloves. You could always pick out the *new* A-1 pilots by the oil on their faces. If you've ever been around a Wright radial engine, you know that oil leaks are normal and extensive. Mission endurance at times became a function of how much *oil* you had on board instead of how much *fuel* you had. Naturally, the entire underside of the fuselage, wing roots, and entire engine section were covered with oil. Flight suits and gloves quickly picked up a share of the mess during preflights. Wipe the sweat from your brow just once with your gloves on and you were marked; forget to have your gloves on during preflight and you were marked.

Preflight of the cockpit began at the left rear, proceeded up the left side across the front instrument panel, across the armament panel beneath the instruments and between your legs, and down the right side. The fuel selector handle on the left console allowed manual selection of internal or external fuel. Special note had to be taken of the manifold pressure gauge before start to determine barometric pressure to be used later during engine run-up.

Starting the A-1 was a real task, especially for those of us who had all-jet experience. No more automatic starting—just push the button, throttle to idle at 12 percent rpm.

The A-1 engine start was normally accomplished using an external source of D.C. power, although aircraft battery power could be used in an emergency. With external power connected, all caution and warning lights were checked—especially the all-important chip-detector light. The chip detector was the device that informed the pilot that metal pieces were present in the oil sump. Metal chips in the sump were normally the only warning of impending internal engine failure. The fuel-boost pump was turned on and pressure checked on the gauge (normally 21–25 psi). With a "prop clear" call to crew chief, the starter was engaged to rotate the engine through four complete revolutions—16 blades. This initial rotation was a check for fluids (oil, gas, or hydraulic) that may have seeped into any of the cylinders. If the engine failed to rotate normally (hydraulic lock), the start would be aborted, and the lower cylinder ignitor plugs would be removed to drain those cylinders. After 16 blades, the ignition switch was turned to "both," and the primer was used intermittently to pump fuel into the engine.

Opposite page: A pilot inspects "daisy cutters" on an A-1.

With a cloud of blue smoke and a burst of noise, the huge engine would hesitatingly come to life, shaking and vibrating the entire airframe. Once all 18 cylinders were going, it felt like you were sitting on the biggest Farmall tractor ever built. The engine was stabilized at about 1,000 rpm on the primer before slowly advancing the mixture lever to transfer to carburetor fuel. With the engine running smoothly, the ground crew was signaled to disconnect external power. Battery, inverters, and radios were turned on, and the aircraft was ready to taxi out. Just prior to taxiing, the fuel selector was placed to the external fuel position to ensure that external tanks would feed properly. Throttle closed, "thumbs out" for chock removal, and the bird was ready to lumber out for run-up.

The A-1 had a couple of unique taxiing aspects. First, the tailwheel had to be unlocked in order to make turns. As in the T-33, the pilot steered by using differential braking. Most of the time the engine produced enough prop blast at idle rpm to make the rudder effective for small corrections. Idle rpm was normally enough power to keep the aircraft moving, depending on the ordnance load; however, the generator would come off the line (not produce electrical power) at idle, with the result that the radios would become weak or inoperative. At about 1,000 rpm, the generator worked fine, but the aircraft would taxi at excess speed. And so it was a game of riding the brakes and jockeying the throttle to keep everything working and at a safe speed. The brakes were very easy to become accustomed to but a "hamhanded" jab on the brakes at almost any speed could bring the tail wheel up off the ground and risk getting a piece of the pavement with the prop. Taxiing could be accomplished with the wings in the folded or extended position, again depending on external loads. Normally, taxi out was with the wings extended and locked, and taxi in was with the wings folded. This ensured that the wing-folding hydraulic system was exercised regularly to keep the seals lubricated.

The aircraft was made with folding wings for the U.S. Navy, to facilitate aircraft carrier operations, and we received our aircraft from the Navy. Because the wing-folding system was connected to the main hydraulic system, the Air Force had a choice of modifying the aircraft or maintaining the existing system, and it was less expensive to maintain the system and practice regular cycling to keep the seals flexible.

Engine run-up was quick and simple. To keep the tail from bouncing or flying up, the control stick had to be held firmly in the full aft position whenever engine power was above idle. With cylinder-head temperature somewhere above 100 degrees Celsius and oil temperature above 40 degrees Celsius, the pilot proceeded to exercise the propeller pitch-changing mechanism from full increase to full decrease. An improperly operating prop control could cause an overboost or overspeed condition, either of which might cause engine failure. Engine power was checked by increasing manifold pressure with the throttle to that manifold pressure noted during cockpit preflight. A check of each magneto for engine roughness or excessive loss of rpm and switching in and out of high blower (the supercharger) completed the engine checks.

The final checks included cycling the oil-cooler door open and closed and visually checking over the left side in front of the wing root to ensure that the door was halfway open. An oil-cooler door stuck in the closed position would cause the oil to overheat. Overheated oil loses its viscosity and can be ingested by the engine, resulting in engine failure. A last check was made of the flight controls (free and clear), wings were checked down and locked (a red, one-inch pipe protruded from the leading edge of each wing when the wings were unlocked), and flaps were set to the takeoff position. The run-up check was then complete.

Takeoff could be made with the cockpit canopy either fully open or fully closed. Carbon monoxide tended to build up in the cockpit if a partially open canopy position was selected. In Vietnam, our squadron was required to take off with canopies closed, and we were required to turn off the cockpit fresh-air nozzles. This procedure resulted from an unfortunate accident when one aircraft on a maintenance test flight developed an engine fuel leak and fire. The fire burned through the cockpit ventilating pipes which are routed from the front cowling to the cockpit. Burning fuel entered the pipes and spewed into the cockpit through the air nozzles, much like a blow torch. The pilot managed to bail out, but his parachute harness had been burned through, and the chute failure caused his death. Takeoff on a hot day was a sweaty experience.

For takeoff, the aircraft was lined up on the runway, tail wheel locked, and a final engine check completed. At brake release, the throttle was smoothly advanced to maximum manifold pressure as 61.5 inches right rudder was applied to control torque. The R-3350 engine, rated at 3,000 hp for the Air Force, produced enough torque to pull the aircraft quickly off the left side of the runway if corrective rudder was not applied. As soon as the aircraft was rolling and everything (engine instruments) looked good, the control stick was pushed firmly forward to fly the tail off the ground. With the tail raised, you felt the aircraft was flying slightly nose down. This attitude insured maximum acceleration and was maintained until reaching takeoff speed (which varied widely from about 80 to more than 100 knots, depending on ordnance load). With a little back pressure, the aircraft would fly smoothly off the ground.

Flying the Skyraider was like living in an earlier era. The noise level in the cockpit was considerable, especially with the canopy open. The cockpit was not air-conditioned, which made for sweating palms and brows on those tropical

missions. For a time in Vietnam, we were allowed to cut off the sleeves of our flight suits to be cooler. But then some "safety types" decided that short sleeves would be hazardous in the event of cockpit fires, so cut-offs were banned. I remember the sheer pleasure of climbing back to altitude after a strike, opening the canopy, and inching a sweat-soaked, gloved hand above the canopy bow into the cooling slipstream. The canteens of ice water the crew chiefs faithfully passed to us before engine start always helped after working a target.

The A-1 had such an aerodynamically dirty profile that its climbing, accelerating, and high-speed performances were poor. I remember taking a clean airplane (except for pylons) and applying maximum power in level flight at about 1,000 feet. Slowly, the airspeed increased and stabilized at about 250 knots. With firm back pressure, I zoomed the aircraft to about 30–40° pitch and held it until the airframe gave warning of a stall. I had succeeded in climbing less than 2,000 feet. The same maneuver in an F-100 had netted me over 25,000 feet.

But what the A-1 could not provide in acceleration, climbing, and speed, it more than made up for in turning and lifting ability. The slower speeds allowed us to complete 60–70° high-angle strafing passes and nearly vertical dive-bombing passes from 3,000 feet above ground level. Weapons delivery accuracy from that level was phenomenal in comparison to that of the F-100s and F-4s.

In setting up for a dive-bomb pass, the A-1 was positioned so that the target was just visible over the side of the cockpit. The throttle was closed as the pilot completed a rolling dive toward the target. It was amazing how that huge prop suddenly became a speed brake as the throttle was closed and the prop blades became aligned flat against the wind. The pilot would feel himself partially hanging forward in the seat as he dived toward the target. From that point, it was a simple matter to track the "pipper" or aiming reticle up to the target (we had an adjustable optical sight), hold it there momentarily for airspeed/altitude parameters, and then release the weapons. The "hold it there" part of the maneuver gave me a thrill on more than one occasion. "Bunting" or pushing forward on the stick was sometimes required to prevent the "pipper" from going above the target on a bombing run. The forward stick pressure was often enough to create a zero G or negative G condition in the aircraft. In a negative G condition, all of the dirt and loose items in the cockpit would be thrown from the floor to the ceiling. Likewise, in the fuel tank, the gasoline would move so that the end of the fuel line would become uncovered, causing the engine to quit. I remember occasions when I pulled up from a dive-bomb pass and pushed the throttle forward only to find that the engine would not respond. Fortunately, the propeller would windmill

Opposite page: A formation of A-1s.

until more gasoline could be sucked up from the tank, and then the engine would start with no effort from the pilot. Believe me, it gives you a "weak in the knees" feeling to think that the engine has failed over unfriendly territory.

Night missions in the A-1 were especially interesting. For ordnance delivery, engine power would be set near maximum, which would cause "torching" from the exhaust stacks. Because this made the aircraft more visible to enemy antiaircraft gunners, the standard procedure was to turn off all lights, reduce throttle, and pull the mixture control to lean before each pass. A night operation with four A-1s and a flare ship was always a bit tense—trying to keep track of everyone and work the target.

Approaches and landings in the A-1 were "no sweat" as long as you were mindful of a few basic precautions. First, the tail wheel had to be in the locked position for landing. Most touchdowns were either three-point or, in some cases, tail wheel first. I took a certain amount of pride in trying to roll the tail wheel on first whenever crosswinds were not a factor. If the tail wheel was free to swivel unlocked, the aircraft could perform some very strange ground maneuvers. Second, you had to respect the throttle when the airspeed was low—like on final approach. Just before I arrived at Bien Hoa in 1965, a pilot was killed when he bounced an aircraft on landing and then throttle-burst the engine (jammed the throttle full open) to make a go-around maneuver. He was unable to counteract engine torque and wound up inverted on the runway.

During my tour of duty in Vietnam, I felt that the A-1 was the best aircraft available for the job. It had the range, endurance, accuracy, and weapons capacity to enable it to go almost any place in-country in support of friendly forces. The UHF-VHF-FM communications radios it carried allowed the pilot to talk with ground forces, the forward air controller, and other fighters. The armor plating on the fuselage and that huge engine up front provided excellent protection for the pilot. And its slower speeds and high maneuverability enabled the pilot to work targets effectively in poor weather conditions.

The motto of the A-1 Skyraider Association is "We flew. We fought." I'm proud to have been one of the men selected to pilot that flying machine.

Maj. Donald E. Jones was commissioned into the Air Force at Memphis State University in May 1959 and went on active duty the following month. He took pilot training at Spence Air Base, Georgia, and Greenville AFB, Mississippi. In January 1965 he began transition training into the AA E Skyraider at Hurlburt Field, Florida. In March he was assigned to the 602nd Fighter Squadron, Bien Hoa Air Base, Vietnam, where he upgraded to instructor pilot and flight leader. Major Jones flew 269 missions over Vietnam and accumulated just under 500 hours in the Skyraider.

Opposite page: An A-1 taking off from the flight deck of the USS Ranger.

B-32 Dominator

Willard S. Ruliffson with Robin Higham

I first met the B-32 one day early in 1945 when I was assigned to learn to command one at Ft. Worth A.A.F., Texas. My first impression was that it was a very big bird compared to the old slab-sided B-24s I had been flying. With the great round fuselage, originally meant to be pressurized, it seemed to be immense, and, in fact, was a little over twice the size of the Liberator. As impressive as the size of the fuselage were the great dual main wheels and the immense single fin which appeared to be at least 40 feet high.

The Dominator's large Wright R-3550-23 engines had 2,200 hp; the B-24s had 1,200 hp. The 32's wing span was 135 feet; the B-24's was 110 feet. The Dominator weighed 113,500 pounds with 5,226 gallons of fuel, giving a range of 4,450 miles in still air with 20,000 pounds of bombs. (The designed flying gross weight could go as high as 120,000 pounds, with a maximum of 123,000 pounds.) In contrast, the B-24D weighed a maximum of 60,000 pounds with 3,664 gallons of fuel and had a range of 2,850 miles with 5,000 pounds of bombs—or a maximum ferry range of 4,660 miles. So here was an aircraft weighing over twice as much as those I had been used to flying.

The B-32 Dominator, a great successor to the B-24, was created as an insurance policy in case the Boeing B-29 did not work out. Originally, it had the same engines as the B-29. It was also pressurized. Otherwise, it was a Convair aircraft with the twin tails of the PB4Y Coronado flying boat and the dihedral tail plane. This was changed in the production models to the single-tail fin and normal tail plane, which had appeared first on the Navy's B-24 conversion, the Privateer. Before the aircraft got to production, tactics in the Pacific changed, and instead of the remote and aloof high-altitude attacks,

---

Opposite page: The Consolidated B-32 in flight.

those from lower levels were envisaged, so the weighty pressurization system was removed, as well as the remote-controlled turrets housing the ship's 20 mm cannon. Thus, by the time I got to it, the Dominator was more like an enlarged Privateer than anything else. It carried ten .50 caliber machine guns in five turrets. Officially, the Army Air Force considered it overweight and unnecessary. They also said that the view from the boombardier's position was poor. But this really was not true, at least that is what we pilots felt when we got to know the B-32 during the spring and summer of 1945. We thought it a pity that only 115 of the 1,713 ordered were completed.

Getting into the B-32 was much the same as getting into the B-24, only the climb to the cockpit seemed to be considerably greater. One could enter the forward of the two bomb bays and then climb the ladder to the intermediate deck on which was located the engineer's station and the galley. The latter was a holdover from the aircraft's PB4Y ancestry. We used it only on overnight flights. Still, it would have been nice on those long bombing runs to Japan from Guam and other overseas bases. Also on the intermediate deck was the trolley, fitted in some models, along which a man could haul himself back and forth across the bomb bay to the rear of the aircraft.

Those of the crew permanently stationed back there (rear top turret, tail turret, and ball turret gunners) got into the aircraft through a hatch located just aft of the retractable ball turret on the underside. The pilots, navigator, radar man, bombardier, and engineer climbed the next ladder onto the main deck. The nose gunner and the bombardier could reach their station through a hatch on the underside of the nose or by climbing down through the pilots' compartment. Chest-type parachute packs were stowed nearby for each crew member, but stowage was not always adequate. On one occasion we had a cabin full of nylon fluffing when the navigator caught his chute on the corner of a stringer or some such thing and popped it open. Luckily, we had a spare on board and equally luckily we did not have to jump on that or any other sortie. The standard procedure for bailing out was for the crew in the rear to exit via their entrance hatch and for the rest of us to jump out the open bomb bay or a hatch forward behind the bombardier.

As soon as you entered the cockpit, you noticed the space—it was wide and had many panels in the windows. In fact, it was enormous—the pilot and copilot could barely touch hands in the middle; and I am not kidding about that, as I am over six feet tall. This great space meant that we communicated via the intercom instead of by shouting as we did in most other aircraft of the day. The other feature of the cockpit was what seemed to be the vast array of instruments and switches. There was a special panel for propeller controls, as this was one of the first aircraft fitted with reversible props to shorten the land-

Opposite page: Another view of the B-32.

ing roll or to abort a takeoff. And there was a panel devoted to deicing gear, for this aircraft was one of the first to be fitted with electrical deicing on the leading edges of the wings and tail empennage. Deicing of the propellers was accomplished by pumping isopropanol through a slinger ring; the fluid then found its way to the cutting edge and the tips of the props by centrifugal force.

If the B-24 represented the aviation revolution of the 1930s with its variable pitch propellers, high-octane fuel, retractable undercarriage, flaps, and all-metal construction, as well as its high-aspect-ratio Davis wing, it also suffered from being in the early years of transition. This meant that there were numerous versions. For example, I flew models C through J during my training days, and not every one was an improvement over its predecessor. The B-32, on the other hand, was the second generation. Most of the bugs had been worked out and many of the refinements, accelerated by wartime needs and research, were already installed in the early production models. Thus, compared to the Martin B-10 of a decade earlier, or even to the B-17 and B-24, this was a very modern machine. Naturally, in a cockpit of this complexity, simply checking that the ground crew had done their job, or that someone else had not, took time. Thus, before entering the B-32, pilot, copilot, and engineer made sure that the pitot tube cover was removed, landing gear and nosewheel tires and oleos were correctly inflated, fire extinguisher discs were intact and had not been accidentally discharged, props were free of unusual nicks and dents, nacelles were securely fastened and free of pronounced oil leaks, no fuel leaks or seepage existed, trim tab positions were correct—and, on reaching the cockpit, remembering to check that tab-control settings were correct; landing lights were fully retracted and flush, and safety locks on main and nose gear had been removed.

After the copilot and I had strapped ourselves in and had adjusted our seats, we started down the pretakeoff checklist printed on a plastic card about eight inches long. One of us would call out the items and the other would look it over and respond "check," as fuel gauges, auxiliary power unit (APU), inverter switch, circuit breakers, propeller selector switches, hydraulic pump, control locks, antiicer switches, *ad infinitum,* were confirmed to be operating properly or in the correct position.

Once all this was done, we would glance out both sides of the cockpit, check to get the thumbs-up signal from the crew chief on the ground, and proceed with engine start-up. This procedure began with #2, the left-hand inboard engine, because it drove the hydraulic system, as did #3—but generally the pilot had better observation and control when starting #2 first. Once #2 was started, #3, #1, and #4 followed, in that order. With all engines running and intermediate checks on oil pressure, cylinder head temperatures, etc., completed, we checked by intercom to be sure that everyone was in place, and, with hardly any warm-up—because it was early summer in Ft. Worth—the chocks were waved away and we started the taxi run to takeoff.

The B-32 was easy to taxi because it had a steerable nosewheel controlled by using throttle and minimum brakes. Normally, engines were set to turn over at 800–1000 rpm—enough to pull the ship at a good clip along the taxi strip. One problem, usually solved by turning on George, the autopilot, was the leg power required to keep the big rudder centralized when taxiing in a crosswind. Once near the runway, we would swing around into the wind and go through the pretakeoff checks. These included running up each engine in sequence to 48–49 inches mercury while standing on the brakes, switching magnetos to watch for more than a 100 rpm drop, and leaving the turbo-boost controls in position to develop maximum takeoff power. The actual pre-takeoff check included closing bomb-bay doors; securing all hatches; checking generator, inverter, and booster-pump switches; setting fuel tank selectors at tank to engine, prop selector to automatic, mixture controls to auto rich, various shutters to open or automatic, and wing flaps to 30 degrees; moving all controls full right, full left, or full forward and full rear; noting critical pressures and temperatures (oil, fuel, cylinder head, hydraulic); and checking that crew members were in position and braced and that all guns were trimmed fore and aft.

Once the pretakeoff check was completed and we were cleared by the tower, brakes were released and the airplane was guided onto the runway using light brakes and outboard engines. When aligned with the centerline, the throttles were walked slowly and smoothly forward to full open (2,800 rpm; 49 inches mercury), and the takeoff run was under way. A fully loaded B-32 took a long time to get rumbling, though a light version had a pretty snappy takeoff with all 9,200 hp available. About halfway down the 10,000-foot runway, the controls would finally begin to bite, and nosewheel steering could be abandoned. At 130 mph IAS it would finally begin to fly, and one could ease back on the stick and begin to climb away. Apart from his sitting higher, for the 24 pilot the 32 had a normal takeoff and climb. It required a fair amount of rudder at the beginning of the takeoff roll, but once airspeed was adequate it was very docile. Off the ground, unlike the B-24, it was not mushy (or at least the lightly loaded planes we flew were not). The wheels coming up made little difference, though you did have to remember to toe the brakes to make sure that the wheels stopped spinning on their way into the wells and the flaps were milked up in the usual small decreases until it was flying clean. The B-32 did not need to be brought down carefully on the step to level out at the desired altitude; you simply flew to the desired altitude and leveled off

smoothly right there. With the Liberator, on the other hand, you climbed up to 500 feet above the desired height and then let down gently to it, or, if diving, you leveled off above and then settled down.

We used the automatic pilot more in this ship than in the B-24, even on climb, and most of the time when cruising, as the aircraft was very stable. It may not be entirely fair to say, but I remember the 32 as being much more stable on an engine-out situation, too. I say it may be unfair to put it this way because of the training we got at Ft. Worth; the instructors only cut one of the inner engines and never an outer one. Why? I don't recall. It may be that they were all combat veterans who could see the end of the war coming and they were darned if they were going to risk a student pilot putting their necks in a noose because the aircraft yawed out of control or rolled over with an outboard engine gone. On three engines the Dominator was definitely stable and needed only a bit of rudder cranked in with the trim to maintain course and altitude. This certainly was not true with the Liberators, they had a tough time on three engines and sank like a brick on two. I know, because one night near Savannah we lost both engines on the left side and we barely made it onto the runway!

Normal cruising for the B-32 required about 34–35 inches of boost and an IAS of 180 mph. Very little allowance had to be made for the weight of the aircraft, though like all machines of the day, it probably jumped a bit if all the bombs were let go at once.

We did only limited formation flying in the bird, perhaps because it was so large and visibility was somewhat limited, perhaps because we never got to operations.

Another peculiarity of our training was that we got very little instruction in power stalls. My main recollection is that with the stiff, round fuselage, the B-32 did not give as clear a signal as the B-24, except possibly for a mild tail shake. When a stall went through, the nose dropped gently but quickly straight down. Once you automatically snapped the control column forward and held the plane straight until the speed built up again to 180-220 IAS (how far depended upon weight), it then was easy enough to recover by easing the stick back and easing on power. To give some idea of the variance in speeds with weights and flaps on this aircraft, the manual shows that with 0 degrees of flap, the stalling speed was 131 mph at 80,000 pounds and 156 mph at 120,000 pounds; with 30 degrees down at 120,000 pounds, the stall speed was 133 mph, varying a bit, of course, from airframe to airframe. Cruising speed was normally 180 mph with the aircraft redlined at 240 mph at 118,000 pounds, or 330 mph at 100,000 pounds.

Opposite page: A B-32 at rest.

The B-32 was easy to maneuver in the rather straightforward Rate I (30 degrees/minute) turns we did and was no trouble to handle in the corkscrew pattern that was developed early in the war as a defense against fighters.

As for landing, it was no trouble at all. You simply made the usual down-wind leg doing your prelanding check: start APU, retract turret, hydraulic pump on, mixture auto rich, generators on, props auto, 2,400 rpm, gear extended, flaps 30 degrees. Then you turned crosswind and reduced power some to set up for the final at 150–160 mph, a little higher (165–170) on three engines, lowered full flaps (40 degrees), and powered right on in with about 30 inches and 130 mph IAS. Once over the end of the runway, you eased the throttles back and slowly brought the nose up until the aircraft set-tled—sometimes so gently that you were surprised to be on the ground. If the runway was long enough and someone was on your tail, your roll was a little longer; but usually, once the nosewheel was hard down, the propellers were reversed and the throttles shoved forward, and slowing down quickly and evenly was no problem.

One oddity about the Dominator was that the photographs show a tail skid. I have no recollection of this—whether or not it was retractable or what its purpose was. My only guess 30 years after the event is that it was there to prevent poor pilots from scraping the after-fuselage along the runway when landing in a too-high nose-up manner, which I suppose was possible if you were an old B-17 pilot used to making tail-down three-pointers. Certainly it was not a problem for those of us who came off the 24.

While at Ft. Worth, we wondered about the shape of things to come as we could see the tail of the B-36 sticking out of the hangar across the field. One day we even got a glimpse of the whole thing. But the war was over, we never went operational, and I walked away from my last flight in the 32, and from the old USAAF, satisfied that I had flown the largest aircraft then available for operations and a worthy successor to the old Convair Liberator.

Willard S. Ruliffson is a biochemist at Kansas State University, Manhattan. He served in the U.S. Army and Army Air Corps from 1941 to 1946 and in the Reserves until 1950.

Opposite page: Overall view of the B-32 in flight.

F-80 Shooting Star

John W. Keeler

We were homeward bound to Britain at 24,000 feet, north of Würzburg, Germany. It was late 1944. Our squadron of Thunderbolts was flying cover for a box of B-24s. Somebody bellowed, "Hey, Daily Lead, we got one of them blow-jobs at two o'clock low!" As we rolled into the attack, I had my first glimpse of a jet aircraft. It was an impressive but short glimpse. At that time there were not many aircraft that could outdive the Thunderbolt, but here was one climbing faster than we were diving. Needless to say, no one got a shot at the German jet, and we would see more of them before V-E Day.

But this is not a story about the famed Messerschmitt 262, nor about the great Thunderbolt. It is a story that, for me, started that day with a burning desire to fly a jet fighter. It is a story about the first combat-tested jet aircraft in the U.S. military inventory. It is the story of the F-80 Shooting Star.

It was six years from that day north of Würzburg before I crawled into the cockpit of an F-80 for my first solo jet flight. In the intervening years I had watched the development of the jet arm of the U.S. Air Force. Lockheed seemed to have the inside track in the fighter business, and while as a "Jug" pilot I had said many uncomplimentary things about their Lightning in World War II days, I was impressed as I learned of the advances of the XP-80. The first XP-80 had flown in January of the same year that I had glimpsed that ME-262. It was 132 days from drawing board to flight; it had reached the almost unheard-of speed of 582 mph and gone to 39,000 feet. The first Army Air Force squadron was equipped with P-80s in March of 1945, and the P-80 had shattered the speed records from coast to coast and at the Cleveland National Air Races.

Opposite page: F-80s of the Kansas Air National Guard.

It was at Williams Air Force Base, Arizona, where I was to train to be a jet flight instructor, that I first came face-to-face with this beautiful and impressive bird, the F-80 Shooting Star. (We were still calling it the P-80 at that time.) The first TF-80s (T-33s) had arrived at Willy, and I had five dual rides before crawling into the cockpit. It was tight even for a 160-pounder like me, and I remember thinking as I strapped in that it was much like a Mustang cockpit.

The plane was 34 feet 6 inches long, 11 feet 4 inches high, and had a wingspan of 38 feet 10 inches. The instrumentation was primitive compared to today's fighter cockpits, but it was a great improvement over our World War II birds. "Toggle switches, circuit breakers, and clocks" was my first impression as I sat there getting familiar with my surroundings. The airspeed read in miles per hour and fuel consumption in gallons per hour. As I was taking in the mass of gauges and switches, I remembered and smiled at a comment I'd heard many years before. My father had owned a Ford car in the 1930s, and a droll friend had asked as he looked over the dash, "George, did you get blueprints with this?"

There was one incongruous item in the cockpit of all the F-80s at Williams. Some months before, a pilot had crash-landed and then burned because he couldn't open the jammed cockpit canopy. Now at Willy each F-80 had a sawed-off baseball bat strapped forward of the left console—a primitive but effective tool to use to batter one's way out of a locked cockpit.

For one raised in the prop fighter era, one of the most startling revelations on that first jet flight was the slow response when the throttle was advanced for takeoff. Anyone who had flown the Thunderbolt or Mustang remembered the immediate surge down the runway when that 12-foot prop grabbed the air and how the bird leaped off after a few hundred feet of roll.

Not so in that pre-afterburner era of jet fighters. On a summer afternoon in that Arizona desert there was always some last-second "puckering" before the bird staggered into the air off the end of Willy's 6,300 feet of runway. Takeoff roll was seldom computed, and a wet finger held in the breeze usually decided go or no-go. On a cross-country flight to Denver some weeks later this was nearly my undoing. The mile-high city on a hot day is never a setting for a short-field takeoff, and I blew dust and sagebrush for what seemed to be halfway to the Kansas state line before getting airborne from Lowry Field. Heavy emphasis was later placed on computing takeoff rolls.

A simultaneous revelation on takeoff for a former propeller driver was the astonishing absence of torque. For one whose right leg was longer than his left from years of holding 2,000 hp straight down a runway, the phenomenon of getting airborne without manhandling the rudder control—indeed with little or no rudder pressure—was nearing the miraculous.

Opposite page: Inside the cockpit of an F-80.

Like all airplanes the F-80 became a beautiful machine with gear and flaps up, airspeed increasing, and climbing skyward. But there was an added beauty for the F-80—its ease of handling. For anyone who had wrestled World War II fighters into steep turns at 400 mph, the fingertip control of the roll axis of the F-80 was also a miracle of the age. In retrospect, after flying Century Series and other high-performance fighters, the F-80 still stands out as the easiest-to-fly aircraft I ever operated. Its hydraulic-boosted aileron control gave a new dimension to fighter performance and fighter tactics.

It was a light airplane, relatively speaking: clean, with internal fuel only, the F-80B weighed 12,744 pounds; with tip tanks full of JP-1 it grossed out at 15,215 pounds. Its J33 engine gobbled up 120 gallons climbing to 30,000 feet and covered 120 miles of ground getting up there. A calibrated airspeed of 260 mph would true out at about 410 mph at this altitude. The flight operating charts said you had enough fuel to escort bombers (and that's what the F-80 was designed for) 530 miles, drop the tanks, fight for 15 minutes at 100% rpm, and turn around and get home with 50 gallons in the traffic pattern—enough for one go-around if you didn't get lined up the first time.

In the pattern the 80 was stable and honest. The 360° overhead approach for jet fighters was out of vogue for a period of time, and the landing pattern in the early operating instructions was rectangular.

Even the published tech orders on the E-80 took on a jet-age appearance. They were the first I had seen with true readability and with any humor. Straightforward instructions such as this appeared in boldfaced type: "WARNING: Do not spin this airplane with drop tanks installed. Jettison tanks if accidental spin develops." And even if redundant, this double emphasis was impressive: "This airplane is controllable up to a Mach number of .8. This limitation must be observed." There was also a loose permissiveness in the flight instructions that doesn't appear in today's manuals: "In general, acrobatics should not be attempted below 10,000 feet until the pilot becomes familiar with the speed at which the airplane can gain and lose altitude."

Every prop driver who has transitioned to jets has had that sinking sensation on his first formation join-up when he has chopped the throttle and continued to streak on past his exasperated leader. The clean aerodynamics of the F-80 took some getting used to, and even the speed brake didn't come close to giving the braking power one had with four 12-foot blades out front. But the 80 was a jewel to fly in formation once it was mastered. It was a stable aircraft, and even with the underslung drop tanks it took a minimum of effort and jockeying of the throttle to hold fingertip alignment.

On several occasions at Williams I flew with the Aerojets, one of the first jet demonstration teams in the world. The F-80 was superb in this role. With

---

Opposite page: At work on F-80s.

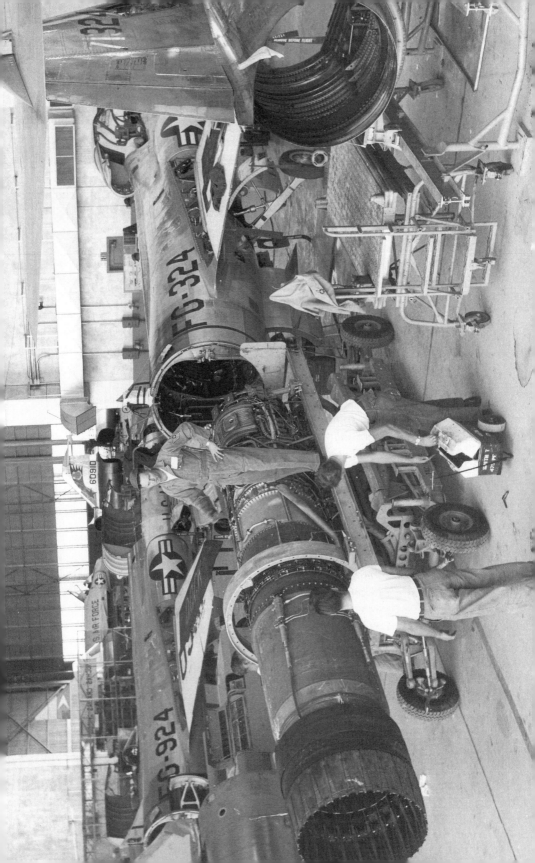

no drop tanks, wings could be tucked in to a four-foot overlap on the lead; the formation performed more as a single airplane than any demo team before or since.

It was early 1952 before I got my orders to the 8th Fighter Bomber Wing, then flying out of K-13 near Suwon. The three squadrons were flying F-80Cs, the latest model of the Shooting Star. If I had been impressed with the F-80 as a jet trainer, my respect for it was increased tenfold in its role as a combat aircraft. As a gun platform and weapons delivery system I found it to be par excellence in the Korean War. Even with an outmoded sight the F-80 was superb at putting bombs on the target and in its close-support role. Designed as a high-altitude air-to-air fighter, the Shooting Star wound up in Korea as a fighter-bomber. Lockheed engineers must have cringed at the loads of bombs, rockets, and napalm that we hung on the wings of this little bird!

While it was no match for the performance of the swept-wing MIG-15 that we sometimes faced in the North Korean skies, as a ground attack machine it was unsurpassed. The six .50 calibers in the nose gave a good concentration for strafing trains and vehicles as well as hosing enemy bunkers and gun positions. The guns were also fine protection for low-level attacks with napalm.

But it was as a bomber that the F-80 excelled, carrying a thousand-pounder tucked under each wing. We initiated dive-bomb runs in echelon from 11,000 to 13,000 feet. A steep run—60–70°—was best for accuracy. The book said to release at 3,500 feet to bottom-out of the dive between 2,500 and 2,000 feet. When it was necessary, the book was forgotten; with an F-80 one could bore into 1,500 feet, release, and still get away without picking up bomb fragments from the plane ahead. Dive-brakes were used in this form of delivery, and speed seldom exceeded 350 mph at bomb release.

Skip bombing in the F-80 was effective against the railroad tunnels in the mountains of North Korea. On one particular mission against a supply train that had taken refuge in a tunnel, I simultaneously released two delayed-fuse thousand-pounders into the tunnel entrance, banked over the tunneled mountain, and saw bomb blast come from both ends of the tunnel. The remainder of the four-ship flight sealed the train in the mountain. A good afternoon's work in any war!

Encountering MIGs in the 80 was not dreaded by U.S. pilots. Quite to the contrary, we welcomed the few tangles we had with them. It was an F-80 that knocked down a MIG-15 in the first all-jet air-to-air battle. The superior speed and zoom capability of the MIG gave it an immediate advantage, but if its pilot made the mistake of slowing to the 80's speed for a fight, the MIG was outturned and outgunned by the straight-winged Shooting Star.

Opposite page: Maintenance men assemble the rocket mechanism of an F-80 before a test flight.

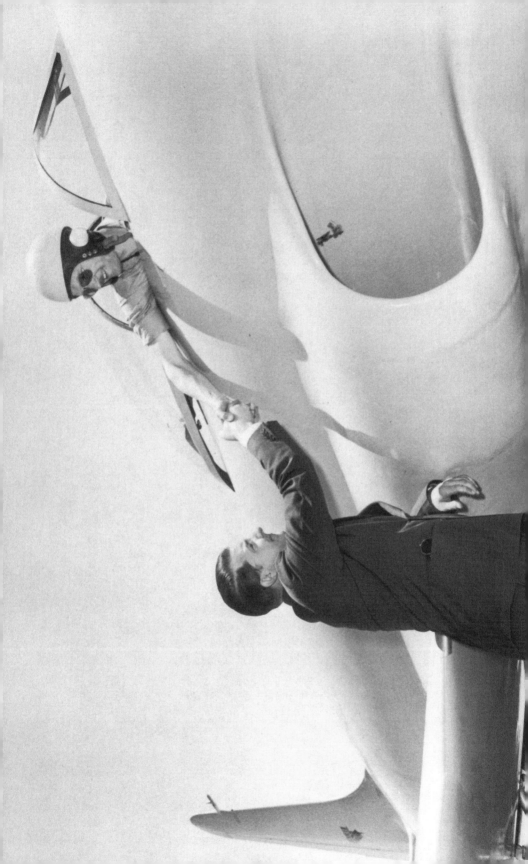

All jet aircraft are supersensitive to battle damage, and the F-80 was no exception. But its simplicity and lack of complicated control and fuel systems gave it a special toughness and battleworthiness. On at least one occasion over Korea a battle-damaged 80 flamed out as it was limping home. Unable to get an airstart the pilot glided southward. His innovative flight leader dropped to the rear, gently nudged the nose of his 80 into the tailpipe of his flamed-out wingman, and "pushed" the crippled bird back over friendly territory. That's togetherness at its best.

The greatest satisfaction for a fighter-bomber pilot in Korea came in the form of a good mission in direct, close support of our ground troops. About 60 percent of our F-80 combat missions were close-support type. I have cherished for more than 20 years a letter from Major General J. C. Fry, then commander of the Second Infantry Division in Korea, which addressed the close-support role of the F-80. The letter came to the 8th Fighter-Bomber Wing the day after a particularly hard-fought ground and air battle for an infamous piece of front-line real estate known as "Old Baldy." The letter is indeed a tribute to the men and to the F-80 Shooting Stars they flew:

> I wish to express on behalf of my command our heartfelt appreciation for the superb combat assistance given us on 5 November. I personally observed the low level attacks made which, without question, hurt the Chinese tremendously. In fact, one ground observer reports seeing a Chinese .50 caliber gun receive a direct hit by napalm. My considered opinion is that the air strikes were extremely effective.
>
> A by-product of the air attack was the tremendous lift it gave the Infantry. I was on "Old Baldy" when some of the attacks were made, and without exception, officers and men alike were pleased and happy over what they saw. I am sure the pilots concerned would have been immensely proud if they could have heard the men say, "It takes real guts to go in and do that job."

The last F-80 came off the Lockheed production line in June 1950. In six and a half years 1,732 Shooting Stars were manufactured. The U.S. Air Force, U.S. Navy, and five South American nations used the airplane as a first-line fighter at some period of time until December 1972. My last flight in an 80 was in 1959, when I ferried one to the Colombian Air Force.

The T-33, the most famous jet trainer in the world, is the dual-control, tandem-seat version of the F-80. In the decade of the 50s, 90 percent of the Free World pilots trained in this aircraft. This "big brother" of the F-80 has been the standard jet trainer in 40 foreign air forces.

Opposite page: Congratulating an F-80 test pilot.

On a recent visit to the Air Force Museum in Ohio, as I stood before the polished Shooting Star on display there, I recalled a story concerning the first test flight of the F-80. As Lockheed designer "Kelly" Johnson approached the plane with test pilot Milo Burcham he said, "She's all yours, Milo. Treat her nice. Find out if she's a lady or a witch."

For one who trained, taught, and fought in the 80 she's a lady—a revered and respected lady.

Col. John W. Keeler is director of information for USAF in Europe with head-quarters in Ramstein, Germany. In World War II he served with the 8th Air Force in England, flying P-47s. Recalled to active duty during the Korean War, he flew 166 missions in the F-80.

Opposite page: An F-80 upon returning from strafing operations.

F-111 Aardvark

Peter M. Dunn

The Air Force has not formally named the F-111, but I suppose it really does not have to; as always, the crews have already done so. Although it deserves a more striking and sinister name to adequately reflect its excellent combat capability, those who fly the F-111 know it as the "Aardvark" (no doubt for its long, slender proboscis, so prominent at first sight). Never before has a flying machine been so highly publicized—for good or ill. The F-111 has been the subject of fierce political and technical controversy from conception to birth, and perhaps it is fitting that the most eloquent testimonials to the combat performance of the F-111 have come from the enemy.

A pilot or weapons system officer (WSO) coming from another fighter would notice several slight variances at first glance. The sheer size of the airplane is impressive; it grosses out at over 80,000 pounds with internal fuel only, compared to, say, an RF-4C's 52,000 pounds with three external fuel tanks. The F-111 may also look somewhat cluttered, what with wing high-lift devices (slats, flaps, rotating gloves) and pylons. The wings are high and set well back; only the outer halves of the wings (which seem to be set very far aft) can be seen from the cockpit. When one first sits in the cockpit the limited visibility is immediately noticeable. Because of the side-by-side seating arrangement the pilot must rely on the WSO to clear the sky visually on the right side, and occasionally cross-cockpit formation flying must be done. EB-66 pilots, who sat on the left and had no right seaters, will appreciate the problem. This matter is really not terribly important, since the F-111 works mainly alone, at night, on the deck, at flight parameters not approachable at present by other fighters.

Opposite page: A camouflaged F-111.

A glance down the top of the aircraft will reveal a broad, flattish back, which generates a great deal of lift. A position about 100 yards behind an F-111 will give you a good view of this very wide dorsal area as it gently slopes down toward you. In the air, at forward wing sweeps and with gear down, the F-111 looks like a great mottled goose with long beak and high wings. But sweep the wings full aft and an incredible transformation occurs. The ugly duckling becomes a graceful, deadly, dartlike creature as it knifes through the sea of air—no frills and all business.

Since the F-111 has no ejection seat but employs an escape module, the usual detailed seat preflight is eliminated. Strapping in is a simple affair, and evidence of foresight and human engineering in the cockpit is readily apparent. It is a comfortable cockpit, and the airplane has often been referred to as the "Cadillac of fighters." There are actually places to stow charts, checklists, and flight publications.

Starting the engines is quite simple—and flexible. In addition to the usual pneumatic start, a starter cartridge can be used, and cross-bleed starts can be accomplished. Hot starts are almost unheard of. Unlike the J-79 engines in the F-4, which idled within very small permissible deviations from 66 percent rpm, the TF-30 can idle from 57 to 69 percent rpm.

Taxiing the F-111 is also a little different. The crew sits directly over the nosewheel, and the large main wheels are fairly close together. When making a tight turn one gets an impression of teetering. On takeoff, nosewheel liftoff averages about 142 knots. At Nellis Air Force Base, Nevada, where base altitude is over 1,800 feet and summer runway temperatures rise to 125 degrees Fahrenheit and higher, takeoff distance is about 4,200 feet. Acceleration is fairly good for such a heavy aircraft. In the early A models maximum engine thrust is around 18,000 pounds per engine; later models have far more powerful engines in the 25,000-pound class. The stick is pulled back at rotation speed, but immediately after nose liftoff a forward stick motion may be required to arrest rotation of the aircraft. The pilot cannot snatch the gear up, as in other aircraft, because of the exceptionally long extension of the main gear struts. If the gear handle were raised while the wheels were still in contact with the runway, a pressure of 750 psi would be routed to the wheels for auto braking, and two blown tires would result.

The variable-sweep wings rotate on individual pivots and literally permit the pilot to redesign the aircraft in flight. The pivots are steel pins 8.5 inches in diameter, set in a solid box which is the structural heart of the airplane. Wings extended to 16 degrees provide a maximum surface area for greatest lift, permitting short takeoffs and landings. As speed increases and lift is converted to drag, wingspan and surface are reduced by sweeping the wings back

Opposite page: The underside of an F-111.

to a maximum of 72.5 degrees, where they lie tucked along the tail. No retrimming is necessary while sweeping the wings or changing speed, since the aircraft automatically and consistently trims itself to one G flight. As the wings move, the four inboard pylons also automatically readjust their alignment to remain streamlined at all times. The versatility and overlap of the system was dramatically illustrated by the four-ship "tiger formation" employed for displays by my old squadron: the leader flew with wings out at 26 degrees, No. 2 and No. 3 set sweep of 45 degrees, and the slot man was swept full aft at 72.5 degrees. It was a pretty impressive sight as we flew over the field. The aircraft will slip through Mach 1 with about a 54 degrees sweep; at Mach 1.7 or thereabouts the wings will be positioned to 72.5 degrees, and the F-111 will punch through Mach 2 and higher. Because of its bulk, the F-111 makes a tremendous supersonic shock wave. Standing in a desert valley bombing range, I have seen the entire valley floor instantly erupt in a cloud of boiling dust, as if sharply struck by the flat of a giant hand, following a low-level supersonic bomb run.

The F-111, although a fighter, can carry an incredible bomb load. It has an internal weapons bay in addition to the wing-mounted pylons. A wide variety of ordnance can be loaded, including various sizes of general-purpose bombs, CBUs (chemical-biological units), rockets, and air-to-air missiles. A six-barrel 20 mm cannon is also installed.

After takeoff it seems to take a long time to clean the airplane up; the gear is raised, then the slats and flaps. Normal cruise wing sweep is 26 degrees. The F-111 handles beautifully in the air. Like the gooney birds of Midway—which appear awkward and ungainly on the ground—it assumes a new personality when airborne, exuding grace and confidence as it glides over the earth. It is a very honest and responsive aircraft, and many pilots comment on the fact that there is no "dead" spot in the stick. A constant G response is commanded for a given amount of stick travel regardless of airspeed, altitude, or gross weight.

The range of the F-111 is astounding, especially for a flyer coming from another fighter. F-111's have crossed the Atlantic nonstop and without inflight refueling, on internal fuel only. At the time of this writing a Nellis crew has just returned from Pease Air Force Base, New Hampshire, a distance of about 2,250 miles. On the trip east they arrived over Pease after five hours and were still able to shoot several approaches and closed patterns before finally landing. This great range is due to another technical innovation in the F-111—the fan engine with five-stage afterburner.

I'm not sure if anyone really knows what the F-111's top speed really is. On my first flight in the F-111 we reached Mach 2 while climbing out from takeoff, still relatively heavy, and had to reduce speed only to keep from running out of the supersonic corridor. A nice turn was made at 1.8, and the aircraft performed exceedingly well (turns, rolls, etc.) while supersonic. It is designed to provide a stable bombing platform while supersonic on the deck, and it does this very well. The advertised top speed at altitude is Mach 2.5, or about 1,640 mph. For sustained high Mach operation a total temperature indicator is provided the aircrew. At very high speeds, when critical skin temperatures are approached, a red warning light comes on and commands the pilot to reduce speed. A digital readout will start to count down from 300 seconds. A "Total Temperature" lamp on the main caution panel will also light up. The pilot had better pull the power back at this time or structural damage could occur.

Should the crew be forced to abandon the aircraft, the only conscious effort required of either crew member is squeezing the ejection handle. Everything after that is completely automatic. Explosive charges sever the module from the aircraft. The module's rocket motor has lower and upper nozzles, and special sensors continually monitor aircraft speed and direct firing of the proper nozzle. At low speeds the lower, more powerful nozzle is fired, with a slight assist from the upper nozzle to maintain correct trajectory. G sensors and barostatic devices initiate deployment of the recovery parachute. The crew can select automatic chaff initiation at module separation to assist ground radars in detecting the bailout area. Center of gravity considerations are critical to ensure optimum escape attitude, and the weight differential between the crew members may not exceed 65 pounds. Even the thermos water bottles stowed above and behind each crew member must be filled and carried aboard, since they have an effect on proper module loading. A Nellis crew bailed out over the rugged terrain near the Grand Canyon not long ago. The module rolled down an incline for several hundred yards. The crew, strapped inside, emerged relatively untouched and stated that they might not have survived had a conventional ejection seat been used. My own experience in bailing out in a conventional rocket ejection seat over similar rugged country, with severe injury to the pilot, confirms this observation. The module will float if it lands in water, and extra flotation bags can be inflated; should high swells cause cabin flooding, the aircraft commander's control stick becomes a bilge pump. The crew can also sever the module from the aircraft while under water. Again, flotation bags inflate to help the module rise to the surface.

Have you ever watched a mallard duck come in for a landing? It comes in with neck taut, wings outstretched, and stubby legs close together and braced. That's the landing F-111 in a nutshell. Those who have landed aircraft like the F-101 and F-104 will appreciate the landing speed of the F-111. It will touch down within a few knots of nosewheel liftoff speed—somewhere around 140

knots, depending on landing weight and wing sweep (which will be 15 or 25 degrees). The F-4 with the boundary layer control system approximates this. Initial approach speeds are standard—350 knots indicated. Pitchout is made with throttles at idle, 10–12 alpha units (an angle-of-attack measurement which is simpler to use than airspeed). Rollout on downwind is still at idle power, using what seems like a lengthy procedure to attain landing configuration. The main gear door is the speed brake. The gear is lowered first, followed by the slats, then flaps. Base turn is made with a bank angle of 30–40 degrees, in contrast to the 50–70 degrees of bank in some other fighters. Halfway through the turn on base, power is usually applied. With the fan engine, which accelerates relatively slowly, the pilot cannot afford to wait until he needs power to apply it in order to arrest sink rate. No matter how tightly he pitches out, once in landing configuration it is always possible to turn inside the pitch.

The final approach is with power on, holding 10 alpha. Ground effect is experienced upon approaching the overrun, which tends to shallow out the angle of attack. This is countered by applying slight back stick, which is definitely not a flare or roundout. As soon as touchdown is achieved and the engines retarded to idle, wing spoilers rise to kill wing lift and assist in slowing the aircraft. The F-111 has no drag chute, but braking qualities are so excellent that short field landings are no problem. The tires are big, and maintenance gets ten times more landings out of these tires than from those on any other fighters.

To those with experience in high-speed low-level flight, one thing that is instantly noticeable is the steady, granitelike ride. Other fighters flying within similar low-level parameters ride "hard"—the aircraft is striving hard and the ride is bumpy in any sort of unstable air. The F-111 glides through the Mach at low level so easily that the crew would never know the difference were it not for the Mach indicator. The reason for this is the stability augmentation system. This flight control system is unique in that it is self-adaptive. Heretofore, the only other aircraft to possess this feature was the X-15. Triple-redundant pitch, roll, and yaw circuits constantly compensate for deviations in aircraft motion; and computer-commanded corrections are performed before the crew is aware of any possible turbulence or gusting. The result is one of the most solid, stable rides imaginable.

The TFR (terrain-following radar) is another system that makes this airplane unusual. With the deployment of the 474th Tactical Fighter Wing to Southeast Asia in September 1972, the United States finally had a full time, credible night low-level strike capability. Terrain-following radar systems were not new; *automatic* TFR systems were. The missions flown by the 474th over North Vietnam could not have been accomplished manually. The crew can

---

Opposite page: The F-111 was capable of both subsonic and supersonic speeds.

select a variety of altitudes as well as kinds of ride desired: a three-position switch directs a soft, medium, or hard ride. Soft ride programs a gentle pull-up over high ground; hard ride brings the aircraft closer to terrain before initiating a steeper pull-up; in hard ride the descent commands up to a zero G pushover. The TFR also has a situation mode, which permits the crew to fly around peaks rather than over them, and a ground-mapping mode which does what the name implies. One can also make excellent fixed-angle bomb runs with the ground-mapping mode of the TFR, which provides a backup in case the attack radar system (ARS) is lost. The TFR system is dual channel; should the operating system fail, another identical system will automatically take over. If a malfunction occurs anywhere in the system, fail-safe circuits will command an immediate and shuddering pull-up.

Both ground and airborne TFR checks are performed to test the radars and the fail-safe circuits. The aircraft will automatically descend on command, hands off, at a rate of about 10,000 feet per minute. At 5,000 feet above ground level the radar altimeter will identify the earth's surface, and the rate of descent will increase noticeably until just prior to the preselected altitude where a smooth level-off is automatically accomplished. The stick will not move as the aircraft climbs and descends over mountain and valley; the climb and dive commands are sent directly from the TFR computer to the pitch channel of the flight control system. Occasionally it may be necessary to apply power as a particularly steep mountain is approached. In the inky blackness of night it is initially unnerving to look out and see the black hulks of mountains slide by above you as the aircraft settles into a valley.

The weapons system officer backs up the TFR with the big ARS and continuously alerts the pilot to the terrain picture ahead. The ARS has outstanding resolution. Its frequency agility characteristic does two important things for the operator: by continuously and automatically shifting frequencies it approaches optimum reflectivity of the wide variety of materials swept by the radar and provides antijamming function as well. After using equipment like this I could never think of returning to other aircraft I've flown—such as the B-52, EB-66, and RF-4C—much as I enjoyed them all.

As the target is approached, the WSO punches a button that recalls target coordinates set into the computer before flight. The radar cross hairs automatically reach out and settle on the target, and the inertial navigation system is generally so good that the usual problem of last-minute radar scope interpretation is eliminated. If the target is a "no-show," offset bombing capability is available.

The TFR system will keep the aircraft at the desired bombing altitude. However, if the BCU (ballistics computer unit) is being used, delivery param-

---

Opposite page: The sleek F-111 in flight.

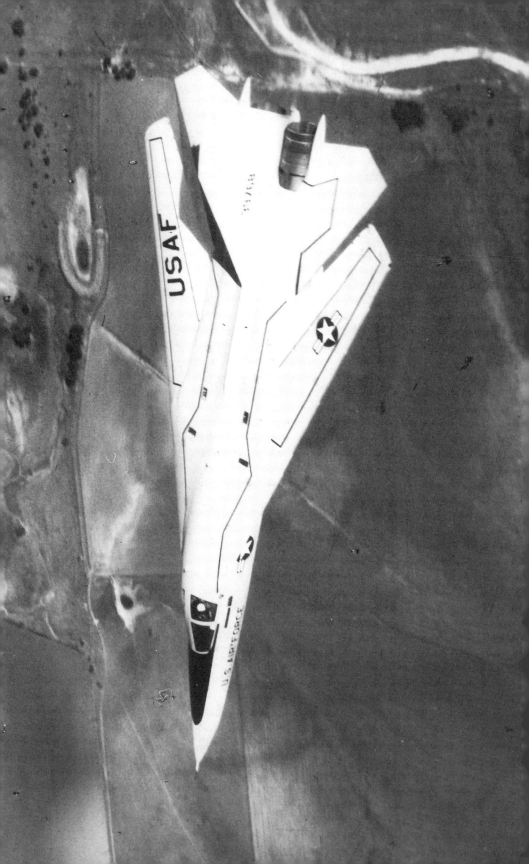

eters are not critical; the BCU will constantly and automatically adjust ballistics for changes in heading, airspeed, and altitude until bombs away. Should the BCU fail, manual ballistics inserted into the system before flight can be instantly used. F-111 crews still debate whether the auto bomb mode using the BCU is as accurate as trail bomb using manual ballistics; it's a moot point, since the bombing circular error averages in both are so good. Visual laydown nuclear bombing attacks can be made at 200 feet and 520 knots minimum airspeed, using the pilot's lead computing optical sight.

While aircrews have always been totally mystified at the bad press the F-111 has received, the aircraft finally began to receive some well-earned praise as a result of the Linebacker I and II campaigns—the air offensives over North Vietnam in 1972. Night after night the F-111s took off from Takhli Royal Thai Air Force Base, Thailand, armed with Mark 82 500-pound bombs or Mark 84 2,000-pound general-purpose bombs, descended over Laos to terrain-following altitudes, flew at low altitudes as far as the northeast railroad, delivered their ordnance, and returned to Laos at low altitudes before climbing out for home. Well over an hour was spent at very low altitudes and high speeds, and the entire mission from start to finish was flown with internal fuel only and no inflight refueling. No other fighter in the world can even approximate this performance. Medium-altitude missions were flown against enemy forces in Laos and against the supply trails along the panhandle, and the great accuracy of the radar bombing systems repeatedly broke the backs of Communist attacks. The legendary General Vang Pao, the Laotian Lawrence, presented the 474th Tactical Fighter Wing with a trophy AK-47 rifle as an expression of thanks. Captured North Vietnamese troops referred to F-111s as "whispering death."

On days when solid undercast would normally have prevented fighter strikes on enemy forces, we rendezvoused with flights of F-4 or A-7 aircraft that released their ordnance on command of the F-111, which was bombing by radar. This technique of pathfinder bombing proved to be very valuable and was employed night and day. While the B-52s rightly earned great praise for their part in the final December blitz over North Vietnam, it was the F-111 aircraft which—singly and largely unheralded—struck the enemy MIG airfields, SAM (surface-to-air missile) and gun sites, and other threats minutes before the big bombers appeared on the scene and directly contributed to minimizing B-52 losses.

It is ironic indeed that it was the North Vietnamese themselves who did a great deal to build the legend that is growing around this airplane. Communist air defense forces never succeeded in solving the problem of detecting intruding F-111s. POWs returning from Hanoi told of Communist target areas sounding the all clear after strikes by other U.S. aircraft, only to be completely surprised minutes later by lone F-111s roaring over and attacking their targets. One of the Nellis crews, who was hit by a "golden BB" in December, told of the Communist prison guard who came up to him and said, "You F-111." Then making a flat horizontal sweeping motion with the palm of his hand, he shook his head in admiration and said, "Whoosh." An amazing compliment by the enemy. I don't think I can improve on that.

Maj. Peter M. Dunn has had three tours in Southeast Asia, including more than 100 missions over North Vietnam. He has flown combat in the EB-66 and the F-111. He recently received the M.A. degree in history from the University of Nevada.

The C-130

Robert Lee Clark

A lot of words come to mind when I try to sum up my feelings about the C-130: rugged, dependable, versatile . . . forgiving. But perhaps the best is faithful. Pilots are noted for their emotional attachment to their airplanes. And almost without exception, the C-130 pilots I have known have loved the C-130 and have had faith in it. No matter how bad the going got, the Hercules would get you through!

There is no doubt in my mind that when they park the last C-5, F-16, and whatever follow-on bomber we build, in storage at Davis Monthan AFB, the crews will be flown home in a C-130.

My love for the venerable Hercules dates from my first practice preflight at Sewart AFB, Tennessee. Although Sewart was in the process of closing down, C-130 and C-7 Caribou training was still concentrated there. The only exception was the C-130A model school at Ellington AFB, Houston, Texas.

When I later attended the A-model school, I found that significant changes in the flight deck arrangement, propellers, flight controls, pneu-draulics, fuel, and other systems in the C-130B and later models separate the C-130A from other C-130s as two very different types of aircraft. Handling characteristics are similar, but systems operation and troubleshooting require a separate course. (The C-130D is a unique exception—it is basically a C-130A equipped with snow skis.)

I graduated from Undergraduate Pilot Training (UPT) in June 1968 with my second choice of assignments: WC-130s to Ramey Air Force Base, Puerto Rico. The sight of my first real, live C-130, dressed up in camouflage, gave the

Opposite page: A C-130 in the service of the Egyptian Air Force.

lasting impression of a rugged, hardworking aircraft—one that you could count on. Years later and, hopefully, a lot wiser, I still feel a tingle when I see or hear a C-130!

Before I was allowed to fly the beauty, I had to take several weeks of classes and then endure long hours in the simulator. There I learned to cope with, or at least remain calm through, every possible malfunction while figuring out all the instruments. Due to the wartime push, the simulator was being worked overtime, and our session began each day at 0300 hours. It was a tribute to the people at Sewart that with minimal facilities and supplies of a partially closed base, we still had full base support for the hectic schedule.

Simulators, at least those of that era, were essentially modern link trainers. You could learn procedures, but not the "feel" of the airplane. No visual presentation or motion was included. Still, learning procedures with two or three fire lights flashing was enough to motivate me deeper into the two-inch thick Dash One!

Teams were set up with two student pilots and one student engineer matched with one instructor pilot and one instructor engineer. My match for student pilot, Capt. Eric Wheaton, was a close friend from pilot training; our student engineer quit the program about half-way through. Eric and I had the rapport to continue and to support each other as student engineer, too, when it came to the actual flying. I really think this arrangement helped us to know the aircraft systems in a way that has spanned the years.

Finally, the magic day arrived: 22 August 1968, my first flight in that beautiful camouflaged turboprop C-130, 62-1839. The "Before Starting Engines" and "Starting Engines" checklists went smoothly, and engine start was a breeze without all the fire lights flashing.

For one thing, the start is very simple: move the condition lever from stop to run and push the start button. High-volume, low-pressure air is used to start the turboprop jet engine.

The air to start the first engine can be obtained from a ground start cart such as the type MA-1A which is used to start a number of jet engine aircraft. Normally, however, the auxillary power unit (APU) mounted in the left wheel well provides the air. The APU is a small jet engine that can be electrically started from the aircraft battery if a ground electrical power unit is not available. Once the first engine is up to idle speed, bleed air from the compressor can then be used to start the other engines. This self-contained start capability is combined with several fueling options. Hydrant or tanker truck single-point refueling with JP-4, or just about anything else flammable, is made at the sin-

gle-point receptacle on the aft end of the right wheel well pod. Over-the-wing refueling makes the C-130 self-sufficient throughout the world.

The start is automatic with only pilot monitor required in the event of malfunction. The scanner (or loadmaster) is positioned out in front of the aircraft with intercom to clear the propellers and monitor the engine starts. The propeller is in fixed pitch directly controlled by the throttle in the ground range. It is almost zero pitch in ground idle as thus it turns quickly up to idle rpm. The scanner also can act as fire guard if the standard Air Force fire guard with 50-pound fire extinguisher is not available.

The automatic and rapid-start capability came in handy countless times in Southeast Asia! I remember a mission just two days before the bombing halt in August 1973 where we launched from revetment alert in eight minutes. We boarded, strapped in, started number three engine, and taxied on one engine while starting the other three engines. Getting the AC-130A gunship with its thirteen-man crew airborne in minimum time required a trained crew and a reliable aircraft.

The nose wheel steering system got a good workout during my first taxi. I was used to the rudder pedal steering of the T-38 trainer or the Cessna 172. The actual miniature steering wheel and "Speed knob" on the C-130 posed new coordination problems for me. It took several flights before I started treating it like power steering and reduced my left-handed inputs—fortunately the nose wheels and strut took my punishment of continual extreme deflection steering!

Probably our greatest fear in flying the C-130 was that we would inadvertently pop the low speed ground idle buttons by pushing the throttles too far forward during taxi. This was briefed as the cardinal sin—and cost a six-pack of beer to blot the memory from the instructor engineer's mind. Actually, it can cause real trouble in the form of an engine compressor stall or turbine section overtemperature if the engine tries to increase rpm while the throttle is forward calling for an extra-high fuel flow and the air drag of an increased propeller pitch.

The low-engine speed is a real help in taxi. The reduced rpm, from about 96 percent down to 70 percent, considerably reduces thrust and eliminates most braking requirements. Oil temperatures stay cool because reverse thrust is not needed as often to slow down. It is also much quieter, which is readily appreciated by C-130 crews. Mastering the low-speed ground idle taxi was no major problem and only cost one or two cases in honorariums!

Opposite page: A Royal Saudi Air Force C-130 in flight.

Engine run-up, so carefully rehearsed in the simulator, was a new and unique experience for the novice. With our luck, the airplane was really bucking pretty good with power set at 8,000 inch-pounds of torque as the propellers generated four small tornadoes. We strained against the set parking brake. With all the noise and movement, it was difficult to read the gauges carefully and check engine performances as we had done in the simulator.

The magic indicators for C-130 engine performance are torque and turbine inlet temperature (TIT). The engine runs at 100 percent rpm in flight, and increased fuel flow simply results in a bigger bite by the propeller. Reducing the throttle reduces fuel flow, produces a flatter propeller pitch, and lowers airspeed. Torque, measured in inch-pounds, indicates the bite of the propeller by showing the torque load between the engine and propeller. Maximum torque for the C-130E with the T56-A-7 engine is 19,600 inch-pounds. TIT then measures engine performance by showing how hot a fire is required to produce the torque. The maximum on the C-130E is 977 degrees Celsius. By matching torque, TIT, and fuel flow between engines, the crew can analyze performance and readily identify malfunctions.

During engine run-up, the power is set for a minimum of 8,000 inch-pounds of torque and above 860 degrees Celsius. Above 860 an automatic temperature schedule is activated, and fuel is fed in at the proper rate to achieve the preset temperatures. This insures smooth and consistent power response among the engines and automatic overtemp protection. By having the power above 8,000 inch-pounds for run-up, we could get a good picture of engine performance before taking the active runway for takeoff.

The propellers have a mechanical control to maintain 100 percent rpm. In addition, there is an electronic system to maintain more accurate rpm and to use for sync of the propellers. With the propellers in sync, the speed of all four is maintained exactly the same and the phase relationship is aligned to reduce propeller beat against the fuselage. Both the electronic and mechanical systems are checked on engine run-up.

I was apprehensive about my first takeoff because we had been warned that like most prop jobs, the C-130 pulls to the left on takeoff. I wanted to be on top of this—and consequently overcorrected nicely for the very subtle pull to the left. Slight positive pressure on the nose wheel steering wheel or slightly reduced power on Numbers 3 and 4 (right wing engines) during the initial takeoff roll is sufficient to keep the nose wheel square on centerline.

Even under extreme loads and with guns protruding out the left side, the aircraft will accelerate smoothly to takeoff speed. On hot days at Peterson

---

Opposite page: The maritime version of the C-130.

Field, Colorado (elevation 6,172 feet), or with a maximum gross weight for takeoff (125,000 to 165,000 pounds depending on model), it may take a little more runway and appear to require an excessive amount of time.

The C-130E was operated routinely in Southeast Asia on unimproved airstrips of less that 3,000 feet. These were fairly close to sea level. A summer day's takeoff from Peterson Field may take 6,500 feet of ground run. On a standard day at sea level, with assisted takeoff rockets installed, from brake release to airborne could take only 20 seconds. Meanwhile, back at Peterson Field, the takeoff run may take an eternity! Still, the C-130 is a flying aircraft and makes the transition airborne nicely somewhere in the neighborhood of 110 to 120 knots.

By the time you finish the simulator phase you know better than to raise your own gear or flaps. So, on my initial takeoff came my first real decision. I decided and then announced: "Gear Up." After a year of pilot training, learning to fly and do it all myself, I had delegated critical action! My instructor, Maj. Ed Yelton, in the right seat, responded as a copilot. He cleaned up the aircraft, (brought gear and flaps up on my command), handled the radios, and away we went to a predetermined area for my first work-out.

I think most recent UPT graduates immediately liken flying the C-130 to flying the "Tweet," the Cessna T-37B jet trainer. For sure, it isn't like flying the supersonic T-38A Talon. Having transitioned back to the T-37 after my C-130 days, I do detect a great deal of similarity in response and other factors such as climb rates and airspeeds, except that the C-130 cruises at higher airspeeds! T-37 climb speed starts at 200 knots at sea level and drops to 180 knots indicated airspeed at 10,000 feet MSL. C-130B climb speed is a constant 180 knots indicated airspeed up to 10,000 feet MSL. Both aircraft achieve about 2,000 feet per minute rate of climb right after the takeoff. The C-130 normally cruises around 300 to 320 knots true airspeed, some 15 to 25 knots faster than the T-37 cruise above 18,000 feet MSL.

The high wing isn't unstable as I had first imagined. The nose tends to hunt, a few degrees left and right, but it is minor and easily accepted. Wing rock in turbulence is a very minor problem and again is easily handled down to touch-down speeds. The yoke feels a little sluggish below 120 knots or so, but control deflection is still more than sufficient. I found that the extra yoke movement required really helped rather than hindered because it dampened out much of my overcorrection!

Four years in weather reconnaissance duty gave me a chance to see the C-130 (B model) perform under varied and unusual conditions. Basic weather

---

Opposite page: A C-123 sprays defoliant in Vietnam.

recce provides everyone the opportunity to build many hours of boredom on the ten-hour-plus standard synoptic tracks. The nitty gritty of hurricane hunting, winter storm recce, and low-level fog seeding provide the proper setting for the "moments of sheer terror" that make flying a challenge and worth doing!

Flying tropical storms and hurricanes is demanding on any aircraft. The C-130 has fared better than most, and I attribute that to the rugged construction and dependable engines. Only one WC-130 has been lost on storm penetration. The engines will handle extremely heavy rainfall without a sputter. The propeller keeps most of the water out, and the slight amount that makes it by doesn't seem to affect performance. Because the aircraft was built for unimproved runway operations, it stands up to most turbulence without even a popped rivet. On one particular night hurricane penetration we inadvertently encountered what I would call severe turbulence and were temporarily out of control. Other than one very wide awake and alert crew, later inspection revealed no defects.

Turbulence penetration airspeed, around 160 knots indicated airspeed, provides a reasonably smooth ride. The rapid power response typical of turboprop aircraft was a big help in keeping us out of trouble in severe weather areas. The usual technique for penetrating a squall line or the wall cloud was to keep the autopilot engaged except for altitude hold. I would use the autopilot elevator wheel to maintain desired pitch attitude and altitude, guarding the yoke with my other hand. With my hand lightly touching the yoke, I could disengage the autopilot and immediately hand fly the aircraft in the event that the severe weather flipped the aircraft on its back or to some other unusable attitude. The flight engineer would hold the computed airspeed with the throttles. The copilot backed up both of us. Altitude might vary by as much as 1,000 feet in the really turbulent areas, but slow steady corrections kept the aircraft well under control and avoided overcontrol. Using the autopilot reduced pilot fatigue, but didn't do a thing for pilot strain!

Most C-130s have extended-range fuel tanks. Underwing pylon or removable cargo compartment tanks—or combinations—are used. The mission endurance thus varies greatly from the 5 hours of the AC-130A gunship to 20 hours on some WC-130H models, to unlimited on the small number of air refuelable models. My logbook reflects my longest mission to be a 12-hour, 42-minute hurricane penetration mission from Ramey AFB, Puerto Rico, to final landing at McGuire AFB, New Jersey. Maintenance problems delayed our replacement aircraft, so we remained in the storm to get the next required position fix.

Opposite page: The Royal Canadian Air Force also used the C-130.

Although the C-130 has a noisy interior, crew bunks are adequate to get a little rest if the mission permits. In the standard C-130 B and E models, the bunks are on the flight deck. In the weather recce models, they were near the rear of the cargo compartment. This could be a long, long walk if a major malfunction occurred! For all the low altitude work, both pilots are in their seats.

I believe that the low-altitude fog seeding mission really demonstrated the versatility and dependability of this airplane. I was associated with the cold fog (fog in below-freezing temperatures) dissipation project in Europe from 1968 through 1972. A similar program was conducted at Elmendorf AFB, Alaska. A grain grinder and six 1,000-pound capacity ice chests were installed in the cargo compartment of the WC-130 (weather modified version). Dry ice was uploaded, and we launched whenever one of the selected airfields was closed down due to cold fog.

The C-130's stability on takeoff permitted zero-zero departures without incident. Most of the seeding was accomplished just touching the top of the fog at a minimum of 300 feet above the ground. Airspeed was 120 knots, with half flaps used to increase stability. Six- to eight-hour missions were not uncommon. The technique of seeding with the roughly ground dry ice proved extremely effective. The dropsonde launcher was removed and the ground dry ice was funneled out of this hole in the bottom of the aircraft. (The dropsonde launcher is used to drop a package similar to the one carried aloft by weather balloons.)

Just as the old faithful C-47 was modified to the attack configuration, the AC-130 was tried and became a potent threat to the movement of supplies along the infamous Ho Chi Minh trail. The initial version had 7.62 mm and 20 mm rapid-fire guns. The AC-130A finally progressed to two 40 mm Bofors and two 20 mm Gatling guns. These 40 mm guns permitted a much higher working altitude (normally 7,500 feet above the ground) to avoid the increasing ground-fire threat. The AC-130H model was finally configured with the more powerful engines (T56-A-15) to carry one 105 mm Howitzer, one 40 mm Bofors, and two 20 mm Gatling guns. Both the 105 mm and the 40 mm on this "Big Spectre" were trainable. The sensor operator could pick up a target and aim or train the gun independently of the aircraft as long as the pilot put the aircraft within certain parameters. The A-model had fixed guns, so that the only way to aim the guns was to move the aircraft.

The AC-130 "Spectre" relied primarily on two sensors for targeting. The low-light-level television used bright moonlight or flares to pick out trucks, boats, and other targets. Infrared was independent of light sources. Both sys-

---

Opposite page: The cockpit of a C-130.

At the controls of a C-130 over Vietnam.

A C-130 delivers equipment using LAPES, low altitude parachute extraction system.

tems were directed—"flown"—with aircraft sticks using transducers, and the images were displayed on small television set monitors enabling sensor operators to search out and track targets along roads or streams. Once a target was located, the sensor operator would hold it dead center and that sensor was selected in the computer. The pilot then used an angle of inclination indicator and an attitude indicator with pitch and bank steering bars to maneuver into a 30-degree bank orbit for firing. The side-mounted gunsight was then used to make the fine adjustments (plus or minus one mil or about one-eighth of a degree of bank and heading) to fire with extreme accuracy. Pilots could consistently hit within a 20-foot circle from a slant range of two miles.

Even in this heavily loaded and high drag configuration (guns, TV camera, sensors, all hung out the left side of the aircraft), the C-130 was an easy aircraft to fly. The initial takeoff was a little bit more sporting, and in the event of engine failure at that point, it would have taken everything to keep the airplane in the air.

For the most part, engine-out performance is no problem from the C-130. Ceiling may be reduced, but sufficient power is available on three engines. Two-engine performance, especially if the two good engines are on one side, varies from good to marginal depending on gross weight and configuration. Many C-130s have limped in on two engines, so we always had hope and took precautions when we had the first engine fail. I have even heard tales of A models flying on one engine in a controlled descent. Unfortunately, I have not had the opportunity to test the theory!

The Hercules is a dream to land. Approach speed varies depending on gross weight from 150 knots down to 115 knots for a maximum effort (short field) landing. Runway threshold airspeed is 10 knots slower, and touchdown airspeed is around 10 knots below that, but not less than about 95 knots. Landing rolls could be as short as 1,500 to 2,000 feet if need be. Even in light to moderate turbulence, a smooth, precise approach is easy to fly. Power response is smooth and almost instantaneous. The joke among pilots is that the throttles are directly wired to the airspeed indicator! If approach speed is maintained and a slow power reduction begun about 200 feet in the air, threshold speed will be right on, and a grease job is almost assured. The pitch change is not drastic and is made slowly.

Two landing configurations can be a problem. A heavyweight no-flap landing can be a tail dragger if overflared even slightly. A very lightweight full-flap landing can float forever. I've seen a touchdown at 64 knots! To mess up other landings takes almost conscious effort!

**Opposite page: Later models of the C-130 were equipped
with computer systems that calculated aircraft data.**

As I think back over the good and the bad times in the C-130s I've flown, I believe the most ridiculous feeling I've had in them was during a practice bailout in the AC-130A gunship. Because the primary mission was flown at night, we had to practice (on the ground) an emergency bailout in blackout conditions to complete our checkout.

After engine shutdown following one of my initial missions, the instructor pilot gave the bailout signal. He turned the jump bell on, killed all the lights, and away I went. I followed the routing each aircraft commander had to take: I unstrapped, cleared the gunsight on my left, climbed over the center console to my right and around the flight engineer's seat. I slipped past the flak curtain and jumped over the TV camera into the cargo compartment. Upon hitting the 20 mm spent brass and running into the 20 mm ammo boxes, I jinked left then back right until I ran into the backslide of the fire control booth. I then veered to my right and made my way down the narrow aisleway tripping on 40 mm ammo cans until I hit the 40 mm guns. I then turned left into the 40 mm ammo rack and back to the right into the flare launcher. A couple of quick trips over the folddown crash landing seats and I was off the ramp.

I would have been safely out of the aircraft reaching for my D ring except that I discovered that I had caught the D ring on something up front and my entire parachute was strung out inside the cluttered interior!

Maj. Robert Lee Clark, a Senior Pilot, is currently the Wing Quality Control Officer (Aircraft Maintenance) at Reese AFB, TX. During his service with the USAF Hurricane Hunters, his first flying assignment, he was credited with 21 hurricane penetrations and logged over 2,500 hours in the WC-130B.

B-57 Canberra

Roy J. Carrow, Jr.

The B-57 built by the Martin Company is the U.S. version of the British-designed Canberra. The original of this twin-jet bomber was designed during World War II but did not become operational until the late 1940s. Various models of the Canberra have been built by Great Britain, Australia, and the United States, and many countries throughout the world have flown and still fly these variants. A unique and perhaps the most ironic event in the history of this aircraft was the Indo-Pakistan War, where the British Canberra and the American B-57 fought on opposite sides.

The Canberra, as originally designed by the British, was built in two versions. One was a tactical bomber and the other a reconnaissance platform. The United States bought the design from Great Britain and built or modified existing airframes into seven different versions. These seven have been further modified to equip the basic airframe for many different missions. The B-57 is truly the "Gooney Bird" (C-47) of the jet age.

The basic airframe as acquired from Great Britain has a wingspan of 64 feet and an overall length of 65.5 feet. The basic weight of the aircraft is approximately 29,000 pounds. With wing-tip tanks installed, it will carry 18,700 pounds of fuel. This is sufficient for 4 hours and 30 minutes of flight time at 41,000 feet, cruising at 390 knots true airspeed. This gives the aircraft a no-wind range of approximately 1,750 nautical miles, for there is no air-refueling capability.

The aircraft's two Curtiss-Wright J-65-W5B engines originally gave 7,220 pounds of thrust each; today, through modifications, the thrust has been increased to 7,660 pounds each.

Opposite page: A pilot and his B-57.

185

The engines are midmounted in the wings approximately 15 feet from the fuselage centerline, a feature that makes flight on one engine a little sporty. If power on the good engine is increased too rapidly, the sudden increase of thrust will result in a violent and uncontrollable yaw and roll. A rudder-power assist system (rudder-power system on B-57E aircraft) was incorporated to lower substantially the minimum single-engine control speed by providing additional rudder deflection when needed by the pilot.

Starting the engines is a rather unusual procedure. A gunpowder cartridge is inserted in the starter, which is mounted in the center of the engine intake. An electrical charge ignites the cartridge and through a gear assembly the starter turns the engine to approximately 20 percent rpm where it can sustain its own combustion. A clutch then disengages the starter. If the clutch fails, the starter will disintegrate at approximately 38 percent engine rpm, throwing fragments all around. A starter housing was later installed to contain the fragments from a disintegrating starter.

One of the most unusual features designed into the aircraft is the rotary bomb door. Most bomb doors are clamshell type which open and close like retractable landing-gear doors. On the B-57, the bomb door rotates 180 degrees and actually exposes the ordnance to the slipstream. This allows ordnance to be loaded either with the bomb door installed on the aircraft or on a spare bomb door that can easily be winched into place.

Four high-drag low-lift flaps were installed on the aircraft for lower landing speeds. There are only two positions for the flaps: up for takeoff and normal flight, and down for landing. Additional drag devices are incorporated in the form of wing speed brakes. These are small fingers on the upper and lower surfaces of the wings which extended into the slipstream. Later versions also incorporate two large speed brakes mounted on either side of the aft fuselage.

Flight controls incorporated into the aircraft consist of the standard ailerons, elevator, and rudder. The primary control surfaces receive assistance from the trim devices and the variable-incidence stabilizer. The conventional elevator, rudder, and ailerons have unique mechanisms that relieve the pilot of heavy-control loads. At high speeds, these mechanisms also prevent excessive loads on the structure of the aircraft by indirectly restricting the travel of control surfaces. Rotation of the control wheel, movement of the rudder pedals, or longitudinal movement of the control column moves push rods to actuate the control surfaces directly or indirectly. On the ground and at low speeds, the push rods directly deflect the control surfaces, but as airspeed increases, the resulting load on the control surfaces resists the action of the push rod. Through assist tabs on the control surfaces, the torque tube in the torque-tube-and-blowback-rod assembly twists to absorb the movement of the

Opposite page: Performing maintenance on B-57s.

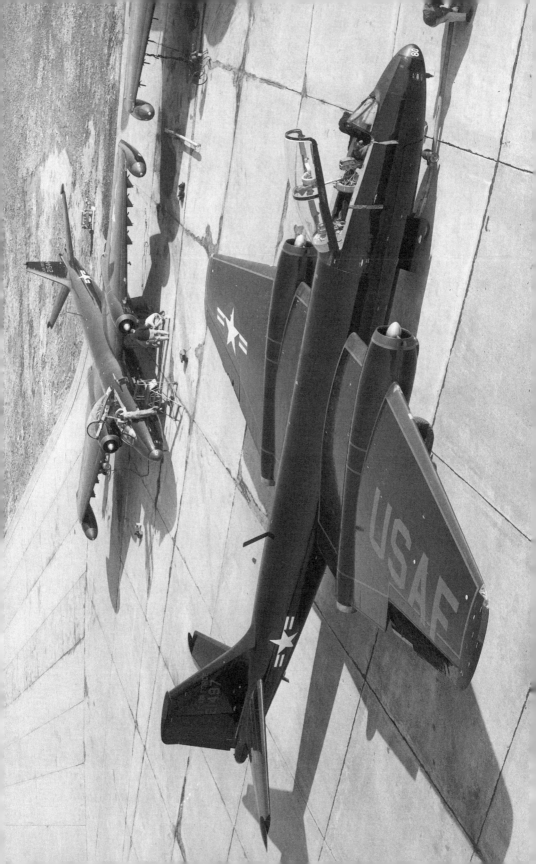

push rod. This system reduces pilot effort and still maintains conventional control feel at all airspeeds. At high speeds, a large tab angle imposes high air loads on the tab, causing the blowback rod to twist in the opposite direction to the torque tube. This increases the control load felt by the pilot, thereby using the pilot's strength as a limiting factor in maneuvering the aircraft. So don't ever let a B-57 pilot talk you into "arm wrestling!"

The first version built in the United States was the RB-57A. This model was designed as a reconnaissance platform and was almost a duplicate of the British version. The crew entered the aircraft through a small door on the right side of the fuselage. The pilot's seat was elevated and included a "bubble" type canopy. The navigator sat back in the enclosed fuselage and had only a small 6-inch window. Both aircrew members had ballistic seats for ejection. This version also had a Plexiglas nose. The navigator would move forward and lie in the nose for more exact high-altitude reconnaissance. The British and Australian versions had a manual bombsight in the nose, which the bombardier used for sighting and releasing ordnance. A photoflash cartridge system was incorporated in the wing bays for night aerial photography. Normally 20 M-123 photoflash cartridges were loaded in these bays. Each cartridge had a peak illumination power of 265 million candlepower. An electrical impulse ignited the propelling charge causing the cartridge to leave the aircraft. This also ignited the delay fuse. The cameras were timed with the delay and operated in unison with the cartridge. This model was phased out of the inventory in 1972 after 20 years of service.

The B-57B was designed as a tactical bomber. The most noticeable change is the forward section of the fuselage (crew compartment). A "clamshell" type canopy was installed and both seats placed on the centerline of the fuselage. The rear seat is elevated slightly to give better forward visibility. Besides the bomb-bay area, this version also includes eight wing stations and a gun-bay area in each wing outboard of the engines.

The B-57C is nothing more than the B model with two sets of controls. It is used primarily as a trainer for checking out new pilots. The instructor occupies the rear seat and has access to all controls necessary for flight. During the Vietnam conflict it was used as a tactical bomber.

The B-57D brought about a rather drastic design change. The wingspan was increased from 64 to 106 feet, and two J-57 engines replaced the J-65s. This version was designed for high-altitude recon naissance and electronic countermeasure missions. A system was incorporated to allow the aircrew to wear pressure suits for the high-altitude flights. Because this version had problems with the pressure system and flew very few high-altitude missions, it was also phased out of the inventory in 1972.

Opposite page: A B-57 taking off.

The B-57E model is basically another version of the B model with a completely different hydraulic system. The two constant displacement hydraulic pumps were replaced by two variable displacement pumps. The rudder-power assist system was replaced with a full-time rudder-power system. This requires an artificial pedal (feel) force to replace the conventional rudder pedal force. This version, like the C model, is dual controlled and was designed originally for sampling and two-target missions. The sampling mission was primarily used in atomic bomb tests in the Pacific.

The B-57F is the "giant" of all the Canberras. General Dynamics converted tactical bombers into high-altitude reconnaissance aircraft. The modifications give the aircraft an increased operating ceiling, greater range, and improved handling characteristics. The conversion, which involved almost complete redesign and rebuilding, makes use of advanced materials, including honeycomb sandwich panels, for the new components. The original 64-foot wing was replaced by a new three-spar wing with a span of 122 feet, 5 inches. The ailerons are inset at about midspan and supplemented by spoilers. New and larger vertical tail surfaces were fitted. All control surfaces were modified to have tightly sealed gaps to reduce drag, and the flaps were eliminated. The J-65 engines were replaced by two TF-33 engines developing 18,000 pounds of thrust each. In addition, two J-60 auxiliary turbojets can be added in underwing pods. This gives the aircraft the capability to fly at extremely high altitudes. The fuselage fuel tank was deleted to make way for equipment, and all fuel is carried in the wings outboard of the engines. In 1976 two of these aircraft were still being flown by NASA.

The B-57G is the most sophisticated of the Canberras. Again, the tactical bomber version was modified, this time by Westinghouse in conjunction with the Martin-Marietta Corporation. Designed as a night tactical bomber, a slightly modified airframe houses a host of electronic sensors and navigation equipment. Changes visible externally include a broad chin fairing beneath the nose which houses much of the new equipment. A window on the left side provides for a low-light-level TV camera and a laser range finder. The window on the right side contains infrared equipment. Multifunction radar, including terrain-following, is housed in the nose of the aircraft, which also is equipped with VOR, TACAN, and ADF for navigation. In addition, it has a multipurpose computer that is used for navigation and for weapon delivery. Where most of the B-57s have only one or, at the most, two UHF radios, the B-57G has UHF, VHF AM, VHF FM, and HF frequencies. This gives the aircrew the capability to talk to any place in the world. This is the first aircraft with the capability to drop and track a laser-guided bomb right to the target with no assistance from another aircraft.

Opposite page: A B-57 in flight.

The B-57s in the inventory in 1976 primarily consisted of EB-57s. These were previously B and E models modified for use in an electronic counter-measure mission and are under the operational control of NORAD (North American Air Defense). One DC generator on each engine was removed and an AC generator with a constant-speed drive was installed to afford adequate AC power for the ECM equipment. Rocket ejection seats and an improved canopy thruster were later incorporated to give the aircrew a true zero-altitude ejection capability. These aircraft are presently flown by two Air National Guard units and one active Air Force unit.

I first became familiar with the B-57 in May 1963. I was assigned to the 90th Tactical Bombardment Squadron at Yokota Air Base in Japan.

My transition into the B-57 was quite an experience. After instructing pilot training for four years, *I* was the student. Ground school taught me the basics of the aircraft systems and the fundamentals and characteristics of the aircraft in flight.

As in most aircraft, one particular item is stressed, briefed, and practiced so thoroughly that more aircraft are lost simulating the emergency than in the actual event. This is also true in the B-57. Single-engine characteristics were stressed and practiced on almost every flight.

There is a twilight area in the B-57 that occurs shortly after takeoff. If an enpoint, it is almost impossible to control the aircraft. Before the modification that installed rocket ejection seats, this emergency was generally fatal to the aircrew.

Once the plane is airborne and has passed through this twilight zone, loss of one engine does not pose any more of a problem than other emergencies. Good throttle technique and proper airspeeds will result in a safe and uneventful landing. The only bad part of a single-engine landing is that if rudder control is lost as the aircraft rolls along the runway, the plane cannot be taxied on one engine except in a circle.

The B-57 is a good flying bird and very stable, but it is completely different from any other aircraft I had flown. The exterior inspection is about the same as for any other aircraft, checking for fuel or hydraulic leaks and overall general condition.

Then comes the interior inspection. The first difference is the spaciousness of the cockpit. Your shoulders don't touch the canopy rails as they do in most aircraft. The rudder pedals can be adjusted to allow full rudder deflection regardless of the length of your legs.

The interior inspection starts with the normal left to right sequence. The armament panel is eye-catching to say the least. There you see an array of 25

Opposite page: A B-57 with its bomb-bay door retracted, preparing to drop its heavy bombs on targets in Vietnam, February 1966.

lights, one for each bomb that can be loaded. In addition, there is a select switch for each wing station and each section of the bomb bay. The system also incorporates an armament-select switch for releasing rockets and bombs. Through the various switches you can select the weapon you want to expend. The guns are relatively easy to set up. A three-position switch turns on the gunsight light reticle or arms the guns or both.

The fuel panel deserves much attention in selecting the tanks to be used. On takeoff the aircraft is very close to the aft center of gravity limits. Therefore, it is imperative to burn fuel from the aft fuselage tank first. If for any reason this tank does not feed, the aircraft will exceed the aft center of gravity limits approximately 10 minutes after takeoff and loss of elevator control will quickly result.

The rest of the interior inspection is merely turning on and off switches and equipment according to the checklist.

The starter exhaust duct is located on the right side of the engines. This allows the canopy to be closed after the right engine is started so that the exhaust fumes from the left engine do not enter the cockpit area. Normally the right engine is started first and then the left.

After the engines are started, the normal flight control, trim surfaces, and system operations are checked prior to taxiing.

You have to use differential power and brakes to taxi. A standard day takeoff with a 47,000-pound aircraft requires approximately 4,000 feet with a takeoff speed of 140 knots. Brakes are used for directional control until the rudder becomes effective at approximately 60 knots. Because the nose has a tendency to rise prematurely, a push force of approximately 30 pounds is applied to the control column. At approximately 100 knots, the push force is relaxed to allow the aircraft to assume a level attitude. The nosewheel is lifted off the runway 10 knots below takeoff speed of 140 knots. Takeoff is smooth, and the aircraft accelerates nicely to the recommended climb speed of 250 knots. It takes approximately 17 minutes to climb to 37,000 feet.

The aircraft can cruise easily at any altitude up to 43,000 feet. The cabin pressurization system keeps the cabin pressure below the 25,000-foot altitude level.

On a normal descent, power is reduced to 80 percent rpm and a descent rate initiated to maintain .70 Mach or 250 knots IAS. At this rate, descent from 43,000 feet can cover 160 nautical miles. For a rapid descent, power is reduced to idle and speed brakes extended. This procedure reduces the distance to approximately 40 nautical miles.

A normal overhead pattern is flown for visual recovery. Airspeed is 250 KIAS and altitude is 1,500 feet. At the "break" point, power is reduced to

---

Opposite page: Interviewing B-57 pilots.

approximately 65% and an angle of bank of approximately 60° is established. Landing gear is lowered on downwind below 200 KIAS and the flaps are lowered just as the base leg is initiated. Airspeed is reduced throughout the turn with 140 KIAS attained when rolling out on final. Airspeed is further reduced during the final approach to arrive at the runway with a touchdown speed of approximately 100 KIAS.

For instrument approaches the aircraft is equipped with "round dial instruments." The approach is flown at 160 KIAS until the descent is started. Airspeed is then smoothly reduced to the best final approach speed, normally 130 KIAS. When the landing is assured, the airspeed is further reduced to the touchdown speed. The plane is very stable on final, unless turbulence is encountered. Under a minimum landing condition, the aircraft can be stopped in less than 2,000 feet.

I am greatly impressed with the weapon payload this relatively small aircraft can carry. There are 21 stations in the rotary bomb door. In addition, the four inboard wing stations can carry up to 1,000 pounds on each station. The four outboard stations are designed to carry rocket pods containing a maximum of nineteen 2.75-inch FFARs each. These are rockets approximately 4 feet long and 2.75 inches in diameter. The fins fold into the case so that the rockets can be placed into the rocket tube. When the rocket leaves the aircraft, the four fins extend into the slipstream to give the rocket stability. Enclosed in the wings, outside each engine nacelle, are the gun bays. A total of four 20 mm cannons with 1,160 rounds of ammunition can be carried in these gun bays. Some of the early versions carried eight .50 caliber machine guns.

Ordnance is delivered by various methods. High-angle dive delivers general purpose bombs and fragmentary ordnance. The base (or perch) altitude is 5,500 feet above the ground. Approximately abeam of and 1–2 miles from the target a rapid wingover-type maneuver is established. Approximately 110 degrees of bank is used for this entry and the nose is lowered in the final part of the turn. As the airspeed increases, the dive angle is changed to arrive at a release altitude of 2,200 feet above the ground with a desired dive angle of 40 degrees and 350 knots airspeed. A 3.5 G pull is initiated immediately upon release. This allows the aircraft to recover from the dive at 1,000 feet above the ground. A total time of approximately 30 seconds from roll-in to pull-out allows about three corrections during the run.

Low-angle dive is used with variations for firing the 2.75-FFARs and for gunnery. Base-leg altitude is the same as for high-angle dive except that it is established 2-4 miles from the target. This gives a release dive angle of 10–20 degrees at a release altitude of approximately 800 feet and recovery at 500 feet.

Opposite page: Another perspective of the B-57 Canberra.

Skip bombing is used for delivering napalm and weapons with a delay-type fuse. Base leg is 1,500 feet above the ground and approximately 4 miles from the target. Roll-in is initiated in the same manner as for dive-bombing. You roll wings level on final at 300 feet and then continue the descent to 50 feet for the weapon release. This method is extremely accurate.

LABS and SHORAN are used for delivering nuclear weapons. LABS is used for low-altitude delivery. A release-angle setting is precomputed and set into the LABS release gyro. Normally, an over-the-shoulder toss is used. The run to the target is made at 100 feet and 420 knots. When directly over the target, you depress the bomb-release button and initiate a $3\frac{1}{2}$ G pull. A LABS indicator with two perpendicular needles keeps a constant pull and maintains a wings-level attitude. At the precomputed release angle, the system automatically releases the weapon. The pull is continued and recovery made by executing an Immelman on top. You then dive back toward the ground to increase airspeed and exit the area prior to weapon detonation.

SHORAN is for a high-altitude release. This system is dependent upon a ground station, normally within 100 miles of the target, which is definitely a limiting factor. Here, again, the LABS indicator is used for steering information. When the proper signal is received from the ground station, the weapon is released.

The aircraft is so accurate in all modes of delivery (with the exception of strafing) that we gladly challenged other units for beer events on the range. We knew we would lose strafing but could easily cash in on dive-bombing, rocketry, and skip bombing. The range officers in Japan were friendly, and any delivery within 30 feet of dead center was classified as a "bull." It was not uncommon to go to the range and score a "bull" on every bomb and rocket delivered on the entire sortie.

The B-57 was to be phased out of the inventory in 1964–65. The Vietnam Conflict altered this. In April 1964, members of the three B-57 squadrons at Yokota Air Base combined into the 8th and 13th Tactical Bombardment Squadrons and prepared to deploy to Vietnam.

This plan was somehow sidetracked and the two squadrons were deployed to Clark Air Base in the Philippines instead. From April until August, the forces at Clark were augmented with aircrew members, maintenance personnel, and aircraft from the States. Equipment was at a peak, and the aircrews flew daily missions to the gunnery range to improve their delivery tactics.

During May 1964, three aircraft and crews were sent to Tan-Son Nhut Air Base, Vietnam, for combat support missions. We then found we were not the first B-57s in Vietnam. Four RB-57s were already on the ramp at Tan-Son Nhut.

The Tonkin Gulf incident in August 1964 shifted the two squadrons into a semicombat role, and with the bulk of the aircraft and maintenance personnel they deployed to Bien Hoa Air Base in Vietnam. A small contingent remained at Clark to continue the transition and checkout of replacement aircrews and maintenance personnel.

Starting with the deployment to Bien Hoa, the B-57 literally took a beating and the personnel were unable to retaliate. One aircraft was lost in an accident during the deployment, and another ran off the runway on landing. Five more were lost when the Viet Cong launched a mortar attack on Halloween night of 1964. The aircrews had to stand by and do nothing. Due to the political situation, we were allowed to fly only unarmed reconnaissance missions over Vietnam. We were being shot at by the Viet Cong, but our guns were not loaded and the bomb bays were empty. Morale dropped, and for six months we sat in Vietnam and could not do what we had been trained to do and had continually practiced.

Frag orders were the normal means of notification for a mission. They included takeoff time, target, and armament load. These were received daily and then cancelled the next morning. Aircraft were up loaded with various munitions and then down-loaded. We would receive the latest intelligence briefings and then be told to stand by.

This continued until 19 February 1965. On that day, two flights of four aircraft each had been fragged for a mission. The aircraft were loaded with nine 500-pound general purpose bombs in the bomb bay and four 750-pound bombs on the wing stations. The guns were loaded and armed. Aircrews were briefed on the specifics of the mission and the frequencies for the forward air controller (FAC). The aircrews went to the flight line for their normal pre-flight. The engines were started and before-takeoff checks were performed. This was the furthest we had been allowed to go since our arrival at Bien Hoa. Takeoff time came and still no cancellation.

The commander of the 13th TBS was in the lead aircraft. He took the runway with his flight. The four B-57s took off, made contact with the forward air controller, spotted their target, and delivered their ordnance as briefed.

What followed in the next seven years must surely be outstanding in the history of combat flying. Even though the aircraft were few in number (there were never more than 36 in Vietnam), the ground troops and forward air controllers were always eager to work with the B-57. The original two squadrons were augmented by an Australian squadron flying Canberras.

The capability of the B-57s and Canberras to deliver ordnance with pinpoint accuracy, the time on station, and their maneuverability made them, in my estimation, the greatest air-to-ground jet aircraft during the entire conflict.

A flight of four B-57s could deliver ordnance continuously for an hour on any given target. Many of the FACs I talked to would rather have one B-57 to work with than a flight of any other aircraft.

One mission in particular demonstrates the B-57s greatness. An ARVN convoy had been ambushed and pinned down by Viet Cong in a pass near An Khe. The B-57s were to give close air support while helicopters flew into the area, picked up the ARVN troops, and exited out the other side of the pass. When the helicopters started through the pass, the first B-57 started a bomb run. The B-57s flew an extremely tight pattern, and bombs and guns were expended continuously on the area for 35 minutes. The Viet Cong turned their weapons against the attacking aircraft. This allowed the helicopters to do their job. During the withdrawal, not one helicopter was hit by ground fire and not one ARVN soldier was wounded.

Aircrews loved the "old bird" in combat. Its design was the primary reason for the small number of aircraft actually shot down. Two engines located apart, straight mechanical flight controls, and the emergency hydraulic reservoir managed to get most of the aircraft back even when they had to be written off the books after they landed. More aircraft were lost due to accidents and just being old than to being shot down. The greatest loss of aircraft and aircrews occurred on 16 May 1965. An explosion on the parking ramp at Bien Hoa destroyed 10 B-57s and fatally injured 7 aircrew members and 20 maintenance personnel.

The USAF B-57s and Australian Canberras flew continuously in Southeast Asia until 1972. The basic mission remained the same but innovations were incorporated into the aircraft. Night missions became a reality in 1965. Flares were dropped from either another B-57 or a C-130 aircraft to illuminate the target and then B-57s would appear out of the darkness and deliver their ordnance.

Test platforms for new improved sensor and weapon delivery systems were sent to Vietnam. These aircraft were designed primarily for night interdiction. The systems proved reliable, and more airframes were modified. These were the B-57G. With its sophisticated electronic sensors and laser-guided bombs, nothing could hide in the jungle, day or night. These aircraft worked primarily at night, patrolling up and down the "Trail." Spotting a truck, the weapons systems officer would lock-on with one of the sensors, track the target, and drop his ordnance—result, one less truck on the Trail.

In 1972, the last of the B-57s left Southeast Asia, thus ending an extensive, worthy combat history.

My own experience with the B-57 did not end when I left Vietnam in 1965. I was transferred to a Defense Systems Evaluation Squadron. This

Opposite page: Gearing up.

squadron was equipped with EB-57 aircraft. The mission then, as it remains today, was to play the part of the "friendly enemy." The EB-57s are deployed throughout the continental United States, Canada, Alaska, and as far away as Iceland to fly against preplanned NORAD installations and try to sneak through the defenses. If detected, they direct their ECM equipment against the interceptor sent up to stop their intrusion. In the simulation we were "shot down" many more times than we were able to "slip" through. We wouldn't want it any other way.

In May 1968, I left the Air Force and went to Kansas as an Air National Guard Flight Instructor. I joined the 190th Tactical Reconnaissance Group at Forbes Air Force Base. The unit was equipped with RB-57A aircraft, and I was able to participate in yet another of the many roles in which the B-57 has been utilized.

These RB-57s are primarily equipped with K-17 cameras for high- and low-altitude day reconnaissance, K-38 cameras for low- and medium-altitude night reconnaissance, and P-2 oblique cameras for low-altitude day reconnaissance.

Missions were flown at altitudes from 500 feet up through 43,000 feet. The lenses on the cameras could be varied from a 6-inch to a 24-inch focal length depending on the resolution required for the photographs being taken. These "old" aircraft worked out well on the reconnaissance flights. The missions were fun for both the pilot and the navigator. The Tactical Air Command required the aircrews to fly extensively on low-level (500 feet) routes and to acquire photographs of specified targets along the way.

In addition to the routine daily training, the unit was tasked several times for special projects, which meant deployments to such places as Puerto Rico and the Panama Canal Zone.

We retained the RB-57s until March 1972. Then the unit converted to the B-57G aircraft returning from Southeast Asia. I had completed a circuit in the B-57 mission roles: I was back to the bombing mission. The biggest differences for me in this change to the B-57G were the new sensors and ordnance delivery techniques. Before I had only a gunsight for ordnance delivery and a navigator to help spot targets and call off altitudes and airspeed during the delivery pattern. This time we had a weapons system officer with us and he was surrounded by sophisticated electronic sensors. He would track the target, lock-on, and set up the weapon panel for an automatic delivery. The information obtained by the sensors was sent to a computer. The computer analyzed the information, set the weapon panel for the release, and relayed the required steering information to the flight director system. When the systems were peaked up, a weapon could be delivered at night with pinpoint accuracy using only the light of the moon to find the target. We kept the range maintenance personnel busy repairing the pylons after a busy night on the range. For the pilot's fun and amusement, we still had a gunsight installed and a requirement to drop ordnance using the old standby dive and skip methods of delivery.

The unit flew the B-57G until March 1974 when we received the EB-57 aircraft and changed from TAC to ADC. Ironically, we had converted twice in two years and still had B-57 aircraft.

What started for me as a short tour in B-57 aircraft in 1963 has extended into a lengthy and enjoyable career. I have more than 6,000 hours of flying time with more than 3,200 hours in the B-57. I feel I know the "old bird" pretty well and certainly feel at home in it. I still enjoy listening to the fighter pilots relate their stories and add at the end, "You probably wouldn't understand that, being an old bomber pilot." I just sit back and listen and every once in a while tell them, "This old bomber pilot will give you 500 feet of altitude and 50 knots of airspeed and bet you a beer I'll be on your tail in less than a minute."

When the last B-57 finally makes it to Davis-Monthan for storage, I would certainly like to be the pilot that delivers it. Perhaps the B-57 and I will retire at the same time.

Lt. Col. Roy J. Carrow, Jr., entered Pilot Training in 1957 and received instruction in T-34, T-28, and T-33 aircraft; he received his pilot rating in 1958. His first assignment was in F-86F aircraft at Williams AFB, Arizona. He later instructed in T-33 and T-37 aircraft until May 1963 and was then transferred to Yokota AB, Japan, where his career in B-57 aircraft began. He now flies the B-57 and C-131 aircraft with the Kansas Air National Guard at Topeka.

F-84F Thunderstreak

Joseph L. Vogel

To say the F-84 almost was the cause of my death even before I flew it would be stretching the point a bit, but the incident did help me to tighten my preflight procedures and that helped to save my life on at least one other occasion.

As a fresh, "newly winged" pilot just out of jet training, I was undergoing the required 10 hours of hood (instrument training) time in a T-33 prior to being turned loose in an F-84F at Luke AFB, Arizona. As I sat in the back seat that February morning in 1957, I busied myself getting the many straps and buckles fastened when a flight of four swept-wing Thunderstreaks taxied past with their four 100-pound "blue boy" bombs under one wing and a brace of rockets and a fuel tank under the other. I paused in my set pattern of strapping in and savored a moment of anticipation, dreaming of the time I would be going to the gunnery range in the real fighter. As I continued, I didn't notice that I had forgotten the leg straps on my parachute. After takeoff, climb, and level-off, at about 80 miles from Luke, the T-33 engine began to vibrate violently from loss of a turbine blade, and it looked like we would have to abandon the bird. In fact, the front-seater even told me to prepare for the ejection. With judicious use of power and the remaining altitude, we managed to land safely at Luke. As I unstrapped, I felt a profound sense of shock when I noticed that my leg straps were hanging freely down in front of the seat. The F-84F had diverted my attention at the precise moment I would have fastened the leg straps. If we had ejected, I would have squirted out of the bottom of a blossoming parachute with only a few moments to contemplate my fatal error. Since that time, I have never allowed my preflight drill to be interrupted nor have I ever forgotten to fasten securely any of my personal equipment.

Opposite page: An F-84 prepares to refuel.

For the pilots who had the privilege of flying the F-84F Thunderstreak, frustration and fascination rode with them in that single-seat, single-engine tactical fighter bomber. The "Thud's Mother," as it later came to be known, underwent a conventional birth and a fretful childhood and finished its service life without a chance to prove itself in combat. Republic built the F-84F with the strength to live up to the reputation of its venerable grandma, the P-47, the Jug. By sweeping back the flying surfaces, the engineers intended to erase the Mach and maneuvering limits that were a drawback for its straight-wing ancestors, the F-84G and E. [On the flying of the straight-wing F-84, see earlier article, page 47.] With a 33.6-foot wingspan swept back 30°, its length of 43.3 feet, and height at the tail of 15.0 feet, the F was a small aircraft by today's standards. It carried a total of 3,575 pounds of usable fuel internally. During its latter stages in the Air National Guard, it was typically fitted with two 450-gallon (2,925 pounds each) external fuel tanks which nestled close to the fuselage on the inboard wing attach points.

The cockpit of the F-84F was straightforward for fighter aircraft of its day; however, any pilot taller than six feet could begin to feel a bit cramped. After attaching the parachute to the seat survival kit and completing the five-item preflight checklist, the pilot climbed a special aluminum ladder, stepped over the cockpit side, and by twisting a knob ahead of the stick, adjusted the rudder pedals usually to the full-out position. The seat had manual adjustment that had to be locked to ensure successful ejection in case that unpleasant necessity occurred. A left-to-right prestart check insured that the fuel was on, the battery and appropriate warning lights all operating.

The F-84F had several features that only now are again being built into first-line fighters. Fighters subsequent to the Thunderstreak have been tied to complicated ground equipment for starting. With the simple press of a toggle switch on the F-84F, high-pressure air (3,000 psi) and JP-4 jet fuel were fed into a small high-speed turbine that was mechanically linked to the main engine. The mixture was lighted and, with a loud explosion, the engine was spun up to starting speed within about five seconds. The aircraft was even fitted with a utility hydraulic-driven motor compressor which, in about 30 minutes of flight, recharged the high-pressure storage bottle. Of course, as with every good thing, this system had its drawbacks. Sometimes the small starting turbine, which had to spin about 100,000 rpm to bring the engine to idle speed (about 5,000 rpm), would not disengage from the main turbine.

When the pilot ran the engine to 100% rpm, the starter turbine went to astronomical speed and quickly disintegrated. Because the starter was attached to the front accessory case, the pieces were promptly ingested, destroying the high-revving engine in one spectacular explosion. At Luke, the story circulated

---

Opposite page: An F-84.

that during the era when Korean pilots were in training, one hapless individual blew his engine on run-up and started a gigantic fire in the aft section. His instructor, in another aircraft, yelled over the radio, "Kim, Kim, get out; you're on fire!" Because all Korean students were referred to as Kim, two others on that frequency abandoned their undamaged aircraft. Needless to say, the importance of flight call signs was stressed from then on.

No warm-up was necessary unless the engine was being started in extreme cold. Pilots then took the precaution not to move any hydraulic controls until the fluids circulated enough to warm the seals. Premature movement was almost certain to cause a leak in the vital fluids and an abort of the mission. A slight increase in power brought the bird out of the chocks and idle power kept it rolling under most circumstances. Because no power steering was fitted to the castering nosewheel, the pilot kept it straight and turned by judicious use of the wheel brakes which were operated by pressing the toes at the top of the rudder pedals. With a tread of 20.4 feet and power-boosted brakes, the F-84 was very easy to steer.

Pretakeoff checks included ejection seat pins out, canopy closed and locked, parachute low-level lanyard attached, takeoff flaps set at 20 degrees, and engine run-up in less than 15 seconds. If the run-up took longer than that, some malfunction such as dragging bearings or slow fuel control was suspected and the flight was aborted. With full power and a heavy load, initial acceleration was anything but spectacular.

The F-84F, on takeoff, suffered from some of the same ills as the straight-wing version. Notable among these was the lack of thrust from its axial-flow J-65 jet engine. Of the 7,800 pounds of thrust advertised, because of a crook in the tailpipe necessitated by the downward tilt of the engine in its mounts, the F-84F lost approximately 700 pounds when installed. With an operational weight of approximately 25,000 pounds and a hot day, high-altitude takeoff became an affair to remember for the hapless pilot. Typically, at the Mansfield, Ohio, airport, F-84Fs had to taxi into the overrun for run-up and full power check prior to brake release in order to have a safe amount of runway ahead. Takeoff run usually went to 6,000 feet on a 60-degree day. On 80-degree days, 7,500-foot takeoff rolls were not uncommon. By retracting engine screens, 4.4 percent more power was available but hardly noticeable. After flying the F-100 with afterburner and the F-4 with two engines and afterburners, I look back on the Thunderstreak as a very slow performer. The acceleration was slow and smooth compared to the "jolt and go" of burner-equipped aircraft. Early in the life of the F-84F, when I was in training at Luke AFB, Arizona, takeoff rolls were a try-and-see affair. Accurate charts for figuring takeoff distance were not available, and acceleration line-speed checks were devised by the pilot through experience and gut feelings. Later charts showed that 120 knots at 3,000 feet of roll assured a safe takeoff; 165 knots was an average takeoff speed. It was not uncommon for the desert dust at the end of the runway to be churned up by the main gear and tailpipe blast while a very frightened pilot nursed a sagging F-84F out of ground effect. Some did not make it.

Landing gear came up within 8-10 seconds of actuation and had to be up before the speed reached 220 knots. Because the main gear retracted inward, no change of pitch was noted. However with the gear up, the artificial feel unit provided a less sensitive stick movement to stabilator-movement ratio so that large stick movements by the pilot were less likely to over-G the aircraft.

Climb power was always 100 percent for a single bird. In formation, the leader kept advancing power until the slowest bird began to drop back. He then reduced throttle slightly until the weak plane could keep up. On hot days, it would take as much as 15–20 miles to effect a join-up and get the aircraft up to climb speed of 320 knots.

Cruise was the forte of the F-84F. At 35,000 feet, a Mach of .78 produced a true airspeed of 465 knots at 92 percent power and 2,300 pounds per hour fuel flow. If you were in a real hurry at 35,000 feet, you could push up the power to 96 percent, burn about 2,600 pounds per hour, and get almost 500 knots for your effort. Cruising at lower altitudes lowered the true airspeed and raised the fuel consumption figures. In combat, the policy was to run at top speed, never get below 450 knots indicated, punch off the external stores, make one pass, deliver the weapons, and egress as fast as possible.

Early aircraft had a conventional horizontal stabilizer and elevator tail known as the "split tail." In the mid-1950s, an all-moving stabilizer, or slab, powered by a dual hydraulic system, replaced the split tail. An electrically powered jack screw provided a third system of control which was dubiously effective even in a dire emergency.

My two-period career with the Thunderstreak began early in 1957 at Luke AFB, near Phoenix, Arizona. My wife and I were driving toward the base on the first of many memorable Fridays and were greeted by a rising column of greasy smoke coming from somewhere beyond the military compound. Soon we spotted a parachute descending toward the hot desert floor. Fridays became memorable because on each of the next five or six someone lost an F-84F at Luke. The Commander was said to have even contemplated cancelling flight operations on Thursday not to fly again until Monday. The major problems centered around the new dual-cylinder hydraulic system. With only hydraulic and no mechanical linkage to the controls, many of the F-51-trained fighter jocks were uneasy when they flew the bird. To them, a loss in hydraulic pressure meant immediate bailout. It was a well-circulated myth

A formation of F-84s.

that jets blew up immediately after a fire warning light illuminated. A flash of the light or a false indication caused the loss of many a perfectly good fighter.

My only in-flight emergency at the time was subtler and difficult to analyze. Our missions typically ran about 50 minutes in length. On one flight, my fuel gauges refused to budge from full. This situation created a false sense of security until, suddenly, 80 miles from base, the gauges dropped to near zero. After descent with engine idling and some fervent prayer, I touched down and taxied to my parking spot. When the crew chief looked in the tank, only one or two gallons remained. It took several years and a lot more incidents of this type to confirm that the self-sealing rubber tank liners were collapsing as the fuel was pumped out, keeping the float-type indicator showing full until the last moment.

The supervisors of today would blanch if they were forced to handle the crew of aggressive, hot fighter pilots that existed in that more carefree and regulation-free day. In the F-100 which I now fly, air combat maneuvering (ACM) is a carefully orchestrated affair with an aggressor and a defender, very well-defined rules of engagement, and firm limits on who may engage and where. I remember as many as three flights of eight F-84Fs plotting to meet over the desert about 100 miles from base for a dogfight session. Eyesight and altitude were the trump cards with no FAA altitude restrictions and, indeed, no radar even to know we were in the area. The only rule was that wingmen (new guys) were to stay in fighting wing position on their leader, look back to see that the leaders' tail was clear, and see that no one flew between them and the leader. The fights typically started at above 30,000 feet and ended only when the cactus took a beating from the jet blast or the fuel state (bingo!) called for a turn toward home base. Bingo fuel depended upon the distance from home and rate of fuel consumption. About 3,000 pounds was average bingo anywhere up to 200 miles from home plate. (Total fuel, with tanks, was 9,425 pounds.)

It was said that you could not over-G an F-84F because it would stall prior to reaching its maximum of 8.67. The aircraft handbook did warn about that fascinating maneuver called the accelerated stall pitch up. If a ham-handed pilot ignored the prestall warnings, he could suddenly find the aircraft trying to swap ends, with the nose rising rapidly and a loud bang announcing a complete stall. If forward stick was not immediately applied, especially at high Mach numbers, pieces of aircraft, including the wings, would soon begin to shred off.

The accelerated stall pitch-up did have one desirable effect. If a particularly aggressive attacker could not be shaken any other way, pulling through the buffet boundary into the pitch-up would scrub off the speed so rapidly that he would zoom right on by. The F-84F pilot then had no choice but to dive straight down to pick up speed to get away, because at low Mach numbers the Thunderstreak was no good at all in combat. Of course, the possibility remained that the old bird would depart controlled flight and go into a spin. Recovery from a spin in the F-84F was a rare event. In fact, the good book stated that if no recovery was evident at 10,000 feet above mother earth, recourse to the ejection seat was the only out.

When a decision to bail out was made, all that needed to be done was raise the seat arm rests and squeeze the triggers. Raising the arm rests released the canopy, slid the elbow retainers forward, and locked the shoulder harness. When the canopy reached full up on the mechanical arms, a squib circuit electrically fired explosive bolts that detached the canopy which then flew off above the tail. Early models had such strong mounting arms that the canopy remained firmly attached to the aircraft when it reached the full-up position. The steel bow was then positioned directly over the pilot's head as he ejected. After several fatal accidents with this bow, holes were drilled in the canopy arm to establish a breaking point. Finally, an explosive squib modification assured canopy separation prior to ejection. A healthy squeeze on either or both of the triggers set off initiators which in turn exploded the charge that shot the seat about 65 feet above the aircraft. An automatic device blew the seat belt open and rolled a web backing tightly against the pilot, his chute, and survival kit, and literally threw him out of the seat. A key device retained the automatic-timer lanyard in the seat belt and if the pilot was above 14,500 feet, he would free-fall to that altitude, delay one more second, and get a chute opening. At low altitudes, the pilot manually hooked and unhooked a lanyard that insured immediate opening if he so desired. Emergency oxygen was provided by a steel bottle about 9 inches long and 2 inches in diameter stowed in the right side of the parachute. A hose piped the 10-minute supply of oxygen to the pilot's mask when he pulled a large round green "apple" on the right side of the parachute. The seat was very reliable, and only the pilots who waited too long were ever disappointed.

Shooting the six forward-firing .50 caliber machine guns (four in the upper nose and one in each wing root) was a fascinating experience. Each gun carried 300 rounds in combat configuration and fired about 1,250 rounds per minute. From the ground, it sounded like an erratic Gatling burping out the bullets. Air-to-air and air-to-ground (strafing, bombing, and rocketry) were fairly accurate affairs with the A-4 gun-bomb-rocket sight and the AN/APG-30 ranging radar. The sight and radar automatically computed the lead for firing on flying targets, but Kentucky windage had to be used by aiming the sight "pipper" upwind for ground targets. Skip bombing was the most fun and the most accurate. The pilot approached the target from about 35 feet (later

---

Opposite page: Another view of the F-84.

raised to stay out of ground fire) at about 380 knots. When the sight slid over the target, the bomb button on the stick was pressed and an immediate pullup was started. I once made 55 consecutive passes over a six-month period without a single miss.

To most pilots, landing was a piece of cake, thanks to the wide landing gear and the powerful control of the stabilator. The pattern was entered at 300 knots, with a break to downwind, accompanied by speed brakes out and throttle momentarily reduced to check the warning system. The downwind speed was 220 knots until gear and flaps were down. On base, 190 knots was used, and the pilots shot for 165 knots (adjusted upward for fuel load) on final. The F-84F was one swept-wing aircraft that had a beautiful flare and landing. Even the tyros were able to make good landings with very little practice if they held the proper airspeed on final. It was possible to over-rotate and scrape the tail skid, which cost the pilot the traditional case of beer for the crew chiefs who had to repair it.

After touchdown, the nosewheel was held high for maximum aerodynamic drag. Drag-chute landings were practiced but usually held to be the mark of a poor pilot who could not hold proper airspeed on final. After the nose came down, brakes were used for steering below 60 knots because nosewheel steering was not installed.

On engine shut-down, only one caution was observed. It was said that turning the battery switch off before the engine stopped might allow hydraulic fluid to leak past the landing gear selector valve and release the landing gear uplocks. Downlock pins were installed by the crew chief to preclude that possibility. It was always a good idea to recheck the installation of the ejection seat pins prior to exiting because an unscheduled trip up the rails, and they happened occasionally, always ended in disaster.

Compared to the T-33, the F-84F was a comfortable, long-legged, reliable fighter aircraft. It was capable of supersonic flight in a dive and could take a great deal of G forces without any fear of coming apart. Many improvements were made over the 17 years that marked my first and last flights in the aircraft. Compared to the F-100, it was slow, did not have enough power, and had considerably less range with a smaller weapon load. The F-100 needed stability augmentation devices such as a yaw damper to be flown safely at high speeds, whereas the F-84F was straightforward and very predictable. With the boom and receptacle-type refueling, it could be flown for long distances with only the oil supply and the pilot fatigue factors entering into the range equation. The refueling receptacle was a simple door-type arrangement that flipped up out of the left wing about 4 feet from the fuselage, much like the headlight doors on some modern sports cars. With the receptacle up, the pilot flew about 20 feet aft and 4 feet to the right of the centerline of the tanker and held position. The boom operator "flew" the boom to the right position and shoved the telescoping boom downward into the hole. Electrically actuated latches held the nozzle in place until either the boomer or the fighter pilot pressed a disconnect switch. If that didn't work, an electrical override was available. If all else failed, a brute force disconnect literally ripped the nozzle out of the receptacle. This could be dangerous if the nozzle bolts failed and left the nozzle in the receptacle. The fuel flow would reverse and drain the entire aircraft in a matter of 15 minutes. An immediate landing was the only recourse.

One idiosyncrasy showed up when the large 450-gallon tanks were installed on the pylons inboard of the wheel wells. During the strafing runs, at about 320 knots, the pressure buildup between those tanks would cause the Thud's Mother to give a saucy wiggle to her tail. The cure was to fire below or above that speed whenever possible.

Mission changes seemed to come quite often for the Thunderstreak. It was designed as a day fighter, used by Strategic Air Command as a nuclear bomber, became a tactical fighter for Tactical Air Command, was recalled for the Berlin and Cuban crises as a National Guard aircraft, and finally ended its career with the last flight taking place at the Mansfield-Lahm Airport on 30 June 1972. The aircraft, number 52-7021, was piloted by Maj. William A. Millson, a Guardsman from Cleveland, Ohio. Now painted in the early red, white, and blue colors of the Thunderbirds Jet Demonstration Team, it resides on a pedestal beside the Headquarters building of the 179th Tactical Airlift Group on the Mansfield-Lahm Airport. Its Guard pilots placed it on a pedestal during its flying life and left it on that fitting place when it passed from active service.

Lt. Col. Joseph L. Vogel is a former jet fighter pilot with the Air Force and the Air National Guard. He is presently flying the C-130B for the 179th Tactical Airlift Group, Air National Guard of Mansfield, Ohio. Lt. Colonel Vogel, who has been flying various types of military aircraft since 1956, has over 3,800 hours of military flying time, is a command pilot, a civilian-rated flight instructor, and a member of the Aviation/Space Writers Association.

KC-135 Stratotanker

Philip C. Brown

"Ready for contact," reported the boom operator over the refueling frequency. Slowly the B-52 Stratofortress edged forward, guided by the "boomer's" instructions.

"Forward ten, up six." Delicately, the aircraft commander of the B-52 advanced the eight throttles to bring his aircraft to the position at which the boom operator would effect the final contact. On the top of the giant bomber's fuselage, behind the cockpit, the slipway doors were open, forming a V-shaped access to the refueling receptacle.

In the cockpit of the tanker, the pilots were alert for the radio call of "breakaway" in the event that the bomber should overrun the tanker or collision appear imminent. Then it was up to them to add power and, when advised by the boom operator that they were clear, to climb straight ahead. Over the interphone, the boomer had been advising the remainder of the tanker crew of the position of the receiver aircraft.

"Fifty feet and closing, thirty feet, twenty feet." The pilots of the KC-135 felt the rear of their aircraft rise as the bow wave of the B-52 exerted its upward push on the tanker's tail. Because most refuelings were done with the tanker on autopilot, this upward movement was noted by the stabilizer trim wheel taking a few turns to the rear as the autopilot sought to maintain level flight.

Although the presence of fighters and smaller bombers on the boom was hardly noticeable, a B-52 was another matter. While the tanker pilots attempted to maintain a constant airspeed during refueling, an increase was usually noted shortly after contact with a B-52 as the giant bomber started to push the tanker. It was truly a case of "the tail wagging the dog."

Opposite page: A KC-135 in action.

As the bomber stabilized in the refueling envelope, aided by the pilot director lights on the underside of the tanker's fuselage, the boom operator made the final contact. Lying on his stomach on a couch in a pod on the underside of the tanker, the boomer flew the boom with a stick in his right hand while his left hand controlled the boom telescope lever that extended the boom to the receptacle. At night, and particularly in rough weather, keen depth perception and a steady hand were required.

"Contact," reported the boomer.

"Contact," acknowledged the crew of the B-52. With a yellow "contact-made" light on the fuel panel in the cockpit, the copilot of the tanker activated the pumps to start the fuel flow. Through bumpy cirrus and with turns to avoid bad weather, a good bomber pilot would hang on for the 30 minutes or so necessary to receive over 120,000 pounds of fuel. Then, with the refueling complete, the bomber would back off, receive a refueling report from the navigator of the tanker, and be on his way. This drama is enacted many times a day in all parts of the world as the Strategic Air Command fulfills its global mission.

In the summer of 1959, as a pilot trainee in Laredo, Texas, I had my first look at the KC-135. As I taxied out in the front seat of a T-33, my instructor, Lt. Carl Wheeler, said, "Brown, if you're lucky, someday you might fly that aircraft." Three months later, I was one of three in my class chosen to fly the KC-135.

In 1959, the KC-135 was regarded by many as the "Cadillac" of the Air Force. It was an outgrowth of the development by the Boeing Company of a four-engined jet transport originally known as the Dash Eighty that had its first flight on 15 July 1954 and was to attain recognition as the 707. Later, the prototype aircraft was fitted with a refueling boom and associated controls, and 350 flight hours were spent to test and demonstrate its feasibility as a tanker. The KC-135 joined the Air Force inventory in January 1957 and set many records in early 1958, climaxing on 8 April 1958 with a record nonstop flight of 10,228 miles from Tokyo to the Azores.

Crew training consisted of ground school at Castle Air Force Base, California, with flight training at Castle or Roswell Air Force Base, New Mexico. Coming from pilot training where the largest plane I had flown was the 15,000-pound T-33, my first impression of the KC-135 was of its size. It was 136 feet, 3 inches long with a wingspan of 130 feet, 10 inches. The top of its fin towered 38 feet, 4 inches above the ramp. It had a maximum takeoff gross weight of 297,000 pounds and could carry 31,200 gallons of fuel, which gave it an endurance of over 19 hours. Although its top speed was .90 Mach, normal cruise was .78 Mach.

It had a large cargo door on the forward left side, but normal crew access was through a crew entry door on the lower left side abeam the cockpit. Climbing a ladder brought you to the flight deck just behind the pilot's seat. Here the crew of four was normally seated. In addition to the two pilots there was a navigator and the one enlisted man on the crew, the boom operator. A small folding jump seat could be let down between the pilots, just aft of the control pedestal. To the rear of the cockpit door was a lavatory and an area in which the crew could live aboard during a wartime situation. In this well-insulated compartment was an oven, two seats, and six let-down bunks. Farther to the rear was a large 6,000-cubic-foot area for cargo or troops, with center-facing letdown canvas seats along the side and cargo tie-down provisions on the floor. A traveling hoist on an overhead beam could be installed to aid in the handling of heavy cargo. At the rear of the aircraft was an auxiliary power unit that provided electrical power and heat while on the ground.

Almost all of the fuel was carried in the wings and beneath the main deck. At the rear of the cargo area and beneath the level of the main deck was the refueling pod from which the boom operator worked the boom during refueling operations.

The aircraft was powered by four Pratt & Whitney J57-P-59W engines that developed just under 13,000 pounds of thrust with water injection when installed on the aircraft. Although I was impressed with what I thought were four rather large engines, takeoff performance proved to be critical at the heavy weights at which we operated. Commercial transports of this type were then limited to maximum weights of about 245,000 pounds. At our normal takeoff weights of from 275,000 to 285,000 pounds, 9,400 to 9,800 feet of runway were required to get airborne.

All crew members were kept quite busy with their duties, particularly during refueling. Without a flight engineer in the crew complement, the pilots acquired many of his duties such as running the fuel and electrical panels and controlling the pressurization and heating systems. Normally the copilot handled most of the communications, often obtaining clearances for the bombers involved in refueling. Besides his normal navigational duties, the navigator was the quarterback of the refueling rendezvous, locating the bombers on radar and vectoring both groups to effect the join-up.

The boom operator, who rode up front during most of a flight, was also the loadmaster for cargo operations and aided the navigator by doing all of the celestial "shooting" with a periscopic sextant that was extended through a sextant port in the ceiling of the cockpit. This was an area in which most boomers took particular pride, usually surpassing the navigators in their ability with the sextant. Usually the boom operator was also pressed into service as the cook of our in-flight meals and here their abilities were not so universally revered.

On our early aircraft we had a fuel-air combustion starter on the number 4 engine that would allow the crew to start that engine without outside aid and then use air bled from that engine to start the remaining three. Later this was replaced with a cartridge-type starter that utilized a ballistic charge that was fired with a resultant cloud of smoke to start number 4, with the remaining three engines again started with bleed air from this engine. Provision was also made for the utilization of an external source of air.

As the starter was engaged, the engine began to rotate, as indicated on a tachometer. At about 15 percent rpm, the throttle was placed to the START position and fuel was introduced to the engine. A successful start was indicated by a rise in egt (exhaust gas temperature), reflected on an egt gauge. Other engine instruments, all of which were on the pilot's center instrument panel, were an oil pressure gauge, a fuel flow indicator (which read in pounds per hour), and an epr gauge (exhaust pressure ratio), the primary power instrument which reflected the difference between the pressure at the inlet of the engine and that at the rear.

After number 4 was started, a matter of a minute or so, it was run up to 90–95 percent rpm to ensure adequate air for starting the remaining three engines. Although normally started in sequence, the air supply was sufficient to start the remaining three simultaneously, as we did when on ground alert. However, initial rotation of the engines was a bit slower with three engines sharing the same source of air.

For a normal training mission, the checklist through starting engines probably took 20–25 minutes. Excerpts from the actual KC-135 checklist, dated March 1960, follow. On alert, the airplane was preflighted daily down to the point of "hitting" the starter so that a start only took 1.5–2 minutes. In the alert situation, all of our airplanes were to be airborne within 15 minutes from sounding the alarm. With the airplanes "cocked" and employing MITO (minimum interval takeoff) procedures, this was a realistic goal.

EXTERIOR INSPECTION
1. Equipment—Stowed (All)
2. Safety Check—Completed (P)
   a. Nose Door—Closed
   b. Defueling Valve Cover—Closed
   c. Refueling Valves Handle—FLIGHT
   d. Single Point Receptacle—Checked

Opposite page: The KC-135 in flight.

     e. Single Point Panel—Switches off, cover closed

     f. Water Quantity—Checked

     g. Ramp Area-Clear

INTERIOR INSPECTION (CP READS)

(Items 2, 3 and 4 for Copilot when Navigator not flying)

1. Crew Inspection—Completed (P)
    a. 781—Checked
    b. Time Hack—Completed
    c. Emergency Procedures—Briefed
    d. Jumpmaster—Designated
    e. Mission and Weather—Briefed
    f. Start Engines Time—Announced
    g. Questions—Cleared
2. Electronics Cabinet—Checked (CP)
3. Navigation Equipment—Checked (CP)
4. Navigator's Oxygen Panel—Checked (CP)
5. Circuit Breakers—Set (CP)
6. BO Interphone Selector—INTER (CP)
7. Instructor's Oxygen Panel—OFF and 100% (CP)
8. Throttles—CUT-OFF (P)
9. Fuel Panel—Checked (P)
10. Starter Switches—OFF (P)
11. Radar Intensity—Full CCW (CP)
12. Overhead Panel—Checked (P, CP)
13. J-4 Panel—Checked (CP)
14. Anti-Icing—OFF (CP)
15. Pilots' Data Cases—Complete (P, CP)
16. Crossover Valve—NORMAL (CP)
17. Alarm Bell—Checked (P, GC)
18. Battery Switch—EMERGENCY (P)
19. External Power—Checked (CP)
20. External Power Switch—CLOSE (CP)
21. T-R Voltage—Checked (P)
22. Battery Switch—NORMAL (P)
22A. Battery Charging Current—Checked (CP)
23. Instrument Gyros—ON (P, CP)
24. Oxygen System—Checked (P, CP)
25. Crew Report—Completed (BO, N, CP, P)

26. Omni, TACAN, Command Radios and VGH—ON (P, CP)
27. Wheel Well Doors—Clear (P, GC)
28. Inboard Spoilers—CUT-OFF (P)
29. Hydraulic System—Checked (P, CP)
30. Pitot Heat—Checked and OFF (CP, GC)
31. OMNI, TACAN and Command Radios—Checked (P, CP, BO)
32. Autopilot—ON (CP)
33. Fuel Dump—Checked (CP, BO, GC)
34. Lights—Checked and set (P, CP)
35. Fire Switches and Warning Lights—Checked (P, CP)
36. Generator Circuit Open Lights—Illuminated (CP)
37. Synchronizing Lights—Illuminated (CP)
38. Inboard Spoilers—NORMAL (P)
39. Speed Brakes—Checked (P, GC)
40. Control and Trim—Checked (P, GC)
41. Inboard Spoilers—CUT-OFF (P)
42. Flap Warning Horn—Checked (P, CP)
43. Fuel Quantity—Checked (P, CP)
44. Autopilot—Checked (P, CP)
45. Instruments—Checked (P, CP)
46. Cabin Pressure Release Handle—In and Safetied (P)
47. Air Cond Override Switch—OVERRIDE (P) 71 > 97
    Left Alternate Pressurization Switch—ON (P) 98 >
48. Emergency Heat and Pressurization Switch—DECREASE (P) 1 > 70
    Aux Pressurization and Heating Switch—DECREASE (P) 71 > 97
    Right Alternate Pressurization Switch—DECREASE (P) 98 >
49. Air Cond Override Switch—NORMAL (P) 71 > 97
    Left Alternate Pressurization Switch—OFF (P) 98 >
50. Air Cond Crossover Switch—OPEN (P) 98 > plus
51. Cabin Temperature—Set (P)
52. Cabin Manual Pressure Control—OFF (CP)
53. Cabin Pressure—Set (CP)
54. Cabin Rate of Change—Set (CP)
55. Auxiliary Pumps—OFF (P)
56. Hydraulic Pressure Switches—OFF (P)

BEFORE STARTING ENGINES (CP READS)
1. External Power Switch—CLOSE (CP, GC)
2. Battery Switch—NORMAL (P)

3. Pedals, Belts and Harnesses—Adjusted (P, CP)
4. Navigation Lights—As Required (CP)
5. Auxiliary Pumps—OFF (P)
6. Hydraulic Pressure Switches—OFF (P)
7. Locks and Pins—Removed (P, BO, GC)
8. Nose Gear Door Actuators—Connected (P, GC)
9. Wheel Well Doors—Clear (P, GC)
10. Hydraulic Pressure Switches—ON (P)
11. Auxiliary Pumps—AUTO (P)
12. Radio—Request Area Coverage (CP)
13. Gear Warning Light—Extinguished (CP)
14. Air Cond Master Switch—RAM AIR (CP)
15. Bleed Switches—OPEN (CP) 1 > 426
16. Windows—Closed (P, CP)
17. Deleted
18. Fuel Panel—Set for Takeoff (CP)
19. Fuel Heater—Check (P, GC)
20. Inboard Spoilers—NORMAL (P)
21. External Power—OFF (P, GC)
22. Battery Switch—OFF (P)

STARTING ENGINES (CP READS)

1. External Power Switch—CLOSE (if auxiliary power available) (CP)
2. Battery Switch—NORMAL (P) (EMERGENCY if no auxiliary power available)
3. Reserve Brake Pressure—Checked (P)
4. Parking Brakes—Set (P)
5. Radio Call—Completed (CP)
6. Check with Ground—Ready to Start #4 (P, GC)
7. Fuel Air Starter—GROUND START (P)
8. No. 4 Throttle—START (P)
9. Fuel—Air Starter—OFF (P)
10. Oil Pressure—Normal (CP)
11. Check with Ground—Ready to Start #3 (P, GC)
12. No. 4 Throttle—90-95% RPM (P) (Do not exceed MRT)
13. No. 3 Starter—GROUND START (P)
14. No. 3 Throttle—START (P)
15. Oil Pressure—Normal (CP)
16. No. 3 Starter—OFF (P)

Opposite page: A KC-135 refuels an A-7.

17. No. 3 Throttle—IDLE (P)
18. No. 3 Generator Breaker—CLOSE (CP)
19. Check with Ground Controller—Ready to Start #2 and #1 Simultaneously (same procedure as No. 3) (P, GC)
20. Starter Switches—OFF (P)
21. All Throttles—IDLE (P)
22. Flaps—UP (CP)
23. Auxiliary Pumps—OFF (P)
24. Copilot's Instrument Power Switch—START (CP)
25. Electrical Panel—Checked (CP)
26. Battery Switch—NORMAL (P)
27. Aileron Lockout—Checked (P, GC)
28. Flaps—Set for Takeoff (CP, GC)
29. External Power, Chocks and Interphone—Removed (P, CP, GC)
30. Taxi Report—Completed (N, CP, P)
31. Engine Anti-Icing—Climatic (CP)

TAXIING (CP READS)

1. Brakes and Steering—Checked (P)
2. Window Heat—NORMAL (CP)
3. Flight Instruments—Checked (P, CP)
4. Cargo Door Light—Extinguished (CP)

BEFORE TAKEOFF (CP READS)

1. Parking Brakes—Set (P)
1A. Pitot Heat—ON (CP)
2. Stabilizer, Aileron and Rudder Trim—Set for Takeoff (P)
3. Speed Brakes—0 degrees (P)
4. Fuel Panel—Set for Takeoff (CP)
5. Flaps—Set for Takeoff (CP)
6. Attitude Indicators—Adjusted (P, CP)
7. TACAN—OFF (P)
8. Radio Call—Completed (CP)
9. Takeoff Data—Checked (P, CP)
10. Takeoff Report—Completed (BO, N, CP, P)

LINE-UP (CP READS)

1. Brakes—Holding (P)
2. Directional Indicators—Checked (P, CP)

3. Throttle Brake—Set (P)
4. Landing Navigation Lights—As Required (CP)
5. Beacon Lights—Both ON (CP)
6. Starter Switches—Climatic (P)
7. Throttles—Advance for Dry Thrust Check (P)
8. Throttles—Set Water Start EPR (P, CP)
9. Water Boost Pumps—START (CP)
10. Engine Instruments—Within Limits (CP)

TAKEOFF

1. Brakes—Release (P)
2. Throttles—Adjust (CP)
3. Engine Instruments—Monitor (CP)
4. Control Column—Hold Forward (CP)
5. Stab Trim Indicator—Monitor (CP)
6. Airspeed Check—Accomplished (P, CP)
7. Decision Point—Checked (P, CP)
8. Critical Engine Failure Distance—Checked (P, CP)
9. Rotate—Called Out (CP)
10. Airplane—Rotate (P)

RUNNING TAKEOFF (CP READS THROUGH ITEM 9)

This checklist will be used in lieu of the normal lineup and takeoff checklists, during running takeoff operations.

1. Landing, Navigation Lights—As Required (CP)
2. Beacon Lights—Both ON (CP)
3. Starter Switches—Climatic (P)
4. Directional Indicators—Checked (P, CP)
5. Enter Runway—(P)
6. Water Boost Pumps—START (CP)
7. Throttle Brake—Set (P)
8. Throttles—Set Takeoff EPR (P, CP)
9. Takeoff Roll—Started (P)
10. Throttles—Adjust (CP)
11. Engine Instruments—Monitor (CP)
12. Control Column—Hold Forward (P)
13. Stab Trim Indicator—Monitor (CP)
14. 70 Knots—NOW (CP, N)
15. Time—HACK (N, CP)

16. S1—NOW (P, CP)
17. Rotate—Called Out (CP)
18. Airplane—Rotate (P)

ENGINE SHUTDOWN (CP READS)
1. Parking Brakes—Set (P)
2. Electrical Equipment Except Command Radio—OFF (P, CP)
3. Air Cond Override Switch—OVERRIDE (P) 71 < 97
   Left Alternate Pressurization Switch—ON (P) 98>
4. Emergency Heat and Pressurization Switch—DECREASE (P) 1 > 70
   Auxiliary Pressurization and Heating Switch—DECREASE (P) 71 > 97
   Right Alternate Pressurization—DECREASE (P) 98 >
5. Air Conditioning Override Switch—NORMAL (P) 71 > 97
   Left Alternate Pressurization Switch-OFF (P) 98 >
6. Boost Pumps—OFF (CP)
7. Battery Switch—EMERGENCY (P)
8. Throttles—75% RPM, then CUT-OFF (P)
9. Oxygen—OFF and 100% (P, CP)
10. Hydraulic Pressure Switches—OFF (P)
11. Command Radio—OFF (P)
12. Lights—OFF (P, P)
13. Battery Switch—OFF (P)

While taxiing, the aircraft commander steered the aircraft by means of a small wheel mounted on the left side wall of the cockpit. Practically all takeoffs were made with the aid of water injection. A tank in the right wheel well held 670 gallons of demineralized or distilled water. Turning onto the runway, the copilot actuated a switch that started two pumps that delivered the water to the engines. This gave added thrust to the engines for approximately 2 minutes and 5 seconds. Unfortunately, one pump fed the left engines while the other fed the right side. Failure of a pump, therefore, gave quite a yaw as well as a loss of power.

At some of the bases we transitted where the KC-135 was not a common sight, we would sometimes get a laugh when we said we needed distilled water. Some well-intentioned staff officer would finally locate a quart or so at the base hospital and ask us how much more we needed. At the heavy weights at which we operated, the KC-135 was noted for its long takeoff runs and gave the B-52 pilots who sometimes rode with us many anxious moments as they watched the green lights marking the end of the runway coming up at us with the aircraft still showing no inclination to fly.

V-speeds varied with weight and they approximated those of the 707, which are:

	Aircraft Weight	
	295,000	**200,000**
V-1 (at which you can safely stop or continue on three engines)	144 knots	116 knots
Vr (rotation speed, nose gear raised from runway)	149 knots	120 knots
V2 (takeoff speed)	166 knots	137 knots

Acceleration was checked by comparing actual performance from 70 knots with a precomputed speed that should be attained after a run of so many seconds. Although I am a bit hazy on the details, I do recall that you started the time at 70 knots and at the end of the precomputed interval you should have accelerated to a certain speed with an allowance of 3 knots. If you were not accelerating properly during this interval, you discontinued the takeoff.

Although loss of an engine at high gross weights did not present much of a directional problem, it certainly could not be taken lightly because of our high gross weights and the loss of thrust that resulted. Our already lengthy takeoff run was lengthened further. Normally after the loss of an engine one thinks of getting the gear up as soon as airborne to reduce drag, but the first thing that takes place in the gear retraction sequence is that the gear doors that have previously been closed drop open, the forward edge of them adding even more drag. Therefore, trying to "suck" the gear up quickly resulted in the aircraft trying to settle back in until the gear was retracted and the doors again were shut.

Particularly at light weights, but also at the heavier weights, the loss of an engine, especially an outboard, resulted in deviations of up to 75 feet from the runway center line. Full rudder and up to 5 degrees of bank were employed to keep the aircraft on the runway.

Takeoff procedures called for us to climb 500 feet and level off, accelerating to 280 knots as the water ran out. Because the surrounding terrain was often higher than the field elevation, a midnight takeoff of three KC-135s was not unheeded by the local populace as we roared overhead at 200–400 feet and rattled the dishes from their shelves. In North Africa, areas quite close to the runways were cultivated by local people using camels to draw their wooden

plows. I can still see the camel who bolted when our water cut in with its result-ant roar as we turned onto the runway. For all I know, he's still running, dig-ging the longest furrow in Africa.

In an attempt to get the SAC Alert Force airborne in a minimum of time, a technique known as minimum interval takeoffs (MITO) was developed. This called for aircraft to take off at 15-second intervals with three aircraft on the runway at the same time. One would be lifting off, another accelerating through approximately 100 knots, and a third just starting his takeoff run. With the smoke resulting from the use of water injection, visibility was severely restricted, and the most desirable takeoff condition was to have a slight cross-wind that would clear this smoke from the runway and disperse the turbu-lence that would be churned up by the preceding aircraft. Although a 15-second interval was desired, occasionally someone would tap his brakes and you would find the interval shortened even further. Needless to say, opti-mum conditions did not always exist, and a nighttime MITO takeoff under calm wind conditions could provide quite a thrill. However, using this tech-nique, eight B-52s and eight KC-135s could be launched in four or five min-utes—an awe-inspiring sight.

The early aircraft were fitted with an unboosted rudder that required quite a high pedal force in the event of the loss of an outboard engine at low weights and low temperatures. Both pilots had to be properly seated and pre-pared for the directional control requirements, and even then large excur-sions from the runway centerline could be expected. Later, three feet of length was added to the fin, and power boosting was incorporated to make a much more satisfactory system.

Dutch roll, a characteristic of swept-wing aircraft (the KC-135 has a 35-degree sweep back), was a possibility in the KC-135. If you encountered dutch roll while hand-flying the plane, engaging the rudder axis of the autopilot dampened it out quickly. The aircraft handled well at high altitudes but did tend to wallow a bit if flown above the optimum altitude for the particular weight and not kept in trim.

Stalls presented no particular problem, as there was quite a margin of warning. Buffeting preceded a complete stall so that you had sufficient time to take corrective action before getting into an aggravated condition. Smoothly lowering the nose and adding power soon drove you out of trouble.

One inherent advantage of the KC-135 was its ability to reduce weight rapidly by dumping fuel through the boom. At least 6,500 pounds of fuel per minute could be jettisoned in this manner.

The boom itself was a telescoping four-inch pipe the boom operator flew by means of a stick that positioned control surfaces known as ruddervators at

Opposite page: Another view of the KC-135.

the end of the boom. A telescoping lever allowed the operator to extend the boom to a maximum length of 45 feet, 11 inches. When in contact with the receiver, toggles engaged the boom, holding it until certain position limits were exceeded by the receiver. Thus, if the receiver got too far to the left or right, too high or too low, too close to the tanker or dropped too far behind, the boom would automatically disconnect and retract. If the receiver aircraft separated from the boom, a poppet valve slammed shut preventing the additional flow of fuel. The copilot of the tanker then turned off the pumps until contact was reestablished.

For refueling certain types of fighters, a funnel-shaped drogue could be attached to the boom to accommodate their refueling probes.

All the fuel on the tanker was available for transfer, with the exception of approximately 1,000 gallons beneath the standpipes in the main tanks. Or the tanker could consume all of the fuel itself. In an emergency the tanker could even take on a small amount of fuel from a B-52 through a procedure known as reverse refueling. Also, in an emergency the KC-135 was capable of towing a fighter on its boom, and in Vietnam at least one case was recorded of a disabled fighter carried in this manner to an emergency base where it disconnected and glided down to a successful landing.

Emergency egress was through the same crew entry chute that served as the primary entrance. An actuating lever known as the "chinning" bar was stowed on the ceiling above the chute. Pulling this bar down jettisoned the crew entry door and extended a spoiler at the forward edge of the crew entry chute to disrupt the slipstream. The crew member then hung on the bar and dropped through the chute. Although there have been successful bailouts, films of dummy drops in tests did not instill much crew confidence, as they showed the subject passing within a few feet of the boom. Needless to say, the "wheels" should be retracted or one might find himself meeting the left main gear at a very inopportune moment.

During approaches and landings, the aircraft handled very easily. Lowering the flaps unlocked outboard ailerons which then gave the aircraft a fine roll response even at slow airspeeds. Although the KC-135 did not have reverse thrust, braking was good on the long runways from which we normally operated.

One shortcoming was the use of engine bleed air to remove rain from the windshield. Just as we rounded out over the end of the runway and closed the throttles, our area of unimpaired vision would disappear because of inadequate engine bleed air available to keep the windshield clear. We attempted to correct this by retaining some power on the inboard engines for as long as possible.

All the time I flew this aircraft I felt it was a fine airplane. Despite the hard usage to which we put the engines, failures were few; more than one every two or three years was more than your share. Between 1956 and 1965 the Air Force purchased 806 KC-135s and used them in a number of roles—as a tanker, as a transport, as an airborne command post, and for various test projects such as simulating weightlessness for astronauts. The aircraft has performed admirably.

Yet, when I went to work for the airlines in 1965 I realized how much more sophisticated the later 707s are than our early "water wagons." Practically the only thing that I recognized in the cockpit was the window latch. Reverse thrust, fan engines with a much greater thrust rating, engine fire extinguishers, advanced flight director systems and instrumentation, Doppler navigation systems, and the addition of a flight engineer, all made our tankers seem simple by comparison.

Still, the KC-135, endowed with the same dependability and ruggedness that has established the Boeing 707 as the flagship of most of the world's airlines, has proven a valuable addition to the inventory of the United States Air Force.

Philip C. Brown graduated from the University of Connecticut, after which he entered the United States Air Force, winning his wings in October 1959. His first assignment was as a KC-135 copilot at Wright-Patterson Air Force Base, Ohio. During a four-year assignment there he represented his unit in the Strategic Air Command's Bombing, Navigation, and Refueling competition and served as an Instructor and Maintenance Test Pilot, winning the Air Force Commendation Medal for his work. He flew the tanker during the initial refueling tests of the F-105 fighter at Eglin Air Force Base, Florida. Following fourteen months at Ramey Air Force Base, Puerto Rico, he left the Air Force to join Pan-American Airways as a 707 pilot on their international runs out of New York. He has written several articles on early aviation.

F-86 Sabre

Cecil G. Foster

I had recently been recalled to active duty and was reporting to Nellis Air Force Base in Nevada when I first glimpsed the F-86 Sabre. It appeared to maneuver like a bumblebee in flight, although I later found that it carried a lot more sting. I was originally assigned to train in the F-80 but was later selected to upgrade in the F-86. This was one of the highlights of my career. I still recall how we F-80 pilots would gaze hungrily at the Sabre as we rode along the flight line to our Shooting Stars.

On the day that the new assignments were made public, we immediately ran to look the Sabre over. To enter the cockpit it was necessary to place the hands and feet in the kicksteps and climb, as on a ladder. The cockpit seemed filled with an enormous amount of equipment. It was a small cockpit with a sliding, motor-driven bubble canopy. The instrument panel had the standard instruments plus an improved airspeed/Mach indicator, altimeter, fuel flow indicator in pounds per hour, and rate-of-climb indicator. The throttle quadrant was located on the left subpanel and incorporated an air start button, a speed brake switch controlled by the thumb, and a microphone button for transmitting on the UHF radio. The stick had a form-fitted hand control with a trigger switch, trim control, nose-gear steering button, and bomb release (pickle) button.

As the pilot looked out of the cockpit, the swept-back wings gave him the feeling of riding well forward on a speeding dart. Visibility throughout the horizontal plane was outstanding. The pilot sat high in the bubble; the only blind spot was underneath the body, wings, and empennage. It appeared to

---

Opposite page: The F-86.

be almost impossible for an enemy to sneak into firing position at the F-86 when there was an alert pilot at the controls.

Early model Sabres had wing slats on the leading edges for improving aerodynamic capabilities at slow speeds; these were manually locked in place after the craft became airborne and unlocked prior to landing. On later models the wing slats moved back and forth automatically, depending on the existing aerodynamic conditions. This caused some difficulties when operating at extremely high altitudes or when flying near the maximum performance levels; however, they provided added lift automatically at high G loading and/or low airspeeds. Later models (F-86F) and modified early models had a slightly longer wing without the wing slats. This modification provided added performance at extremely high altitudes with a decrease in turn capability in the lower altitudes.

Six .50-caliber machine guns, located three on each side of the nose, provided awesome power. They were synchronized to a point approximately 1,000 feet in front of the aircraft, but their effective range exceeded 2,000 feet, and on a few occasions enemy aircraft were shot down at ranges exceeding 3,000 feet. These successes were undoubtedly attributable to the assistance provided by the computing radar gunsight. The ammunition was linked and the mix consisted of armor-piercing incendiary, tracer, and high explosive.

Starting the engine was a simple and rapid operation. As an example, one day in 1952 as I was passing through the squadron operations area at K-13, Korea, I was unexpectedly called to assume alert duties. Moments after selection, I was told to scramble—before changing into flight gear! While getting strapped into the cockpit, I was assisted by a fellow pilot who climbed astraddle the nose of the fighter facing rearwards, reached into the cockpit, started the engine, and then jumped off to the side. I became airborne in less than three minutes from notification. No warm-up was necessary for the aircraft or its component systems—a tremendous asset to a forward-based fighter. Taxiing this aircraft was simple; nosewheel steering used the utility hydraulic system and was instantly available by activating a button on the stick grip. In the rare event of a utility hydraulic system failure, the aircraft could be steered by the use of wheel brakes.

Most missions were initiated with a formation takeoff, usually in elements of two. The control surfaces were hydraulically operated, giving the F-86 instant response to control inputs, and throttle response was outstanding. A perfect wing position takeoff was quite easily flown and was a very enjoyable experience. The lead aircraft would signal engine run-up for his element by rotating a raised finger, then signal for a simultaneous brake release by a head

Opposite page: A precision demonstration by F-86s of the Sabre Knights, an aerobatic team.

nod, followed by a smooth throttle advance to about 98 degrees. This permitted the wingman sufficient leeway in power to maintain good wing position throughout the takeoff. As airspeed increased, a slight back pressure on the stick lifted the weight off the nosewheel and permitted an extremely smooth takeoff.

Instant and positive control was always available from takeoff through landing. The F-86 was the only aircraft I have flown that gave the pilot confidence that he could do any maneuver he desired, at any time, with full assurance of safety throughout. For example, while flying at cruise power settings, the pilot might want to perform a loop; he need only pull back on the stick, push forward on the throttle, and casually complete the maneuver. Although the airframe had G limitations, it could sustain more than the pilot—even when he was augmented with a G suit.

Fuel for the F-86 had a kerosene base with a maximum internal load of 3,000 pounds. Fuel consumption at 45,000 feet was 1,200 pounds per hour (the same as idle on the ground). The effective range was increased considerably with the use of two drop tanks. Normally, taking off from K-13, Suwon, Korea, a climb to and cruise at 38,000–40,000 feet to the Yalu River would consume all of the fuel from the drop tanks. These tanks were retained unless enemy aircraft were engaged, in which case they were jettisoned by simply pushing a button (commonly referred to as the panic button).

Once free from the tanks, the F-86 maneuvered magnificently. Our Fighter Wing instructions were to leave the Yalu River area with no less than 1,000 pounds of fuel, since the distance to K-13 was 250–300 miles. Once we were chasing a MIG-15 at 1,000 feet near the Yalu River when the wingman called, "Bingo fuel" (meaning 1,000 pounds of fuel remaining). Disengaging the enemy, we climbed at Mach .93 to 45,000 feet, cruised to within 100 miles of K-13, then pulled the throttle to idle and left it there until after landing. We still had 250 pounds of fuel remaining! For comparison purposes, modern jet fighter aircraft are in an "emergency fuel" state even in the traffic pattern with only 1,000 pounds of fuel remaining. Top speed for the F-86 was Mach .97–.98; however, normal cross-country cruise varied from .86 to .93.

Landing techniques were similar to conventional fighter aircraft: enter initial (350 KIAS [knots indicated airspeed] would do quite well) and when reaching the near end of the runway, enter an 80-90-degree bank while simultaneously extending the speed brakes and reducing the throttle to idle. The bank was maintained, and when the proper speed was reached, the gears and flaps were extended and checked. The 360-degree idle-power pattern was usually very comfortable and easy to complete for the flight leader; however,

---

Opposite page: An F-86 off the runway.

An F-86 fires ten of its twenty-four rockets in a test over the Gulf of Mexico.

F-86s flying in formation.

strong wind conditions or wingman position required an adjustment in technique. Throttle response, if power was needed, was readily available.

Later techniques were developed that required establishing a downwind leg prior to entering base leg. This was necessitated by wind miscalculations or weak pilot techniques that resulted in aircraft mishaps; the change provided additional time and a chance to adjust the pattern to fit the conditions. The F-86 had a good glide ratio (although not as great as the straight-winged jets) which provided a nice flare prior to touchdown on the two main gears. The nose lowered gently to the runway as the airspeed decreased. Positive control was available throughout the landing roll. Wheel brakes were very efficient and greatly reduced the landing roll but were seldom needed on a 6,000-foot runway.

Training for combat in the Sabre consisted of ten sorties at Nellis Air Force Base; these included a solo checkout, aerobatics, engineering, formation, high and medium altitude air-to-air gunnery, and air-to-ground gunnery missions. It was possible in the early models to pull too many Gs in the gunnery patterns, resulting in a violent high-speed snap roll frequently followed by a spin or spiral. Later models were improved with the automatic wing slat action, eliminating this undesirable trait.

The F-86 became an extension of the individual at the controls. It could be as docile, smooth, beautiful, vicious, deadly, speedy, daring, or safe as the pilot desired. The redundant systems throughout the aircraft provided safety margins which encouraged the pilot to go anywhere, anytime, against all odds, for he was confident that he had the best and safest fighter ever built. I never sustained damage from either enemy aircraft or antiaircraft gunfire throughout my Korean tour of 100 missions, including approximately 35 dogfights.

Combat maneuvering was superb. The Sabre excelled or equaled the MIG-15 in all aspects except for service ceiling. The MIG-15 could climb higher and in some cases faster than the Sabre, but it was no match for the F-86 below 40,000 feet. In one dogfight beginning at 38,000 feet, my wingman and I attacked a group of 24 MIG-15s flying in three flights of eight. The resultant action lasted over 45 minutes and produced one MIG-15 destroyed and one damaged. Many other battles involving similar odds were experienced, and in each instance the F-86 proved to be a superior aircraft.

Defensive/offensive tactics were universally referred to as "fluid four" maneuvers. A thorough description of these tactics would require more space than available here: briefly the basic unit is an element of two air craft flying approximately line abreast. Each of these is augmented with a wingman, greatly enhancing the defensive capability. Several flights of four can be used in a single formation, but the most effective use is achieved by retaining the

Opposite page: Another view of the F-86.

Top view of the F-86.

flexibility of flights of four. The distance between aircraft within a flight expands as the altitude increases, thus compensating for the change in radius of turn at higher altitudes.

When used in a ground-support role, the Sabre compared favorably in payload with the F-80, while retaining its excellent defensive capability after releasing the payload.

Ejection was a simple action—pull up the armrest (which jettisoned the canopy and locked the shoulder straps) and squeeze the trigger in the armrest. I had supreme confidence in the system and cannot recall a single instance when it failed.

One idiosyncrasy of the F-86 was the necessity of physically entering the nosewheel well to reset the emergency hydraulic system after it was activated from the cockpit. It was common practice for the crew chief to use this system to open the gear doors for maintenance on the aircraft, but if the system was not manually reset it was impossible to raise the landing gear after takeoff. This occasionally occurred when actions were rushed prior to a combat mission, resulting in the annoyance and embarrassment of an aborted sortie.

There should be no doubt in the reader's mind that I thoroughly enjoyed every minute in the F-86. Although by today's standards the Sabre was small and slow with minimal firepower, there never was an airplane so beautiful, dependable, maneuverable, and deadly when in the right hands. What more can I say about the airplane that made me the top living jet ace at the time of my rotation from combat?

Lt. Col. Cecil G. Foster flew the F-86E in the Korean War, the F-86D and F-101B in the all-weather interceptor career field, and the F-4D over Vietnam as commander of a tactical fighter squadron.

F-105 Thunderchief

Jerry Noel Hoblit

The target was in the vicinity of Thai Ngyen. Leo Thorsness was leading the Iron Hand Flight; Tom and I were flying No. 3. Our plan was to split the elements about 50 miles out from the target: Leo would cover north of the target and Tom and I would take the area to the south. But the flight plan fell out as soon as we entered the package, since the weather was very poor. Leo didn't call for the element split, and I assumed that he wanted to keep the flight together until we either weather aborted or found suitable weather right next to the target. Very suddenly we broke out of the cloud-covered hills and I saw the missile.

The missile was tracking Leo, and it was obvious from his transmissions that he was well aware of it. He was in a hard left turn going over some very small hills. The missile was in a hard right turn. From the geometry of it, it looked as if the missile had been fired at a nearly tail-on aspect to the flight. We were very low. Leo hugged the ground and the missile scraped off on one of the hills. I looked in the direction the missile had come from just in time to see a large splash in the klong, probably the booster, and just past that point I saw something I never expected to see: the side view of a camouflaged missile site. I was looking under the netting and could clearly make out the launchers, although it seems hard to believe since my range had to be 4–8 miles. The next action was obvious and automatic. I advanced the throttle and brought in the afterburner, forgetting about Leo. I kept my eyes on the site, because I knew that as I gained altitude I'd lose it if I didn't keep the position firmly fixed.

I had six CBU-24s, and the sight was set for a manual 45-degree 5,500-foot AGL (above ground level) delivery. In combat you never hit your conditions

Opposite page: An F-105 bombs a missile site in North Vietnam, 1967.

247

exactly and normally make aim point corrections to compensate for dive angle or airspeed variations, but I was so preoccupied with keeping the target in sight that I just put the pipper (gunsight) on the center of the site and reacted when it looked about right. As soon as I felt the ordnance leave, I started a jinking pull-out; when the time came for bomb impact, I rolled up to take a look. I never had such a lucky hit in my life. The pattern covered the site exactly, and immediately two missiles blew up on the launchers; there's no mistaking the characteristic orange smoke when an SA-2 explodes. I didn't see where the wingman's bombs hit. He had six Mark-82s, and he said at the debriefing that he saw his bombs go off on the site also. That was the first missile site "kill" we had made. It came in March 1967 on my sixty-ninth mission—my thirty-fourth as a Wild Weasel.

In 1960 the F-105 had not yet received its final epithet of "Thud"; it had various—mostly unkind—nicknames such as "Squat Bomber" or "Hyper Hog." The majority of fighter pilots believed the bar story that Pentagon bomber generals had selected the Air Force's next fighter over the objections of the one or two resident Air Staff fighter pilots, disregarding a host of better aircraft in the process.

My first impression led me to believe these stories. The airplane was on the Nellis ramp—out of commission—after an eventful flight from Seymour-Johnson, where the Fourth Wing had the first F-105Bs. It was huge. My education up to that point, at the hands of former F-86 pilots, had led me to believe that the F-100 was a big airplane. The F-105 was much larger—more than 60 feet long and weighing more than 36,000 pounds without external fuel or stores. Contributing greatly to the aircraft's impression of size was the extreme length of its main gear, caused by the midwing configuration and the necessity to have tail clearance on take-off rotation.

Jim Sears and I approached the aircraft with the proper awe expected of young Nellis studs (a term referring to our student rather than bachelor status) who were first laying eyes on the "Air Force's Future Tactical Fighter." I tried to chin myself up on the intake to see what that looked like and found myself unable to reach it even with a running leap. Jim, although shorter, was more athletic and did manage the feat; I made a mental note that preflight checking of intakes for possible FOD (foreign object damage)—standard on every jet—was going to force me to get into shape. We were impressed by other unusual external features as well as by the size of the craft. The rakish intakes appeared very radical. The aircraft had a bomb bay designed for a nuclear weapon; a large piston driven by an aircharge ejected the bomb from the aircraft. The speed brakes consisted of four petals aft of the vertical stabilizer that completely surrounded the fuselage. Few airplanes up to then had

---

Opposite page: Performing maintenance on an F-105.

incorporated spoilers for roll control. The canopy looked strange, and the port for the M-61 Gatling gun had an ominous and effective air about it.

Later I learned that the intake design was used to incorporate a movable plug which changed the intake's geometry (automatically) above Mach 1.4 so that intake shock waves were properly positioned up to Mach 2.0. Checking the intakes was not a preflight item; the external preflight consisted of little more than a general viewing of the aircraft from four sides. During most of the Thud's productive lifetime the bomb bay was filled with a 390-gallon fuel tank, and the bomb bay turned out to be an unnecessary design that detracted from the aircraft even in its nuclear mission. The speed brakes were very effective and caused no pitch or yaw transits at any speed, including Mach 2. There was, however, something inherently spooky about an airplane that automatically opened the speed brakes a few degrees to allow the afterburner to light. The spoilers contributed greatly to the honesty of the aircraft's control, particularly at slow speeds. I often wondered if the F-100's adverse yaw characteristics could not have been improved with spoilers instead of the more conventional ailerons. The canopy was of double design that circulated air between the layers to prevent fogging. The M-61 was, and remains, an effective air-to-air or air-to-ground weapon, not only on the F-105 but on the A-7 and the F-4E as well.

After that first view of the F-105B in 1960, I went to Germany to fly F-100s with the 49th Tactical Fighter Wing; in the fall of 1961 I returned to Nellis to check out in the F-105D. That began my gradual conversion to "Thud driver" both in spirit and in fact. The airplane had been optimized for low-level penetration and delivery of nuclear weapons, and the D model was equipped to accomplish this mission in all weather conditions. The airframe, armament, and electronic equipment also permitted the F-105D to perform day-fighter, limited-interceptor, close-support, and conventional interdiction missions.

At Nellis we learned to fly the aircraft and all the basics of the aircraft's systems, and on returning to Germany we completed weapons qualification and became alert-qualified in the aircraft. To become fully combat ready required that we learn new techniques of radar navigation and bombing, and in the European F-105 wings a great deal of emphasis was correctly placed on this aspect of flying the Thud.

While still at Nellis I noted the first indications that pilot acceptance of the F-105 was growing. Former F-104 pilots were heard to say an occasional kind word about the aircraft. No one could fail to be impressed by the aircraft's stability and control characteristics, low-altitude performance, or systems integration and cockpit layout. The D model had much more sophisticated electronic

Opposite page: A pair of F-105s.

systems than the B and was easier to maintain—although still ahead of it were numerous groundings and non-pilot-related accidents.

Despite the airplane's size, the impression from the cockpit was fighter-like. The cockpit was of average size, and visibility except to the rear was good. In its day the F-105 was the most complex single-place airplane ever built, and even today few aircraft can match the Thud's range of capabilities. Yet its cockpit was very logical, easy to learn, and easy to manage. Airframe-related systems were simple, and most of the cockpit was devoted to weapons systems and navigation equipment.

To accomplish the aircraft's primary design mission, four essential pieces of gear were integrated and displayed to the pilot: a ground-mapping and terrain-avoiding radar, a doppler and navigation computer, an auto pilot, and a bombing computer. The pilot's displays were arranged in a T in front of him, along with integrated tape and gyro instruments just above the radar scope. The ground-mapping radar was used in conjunction with the doppler and navigation computer to navigate to and identify a target. The radar scope used a 90-degree sector scan with variable ranges from 13 to 80 miles. It was the designer's intention that the majority of flight time would be spent with the scope in a contour-mapping or terrain-avoidance mode, allowing the pilot to maintain the closest possible profile to the ground. Ground mapping was to be used selectively for navigation point and target identification. In practice we found that the allotted flying time allowed us to be barely proficient in radar navigation using only the ground mapping and usually flying our legs on MEAs (minimum en route altitude). The autopilot was designed to be used in at least a stick-steering mode from takeoff to landing and was essential for the low-level, all-weather mission. In Southeast Asia an attempt was made to used the F-105 as a night or adverse weather, low-level bomber—without outstanding success. My experience with the F-105, A-7, and A-6 leads me to believe that radar, low-level, conventional bombing is generally unproductive and a waste of time in a single-place aircraft. It is a very viable tactic, however, for nuclear ordnance.

The Thud, along with several other aircraft, employed the integrated tape instrument display. The instrument cross-check was so easy with this display that new Thud pilots would frequently perform better after one flight than they had after many in their old airplanes.

The toss-bombing computer (TBC) was an analog device tied into the other aircraft systems and was meant to be used for both conventional and nuclear delivery. We seldom used the TBC for conventional bombing but relied on the manually depressed sight instead. In retrospect, I believe that we

---

Opposite page: An F-105 in flight.

erred in this and should have spent more pilot and maintenance time on this system and used it as the primary bombing system in Vietnam.

Engine and aircraft flight systems were not complex. The J-75 engine was started either by pyrotechnic cartridge or external air source. Once rpm was developed, the pilot brought the throttle to idle and starting fuel was automatically sequenced. Idle rpm was 68–71 percent. An air turbine motor (ATM), driven by compressor air, supplied power for both the AC generator and the utility hydraulic systems. This ATM was located forward and to the right of the cockpit and was very noisy, especially on the ground. Once started, with the ATM and AC generator on the line, all subsequent checks were straightforward and could be accomplished in less than five minutes in coordination with a crew chief, by hand signals or through ground interphone. I have been wheels in the well (gear up) in four minutes in an alert aircraft—starting from the Officers' Club!

The F-105 carried large amounts of varied armament and was capable of being refueled either by probe and drogue or by boom. Engine-driven pumps provided power to the dual hydraulic flight controls. A ram air turbine was available for emergency electric and flight control hydraulic power. Unfortunately a hit that caused loss of one flight control hydraulic system usually got them both. I later came to appreciate the manual backup system in the A-4 and consider it essential that flight control hydraulic lines be physically separated and that fly-by-wire systems be thoroughly investigated.

Although the F-105 was optimized as a fighter-bomber, it had day-fighter and limited-interceptor capabilities. At one time it had the best MIG-killing record in Southeast Asia. Its antiaircraft armament consisted of an interceptor-type radar display, lead computing sight, M-61 gun, and Sidewinder missiles. In terms of performance it was usually outclassed by the F-80, F-4, MIG-19, and MIG-21 but generally superior to the F-100 and MIG-17. It could beat the MK-6 (Canadian Sabre), F-86, and MIG-15, providing the Thud driver did not try to slow down and turn with his adversary and generally kept his head above his emotions. In the Southeast Asia campaign over North Vietnam the Thud's day in the sun arrived, and it was the mainstay of Rolling Thunder operations until the 1968 bombing halt. Two-seat F-105Fs were equipped for a surface-to-air missile hunter-killer mission. These Wild Weasel aircraft have added an interesting new dimension to aerial warfare.

The F-105 was an easy aircraft to fly as long as you did it fast. It was built to operate at low level and very high speed. This it did exceedingly well. It did not do well at altitude (in terms of performance, stability and control were excellent in all flight regimes) and demanded high speed in the traffic pattern. Takeoffs were frequently above 200 knots. Landing approaches, although

Opposite page: A formation of F-105s.

flown with an angle of attack instrument, were sometimes in the 200-knot range also. Nevertheless, its good brakes, drag chute, and power response were such that such speeds were no particular problem. I can remember few takeoff rolls over 6,000 feet. A no-drag-chute landing seldom ended in a barrier engagement.

In the air the aircraft simply had no peculiarities. A spin or out-of-control situation, such as an adverse yaw induced out-of-control maneuver, was almost nonexistent. It took extreme, usually intentional, mishandling to get the bird to spin. Few pilots succeeded, and fewer still were fast enough to beat the airplane in doing its own spin recovery. The only control anomaly was a tendency for a nose-down pitch change when the gear was retracted forward into the swept wings.

When the airplane was new it could achieve Mach 2 easily. As the airplane grew in service, however, the expected thrust uprating of the engine did not materialize. The craft did grow in weight and drag because of various modifications, so both its top speed and range were substantially reduced. Above Mach 1.4 it was slowed with speed brakes instead of with a throttle reduction. In 1961 a man chasing me on a Mach 2 run had to put out his speed brakes to stay behind my slower aircraft. By 1967 few F-105s could achieve Mach 2 on a test flight.

There is no question in my mind that the F-105 and her pilots and EWOs (Electronic Warfare Officers) wrote a page in the history of aerial warfare in Vietnam. Whether they did so because they were inherently great or just happened to be there when it all happened is a judgment I cannot make. This, however, I know: it was an honest aircraft—one that reflected care in design and engineering, and it was a credit to all who conceived and built it. It educated us and remains the standard according to which I judge other airplanes. I prefer the A-4's size and economy, the A-7's digital integration and accuracy, and the F-4's excess power for a fight; but if I had to choose one airplane today to go to war tomorrow, it would have to be my Thud.

Lt. Col. Jerry Noel Hoblit flew the F-105 at USAF bases in Germany, Japan, Thailand, and the United States between 1961 and 1967. His subsequent duty has been with the Air Force Test Pilot School, the Navy Air Test and Evaluation Squadron, and the Office of the Deputy Chief of Staff for Research and Development at Headquarters, USAF.

Opposite page: An F-105 dives on a target in North Vietnam, firing a volley of 2.75-inch rockets.

O-2A Super Skymaster

Timothy Kline

A high-wing, all-metal aircraft with retractable tricycle landing gear, the O-2A possessed uniquely designed centerline mounted twin engines—one on the nose and one between the twin tail booms. Cleverly eliminating the often hazardous asymmetrical thrust problems of conventional twin-engine aircraft, the plane provided excellent handling characteristics throughout its speed range of 80–200 mph. A far cry from the "fork-tailed devil" of World War II fame (the P-38), this twin-boom, push-pull prop plane endeared itself to pilots in the low and slow combat environment of Southeast Asia. Known affectionately and unofficially as the "Oscar Deuce," it acquired less respectable titles with remarkable ease. Forward Air Controllers (FACs) who labeled it "Oscar Pig" and "Oscar Deuce" bemoaned its sluggish performance, poor visibility, and lack of power. In a climb the two 210 hp Continentals strained for altitude. In a dive the heavily laden craft (maximum gross weight 4,850 pounds) threatened to overspeed the props. Still, all things considered, few FACs complained about the plane's best feature—the second engine.

Twice in my experience that other engine enabled me to bring the bird home in appropriate style. Both times I had been conducting visual reconnaissance over heavy jungle with no place below me suitable for a forced landing; but for a second chance my plane and I might have been converted into a decorative ornament for the high branches of the ominous trees which beckoned below. On one of these occasions I had thrown a rod on the rear engine. More powerful for mysterious reasons relating to aerodynamics and airflow, it was generally conceded to be the wrong one to lose if you had the choice. There were persistent rumors that without a rear engine the O-2 would be

Opposite page: The O-2A.

259

unable to climb, might even be unable to hold its own altitude, and might possibly give you a nice controlled glide eventually bringing man and machine to an unwelcome greeting with terra firma. I am happy to relate that you can maintain altitude with only a front engine operating at full throttle. Of course I had to close the small cowl flaps on either side of the rear engine and below the forward engine. I had, in addition, the unpleasant task of dropping my two rocket pods and fourteen rockets over enemy territory, to reduce the drag and to streamline things a bit. Fortunately the terrain below me was the flat land of sea level swamps near Saigon. Had I been over the rugged mountains of I or II Corps, my tale might not have ended so propitiously.

Originally built by Cessna as a "doctor's airplane" and designated the 337 Super Skymaster, the O-2 was packed with 600 pounds of UHF, VHF, and FM radios; painted gray and white; fitted with four pylons for rockets, flares, and even a set of 7.62 mm miniguns (which were apparently never used in anger); and then sent off to war with minimal fanfare. Its primary virtues—as a replacement for Cessna's older FAC aircraft the O-1 Bird Dog—were twin engines, higher cruising speeds, and the capability of carrying more rockets (especially important for putting in multiple air strikes or even a single strike where high winds might blow the smoke away too quickly, requiring frequent marking passes by the FAC). For these beneficial features it sacrificed visibility, ruggedness, and the ability to operate off grass strips. It has always seemed to me that the O-2 was simply an uneasy compromise between the low-cost but limited Bird Dog and the high-priced but far more talented Bronco (OV-10).

In many ways the O-2 reminded me of a dwarfed scale model of some real airplane. The wing pylons were tiny, the main wheels were small black orbs, and the plane was built low to the ground. One day I watched four O-2s taxi out for takeoff and line up behind an AC-119 gunship. The collective group gave the appearance of four ducklings following mama to the lake.

While the aircraft was indescribably ungainly on the ground, it was almost sleek and swift-looking in flight; the main problem was getting it airborne. After entering through the right-hand door you crawled across the seat gingerly, avoiding the radios and instrument panel. Because of an uncomfortably long takeoff roll (anywhere from 1,000 to 3,500 feet), I was always careful to line up with plenty of runway ahead; when the plane was loaded with full rockets and flares, the takeoff process could be lengthy. Once free of earth's friction the O-2 behaved distinctively. When the tiny gear handle was placed up, a remarkable thing would happen: the nose gear behaved normally; but the main wheels, after starting up quite regularly, would stop abruptly halfway through the procedure and rotate fully flat into the windstream, causing the airframe to shudder in protest and the airspeed indicator to hesitate as if speed brakes had been applied. After half a heartbeat the main wheels would resume their upward movement and tuck neatly below the aft engine. Normal climb could then be resumed. From the vantage point of a ground observer it reminded me of a great gander getting aloft—with webbed feet first dangling flat and back, then knees up and finally into the up-and-locked position somewhere in the tail feathers.

The O-2 will never find service in the high-spirited stable of the Thunderbirds, nor will it be lauded by the Air Force as the final answer to the problematical needs of forward air control. But it did perform well in skilled hands. It seated two side by side, or four with passenger seats added, and possessed two sets of controls; but I'm convinced it was the most difficult FAC aircraft for controlling air strikes. Visibility from the left side of the cockpit was so bad that most jocks found themselves invariably in left turns favoring the nearest window. To improve vision Cessna had cut a window in the lower right door and one just forward in the right-hand wall. Two more windows had been cut into the roof. Despite these modifications, most FACs were seen circling left over target areas.

Then there was the not inconsiderable aggravation caused by the control wheel. Not a bad fixture in an executive's cross-country aircraft, it was out of place in the gyrating world of the constantly turning, climbing, and diving FAC. To keep the fighters, friendlies, and target in sight in a plane with zero visibility to the rear (there was an engine in the way) and precious few windows while wheeling, talking, and setting up armament switches was no mean task. The O-2 driver had his hands full controlling a strike; during these hectic moments a stick, a turboprop, and a bubble canopy would have been welcomed.

To its credit I must admit the O-2 was reliable and sturdier than I had expected. Even the tinker-toy landing gear system rarely caused grief. The bird could get to distant targets more quickly than the O-1, preventing unnecessary frustration for fighter pilots, but its vaunted speed advantage was certainly no quantum jump. The O-2 cruised at 160 mph maximum, with normal cruise of nearly 140 under combat loads; the O-1 cruising speed was 85–90 mph.

Most effective at night, with a lusty roar and an exceptionally fine instrument panel, the smooth-cruising aircraft loaded with flares and rockets could be remarkably potent. I once ferried an O-2 to the people at Pleiku who did most of their business at night over the Ho Chi Minh trail. Their O-2s were painted solid black and looked quite lethal in the revetments.

Having flown the F-4C for four years I was pleasantly surprised to find the O-2A equipped with a very similar gunsight. Basically a noncomputing, pipper-and-ring projecting type with manual mil adjustment, it made a handsome

addition to the glare shield of the left instrument panel. Immediately beside it were rocker-type arming switches. I soon discovered the O-2 was a stable platform for rocket firing and, once I had adjusted to the parallax problem of firing from a side-by-side cockpit, was able to fire with good accuracy. Toward the end of my tour, while checking out an instructor pilot in a free fire zone, we came upon an enemy soldier paddling surreptitiously along a tributary of the Mekong. We attempted some single shots with the few rockets we had left in the tubes and hit fairly close to his sampan. The enemy reacted by beaching his small sampan, uncovering an AK-7, and returning our fire. While unable to hit the Vietcong soldier standing at the water's edge, we probably succeeded in unsettling him. A rocket failing to hit its target still makes a nerve-shattering crash as it breaks the sound barrier prior to impact. The 2.75-inch rockets with phosphorus warheads can be lethal if they hit close enough, and having witnessed many aerial demonstrations of target marking, I can attest to their aural ferocity.

One aspect of flying the O-2 was particularly strange. Although many modifications had been made to adapt the airplane to its combat role, one item was conspicuously overlooked by the Cessna engineers. The seats were flimsy, without the slightest bit of armor plating, and generally uncomfortable. In addition, once the Air Force decided to make the parachute a mandatory part of the FAC's flight equipment, there was even less room on the seat.

Parachutes were not liked. They made the already difficult problem of exiting the aircraft, which had a door only on the right side, more difficult. Still it must be acknowledged that the parachute did save some lives. One young FAC ran his O-2 into another O-2 while relieving his partner over a target area at nearly 13,000 feet above the ground. Thanks to his altitude, he had time to kick the left side window out and squeeze himself out of his uncontrollable aircraft. Miraculously he survived. Most pilots were rather skeptical about their own ability to carry out such an emergency procedure, however. The other technique was to unstrap, cross the cockpit, and exit via the right door—no small task in my opinion.

Handicapped by its civilian origins, the "Oscar Deuce" nevertheless has earned a niche in the ranks of illustrious combat aircraft. It served well above the jungles, swamps, and mountains of Vietnam and Laos; and courageous pilots did remarkable things with it.

Capt. Timothy Kline flew F-4Cs for four years (1966–69) at RAF Woodbridge, U.K., and later served as forward air controller and air liaison officer to the Royal Thai Army at Bearcat, Republic of Vietnam. He is currently an instructor in history at the USAF Academy and flies the T-33 aircraft.

Opposite page: Another view of the O-2A.

Top view of the B-47.

B-47 Stratojet

Earl G. Peck

The Boeing B-47, officially the "Stratojet," was one of those airplanes that never seemed to acquire any sort of affectionate nickname. Although pilots may refer nostalgically to the "Spit," "Thud," "Hun," "Jug," or even "Fort," the B-47 remains just that. This probably stems from the fact that although it was often admired, respected, cursed, or even feared, it was almost never loved. In fact, I think it would be fair to say that it tended to separate the men from the boys!

It was relatively difficult to land, terribly unforgiving of mistakes or inattention, subject to control reversal at high speeds, and suffered from horrible roll-due-to-yaw characteristics. Crosswind landings and takeoffs were sporty, and in-flight discrepancies were the rule rather than the exception. All in all, the B-47 was a very demanding machine for its three-man crew.

None of this, however, should seem very surprising when one considers the near-revolutionary nature of the beast. It was, in fact, the first large, swept-wing American jet aircraft. Landing gear consisted of two tandem centerline trucks in the fuselage, so located because there was no room in the thin, high wings, which angled back at 35 degrees. Because the landing gear was directly under the longitudinal axis, outriggers in the inboard nacelles were needed for ground stability. And because neither of the main gear trucks was near the center of gravity, the aircraft was designed to *rest* in a takeoff and landing attitude rather than rotate conventionally. The margin for error in landing attitude was thus extraordinarily small—a front-truck-first touchdown produced an olympic-sized bounce!

Obviously, therefore, great care was required in deploying the 32-foot ribbon-type brake chute which was installed to offset, during landing roll, the relatively poor deceleration characteristics of the bird. It was worse than embarrassing to have that chute blossom about the time you reached the apex of a bounce after thinking you were properly on terra firma.

The brake chute was not to be confused with the 16-foot approach chute designed for use in the traffic pattern. The approach chute enabled the pilot to keep the engine rpms in a responsive range, both for more precise control of descent rates and to make thrust more readily available for go-arounds.

But, its idiosyncrasies notwithstanding, the B-47 served as a mainstay of the SAC deterrent posture during the darkest years of the protracted Cold War. Thus a typical B-47 mission was comprised of all those activities that the crew had to master if the system was to serve as a credible deterrent. They were also the same things that would be required during a nuclear strike mission if deterrence failed: high- and low-level navigation (celestial, radar, grid) and weapon delivery, aerial refueling, electronic countermeasures against air and ground threats, positive control procedures, exercising the tail-mounted twin 20 mm guns, emergency procedures, cell (formation) tactics, and others I am sure I have forgotten. Crew planning for a mission took up *most of the day prior* and was elaborately precise and detailed. The crew was expected to approach each training sortie with the same meticulous professionalism that would be required for an actual strike launch.

And professionalism keynoted the mission attitude that prevailed from inception to completion. On the day of the flight, the crew (pilot, copilot, and navigator) checked in at the airplane, with all of their personal equipment (parachutes, survival gear, helmets, oxygen masks, etc.), *three hours* prior to takeoff. There followed an exhaustive series of inspections—station, exterior, and interior—which consumed about an hour and a half and satisfied the crew that the airplane was ready to go.

The station check included the usual perusal of forms, equipment, and safety items, and preceded a rather detailed "walk-around." Normally, the pilot and copilot split the inspection to examine the (for its day) massive exterior (length 107 feet, wing span 116 feet). Generally, they were looking for fuel leaks, hydraulic leaks, loose panels, and tire condition.

Following the exterior inspection, the crew members assumed their respective positions in the crew compartment for a system-by-system interior inspection. Ingress was gained via a self-contained retractable ladder (which according to alert shack rumor cost the Air Force $1,700 each). Pilot and copilot sat in tandem under a Plexiglas clamshell canopy, while the navigator sat in the nose. Virtually nothing escaped the interior inspection—fuel system and loading, hydraulics, flight controls, escape systems (for bailout, the pilot and copilot ejected upward and the navigator downward), switch positions,

---

Opposite page: Front view of the B-47.

electrical systems, oxygen, instruments, aerial refueling system, navigation equipment, and so on, through a seemingly endless array of checks.

But we finally would finish and, finding the bird fit, would leave it and wend our way to base ops for a weather briefing and to compute takeoff data and file a clearance.

It should be noted at this point that the SAC B-47 units relied heavily on the crew members' private autos. First, we'd meet at the Personal Equipment Shop, load our gear in the trunk of one car, drive out to the airplane, and unload. After the interior check, we'd drive the car to base ops and then drive back down the ramp and park opposite our assigned airplane. After the flight, the route was retraced, with an added stop at maintenance debriefing. From start to scratch, the crews' own vehicles enabled the system to work!

In any event, we would return to the airplane from ops, strap into the chutes and ejection seats, and run a lengthy "before starting engines" checklist in order to be ready to crank about 20 minutes prior to launch. Engine start was a frantic exercise requiring dexterous manipulation of switches and throttles beginning with number four and followed by five, six, three, two, and one in rapid-fire sequence. After removing external power, the aircraft hydraulic and electrical systems were energized, the bomb-bay and entrance doors secured, and the airplane was ready to taxi.

Taxiing the B-47 was relatively easy. Turns could be smoothly negotiated through the steerable front truck with one steering ratio available for taxi and another, less sensitive, for takeoff and landing. Despite the three-point attitude, visibility was good—S turns were not necessary. At heavy gross weights, however, taxi speed was severely limited to preclude undue stress and tire overheating.

When the end of the runway was reached, our heroes would accomplish a routine before-takeoff checklist, recheck takeoff data, and be prepared to cross the threshold precisely on scheduled launch time. Takeoffs were of the rolling variety with all six throttles advanced to 100% rpm shortly after alignment.

Takeoff in a B-47 was, to my knowledge, unique in its day, for the airplane was in effect "flying" shortly after beginning the roll. This was attributable to the flexible wings which permitted the outriggers to lift off as soon as the airflow generated any appreciable lift. The pilot then had to maintain a wings-level attitude through the flight controls, while steering primarily with the front gear truck. In fact, it was possible, at that point, to steer the aircraft by "bicycling" as it would turn left or right on the runway as the wings were tilted.

During the takeoff roll, aircraft performance was checked by timing the acceleration from 70 knots to a precomputed decision speed. At that point

Opposite page: A B-47 in flight.

the pilot made an irrevocable decision to continue the takeoff or abort. Lift-off was achieved at a calculated speed (typically about 160 knots) dependent on weight and conditions and in very nearly the ground attitude.

Gear was retracted immediately and the flaps raised on a schedule linked to acceleration. Normal initial climb speed was 310 knots indicated which was maintained to 20,000 feet and then decreased gradually in accordance with a charted optimum schedule.

Somewhat ungainly on the ground, the B-47 assumed a classic grace in flight. Control response was positive throughout the performance envelope, except at the extremes. At low speeds and high angles of attack, it was possi-ble to induce virtually uncontrollable roll-due-to-yaw, a characteristic respon-sible for several disastrous takeoff crashes after outboard engine failure near unstick speed. At the other end of the spectrum, indicated airspeeds in excess of about 425 knots produced aileron reversal. This condition was actually due to warping of the flexible wings in which the wing tips functioned as ailerons and the ailerons functioned as trim tabs. In between, however, the B-47 was reasonably docile.

My own experience with outboard engine failure during takeoff was rep-resentative except that I was luckier than most. Number six quit about halfway between decision and lift-off, producing a violent yaw toward the dead engine. This was followed by a strong rolling tendency which further aggravated a dis-mal directional control problem. With rudder and yoke fully deflected, I man-aged to struggle into the air just prior to leaving the side of the strip. Things weren't looking much better, however, because after retracting the gear, we were headed across the boondocks in an uncomfortably skewed condition, gaining neither airspeed nor altitude. In fact, the navigator, Jim Gravette, said later that he would have ejected except that his downward-firing seat would have driven him into the ground from our precariously low altitude! It's just as well that he couldn't eject, because we were able to gradually nurse a few more knots out of the beast, milk the flaps up, and get the thing flying. From then on, the dead engine posed little problem.

Aerial refueling with the B-47 presented difficulties stemming principally from incompatibility with the piston-driven KC-97 tankers then in use. Very high wing loading and associated stall speeds in the B-47 meant that the KC-97 was taxed to provide any respectable margin above stall while hooked up. On one particularly dark night my airplane stalled off the boom and fluttered gracefully down through 5,000 feet of murk before it became a flying machine again! In retrospect, of all of the airplanes I have refueled in flight—F-84, B-47, B-52, F-4—the B-47 was easily the most challenging.

Also challenging were the combat bombing tactics practiced by the B-47 force. A typical mission involved a low-level, high-speed penetration of "enemy" territory, a pop-up to about 1,500 feet for the simulated delivery of a drogued nuclear weapon, and descent back to the "deck" for escape. It took a skilled navigator and good crew coordination to "hit" (electronically) within the allowable circular error. Although they never dropped a bomb in anger, the ability of the B-47 crews to do so effectively helped make it unnecessary.

Approach and landing were predicted on a "best flare" speed, which varied with the landing gross weight. On a typical landing, "best flare" speed would run about 135 knots, and all other pattern speeds were computed from that base. Thus the downwind leg was flown at "best flare plus 30," approach chute deployed, and gear and flaps extended. Airspeed was further reduced to "best flare plus 20" during the descending turn to base leg, and again to "best flare plus 15" turning final.

Airspeed was gradually dissipated on final approach in order to reach the end of runway at precisely "best flare" speed. Throttles were retarded when landing was assured and the aircraft rotated in order to touch down on all main gear simultaneously or slightly aft truck first. The situation to be assiduously avoided was the nosewheel-first landing which put you back in the air with something less than desired velocity!

The brake chute was deployed as soon as the aircraft was firmly on the ground and was a great assist in deceleration. It could be extended by either the pilot or copilot, but, for most of us, wisdom dictated that the pilot do it himself to preclude a disastrous, untimely deployment.

Looking back, although much of the flying I did in the B-47 was not particularly enjoyable—it was in fact tedious, demanding, even grueling at times—it was rewarding in terms of professional satisfaction. I felt I was doing an important job and took great pride in doing it well in a machine capable of performing. As with most airplanes, the advertised performance figures (4,000 nautical mile range, 600 mph speed, 40,000-foot service ceiling) didn't mean much to the guys flying the B-47. It was important only that it go fast and far enough to enable a group of professional, dedicated, and gutsy SAC crews to provide the bulk of American deterrent strength during the middle and late 1950s.

At that time the SAC B-47 armada numbered more than 1,400—principally E models. The balance of the inventory included EBs, RBs, and TBs, each with its own specialized role. As the decade waned, the B-47 was gradually supplemented and later supplanted by the B-52 as SAC's "big stick," but the Stratojet had written an important chapter in the history of military aviation.

Brig. Gen. Earl G. Peck is Deputy Chief of Staff for personnel, SAC, Offutt AFB, Nebraska. He is a graduate of the University of Texas and the Industrial College of the Armed Forces and holds the master's degree from George Washington University. His 6,000 hours of diversified flying experience span 24 years and are evenly divided between fighters (F-80, F-84, F-4) and bombers (B-47, B-52).

Opposite page: Another look at the B-47.

F-100 Super Sabre

Garth Blakely

My initial training in the North American F-100 Super Sabre began in the summer of 1964 with the 188th Tactical Fighter Squadron New Mexico Air National Guard (TFSNMANG) at Kirtland AFB, Albuquerque. Time was of the essence; the squadron needed combat-ready fighter pilots, and the check-out process went quickly. For the first several days we read, reread, and memorized the Dash One, concentrated on emergency procedures, made practice walks around the aircraft, and spent time getting thoroughly familiar with the cockpit and normal procedures.

After a week that seemed like months, flying actually started. With my instructor we had a briefing on exactly what we were going to do throughout the mission and then walked across the ramp to our waiting F model—our one aircraft that carried two pilots. Flying the F would be the same as flying the single-seated A or C models which the squadron was equipped with, except that an instructor would be along to get me acquainted with the bird before going solo.

We made our normal walk around, checking the nose wheel steering, panel security, tire condition, hydraulic or oil leaks, brake condition, engine condition, and the all-important drag chute for proper installation.

We were satisfied with the exterior condition of the aircraft and thus climbed the ladder, put our back-pack type parachutes in the seats, and connected them to the survival kit that we sat on during the mission. Settling myself in the front seat, I made a check around the interior starting on the left and working around to the right. The radio was checked off, the gear handle down, all warning lights tested, engine and flight instruments checked

Opposite page: An F-100 takes off from a zero length launch.

for proper indications, oxygen system tested, navigation radios set, and all circuit breakers checked in. Power was then applied to the bird and the UHF radio turned on and checked.

Starting the engine was a simple matter. With clearance from the crew chief on the ground, externally developed air was applied to the engine, which started it rotating. At 12 percent the throttle was brought "around the horn" supplying ignition and then fuel. All engine instruments were monitored closely, and within about 30 seconds the Pratt and Whitney J-57 was stabilized at idle, and all external power and air was removed.

After another check of all systems including hydraulics, electrical, and engine, we were ready to taxi. With the nose wheel steering engaged, we taxied out of the line and down to the end of the runway. With clearance from the tower for takeoff, we lowered the canopy and lined up on the runway. Holding the brakes firmly, the engine was run up to full power and all engine instruments checked again for normal readings. At this time, the EPR gauge was monitored closely as it indicated the amount of thrust the engine was actually producing. We were within limits, and we were ready to roll.

With relaxed toe pressure on the rudder pedals, the 33,000-pound fighter was on its way. As soon as the takeoff roll was started, the throttle was pushed outboard and the engine went into afterburner, developing 16,500 pounds of thrust with a load bang and a surge that set both pilots back in their seats. Checking at the 1,500-foot marker that our acceleration was within limits, the roll was continued to about 145 knots when the nose was rotated; at about 155 knots the aircraft became airborne.

With a rate of climb established, the gear and flaps were retracted and the bird accelerated quickly while climbing at 3,000 feet per minute.

At about 3,000 feet, the afterburner was cut out to conserve fuel as we climbed to 18,000 feet and put the bird through its paces. It was very light on the controls and took constant attention to keep in rein. This would become second nature as time passed. All control surfaces were hydraulically operated with two systems powering each surface at the same time. In the event of engine or pump failure, there was a wind-driven pump to insure control for an emergency landing or bailout.

After about an hour of lazy-eights, chandelles, loops, and any other maneuver we could come up with, we returned to the traffic pattern for the all-important landing practice. This was the area that required the most concentration, as testified to by the number of pilots who "bought the farm" somewhere in the final turn or on final approach.

The F-100 was a highly maneuverable and stable aircraft at intermediate to high speed, including supersonic, but at pattern speeds of 230 knots or less it

Opposite page: The F-100.

began to exhibit some mind of its own if not handled with some care. Adverse yaw, a situation where the aircraft yaws and rolls in the opposite direction to the control inputs, could be encountered in the traffic pattern when large control inputs were used, and a stall could be induced by pulling excess Gs at low speeds because of the high loading on the 45-degree swept-back wing. Either of these when in the pattern could be fatal, for it took considerable altitude to recover—altitude which might not be available before touching Mother Earth.

The pattern was entered from over the approach end of the runway at 300 knots and 1,500 feet. At this point, the pitch out was initiated with a sharp 45-degree angle of back turn to downwind, pulling as many Gs as possible without getting into a low speed buffet. This maneuver, with the addition of deploying the speed brakes as the turn was commenced, placed the bird on downwind at 230 knots or less. Approaching abeam the end of the runway on downwind, the gear and flaps were dropped and the final turn was started in order to end up one mile from the end of the runway at 300 feet above the ground and at a speed of about 165 knots, depending on the amount of fuel remaining. From this point it was a shallow power-on approach to the touchdown point; however, the nose of the aircraft was so high in this final phase that it was all but impossible to see directly out the front of the cockpit. Peripheral vision had to be used increasingly as the plane approached and slowed to a touchdown at about 135 knots. The nose was so high, in fact, that a tail skid was added to the afterburner section and came in contact with the runway on touchdown occasionally when an on-speed landing was made.

In this last phase of final turn to touchdown, the flying characteristics of the aircraft changed somewhat. No large or abrupt variations in controls could be made without general aircraft instability. In addition, when getting close to landing and landing speed, the rudder became much more important than the ailerons in controlling bank. If wake turbulence or crosswind gusts raised the right wing, right rudder had to be used to get it down—using right aileron could aggravate the problem, and in extreme cases cautious use of opposite aileron was effective in controlling the angle of bank.

After touchdown, the throttle was brought to idle, the nose lowered, and the 8-foot drag chute deployed from under the left side of the tail section. This was very effective in slowing the craft to about 60 knots or so, depending on the wind, but in the event of a chute failure, even a 10,000-foot runway quickly began to look very short. As light braking as possible was used down to taxi speed to preclude heating up the brakes and tires which could cause tire explosion shortly after landing.

After clearing the runway, the flaps were retracted and we taxied back to the ramp and parked. All systems were shut down as well as the engine finally,

Opposite page: Two F-100s join up "back to back."

F-100s off the runway.

An F-100 uses a parabrake while landing.

after a pin was inserted in the nose gear to keep it from folding under when hydraulic pressure was reduced.

Then, just before stepping over the side, the prudent pilot checked to be certain that he had inserted a seat safety pin in the ejection seat so that if his foot hung in one of the handles on either side of the seat he would not be given a swift kick about 200 feet in the air. The ejection seat was modified several times, starting out with a simple explosive shell that kicked the seat out of the aircraft after the canopy had been jettisoned and culminating in the later stages with a rocket-propelled seat that would enable the pilot to bail out at ground level and survive. When ejection was initiated in this later seat, several things happened in sequence: the canopy was blown off the aircraft, then the seat rocket ignited sending the seat into the air. At the top of its trajectory the lap belt and shoulder harness were released and the pilot automatically was kicked from the seat. This armed the parachute he had on his back, which automatically deployed if he was not above 14,000 feet. It all worked with only initiation on the pilot's part being needed and it was proven to be reliable.

After four or five flights in the F model, it at last was time to be cut loose for my first solo flight in one of the squadron's A or C models. These aircraft were essentially the same with the exception that the C carried more fuel and could be aerially refueled by either a KC-97 or a KC-135 tanker aircraft.

After the preflight briefing, my instructor and I went to our assigned aircraft and prepared for flight. With only a few exceptions, everything was the same as in the F model, until the beginning of the takeoff roll. The single seated As and Cs had no flaps, increasing the takeoff rotation speed to about 158 knots, and they were about 4,000 pounds lighter, making the 16,500 pounds of thrust much more effective. The flight itself was much like the previous ones in the F, with the exception that the aircraft was much more agile, and it responded, even at low speed, to the controls much more quickly. Back in the landing pattern, a major difference was that final approach was flown at 183 knots, with speed brakes down to insure that the engine was at a high enough rpm to provide quick response to throttle advances, bleeding down to a touchdown speed of 155 knots—quite a bit higher than the F, as the A had no trailing edge flaps, only leading edge slats.

Being designed originally as an air superiority fighter, the F-100 was the first operational fighter with the capability of attaining supersonic flight in level flight. Transition from subsonic to supersonic flight was very smooth, with the only noticeable changes being a jump in mach speed and a momentary fluctuation in both altimeter and vertical velocity. Later, the C and D models were developed to carry ordinance for air-to-ground delivery. The

---

Opposite page: An F-100 maneuvering.

F model was developed more as a trainer than anything else, but also had an air-to-ground capability.

After becoming combat ready in the F-100, my unit was sent to Vietnam for a one-year tour of duty, and the C models we took with us served well. We had the capability of carrying any combat load of munitions required to any place they were needed, and the accuracy of the Super Sabre's delivery system proved to be second to none and reliable. I have heard the F-100 called a "Lead Sled" and innumerable other names, but after over 1,800 hours of flight time in the A, C, D, and F models, it remains that "sleek and shiny, sexy, single-seated, Super Sabre" to me.

Capt. H. E. Garth Blakely (NMANG) is presently a Continental Airlines copilot with 3,800 hours in the B-707 and B-727. He has flown 135 hours in the A-7D for the New Mexico ANG since 1974.

Opposite page: An F-100 in action.

F-94 Starfire

Wayne C. Gatlin

One cannot describe flying the F-94 Starfire without separating the story into two distinct parts—the F-94A/B and the F-94C—for the two aircraft were vastly different with only the center section of the C common to the earlier A model.

The original F-94A was developed in 1949 from the T-33 jet trainer which, in turn, had been developed from the F-80 Shooting Star. The F-94B was nearly identical to the A model except for the A having a low-pressure oxygen system, a 1,000 psi hydraulic system, and a 2.75 psi cockpit pressurization, whereas the B had high-pressure oxygen, a 1,500 psi hydraulic system, 5 psi cockpit pressurization, and windshield deicing, zero reader (the automatic flight instrument that combined all information needed to fly the aircraft on a predetermined flight path), glide-slope receiver, localizer receiver, and automatic cockpit temperature regulation.

Anyone who has had the pleasure of flying the T-33 can readily get the feeling of the F-94 just by remembering what a delight the T-33 was to fly (and still is) and then realizing how great an afterburner would have been on the T-bird. I still fly the T-33 and it continues to be as enjoyable an aircraft as anything taking up ramp space these days—that is, if it doesn't have stuff like pylon racks loaded with Chaff and ECM pods on board, and if .8 Mach is fast enough for you, and if you are satisfied with the 3 G limitation. One's appreciation of the T-33 (or F-94 for that matter) seems also to be somewhat tied to physical size. Both cockpits, being somewhat cramped, made us little guys a bit more prone to sing their praises than did the giants who had to be eased in with a shoehorn and were reluctant to eject for fear of leaving kneecaps under the instrument panel. I understand their fear: I was recently grounded for

---

Opposite page: The F-94.

about six months from the loss of a kneecap sustained ejecting from a T-Bird. My luck ran out over Lake Michigan when my engine failed and, unable to get a relight or find a suitable place to flameout land the bird, I had to "punch out." Unfortunately, I whacked my knees on the windshield bow going out and thus became a reluctant member of the Caterpillar Club after 30 years in fighters. I got back in the T-33 and F-101 on schedule, though.

My first contact with the Starfire came in late 1951 when, as an F-51 driver, I got a class assignment to the F-94 All-Weather Interceptor school at Tyndall AFB, Florida. Before that, my jet experience had consisted of about 20 hours of T-33/B-80 time at Williams AFB earlier the previous summer. The course at Tyndall consisted of 22 sorties for a total of 37 hours. Afterwards I returned to my outfit, climbed back in the F-51, and forgot about the Starfire for about two years. During this time, my 179th Fighter Squadron, ANG, completed its 21 months of Korean Conflict service and was returned to States control, and it was back to the Air National Guard for most of us. Then, in July 1954, the first F-94s arrived on our ramp, the first of 15 A and B models we were to receive. At this time, the F-94A/B was to receive my undivided attention until April 1957 when we ferried all 15 of the original birds to the 109th Fighter Interceptor Squadron (Minn ANG) at Holman Field, St. Paul, Minnesota, and the F-94C became our new "bird" in hand.

The F-94A/B had the same wingspan as the T-33 (38 ft., 9 in.) but was longer (40 ft., 2 in. versus 37.7 ft.) to accommodate the radar in the nose and the afterburner. The top of the fin was also higher (12 ft., 2 in. versus 11.7 ft.) because of the afterburner. Its loaded weight was 16,675 pounds versus the T-33's 15,330 pounds. Armament consisted simply of four .50 caliber machine guns in the nose, though late in the life span of the aircraft some were modified to carry a wing pod under each midwing span. Each pod, weighing 420 pounds, contained two .50 caliber machine guns and ammunition capacity of 265 rounds per gun and upped the gross weight to 17,615 pounds. Naturally, the addition of these pods reduced the maneuverability and performance of the aircraft.

The F-94A/B engine was the Allison J-33-A-33, a centrifugal compressor designed for use with an afterburner for thrust augmentation. Normal rated thrust was 4,600 pounds, but use of afterburner increased it by about 30% to 6,000 pounds. Afterburner was used for takeoff and for periods of climb or level flight when rapid acceleration was required.

Fuel was carried in four groups of tanks. Internally, two leading-edge tanks (52 gallons each), two wing tanks (77 gallons each), and a fuselage tank (65 gallons) totalled 323 gallons. Externally, two centerline tip tanks (230 gallons each) upped the total fuel to 783 gallons. Early models had underslung tip tanks; however, they were all eventually modified and the centerline tank became standard. Normal fuel sequencing was from the tips, then from the leading edge and wing groups, and, finally, from the fuselage tank. If one tip tank failed to feed or only partially emptied, a very serious wing-heaviness condition resulted and it was necessary to jettison the heavy tank; if this failed, abandoning the aircraft was recommended.

The Starfire had conventional stick and rudder controls, and the ailerons were augmented by a hydraulically powered aileron boost. The stick mounted a gun trigger, trim-tab controls, bomb (tank) release switch, and the emergency hydraulic pump switch. The aileron boost provided a 15:1 ratio; without it the ailerons were extremely stiff.

Wing flaps were electrically actuated, and when fully extended were at 45°. For takeoff, you used 32° (70%) of flaps; for landing, you used full flaps. Dive flaps located under the center forward fuselage were used for increasing drag and could be opened at any speed. A slight nose-up tendency occurred whenever the dive flaps were extended.

The tricycle landing gear was hydraulically operated and had provisions for emergency extension. The wheel-brake system was an independent manually operated hydraulic system worked by conventional toe pedals; differential braking was required for taxiing—a sometimes difficult task that required a lot of getting used to.

Each crew member sat in an ejection seat. Raising the right arm rest bottomed the seat and positioned the trigger for firing. Raising the left arm rest locked the shoulder harness. The canopy jettison system was not part of the ejection seat system, as it is in ejection systems now in use, and it was necessary to reach forward with the right hand to pull the canopy jettison handle. Squeezing the trigger on the right-hand grip fired the seat. Standard procedure was for the radar observer to eject before the pilot.

Because the aircraft sat fairly low to the ground, entrance to the cockpit could be made by climbing onto the wing; however, ladders were normally available at bases around the country. The cockpit was snug to say the least—especially with winter flying gear on. Starting the engine consisted of pushing the starter switch to "start" for three seconds and releasing. The starter motor would get you about 10 percent rpm. At 9 percent rpm the ignition switch was pushed to "normal" and then the starting fuel switch was pushed to "auto." You would get a stabilized speed of about 25–35 percent rpm, and then you would put the throttle at "idle" and turn the starting fuel off. No warm-up was required; if you had oil pressure and could get 100 percent rpm, the engine was ready for takeoff. In severe cold, it was usually necessary to allow time for oil pressure to drop within limits prior to takeoff.

You had to taxi using differential braking steering, and forward movement was necessary to negotiate any kind of a controlled short radius turn. Prior to takeoff, your cockpit check included: flaps, 70 percent (32 degrees); trim, neutral; canopy, closed and locked; controls, checked for freedom of movement and proper direction of movement; emergency fuel switch, set for "take-off & land"; throttle, open; and engine instruments, checked. You needed 98 percent for a good afterburner light, and after releasing brakes, you maintained directional control using minimum braking until about 65 knots when the rudder became effective. Nose gear was lifted off at about 125 knots, and the aircraft was flown off the runway in one continuous motion. Once definite climb was established, you raised the gear; the wing flaps were raised between 140 and 175 knots. Climb was at 175–215 knots to a safe altitude, and then you accelerated to your best climb speed. Takeoff ground roll distance for a 60 degrees Fahrenheit, no-wind day, with tip tanks and afterburner, at sea level was 2,400 feet. At 5,000 feet above sea level, it was 3,600 feet. Without afterburner at sea level on the same day, ground roll was 3,400 feet and increased to 5,300 at 5,000 feet above sea level.

Best rate of climb was at 100% rpm nonafterburning, which would get you to 30,000 feet in about 15 minutes using 180 gallons of fuel, the aircraft traveling 77 miles. At 100% in afterburner, it took only 6 minutes to reach 30,000 feet, although you used 260 gallons of fuel and traveled only 37 miles. Best cruise at 30,000 feet was with 93 percent rpm, giving a 287 gallon-per-hour fuel flow and a no-wind ground speed of 377 knots. As your fuel reduced, a cruise climb to 35,000 feet could get your fuel use down to about 217 gallons per hour with only a slight ground speed reduction to 365 knots. You could usually figure about 850–1,000 miles of range for a "no wind-no alternate required" destination.

The Starfire was directionally and longitudinally stable. Uneven feeding of the tip tanks was easily trimmed out, and once the tips were dry the plane handled beautifully. It had a very high rate of roll, and the stall was preceded by a noticeable mushing and buffeting; you could break the stall just by releasing a bit of back pressure. It was fully aerobatic and a delight to fly. Intentional spins were prohibited as well as extended inverted flight over 10 seconds. It had an airspeed limitation of 505 knots or .8 Mach. Above this speed, aileron buzz occurred, and lateral control was difficult and uncertain.

When we first got the 94A/Bs we had no trained radar observers, so initially we had to treat it as a day fighter. Anxious to see how we could do in air-to-air gunnery, we were quick to load the four "fifties" and head out for our gunnery range over Lake Superior. Pegging the range on the gunsight (i.e.,

Opposite page: An F-94 of the Minnesota Air
National Guard in landing configuration.

setting a fixed range input into the computing gunsight), we were quick to learn that we couldn't do as well as we had in the F-51 Mustang. We did, however, after only three months in the bird, win the F-94 Fighter Interceptor Category of the Air National Guard Gunnery and Weapons Meet in October 1954 at Boise, Idaho. Flying without radar observers and pegging the gunsight, we performed like day fighters, firing high- and low-altitude air-to-air gunnery, panel gunnery (air-to-ground gunnery on a 10 ft. x 10 ft. target), and dive-bombing (the dive-bombing consisting of scoring miss distances of .50 bursts from an overhead dive-bomb run.) It was great sport; however, we weren't really utilizing the F-94 and its weapon system to the best advantage. Once we got some experienced radar observers and began using the weapon system as it was designed, our scores increased considerably and we really attained an "All-Weather Capability."

We still flew our gunnery pattern from a basic "high perch" position to the side and abreast of the tow target as we had in the Mustang days. Once in position, we would peel off into and down toward the target which was a 6 foot x 30 foot mesh material attached to a tow bar with a metal reflector. The reflector gave the radar observer a better radar return to lock on to. This target was towed 1,000 feet behind the target aircraft (another F-94). As we reached a 90-degree angle to the target travel, we would reverse our turn and smoothly bring the "pipper" through to where we wanted it on the target. During this time, the radar observer would ascertain the target on the radar set and get a "Reno" or separation of radar returns of the tow aircraft and the target. He would complete the pass. He would call range and we would eyeball the range using the size of the pip in regard to the 6-foot width of the target to reach the best firing range (normal, 600 down to 200 yards). The pip was 2 mils in diameter and, when superimposed on the target, would cover two feet or one-third of the target width at 1,000 feet. After we fired our burst, we would roll away and pass on the opposite side and parallel to the target. If we had a good pattern and were firing a bright-colored ammunition, we could see exactly where the burst had gone into the target. The tips of the rounds of ammo were dipped in a waxlike paint that heated and softened when fired and then left the color around the hole in the target as it broke through the mesh. I preferred red because it was so easy to distinguish. A good crew with a well-harmonized aircraft could put 50–75 percent of the rounds into the "rag" with the Starfire.

We proved this in 1955 and 1956 when we also won the Air National Guard All-Weather Interceptor Phase of the Annual Gunnery and Weapons exercise and our scores were markedly improved from the days of fixed or pegged firing.

Opposite page: The F-94 in flight.

We flew up to four ships in a gunnery pattern, each with different-colored painted ammunition. Proper pattern spacing had one aircraft firing on target, one just reversing its turn, another leaving the perch, and the fourth off target and climbing to the perch. In order not to perforate the rag too badly, we normally fired only two guns, with each having only 100 rounds of ammo.

Of course, the least sought-out job when we were firing gunnery was towing the target (we called it "dragging the rag," and the target call sign was always "ragmop"). It took a bit of skill to get the target air borne without smashing runway lights or losing the weight off the tow bar (which kept the target vertical in flight). However, once airborne, the target pilot had a rather long, boring mission ahead, towing at low speed the entire time. He brought the target home and dropped it in a "drop zone" so it could be recovered for scoring. He kept pretty alert during the actual firing on the "rag" to make certain spacing in the gunnery pattern was good and that none of the radar observers missed their Reno calls and locked into the tow plane rather than the target. He could readily tell a proper pass by the position of the firing aircraft as it reversed its turn coming off the perch. If the pilot looked at all like he was pulling his nose (and guns) through the tow plane, the target pilot broke him off, pronto.

Being Squadron Operations Officer at the time, I made it a point not to get nailed as target pilot very often; however, it happened occasionally. The one mission I towed that still remains vivid in my memory involved one of our fighters colliding with the target. I was tooling along fat, dumb, and happy as "ragmop." I had Arthur Godfrey's morning radio program tuned in low on the AN/ARN-6 Radio Compass and his orchestra was playing "Don't Blame Me."

On the mission we had a pilot who had little fighter experience and even less gunnery experience; in fact, it was his first (and last) firing mission. In his exuberance to get some hits on his first outing, he pressed a bit too hard and collided with the target, wrapping the tow bar over his horizontal stabilizer. I was unaware of this collision because he had disappeared behind me. However, I learned about it rather abruptly. The tow line did not break at the time of collision but acted like a fish taking the slack out of a fishing line as it hits the lure. The pilot, after realizing he had hit the target, immediately started a climb, and, as I was on the other end of the line at a slow speed, the tow cable just lifted my tail to what seemed to be nearly vertical, and there I was looking straight down at cold Lake Superior some 10,000 feet below. The tow cable finally broke, and I frantically recovered from my unusual attitude as "Don't Blame Me" ended. The bird involved in the collision made it home safely with the tow bar still wrapped around the stabilizer. I guess the relatively slow overtake speed of fighter over target was the only thing that kept that bird from losing the stabilizer and plunging into Lake Superior. I didn't tow for a while after that either.

Toward the end of our 94A/B era we modified some aircraft by hanging the two gun pods, one under each wing. This gave us eight guns. However, we never got to try them in air-to-air gunnery. Maneuverability was so eroded by the addition of the pods that I seriously doubt any decent scores could have been attained in this configuration.

Of course, in the actual application of the F-94 in a true all-weather or night intercept, a stern position with no angle-off was ideal for destroying an enemy airborne target. In fact, the F-94 gained a place in Air Force history when during the Korean Conflict a F-94B became the first Air Force jet to gain a night radar kill over an enemy plane when it knocked down a marauding Russian-built LA-9 fighter.

The 94A/B was a good aircraft to land. You touched down on the main gear with the tail slightly down. Excessive tail-low attitudes got the sheet metal men mad because you'd scrape the afterburner shroud on the runway. A standard 360-degree overhead pattern was flown with initial approach at 270 knots, 1,500 feet above the ground. Over the end of the runway, you'd go into a 90-degree bank, chop power, and extend your speed brakes. Continuing your turn, you'd extend your gear when under 195 knots, put full flaps down under 175 knots, and roll out on final about 140 knots. You'd come across the fence with at least 120 knots and touch down between 95 and 105 knots. The F-94 was excellent in a crosswind, and you could put the up-wind wheel on the runway first and then ease the other main on. To quote one of our former pilots, now long-since retired, in a strong crosswind you "get ahold of the runway and don't let go!"—a truism that cannot be denied.

In April 1957 we ferried all 15 of the aircraft we had originally received to the 109th FIS (Minn ANG) at Holman Field, St. Paul, Minnesota, ending the era of the "bird with a gun" for us. Our efforts turned toward the F-94Cs which were appearing on our ramp in numbers.

In 1949 Lockheed further exploited the basic F-80/T-33/F-94A design with a view to improving performance and brought out the F-94C. The F-94C was once known as the F-94B, then as the F-97A, and then redesignated the F-94C when the B model designation was assigned to the improved F-94A. The J-48-P-5 engine with more power was introduced to improve high-altitude performance. A thinner wing was also used. The C first flew in 1951, and when production ended in 1954, 387 had been built. It was the first U.S. fighter to be designed without guns (a mistake, I believe, that has taken over 20 years to rectify).

The wings had been shortened to 37 feet, 4 inches, and had a very definite dihedral. The tailplane was swept back, the intakes reshaped, and the nose lengthened. The C was 42 feet, 6 inches long, 14 feet, 10 inches high, and weighed 24,000 pounds fully loaded with tip and pylon tanks. It acquired another "first" with its use of a braking parachute. For armament it carried 24 2.75 FFAR (folding fin aerial rockets) in the nose and 24 2.75 FFAR in wing pods. It was powered by a Pratt & Whitney J-48-P-5 continuous-flow, centrifugal-type, turbojet engine designed with an afterburner for thrust augmentation. It was a rugged engine and had a good afterburner that gave 33% more thrust at sea level for takeoff and 80% at flight speed. The J-48 produced 6,350 pounds of thrust without afterburner and 8,750 pounds with it. All in all, it didn't look, shoot, or fly like the F94A/B. It went faster and higher, but not farther.

The C (as I'll call it) had a more aesthetic design than the earlier model. With the marked dihedral and swept-back tail, it had a "cocky" look.

Fuel was carried internally in two wing tanks, a fuselage tank, and an engine feed tank, which together carried 366 gallons of usable fuel. Centerline tip tanks added another 503.8 gallons, giving 963.8 gallons (6,064.7 pounds) of fuel for normal operations.

Should you elect to carry pylon tanks, another 460 gallons (2,990 pounds) of fuel could be added, giving a total of 1,329.8 gallons (8,643 pounds). The added weight of the pylons combined with the vastly diminished handling characteristics rarely warranted flying with pylons. The range increased a bit, but the bird really got "doggy" with pylons.

All of the fuel tanks except the pylon tanks (which we rarely carried) could be refueled through a single-point filler well located on the left side of the nose section. Fuel under pressure (up to 50 psi) entered the single point and was directed to the internal fuel tanks and tip tanks through normal fuel transfer lines. This was a vast improvement over the F-94A/B system which required that each tank be filled individually over the wing—a slow, tedious process.

The aircraft hydraulic system operated aileron boost, elevator boost, speed brakes, landing gear, and rocket doors. An emergency system was incorporated to lower the landing gear in the event of normal system malfunction.

The primary flight controls moved manually by conventional stick and rudder pedals or remotely through the electrical and hydraulic systems of the automatic pilot. Hydraulic boosters reduced control-stick forces on the ailerons and elevator. The C was trimmed by electrically operated aileron and rudder trim tabs, ground-adjustable rudder and aileron bend tabs, and electrically repositioned springs to control lateral stick movement. The stick grip mounted a trim switch, external tank release button, rocket-firing trigger, automatic-pilot disengage button, and interphone button.

Electrically operated split-type wing flaps lowered to 45 degrees in the full down position. Two pairs of hydraulically operated speed brakes were used for increasing drag. The forward pair was located in the underside of the forward fuselage and the aft pair in the fuselage behind the wing fillets. The drag chute was packed in a housing above the fuselage tail cone. The 16-foot ribbon-type chute reduced landing roll approximately 40 percent; however, it would shear if released in excess of 200 knots. The gear and brake systems were essentially the same as on the A and B models.

Ground start consisted basically of placing the ground starter switch to "start" for 2–3 seconds then releasing it, the igniter master switch to "normal" when 7% rpm was reached, and the throttle to "idle" at 9 percent rpm and of checking that tail pipe temp was within limits and that idle rpm stabilized at 26–36 percent.

The C taxied easier than the A/B; however, differential braking was still required for turns.

Pretakeoff check was essentially: canopy locked, speed brakes up, AB (afterburner) nozzle closed, flaps 32 degrees (70 percent), trim neutral, elevator and aileron boost on, engine checks complete, and you were ready to go. With brakes depressed, you'd advance to full power, then release brakes, using minimal braking for directional control to 40–60 knots when the rudder became effective. You'd move throttle outboard to afterburner position and check for proper afterburner light, which was a momentary loss of thrust (interval between cock of afterburner nozzle opening and ignition) and then a definite kick in the pants as the afterburner ignited. The afterburner nozzle opened during afterburner operation to prevent excessive tail pipe temperature and pressure from building up in the tail section. This, in effect, gave the tail pipe a larger diameter, and as it opened approximately three seconds before afterburner ignition, there was a resultant loss of thrust.

You raised the nosewheel and flew the aircraft off the runway in one continuous motion at about 147 knots when using afterburner and having full tip tanks and rocket pods. Once definitely airborne—gear up, flaps up to 160–175 knots, and out of afterburner detent for a nonafterburner climb—initial climb was 200–225 knots to a safe altitude and then you gradually accelerated to the best climb speed, which was 315 knots at sea level, dropping off 15 knots for each 5,000 feet up to 30,000 feet where you indicated 225 knots. A no-wind, nonafterburner takeoff distance for a 60-degrees-Fahrenheit day at sea level with tip tanks and rocket pods was 4,200 feet; at 5,000 feet, pressure altitude

was 6,200 feet. With afterburner on the same day at sea level, takeoff roll was 3,800 feet; at 5,000 feet, pressure altitude was 5,100 feet.

For a good many pilots, this was the first jet they had flown that was capable of going supersonic; but to do it, you had to climb to 45,000 feet, plug in afterburner, and roll the nose over and start down. You knew you were supersonic only when the airspeed indicator "jumped" across the Mach meter and you sensed a slight wing drop; when that happened you had to chop throttle, extend your speed brakes, and start back on the stick so as not to put a hole in someone's back yard.

Maximum allowable acceleration for symmetrical maneuvers was plus 8.67 Gs and a minus 3.0 Gs for all configurations except with pylons on. Full pylons installed reduced the G load limitation to 3.85 Gs. Rolling pullout limitations were plus 5.78 Gs and minus 1.0 G, except for aircraft with pylons installed.

We flew the standard 360-degree overhead landing pattern with the C entering on initial approach at 270 knots; 1,500 feet above the ground and over the end of the runway you would break into a steep bank, chop throttle to 55–65 percent as you simultaneously opened your speed brakes. Once under 215 knots, you would drop the gear, get full flaps, and maintain 150 knots in your final turn. Holding a minimum of 145 knots on final approach, you would retard the throttle to idle when the landing was assured. The C was peculiar on touchdown for it really "paid off" or quit flying quite abruptly, and no two birds were alike. Obviously, it was best to be near concrete when it did quit flying. After touchdown, you pulled the drag chute handle and braked to a stop. Use of drag chute was recommended for all landings except those in strong crosswinds. In a strong crosswind, the drag chute would weathervane or swing to the downwind side of the runway, causing the nose of the aircraft to swing to the upwind side. To keep the aircraft on the runway took all of the opposite rudder, aileron, and smooth braking one could muster.

The C had deicing boots installed on the leading edge of the wings and horizontal stabilizer. High-resistance wires embedded in rubber provided continuous heat for the leading edge of each boot. Deicing was not often needed in the F-94C. The J-48 engine, a centrifugal compressor type, was relatively free of icing problems. Surface icing was usually avoided and the best system was to place wing and empennage deicer and pitot deice systems in operation before the ice actually formed.

The C was the first jet I flew that had an automatic pilot. It could be used for cruise, coupled ILS approaches, and radar-coupled attacks. I remember the radar-coupled attacks quite vividly as they sometimes gave a really wild ride; and after a few of these, aircrews were prone to prefer steering the attack

Opposite page: Three-plane echelon of F-94s.

manually. Once you coupled the autopilot with the radar, the aircraft reacted immediately to center the steering dot on the pilot scope. This more often than not caused high G forces, rapid wing roll, and a rather uncomfortable ride as the controls were trying to respond to inputs from the radar system. A "hot" or jumpy dot was really amplified on the controls, and the pilots much preferred using basic "stick and rudder" techniques to center the dot. The state of the art on "coupled" attacks has improved vastly over the years and now many aircraft automatic flight-control systems (the F-101 in particular) are capable of performing smoother coupled attacks than a highly competent pilot using basic control movements.

The primary armament consisted of 48 2.75 folding fin aerial rockets (FFAR). Twenty-four were carried in closed-breach launching tubes in the nose of the aircraft, and 12 were in rocket pods on each wing. Rocket firing was normally controlled automatically by the E-5 rocket-firing control system employing radar tracking and computing combined with a rocket-firing computer. A standby fixed optical gunsight for manual firing was available in the event of a radar system malfunction.

The nose section had four circumferential doors hinged at the forward end that moved inward simultaneously by hydraulic pressure, exposing the launching tubes prior to firing. The doors opened when the trigger was squeezed and closed three seconds after the trigger release by an automatic timing delay. Each rocket pod had 12 rocket tubes. A rocket pod nose of plastic was shattered by the rocket exhaust gases when the rockets were fired. Rocket selection was in salvos of 6 or 12 from each pod, and they could be fired manually or automatically, in conjunction with a corresponding number of 12 or 24 nose compartment rockets.

The F-94C brought us into a new arena for weapons firing. Instead of the usual aerial gunnery pattern where we combined radar tracking, a gunsight, and eyeballs to put bullets into a towed target, we were vectored on to a 90-degree beam rocket attack by ground radar control.

We fired at a Delmar target which was aerodynamically shaped, made of lightweight Styrofoam, with a radar reflector built into it. It was about eight feet in length, looked like a large bomb with fins, and weighed only a few pounds. We carried it cradled in a basket under the left wing of a T-33, and once airborne, it was reeled out to 5,000 feet for the firing runs.

Uniquely, the F-94C enabled us to fire over an undercast: once we ascertained that the Lake Superior range was free of vessels, we could be on top of the clouds and the Ground Control Intercept Station could set us up on firing passes and keep both fighters and target aircraft within the confines of the range limits by radar vectors.

Opposite page: An F-94 and its pilot posing for the camera.

The target ship would normally traverse the length of the range, and the ground controller would space the fighter so that each one turned in on its firing pass at about the time the fighter ahead had broken off of the target. Once the radar observer got an initial contact on the target, he would establish a "Reno" or separation between target and tow ship and then "lock on" to the target. After the "lock on" was solid, the pilot would then steer the aircraft to center the dot on the pilot scope. The pilot of the target plane was the only person who could give clearance to fire, for he was the only one able to ascertain absolutely that the fighter was in fact "locked on" to the target and not the tow ship. He, of course, would have to get a visual sighting of the fighter and then watch for movement of the fighter to the aft as it closed in range. There was a standard radio call "20 seconds to go" when pilot radarscope presentations started shrinking, and it was about this time that the target could detect the fighter drifting aft toward the towed target. Once this drift was perceived, then and only then would the target pilot give a "cleared to fire." Once cleared to fire, the pilot would concentrate on centering the dot, getting the wings level, and trying to make a smooth firing pass. You'd squeeze the trigger and the computer would fire the rocket salvo at the optimum range. You would then break up and into the direction from which the target came. Normally, the rockets would create a good pattern, and we destroyed a number of Delmar targets; but occasionally a fin would hang up on one of the rockets and they would gyrate all over the sky. If no "kill" of the target was made, the tow reel operator could retrieve the Delmar into the basket and bring it home for another mission. The retrieve took skill and deftness, for if the target came in just a "tad" fast, it was knocked off as it banged into the basket.

You could always tell when a flight was returning from a successful rocket mission, for with the plastic nose covers off of the rocket pod and the rocket tubes empty, the F-94C made a weird sound that someone likened to the "howl of the banshees."

As with the A/B model, we were equipped with the C for about three years; then as our ramp started to tilt from the weight of our newly arriving F-89J Scorpions, we ferried the fleet of Cs to the "bone yard," except for those that stayed in the local area to be mounted on pedestals.

Thus ended the F-94 days for us. However, we have retained the T-33, and it is still providing great service. We use it primarily as a target aircraft carrying Chaff and Electronic Counter Measure (ECM) pods in our daily intercept training. It is still a delight to fly, and I can still hear my instructor pilot yelling at me (from way back in 1951), "Dammit Gatlin, you are done with that yank and bank flying, now you've gotta be smooth!" Nor will I ever forget the sensation of smoothness and the quietness of that first jet ride.

The T-33 has been to jet fighter flying what the T-6 was to conventional fighter flying during World War II. Its progeny, the F-94 A/B and the F-94C, fulfilled a vital role in air defense and earned a place of honor in the exacting mission of all-weather fighter interceptor flying.

The T-33s and F-101s are now gone and we are into a conversion to the RF-4C and the Tactical Reconnaissance Mission. As for the RF-4C, all I can say is, "What a beautiful bird to fly!"

Col. Wayne C. Gatlin, World War II veteran, is commander of the 148th Fighter Group, Minnesota Air National Guard, stationed in Duluth. He has logged nearly 6,000 flying hours, mostly in fighters.

F-4 Phantom II

Alexander H. C. Harwick

The F-4 is a two-place (tandem), supersonic, long-range, all-weather fighter-bomber built by McDonnell-Douglas Corporation. Mission capabilities include: long-range, high-altitude intercepts utilizing air-to-air missiles as primary armament; a 20 mm gun as secondary armament; long-range attack missions utilizing conventional or nuclear weapons as a primary armament; and close air support missions utilizing a choice of bombs, rockets, and missiles as primary armament. Aircraft thrust is provided by two axial-flow turbo-jet engines with variable stators and variable afterburner. Airplane appearance is characterized by a low-mounted sweptback wing with obvious anhedral at the tips, and a one-piece stabilator with obvious cathedral. Dual, irreversible power control cylinders position the stabilator, ailerons, and spoilers. A single, irreversible hydraulic power control cylinder positions the rudder. An integral pneumatic system, charged by a hydraulically driven air compressor, supplies compressed air for normal and emergency canopy operation, as well as emergency operation for the landing gear and wing flaps. The wings can be folded for ease of airplane storage and ground handling. A drag chute, contained in the end of the fuselage, significantly reduces landing roll distances and an arresting hook, that is hydraulically retracted, can be utilized to stop the airplane under a wide range of gross weight-airspeed combinations.

The aircraft is powered by two General Electric J79-GE-17 engines. The engines are lightweight (approximately 4000 pounds each), high-thrust, axial flow turbojets equipped with afterburner for thrust augmentation. Under sea level, static test conditions, the engine is rated at 11,870 pounds thrust at Mil power, while at Max power it is rated at 17,900 pounds thrust. The J79 features

Opposite page: The F-4.

variable stators (first six stages), a 17-stage compressor, a combustion chamber with 10 annular combustion liners, a three-stage turbine, a variable area exhaust nozzle, and modulated reheat thrust augmentation (afterburning). A turbine-type starter, operated by air from an external source or by the expanding gases of a solid-propellant cartridge is used to crank the engines for starting. Either the aircraft battery or an external electrical power source is used to provide electrical power during starting. Engine bleed air, taken from the 17th stage of the compressor, is ducted to the boundary layer control system (aircraft without slats), the cockpit air conditioning and pressurization system, and the equipment air conditioning system. From these systems, it is further ducted to supply air to the air data computer, the engine antiicing system, the fuel tank pressurization system, the pneumatic system air compressor, and the windshield rain removal system.

The preceding paragraphs are from the aircrew flight manual and serve as an introduction to the Phantom and its engines. My own introduction was on a bright summer day in 1963 at Craig Air Force Base. I had finished another day of flight training in the T-33 and was on the way home when I became aware of a distinctive and piercing whine in the visual traffic pattern. The aircraft made several patterns which gave me time to watch it land. My first impression, other than the excitement of seeing the aircraft I hoped to fly one day, was how large and powerful it looked in comparison to the T-bird. After the crew shut the Phantom down, we were allowed to crawl all over it. I remember first impressions of all the lettering on the panels, the brushes on the throttles, and the complexity of the equipment.

As luck would have it, my class, 64-C, became the first allowed to attend back-seat training in the Air Force's newest and hottest fighter, holder of fifteen world speed, altitude, and time-to-climb records. (Only recently have some F-4 climb records been broken by the F-15 Eagle.) Quite naturally, all the allotted slots were taken by the upper portion of the class starting with the top graduate.

In October 1963 we headed to MacDill AFB, Florida, to become GIBs, "guys in back." Our first flight was in February 1964 after completing radar training. At that time the Air Force had 28 F-4Bs on loan from the Navy. The F-4C, the first Air Force version, was just coming into the inventory, so our training was in both types. The first flight was sensational! We were passing 20,000 feet in what seemed only long enough to get the T-bird airborne. After level-off, my commander gave me the aircraft. It felt like a refined sports car compared to the tired T-bird, but it was hard to maintain level flight due to the forward sloping canopy rails and the excess power.

Opposite page: An F-4 being refueled by a KC-135.

The rear cockpit of the F-4B was designed for a radar operator rather than a pilot. It was cramped by circuit breaker panels on the sides and by pull-out radar controls. The stick had to be removed in order to pull out the radar scope. Needless to say, after two consecutive radar failures, I quit removing the stick prior to flight and learned to work the set in the stowed position. The F-4C was a much better aircraft for the GIB because it was designed with permanent flight controls in the aft cockpit.

The first year after our checkout in the Phantom was spent upgrading to combat-ready status and giving numerous air shows across the United States. These shows were both official and unofficial. It was always a joy showing off our Phantoms. Once, after a hurricane evacuation from MacDill, our entire contingent of 52 aircraft made consecutive maximum performance takeoffs and climbs using one-minute spacing for the benefit of the F-100 pilots stationed at England AFB. That had to be an impressive sight!

In 1965 we deployed to Naha Air Base, Okinawa, to replace the F-102 unit there and provide air defense for the island. During this time, I began front-seat upgrade training. Although I had enjoyed the "pit," the front seat was and is infinitely better.

The aircraft preflight inspection is really nothing more than a check for leaks, cut tires, unexplainable skin damage, engine condition, ordnance security, and condition. The interior inspection consists of a complete check of switch position followed by engine start during which various systems are brought on the line and checked for proper operation.

After the walk-around inspection, both crew members climb up a special ladder or use a boarding step that can be lowered from the aircraft fuselage. Because the parachutes are built into the Martin-Baker ejection seats, crew members wear a special harness that attaches to fittings on the seat. This is a major improvement over earlier systems when fighter pilots had to lug a cumbersome parachute across the ramp. As a result, it is easy to get into an F-4.

After electrical power is put on, the GIB begins alignment of the inertial navigation system. It takes from 5 to 10 minutes to align the system unless the heading memory mode is used. The system is one which gives the Phantom many of its capabilities, so this apparent long wait is worth it. While the GIB is setting up his systems and computers, the GUF, "guy up front," is getting ready to start the right engine.

Engine rotation is brought about by applying air from an external cart or by use of black powder cartridges. At 10 percent rpm, the ignition button on the appropriate throttle is depressed and held while the throttle is moved forward to get fuel to the engine. The engine then begins to come up to speed. External air is disconnected at 45 percent rpm, and the engine continues a rapid increase to idle rpm of 65 percent. The generator comes on the line at 53 percent rpm, accompanied by a flicker of cockpit lighting and the telelight panel, which has various lights designed to warn of system malfunctions and to relay information concerning fuel transfer, etc. After checking the electrical system and the flight controls, the left engine is started. Again flight controls are checked and all systems including the radar may be brought on the line. Each crew member checks weapons systems, flight instruments, and begins crew coordination procedures which have been briefed beforehand in order to maximize mission effectiveness.

After the inertial navigation system is fully aligned and switched to "navigate," the GIB clears the aircraft commander to taxi. The aircraft commander makes sure the ground crew is clear and gets clearance to taxi from the tower. All Air Force Phantoms have nosewheel steering which simplifies taxi; however, this system periodically has spurious signals, and thus caution must always be used.

Prior to takeoff, the aircraft is generally looked over by a special ground crew to check for cut tires and leaks. Takeoff roll and speed are a function of gross weight, wind, and temperature. Roll may be as short as 2,000 feet for a light takeoff on a cold day or as long as 7,000 feet at maximum gross weight of 58,000 pounds on a hot day. A 3,000-foot roll with nosewheel lift-off at 140 knots and takeoff at 170 knots is fairly standard for a normal training configuration of two 370-gallon drop tanks, a gun pad, and two bombing dispensers.

Afterburner, which had been selected at brake release, is cut off at 300 knots. The standard climb speed is 350 knots calibrated airspeed to cruise Mach. The F-4 actually climbs better starting at 370–380 knots decaying 2 knots per 1,000 feet of climb until reaching cruise Mach. A very steep climb, although not rapid, can be attained at 180 knots. A maximum climb on instruments is performed at 250 knots. The fastest climb can be attained by accelerating to .92–.94 Mach with a constant Mach climb to about 27,000 feet. The nose is then lowered, a slight dive established to accelerate to above 1.2 Mach to open the vari-ramps and close the engine intakes, the nose raised to maintain slightly over 600 knots calibrated at a low G reading until passing the tropopause which is in the vicinity of 37,000 feet, and a slight "dipsy doodle" performed to exceed Mach 2. All this takes about three minutes from brake release. From this point it is easy to pop up to high altitude to engage a highflying target or to run out to intercept a target at long range.

My first front-seat takeoff was memorable. In the back seat I had the habit of running the rudder pedals all the way forward because of the cramped leg room. Although this was satisfactory in the back, in the front it caused a bit of personal embarrassment, for when the aircraft accelerated on takeoff, I slid

down in the seat and had to look out the side to stay aligned on the runway as the nose came up. After vowing never to make that mistake again, I became aware of how much better the visibility from the front really was: no intakes on the sides hinder downward vision; no metal bulkhead or ejection seat in front obstructs forward vision. After a couple of quick intercepts, we spent the first portion of the mission on stalls and aerobatics. Then we found a large rock jutting out of the Pacific and proceeded to make multiple simulated air-to-ground deliveries. The next mission was an air-to-air training sortie in a clean aircraft against another GIB also on his second front-seat mission. At that time there were no GIB upgrade programs in existence, so we were trained to be fighter pilots in the old tradition.

After this introduction to the front, I was reassigned to RAF Station Woodbridge, to the first USAFE wing converting to the Phantom. Flying in Europe during this tour was not only enjoyable but also excellent preparation for combat. The fun included an exchange with a Belgian F-104 squadron, flying crew chiefs in the back seat at Wheelus, being combat-ready in the front, and cross-country missions to Italy, Spain, Germany, and Denmark. Although the normal cruise speed at altitude is .88–.92 Mach or 310 knots calibrated, on one occasion I returned from Aalborg, Denmark, to Woodbridge in 25 minutes, measured from brake release to touchdown at destination. That's an average speed of just over 1,250 mph or slightly more than double our normal ground speed. And part of that flight was subsonic due to supersonic flight restrictions along portions of the flight path.

The preparation for combat included over 1,500 flight hours in three years, realistic training in all phases of tactical fighter flying, and an opportunity to experiment. During my European tour I had the opportunity to fly against the Lightning, Hunter, F-84, F-100, F-104, Mystere, and Mirage. This experience confirmed two basic facts about the F-4: using proper tactics it can defeat any of these fighters, and any of these fighters can defeat an F-4 using tactics that would be employed against another F-4.

The Phantom is an honest airplane that gives more than ample warning when it is being pushed too hard. When it is accelerated properly, the pilot feels both the seat belt across his lap and the seat cushion beneath him. A very mild rumble is felt in the seat when the aircraft is in an optimum turn, a turn that tends to conserve energy. In a maximum turn the aircraft gives a distinctive buffet. Beyond this rate of turn, it goes into hard wing-rock before it lets go and chases its tail. All that is required to stop the fuss is to release back pressure on the control stick. To spin a Phantom takes an asymmetrical load, an out-of-trim aircraft, a bent airframe, or a ham hand. Should one meet any

Opposite page: A formation of F-4s.

of these conditions, he needs only to break the angle of attack by putting the stick forward and/or using the drag chute.

We also had ample opportunity to learn about air-to-ground. We flew radar low levels in the fog using crew coordination, the radar altimeter, and *precise* navigation. The land-water contrast, which shows up well on a radar set, aided this effort. England also has excellent low-level flying areas where we practiced flight tactics against abandoned World War II airfields. The F-4C does not have a computing sight or automatic dive-release system as do later versions of the Phantom. It is, however, a stable air-to-ground platform. Proper use of the GIB makes the F-4 superior to the F-100 and to other previous systems because with proper crew coordination it is possible to eliminate certain variables in the gunnery pattern. I know this comment will offend some single-seat jocks; but it is a fact that we never lost a gunnery competition to either the F-100s or the F-105s at Wheelus. On one occasion I scored six consecutive bulls in a 45-degree dive-bomb during a competition. Our wing circular error average (CEA) for all bombs dropped in 1968 was 80 feet, which is considered very good for manual dive-bombing.

My next assignment was to the USAF Fighter Weapons School at Nellis. In addition to honing our air-to-air and air-to-ground skills, we learned how to optimize usage of the F-4 navigation systems on the combat profile missions. The F-4 has a TACAN like most modern aircraft; but this may be of little value in a combat environment. The inertial navigation system gives the F-4 the ability to navigate in a hostile environment without emitting any detectable signal. This system also provides information to the weapons-release computer system (WRCS), which can be used to correlate navigation information obtained from the radar set. Some F-4s also are equipped with LORAN. Upon completion of the school, I was sent to the 555th Tactical Fighter Squadron at Udorn Royal Thai Air Force Base as a weapons officer.

Flying fighters in combat has to be the most exciting and rewarding flying there is. During the year tour I flew 800 hours—over 750 hours combat time, of which 500 hours were flown as an F-4 forward air controller. During that year the Phantom proved its versatility, reliability, and lethality.

In general, our missions were flown as a four-ship flight assigned to a Forward Air Controller who would control us in the target area. We generally refueled from a KC-135 on the way to the target in order to extend our station time in the target area. The off-load was generally 3,000–4,000 pounds to make up for takeoff and climb fuel. The forward air controllers took 13,000–17,000 pounds at a time. The higher figure was the result of tankers out of position, working a strike farther away than originally planned on some

priority target, or getting involved in a search-and-rescue mission. The F-4 takes on fuel at the rate of 3,900 pounds per minute from a KC-135. During refueling it burns from 400 to 700 pounds. Considering an F-4 with two tanks can hold only about 17,500 pounds of fuel, some of the refuelings were critical. Our normal refueling altitude was 24,000 feet at 310 knots, the standard refueling speed, which meant that as we became heavier with the extra fuel, the Phantoms became sluggish like tired old nags heading for the glue factory. Refueling at night under the above conditions was very tedious.

Our ordnance generally consisted of some combination of 500-pound or 2,000-pound bombs, Bullpups, cluster bomb munitions (CBU) of assorted types, or the Rockeye, which is sometimes regarded as a CBU munition. We also carried the Sparrow missile for air-to-air and electronic jamming equipment. Even though the F-4Ds we flew had dive-toss equipment, we seldom used it.

Dive-toss is an automatic release mode that compares radar range and proper delivery parameters during a diving attack. It integrates input from several sources including the inertial navigation system. Each contributing system must be kept peaked if the dive-toss mode is to consistently deliver ordnance on or near the target. As a rule, dive-toss will put ordnance closer to target than manual dive-bombing in a hostile environment when concentration on exact delivery parameters is difficult. Our wing did as well as the wing at Korat, which had ". . . hot from Korat" as a motto, and delivered almost exclusively using dive-toss. Their bombs were like the little girl with the curl in the middle of her forehead: when they were good, they were very, very good; but when they were bad they were horrid! Some of the best bombing from F-4s I saw while I was a FAC was delivered using dive-toss. Dive-toss was also responsible for the worst bombing I ever saw, including some that missed by spectacular distances, well over a mile on some occasions. As a result, dive-toss was never used when "friendlies" were near or during search-and-recovery missions, when we were recovering downed crew members.

Dropping bombs and CBUs and shooting Bullpup radio-controlled missiles was good sport; but flying FAC missions in the F-4 had to be more fun than anything except the thrill of downing an enemy fighter. The F-4 was and is well suited to the forward air control role for several reasons. It has good response at both low and high airspeed with very good acceleration. The FAC mission in a high-threat environment is enhanced significantly by the backseater; tandem seating is the only acceptable arrangement. The inertial navigation system (INS) and the weapons release computer system (WRCS) add a vital tactical capability because it is possible to "memorize" a target position

Opposite page: An F-4—and its armament.

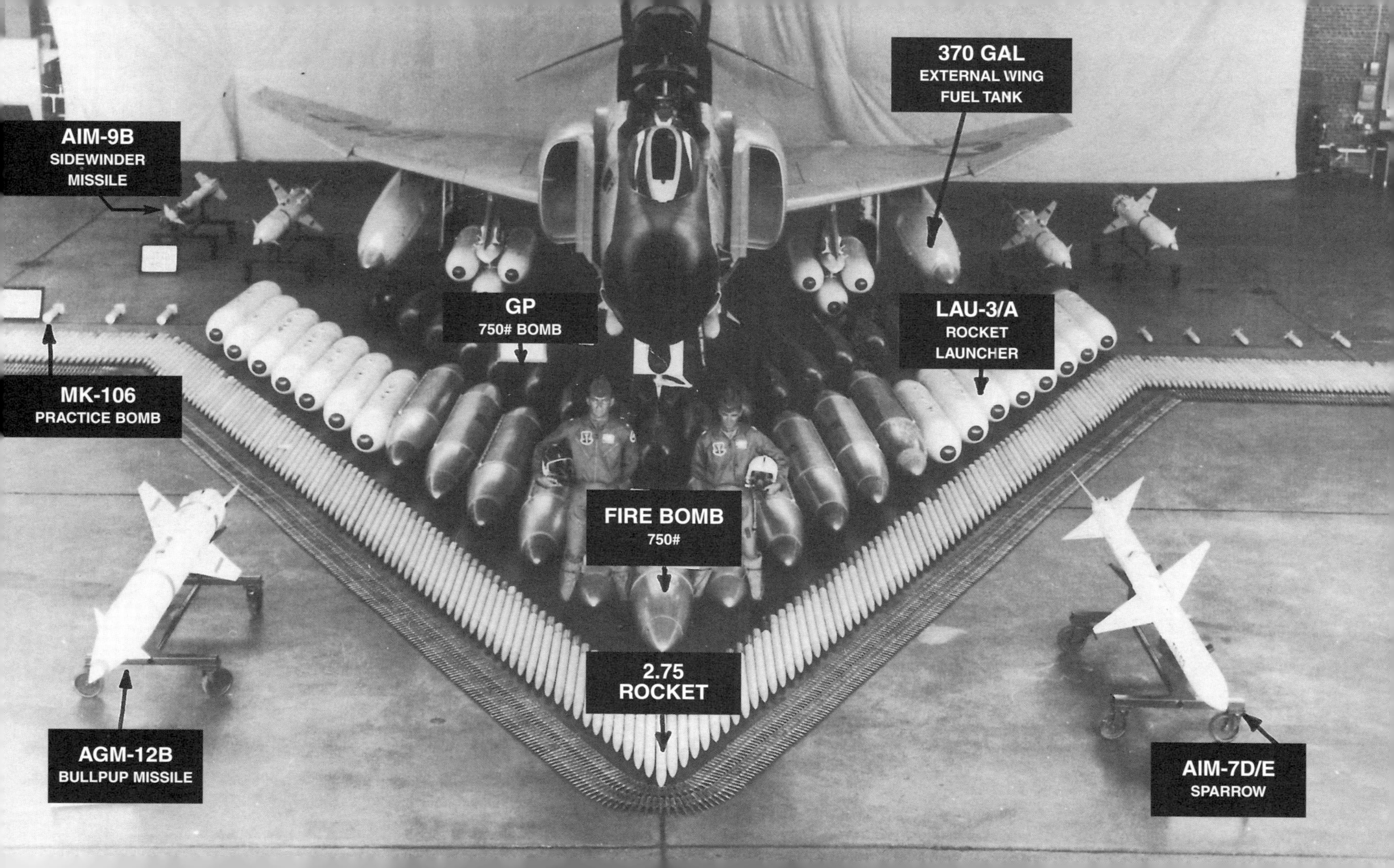

370 GAL
EXTERNAL WING
FUEL TANK

LAU-3/A
ROCKET LAUNCHER

AIM-7D/E
SPARROW

FIRE BOMB
750#

2.75
ROCKET

GP
750# BOMB

AIM-9B
SIDEWINDER
MISSILE

MK-106
PRACTICE BOMB

AGM-12B
BULLPUP MISSILE

and get steering initially to locate it or find it again without having to hang around the target area and get shot at.

The normal F-4 FAC mission lasted about four hours and included four refuelings, one en route to the target area and one each hour for the next three hours. The standard load was two external fuel tanks, an externally mounted 20 mm gun pod on the centerline station, two or three pods of 2.75-inch phosphorus marking rockets, fuselage-mounted Sparrow missiles, and a jamming pod. Though not a frisky colt like a clean Phantom, the F-4 with this FAC configuration was a thoroughbred capable of impressive performance. On one occasion, to mark a target for a succession of fighters in dismal weather, I flew seven consecutive loops to score or assess ordnance effectiveness and to be in a position to fire a rocket as the next fighter was attacking the target area with the exact target not yet in sight. That the Phantom could be flown in this manner attests to its performance.

In addition to being agile, the F-4 is durable. An F-4D I was controlling one day had the outer portion of its wing, from the fold outward, shot away during a pass. The pilot recovered the aircraft and returned to base with no further difficulty. I had a tank fail at 5 Gs in a 45° dive while marking a target only seven minutes after a full load of fuel. The aircraft pitched up and rolled but was easily recovered by releasing back stick pressure and applying proper aileron and rudder. On another occasion I had an engine blow apart resulting in little fuss other than a single-engine landing.

My own F-4 was named *The Naughty Lady*. During the course of the war it was awarded a purple heart with three oak leaf clusters, having survived a 23 mm shell through the wing, a 37 mm between the front and rear cockpits that sent the plane out of control and the GIB out via the ejection seat (he was later picked up after a gun battle on the Plaine des Jarres), an AIM-9 Sidewinder missile that impacted the left main gear during a loading accident, and a terrorist attack that resulted in damage to the belly from several hand grenades thrown under it. In spite of all this, F-4D #65-708 flew smoothly and with very few write-ups for malfunctions.

The F-4 seems to have fewer malfunctions the more it flies. When it sits on the ramp for a couple of days, it begins to leak and develop mystical maladies. Although plans call for 35–40 maintenance hours per flying hour, the plane can be turned around rapidly and flown three or four times per day if need be. Unfortunately some of the "mirrors and magic black boxes" are located in out-of-the-way places, requiring removal of the aft cockpit ejection seat bucket when they pack up.

Everyone who has flown combat has memories of his missions. Mine include the joys of watching SAM (surface-to-air missile) sites get blown away, controlling laser bombs on gun pits and seeing direct hit after direct hit, watching large caches of fuel go up in gigantic flames, emptying in two strafe passes all 7,200 rounds on 13 trucks stuck in a ford, and watching the Thuds consistently drop good bombs on whatever target they were assigned. I also saw horses stampede and men fall off bicycles when they became aware of a high-speed FAC looking over a road, as well as a Ping-Pong game in the jungle. It was also great sport on murky days flying supersonic at very low altitude through the mountain passes without ordnance. This scattered repair crews and on one occasion disrupted a picnic beside a waterfall we had created in repeated bombings along the road segment.

After my Southeast Asia tour, I was assigned as an instructor at the USAF Fighter Weapons School at Nellis. During this tour I instructed Southeast Asia-bound crews in the finer points of employing terminally guided munitions. "Smart bombs" as they are sometimes called were and are being pioneered on the F-4 weapons system; they mark a very significant technical advance. These weapons increase the already excellent weapons capability of the Phantom and ensure that the F-4 will be a major weapon system for a considerable time.

During my tour at Nellis, I was able to fly and compare the C, D, and the E—sometimes all on the same day. The F-4 has the same engines as the C but weighs more. As a result it is significantly slower than the other two. In fact, few Ds will reach Mach 2 without running out of fuel, but both the C and the E will reach Mach 2 fairly easily. The C will keep up with the E in a drag race with less thrust because of less weight. The RF-4C, in which I also have a little time, will match the E.

With just over 700 hours in 11 months, I returned to Europe as a weapons officer with the 32nd Tactical Fighter Squadron at Soesterberg Air Base, the Netherlands. The squadron flies F-4Es and is responsible for providing air defense. The flying in Holland can also be quite good, particularly during exercises when targets range from supersonic, high-altitude to Harriers on the deck. The rules require not only gun-camera film, which confirms weapons parameters, but the tail number, which gets sporting when a Harrier wants to try to deny the information. Once again the Phantom proved that if flown properly it is a match for anything other than our very newest fighters such as the F-15 and F-16.

When USAFE created a tactics school at Zaragoza Air Base, Spain, I was reassigned there. During this tour I had the opportunity to fly the "slatted E," which is the latest USAF Phantom variant. This new model has a beautifully redesigned cockpit, made to be used by a fighter pilot to bring ordnance to bear on the enemy rather than by some human engineer who mans a mahogany bomber for a living. The slats were added to improve the turning performance. They do this, but at the price of higher drag with resulting high-energy decay. Because the amount of energy available defines the limits of options available in an air-to-air engagement, it is imperative to manage energy extremely carefully in this new Phantom.

Although not a single-seat, single-engine aircraft, the Phantom is a fighter in the truest sense with a name and a tradition that will long be remembered in the annals of aviation history. I am fortunate to have been able to fly it since its introduction into the USAF. It is not as pretty as the P-51, as smooth in roll as the F-104, as stable at low altitude as the F-105, or as light feeling as the F-106, but it is a beautiful blend of all these and others. It has done its job well in every classic fighter mission and will continue to serve the free world as a versatile and reliable front-line fighter. It has been the standard against which all other fighters in the world have been measured for a decade and a half.

Maj. Alexander H. Harwick has more time in the F-4 than any other person in the world—3,900 hours. He has flown the F-4B, C, D, E, slotted E, and RF-4C. He has been an instructor at Nellis AFB and the USAFE Tactics School. He was head of the F-4 FAC program at Udorn and flew 257 missions and more than 750 hours in the F-4 in combat. He has spent seven years in Europe flying the F-4.

The RC-121D "Warning Star" Constellation

Russell E. Mohney

For a pilot who had just come from an operational assignment flying jet fighters, reassignment to the RC-121D aircraft certainly didn't represent an ego trip. Such was my predicament in late 1957 as I signed into the 961st Airborne Early Warning and Control Squadron at Otis Air Force Base, Massachusetts.

Anyone who appreciates the clean, sharp lines of modern aircraft suffers a period of shock when first viewing the RC-121D. The basic aircraft was designed as a commercial airliner with clean lines, and it was graceful in flight. The D model, however, was converted into an airborne radar station—and I never saw a pretty radar station. Functional in appearance, yes, but a thing of beauty, never. A bulbous radome had been attached to the bottom of the radar "Connie," making her appear pregnant. Feeling they had not yet added enough drag, the engineers placed another radome on top for the height-finder radar. Because the bird still could get off the ground, they added antennas (top and bottom) for eight UHF radios, TACAN, and Transponders, lightning arrestors on the tip tanks, and assorted other wire. Despite all their efforts, however, the RC-121D could still fly—and fly it did!

Designed and built by the Lockheed Aircraft Company in Burbank, California, the first Constellations had their origin in commercial aviation in the late 1930s. Using the basic technology of the earlier versions, Lockheed introduced the Super Constellation design by the mid-1940s. Under the designation WV-2, these aircraft were purchased by the U.S. Navy in the early 1950s for weather, search, and reconnaissance use. Later, some of these Navy aircraft

---

Opposite page: The RC-121D.

were transferred to the U.S. Air Force. By the mid-1950s, Lockheed's Connie had joined the Air Force in numbers with the purchase of approximately 200 C-121 aircraft in two basic configurations: passenger/cargo, operated by Military Air Transport Service (MATS), and early warning and control, belonging to Air Defense Command (ADC).

Simply stated, the RC-121D was a flying radar station, an airborne part of the U.S. coastal early warning system. Primarily, the RC-121D extended and complemented radar detection beyond the coverage available from ground stations, ships, and the ocean-based "Texas Towers."

What is it like to pilot a radar station? Let me begin by saying that for all its bulk, added drag, and apparent ungainliness, the RC-121D was in fact a great flying machine. Like most large transport aircraft of the time, it was heavy on the controls and slow in response to pilot inputs, but it also was extremely forgiving and airworthy.

Powered by four Wright R-3350-91 engines equipped with power recovery turbines and rated at 3,260 bhp at 2,900 rpm, SL (sea-level), the bird had a lot of power. The normal maximum weight for the radar warning mission was 139,000 pounds, which included 8,750 gallons of AVGAS and a crew of 18: aircraft commander, co-pilot, two flight engineers, two navigators, two radio operators, eight radar operators, and two radar mechanics.

Identifying the Connie was an easy task: all you had to do was count the number of vertical stabilizers—three of them. Rumor has it that when the Connie was undergoing design, one of the specifications laid on by the commercial airlines was that the aircraft had to fit into existing hangar facilities, so Lockheed replaced one tall fin with three smaller ones. The clean C-121 aircraft was very responsive to rudder inputs, but since it was thought the upper radome on the RC-121 series would break the airflow for the center rudder, that rudder was fixed in place. Surprise! No difference. The pilot still had to apply heavy pressures to make a smooth, coordinated turn, and the measure of an RC-121 pilot was how well he could keep the ball centered during a turn under instrument flight conditions.

Although there was a cockpit entrance door on the right side of the aircraft, normal practice was to enter via a boarding stand at the rear entrance on the left side. Height above the ground at this point was 14 feet, certainly no place for a misstep. Upon entering the aircraft, you proceeded to walk through the aft crew rest area and the airborne operations center, past the radio operator and navigator positions located on the left and right respectively in the center wing area, on through the galley and forward rest area, and, after 116 feet of travel, you finally reached the cockpit.

Opposite page: Another view of the RC-121D.

For a large aircraft, the RC-121 had a small cockpit. There was a full panel for the flight engineer located on the right side, and the pilots found it necessary to twist and turn a bit to get into their seats. Once in, it was comfortable, and the closeness enhanced flight deck crew coordination. Intercom/loudspeaker operation was the norm for radio and the other crew positions, but the flight deck ran with unaided voice conversation.

Cockpit checks consisted of checking for mag switches off, proper presentation on the flight instruments, parking brakes set, and emergency hydraulic pressure. Radio operators and flight engineers did all the rest; piloting was an executive job! With all crew compartments secured, engine start was accomplished with ground crew on headset. Starting sequence was 3,4,1, and 2, with the engineer doing it all and calling for mag "switch on" by the pilot after eight blades. As was common with most reciprocating engine aircraft employing a full engineer's panel, the flight engineer worked the throttles, engine prime, and mixture controls during the starting sequence. If one ever backfired, that engineer was in for a miserable 12 to 14 hour trip! The pilots were mainly occupied with checking hydraulic pressures as the pumps came on line and with that myriad of other duties necessary prior to taxi, such as checking compass systems, flight instruments for proper presentation on normal and emergency power, hydraulic pressures, windshield (NESA) heat, pneumatic deicing system for proper pressure/timing sequencing, and making various radio calls to command post, control tower, etc.

When taxi clearance was received, the pilot called for "pilot's throttles," and they were his until taxi speed was established and he elected to give control over them back to the flight engineer. The aircraft was steered by a hand wheel located on the lefthand side of the pilot's seat. Taxiing the bird was a bit tricky until one became used to the landing gear system, which employed a walking principle that normally made the aircraft assume a nose-high attitude. (What is the gear walking principle? The main landing gear consists of an upper and lower strut. The upper strut is composed of two rigid forgings which are bolted together with pivot points at each end. The lower drag strut is a hydraulic cylinder that absorbs forward and backward shock loads of landing and taxiing—a very effective design that insures smooth landing/taxiing operation.)

More than one inexperienced pilot found himself "going on" and "coming off" the step because of poor braking technique—and from a crew comfort standpoint, there is nothing more disturbing than sitting in the tail and finding yourself being rocked to death by some dumb pilot.

Pre-takeoff checks consisted of checking propeller reversing, magneto grounding, and other engine performance using primarily the cathode tube

engine analyzer. This, too, was mainly the engineer's show, with the pilot acting as an interested observer. Taking the throttles once again from the flight engineer, the pilot lined up with the runway center line, keeping power up to stay on the step and prevent plug fouling. When cleared, he called for "max power," and released brakes. He steered with his left hand and followed throttles lightly with his right in case of an abort situation. Three speeds were important during takeoff. The co-pilot called out "70 knots" and relinquished the yoke to the pilot, who discontinued steering and transferred his left hand to the yoke once the rudders were effective.

At V1 speed, after which abort was not possible, the pilot moved his right hand from the throttles to the yoke as well. (V1 speed was usually around 117 knots for a mission-loaded airplane.) At the co-pilot's V2 call, "takeoff speed" (128–132 knots), a steady back pressure on the control column caused the plane to hop right off the ground. A visual and oral signal started the gear up, and after acceleration to 140 knots, a respectable rate of climb was started. A power reduction to METO (maximum except for take-off) was called for, and once it was set, the flaps were retracted, somewhere around 600 feet. It was time for George to fly, and the pilot to have a cup of coffee, but work wasn't over, for while all the necessary traffic procedures were being broadcast and complied with, the speakers also blared requests for permission to turn on the search- and height-finder radars. Preparation for station keeping started early in the two hours en route.

Cruise speed at 15,000 feet was 180 KIAS (knots indicated air speed) /2,500 rpm/182 BMEP (brake mean effective power) on high blower operation at an operating weight of 129,000 to 133,000 pounds. Single-engine failure was a fairly common occurrence on the RC-121D. Many were caused by failure of the Power Recovery Turbine and many were precautionary shutdowns due to excessive oil leaking, etc. The best means of identifying a failed engine was by referring to the BMEP indicator which displayed engine torque. Flight characteristics of the aircraft with either inboard engine inoperative remained unchanged, and rapid trim changes were not required. With either outboard engine inoperative, a slight yawing of the aircraft would be noted, thereby requiring rudder trim. When shutting down an engine, the flight engineer feathered the propeller, placed mixture control to off, and placed emergency shutoff lever to full off after the rpm reached zero. (Note: The emergency shutoff lever actuated valves that shut off hydraulic oil, fuel, generator blast air, and lubricating oil to the engine.) There was no altitude loss at 15,000 feet with normal operating weights.

An Atlantic run below 15,000 feet—where the radar was designed to operate—was usually a weather run. Thankfully, the Connie was an excellent

Opposite page: At work inside an RC-121D.

instrument airplane, very stable, and easy to trim up for hands-off flight. Three-engine operation was the same as four-engine except for trimming the rudder to account for the lost torque. If you got down to two-engine operation, though, you would have your hands full, especially if two engines on one side were lost. A go-around at MAX power under these conditions was impossible, since you would run out of the rudder control required to maintain a controlled flight path.

A unique aspect of the radar Connie was that we flew a deck angle of 4.5 degrees nose up during radar operations. This was to provide the fixed-search radar antenna the proper tilt for maximum range. We flew this angle off of a ship's inclinometer attached to the panel of the engineer's station. (An inclinometer is a curved glass tube about 4 inches long filled with liquid and holding a ball that moves back and forth as the nose goes up or down. Graduations on the edge of the case provide deck angle.) The 4.5 degrees nose up always made walking to the back of the airplane a snap. Cruise control techniques were rigidly enforced, as airspeed was not a factor. Engine power was changed every 3,000 lbs. of fuel burn-off to maintain that all-important 4.5 degrees, roughly every hour.

Our radar patrol mission usually ran about 12 to 14 hours, with two hours en route each way and eight hours on station planned. That sort of back and forth flying around the one spot in the ocean from which the radar was calculated to read really turned a pilot off. But there was a saving grace; in addition to that coveted title of "Aircraft Commander," in the Airborne Early Warning business you were also a radar site commander.

Decisions, Decisions! Questions from the intercept director, the ground tracking stations you report to; unidentified tracks; alternate communications because you can't get through normal HF frequencies; assistance and advice to aircraft in emergency—and, oh yes, to your own airplane. "Overseas air traffic control wants you to move so that a Pan-AM DC-6 can come through on your altitude; the navigator wants to move the track out 25 miles to avoid thunderstorms; 'Stand by TWA'; 'What's that engine the oil leak is on engineer?' Control wants you to extend one-half hour on station because your replacement is late; East Coast weather is going down; maybe you'd better recover at Bermuda." That's the way those patrol missions really were: never long and never boring for the pilot in command.

Although the RC-121 pales in comparison with today's modern jet aircraft, it was a fine machine. Fully pressurized, it had the power and fuel capacity to go coast-to-coast, nonstop, in eight hours—eastbound that is. In fact, on a trip from the West Coast one time, we got into the bottom of the jet stream at 20,000 feet and were making good a ground speed of 375 kts. This

Opposite page: The underside of an RC-121D.

prompted air traffic control to inquire if we were turbo equipped. To an old fighter guy, that was quite a joy!

After being airborne anywhere from 12 to 14 hours, the crew would be eagerly looking forward to landing—particularly the radar crew if you had been subjected to eight hours of battling your way through thunderstorms. The Connie couldn't fly over them as today's jets do, and besides that, the desired radar coverage dictated the altitude at which we would operate. Anyone who has flown the North Atlantic in the wintertime knows that 10,000 to 15,000 feet altitude in thunderstorms isn't going to guarantee passenger comfort! It was standard practice to pass out the airsickness pills shortly after takeoff if the Met guys had forecasted a rough time on station.

Another point about the RC-121D—could it ever collect the ice! Those upper and lower radomes could accumulate it by the ton. Icing of the radomes constituted two-thirds of the total performance loss experienced by the aircraft in icing conditions. Fortunately, the old girl had an adequate automatic pneumatic de-icing system on all flight surfaces and on the radomes, plus propeller de-icing fluid.

If you weren't in a hurry, descent from altitude was made at standard power settings of 1,800 rpm and 120 BMEP, or 1,700 rpm and 110 BMEP giving 1,000 feet per minute at 180 KIAS, or at cruise setting with continuous manifold pressure reductions to keep the engine within limits. On the way down, the crew would accomplish the descent checklist, with the flight engineer again getting most of the action in adjusting cowl and oil cooler flaps, setting up the carburetor air, retarding spark, monitoring and adjusting pressurization controls, setting the rpm to 2,400 on call, and placing the mixtures in auto-rich as landing pattern altitude was reached.

Cowl and oil cooler flaps were utilized to maintain best engine operating temperature. Failure to position them properly would result in exceeding operation limitations, and leaving cowl flaps full open on takeoff would increase drag, thereby causing a longer takeoff roll than predicted. However, I never have heard of an accident caused because of improper cowl flap positioning. The Connie was basically a foolproof aircraft.

Instrument and VFR pattern speeds and techniques were pretty much the same. As a rule of thumb you bled the airspeed off to 150 KIAS (knots indicated air speed) set flaps at 60%, and called for 2,600 rpm and gear down at glide slope. Then the pilot took the throttles and the rest was his act.

In landing, the RC-121 was no different from any other aircraft. You played off airspeed and altitude until you knew you had it made. The RC-121 was responsive and contained no built-in bounce; if you had your act together, you just couldn't go wrong. With the field in sight and full flaps, you came

Opposite page: Inside the cockpit of an RC-121D.

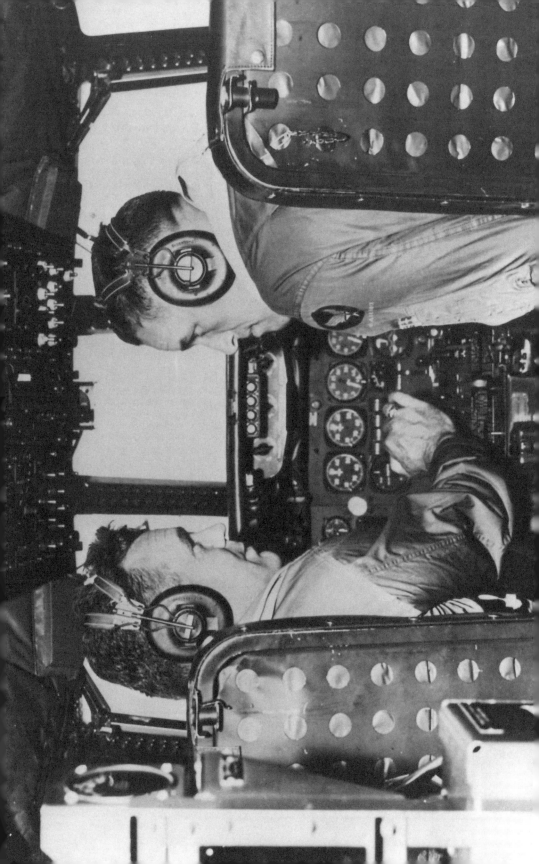

over the threshold at 124 KIAS (weight 110,000), gradually eased the power back, and set her down at about 97 kts. Crosswind was no big problem if you practiced differential power technique and stayed ahead of the airplane.

There are several techniques for making a crosswind approach. The main thing for the pilot to do is establish a definite ground track in line with the extended runway center line. This can be achieved by lowering the upwind wing, crabbing into the wind, and reducing power on the upwind wing and carrying more power on the downwind wing—or a combination of all three. The effectiveness of each technique varies with the type of aircraft. With the high dihedral angle wing of the Connie, I personally preferred the differential power, upwind wing-low technique as opposed to crabbing the aircraft. After touchdown, throttles were brought to idle, the nose-wheel lowered, and directional control maintained by rudder until about 70 KIAS when nose-wheel steering became prime. Stopping was no problem either, as those R-3350s had a lot of reversing power. Cocking the reverse throttle levers brought the propellers into reverse, and 1,500 rpm would provide approximately 60 percent of full braking effectiveness.

As with taxiing for takeoff, the bird had good handling characteristics after landing. Normal after-landing checklists were pulled (hydraulic rudder auxiliary booster pumps off, pitot heat off, wing flaps up, and transponder off), and it was time to hit the chocks with anywhere from 12 to 14 hours in the log book.

I flew the RC-121D for about seven years all told, and at the time of this writing (1978), they still are flying active radar missions with the Air Force Reserve. An aircraft that can fly for three decades has to be rated *great* by any standards. We don't build them that way often, but we did this time. It looked funny, but it flew fine, and long after its sleeker contemporaries have faded into obscurity, the Connie will be remembered as one of the greatest—perhaps a "super" gooney bird!

Brig. Gen. Russell E. Mohney is Assistant Deputy Chief of Staff, Logistics Operations, HQ Air Force Logistics Command, at Wright-Patterson AFB, Ohio. General Mohney served his first operational assignment as a radar observer with the 46th Fighter-Interceptor Squadron at Dover AFB, Delaware, in 1953. He later was a line pilot and Chief of Standardization/Evaluation for the RC-121D.

F-84 and F-5

William F. Georgi

When the comparison of the F-84 in Korea and the F-5 in Vietnam was first proposed, it seemed an easy task. However, when I looked at a model of each fighter, just the external appearances emphasized the complexity of the task. The F-84 was an old functional battlehorse and one of the heavyweights of its day, whereas the F-5 was a sleek "racer" and one of the smallest jet fighters built. Nevertheless, both were good at their particular jobs, and both generated a lot of affection from the pilots who flew them.

There is no simple way to compare different aircraft operating in dissimilar wars. To begin with, their design technologies were separated by approximately 15 years. Of even greater import, each plane was designed to a different primary concept. In one important aspect, however, these fighters were similar. The F-84 was a relatively simple and functional fighter designed for a multipurpose role. Similarly, the F-5 was a reversion to the simple, functional fighter in a later age of more complex weapons.

The F-84 was one of the early production jet fighters and was built in quantity to enter the United States Air Force inventory in 1948. Although it started its career as a long-range escort fighter, the F-84 evolved through its life-cycle into a fighter/bomber. To the credit of the designers, it has the built-in capability to take this transition. As it progressed through a normal test and development cycle, it acquired a substantial operational history prior to its entry into combat. Nevertheless, as with many multipurpose fighters, it suffered the usual design compromises that kept it from enjoying the role of a first-line air-superiority fighter.

Opposite page: An F-5 during a test flight in California.

The F-5 was an entirely different animal. It owed its origin and part of its design to the T-38 trainer. It was designed to meet the demand for a simple, reasonable, multipurpose fighter that could be sold in the free-world market. Unlike the F-84, the F-5 was neither designed nor procured for the United States Air Force inventory.

The environments in which these aircraft saw combat were in many respects as different as the aircraft themselves. The Korean War was fought in a climate and over a terrain reasonably similar to that of the United States. The vegetation of Korea was moderate and supply routes were reasonably well defined. In Vietnam the environmental factors of heavy tree cover and poor visibility produced one of the world's areas least suitable for air attack.

Even the opposition and the tactics were considerably different. In Korea the F-84 was consistently used to strike targets in areas where it was subject to attack by North Korean fighters. It was often engaged by enemy aircraft and could defend itself fairly well. Because the formations were usually large, flights in a "fluid four" configuration could effectively provide low-altitude defense for themselves and for aircraft rolling in on targets. Furthermore, the higher altitude F-86 coverage made the MIGs reluctant to engage the F-84s. Fighters in Korea were also subjected to heavy ground fire, but luckily this was the age AAA (antiaircraft artillery) and SAMs (surface-to-air missiles) were not a part of the enemy defense. In contrast, while the F-5 operated in North Vietnam for approximately 2 of the 6 months it was tested, it was not engaged by enemy aircraft or by the SAM batteries; its primary competition was the AAA in the North and the small arms fire and occasional AAA in the South.

Reminiscences of experiences with both aircraft begin at Taegu, Korea, early in 1952. The day after my arrival there I had my first close look at the F-84. I had been flying the F-80, and to me the F-84 looked like a beast. Luckily, first impressions are not always completely correct.

Talking with the rest of the jocks during my first days at Taegu didn't improve my first impression. As in any unit, the new guy gets the horror stories first thing, and the 49th Wing was no exception. I was told how the F-84 was the most ground-lovin' aircraft known. With great elaboration they told how one per week never got off the ground on takeoff and trundled off into the rice paddy, with the usual dire results. I learned there was some fire for this smoke, but it was vastly exaggerated. The F-84, like most early jet fighters, was underpowered for the load of munitions and fuel it carried in Korea. Add two other problems—that the engine in both the D and E models tended to have loose turbine buckets and that Taegu (K-2) had one of the roughest PSP (perforated steel plate) runways existing—and you had all the makings of a catastrophe. Takeoff with a loaded F-84 at K-2 on a hot summer day was prob-

Opposite page: Another look at the F-5.

ably the "hairiest" part of the entire mission. As the weather warmed up in the spring of 1952, we used two 1,000-pound JATO (jet-assisted takeoff rockets) bottles to assure takeoff. Although JATO got us off the ground, takeoffs were still exciting. Everyone from number three man back in the string was zero visibility and had those added moments of panic wondering if the bottles would light and if the man ahead had lost his radio and aborted. When we progressed to the later models E and G aircraft and finally got a hard-surfaced runway, these problems diminished.

In most respects the F-84 was an honest aircraft. It had little tendency to flame-out, stall, spin, or indulge in other undesirable flight characteristics. To its credit, it had relatively long range for its day, could carry a heavy load, and was an exceptionally stable gun and weapon delivery platform. But it badly needed more thrust.

The cockpit was fairly well organized and large enough to be comfortable, but space for maps, etc., was at a premium and the seat must have been contrived by a sadist. Another minus was the positioning of some of the radio and fuel control switches where they were partially blocked by the canopy rail. Visibility wasn't a plus either. However, the A-14 computing sight was welcome, and most of the important controls were readily accessible.

The F-84 sustained some of the higher loss rates of the Korean War. This is sometimes misconstrued to reflect a weakness in the aircraft. In reality, considering the types of missions the F-84 flew, the deep penetration targets, and the high-density defenses, it was one of the more survivable planes. Most of the losses resulted from heavy AAA during the ground-attack phases; loss rate to MIGs was minimal. Although not precisely recorded, the kill ratio against the MIG favored the F-84. (Of course it probably would have been less favorable had we not had F-86 cover.) The F-84 could defend itself, but because of its comparable lack of acceleration and climb it was very poor offensively.

The F-84's greatest attribute was probably its toughness. In one instance, Tom Titus was hit by a MIG that put three 23 mm explosive cannon shells into his aircraft; one exploded in his tailpipe, another lodged unexploded behind his seat, and the third blew a medicine-ball sized section out of his main fuselage tank and fuselage. Tom had to do some fancy fuel management to get the leaking aircraft back to base. On another sortie I picked up more than a hundred various sized holes from ground fire and the aircraft still made it back. A Captain Barnes demonstrated the structural strength of the cockpit while attempting to recover an aircraft after takeoff. He experienced engine and electrical malfunctions, turned final to K-2 at minimal control speed, lost his high-side tip tank, and spun into the ground. We rushed out to the fireball marking the completely disintegrated airplane to find the cockpit fairly intact

---

Opposite page: Five F-5s in a demonstration.

and a badly bruised Captain Barnes sitting on a paddy wall trying to light a cig-
arette. Although mildly nervous the following day and turning several shades
of purple and green from bruises, he suffered no other disabling effects and
was back in the business within a couple of days. Although the F-84 may not
have been the most loved airplane in the world, a number of fighter pilots
owe their good health to the ruggedness of this aircraft.

I mentioned that the F-84 was developed and introduced into combat in
a conventional manner and that the F-5 had a markedly different history. The
usual process is to subject a new weapons system to arduous testing followed
by an evaluation in operational units. The F-5's introduction to combat was
the first attempt by the Air Force to run a full operational evaluation on an
aircraft in combat. Although the F-5 test conditions could not, in all fairness,
be described as "controlled," they were at least carefully directed and fully
documented.

The test project, formed in the summer of 1965, consisted of a squadron
of 12 F-5s to be evaluated under combat conditions in both North and South
Vietnam. Lieutenant Colonel Hopkins, the Operations Officer, tagged the
project "Skoshi Tiger," and this title was picked up as the official designation.
The F-5s were to be evaluated to determine their capability in both air-superiority and ground-attack roles. The evaluation team, operated from Saigon,
consisted of an analysis section and field teams with photographic and other
technical support.

Because the F-5 was not in the Air Force inventory, we had no prescribed
training or maintenance programs and no technical orders or manual. One
of our first actions was to devise a training and support program. From July
through early October 1965, we trained at Williams Air Force Base, using the
Gila Bend gunnery ranges and devising tactics as we went along.

We deployed to Vietnam via Hickam and Anderson, with all 12 aircraft
arriving at Bien Hoa in good shape on 25 October 1965. I might also mention
that the F-5s we took to Vietnam had a number of modifications to fit our
requirements. Principal among these were a refueling probe, armor plate,
double-gyro flight-instrument platform, modified engine, and pylons and
racks capable of handling a number of munitions as well as the TER.

Bien Hoa was a far cry from Taegu. Although our living facilities were not
as good as those in Korea, the runway and other airfield facilities were far
superior. All of the personnel involved in Skoshi Tiger had trained together,
and morale was exceptionally high. It was an effective unit, with a great deal of
initiative and eagerness to get on with the job. I find it difficult not to go over-
board in praise of the F-5, for going to it from the F-84 is similar to climbing
into a hot Porsche after stepping out of the family station wagon. However,

Opposite page: Three F-5s.

there was one difficulty: as in a sports car, the F-5 has little room for goodies such as electronics, fuel, etc. On the other hand, the F-5 was designed with the pilot in mind. The cockpit has ample space, and the arrangement and controls are as simple as you will find anywhere. Starting and emergency procedures are just as simple. For instance, on an airstart all you need to do is check your fuel selector, set the throttle, and hit the airstart. For that matter, the throttle could be in afterburner and the result would be a normal airstart ending with the engine at afterburner power.

Under normal load conditions the F-5 had none of the F-84's tendency toward extended ground roll to an uncomfortable degree. However, takeoff roll was affected with some of the heavier experimental loads. For example, when carrying TERs and full fuel, the F-5 center of gravity shifted forward enough to make low-speed stabilator control questionable. This forced us to higher takeoff speeds and almost doubled our ground roll. The problem was solved by the comparatively simple expedient of installing a two-position nose strut. Controlled from the cockpit, the extended nose strut was about a foot longer, thereby increasing the ground angle of attack and reducing the stabilator force required for rotation. On gear retraction, the two-position strut returned to normal extension.

Unlike the F-84, the F-5 has sufficient thrust to maintain a good rate of climb after takeoff and can maintain control speed on one engine even when loaded. Whereas the F-84 had no drag chute, deploying the F-5 chute during a takeoff abort brought immediate results. Because the F-5 chute was the same size as that of the F-100, there was no question of stopping; rather the problem was remembering to brace yourself so that you wouldn't end up in the windscreen. Consequently, although we had a few takeoff emergencies in Vietnam, we never had any serious problems like those the F-84 encountered in Korea.

In flight the F-5 has to be forced to go out of control and has no tendency toward surprises. If you keep a little speed on, it will do almost everything you have the nerve to try. At low and moderate altitudes it will fight anything, including the MIG-21. Later versions with modified controls and larger engines should be competitive in any theater.

By the time we got to Vietnam, the Skoshi Tiger pilots were firmly convinced they had the best aircraft in the world, but it was readily apparent that the others in Southeast Asia did not share this enthusiasm. This is understandable, considering the peculiarity of air operations in the Southeast Asian war. At the time, operations in the South relied heavily on the A-lE with its varied loads of munitions and its notably long endurance. Common practice was to launch the A-lE and, once it was within visual contact, have the spotter point

Opposite page: The F-84.

out targets as they were observed. Because the A-1E could spend considerable time in the target area, numerous targets could be struck. In contrast, the F-5 was not capable of long loitering with heavy munitions loads. Operations planned around the A-1E's capabilities did not exploit the best features of the F-5. Nevertheless, the F-5 could carry four 750-pound bombs or equivalent, plus a full load of 20 mm a radius of 200 nautical miles, remain in the target area 5 minutes to deliver its ordnances, and then return to base. Although this was less than the A-lE or the larger jet fighters were capable of accomplishing, it was an average load for many aircraft during this period. Turn-around time in the F-5 also was excellent and resulted in a good sortie rate.

We did find a number of items on the F-5 that needed further work. Many munitions had been tested, but the pylons and racks had not been used under the rapid turn conditions of combat. Consequently, we had instances of faulty releases, in which napalm tanks or drogued bombs struck the aircraft or failed to release. A rapid redesign on the pylons solved this shortcoming.

Another problem we encountered was self-inflicted. A principal reason for the F-5's accuracy was that a small, maneuverable aircraft can get quite close to the target prior to the release. In consequence, pilots often pressed too hard, particularly in gun attacks. Debris blown into the air by 20 mm shells was often ingested by the engines with the usual dire results. On the good side, all aircraft made it back to base, even after engine failure; unlike many other engines, the J-85 had little tendency to disintegrate after ingesting debris. During an attack on AAA positions in Mu Gia Pass, my aircraft was hit by a 14.7 high-velocity shell that penetrated the right side of the forward belly, passed through the aircraft, and entered the left ammunition bay, exploding two rounds of 20 mm. The explosion blew the ammunition door open and dumped links and assorted hardware into the port engine. Although the engine ceased providing much thrust, it continued running in idle range for the 35-minute return to base and still was repairable.

We also found that when operating on the same targets, the F-5 took fewer hits than the F-100 or the F-4. We believed this was because of the F-5's small size and lack of an exhaust trail which gave it low visibility. Although the aircraft took a number of hits during the project, we lost only 1 pilot and plane in action. However, this may have indirectly resulted in the loss of another pilot's services. Col. Burt Rowen, the project Flight Surgeon, was also a fully qualified pilot flying sorties in the F-5. But when the Air Force medical high command discovered this, they forcefully suggested that his duties were not those of squadron pilot and that the project could not afford to lose its Flight Surgeon. So he was grounded. Burt never seemed quite as happy after that.

In South Vietnam, sorties were varied and results were consistently good. In the North we were less successful, not because of the F-5, but because of a number of factors over which we had little control. We lost a good part of the value of our early operations at Da Nang when all bombing sorties to the North were cancelled. This reduced us to escorting patrol aircraft and providing out-country sorties. In the spring of 1966, during our second month at Da Nang, we still encountered problems in attempting to get a complete evaluation. We hit ground targets in the North, in a number of cases within SAM range, but did not have any missiles fired against us.

Attempts to induce a response by North Vietnamese aircraft were a dismal failure. Fighter encounters during this period were fairly low for all aircraft and we had none with the F-5. We escorted patrol aircraft and airborne early warning aircraft, hit some targets close to Hanoi, and tried providing low cover for F-4 and F-105 aircraft on their bombing sorties. At this time the North Vietnamese fighters were flying on the deck into the Red River area then popping up to hit the fighters during their bomb run. In an attempt to counter this tactic, we flew low-level tracks at approximately 500 feet in the mouth of the Red River Valley. No MIGs were launched during the periods we were there; they showed only after we left. Apparently they weren't going to chance an encounter until they found out more about us. On our part, we were confident that we could have scored against the MIGs. The F-5 had been flown against a number of aircraft air-to-air while still in the CONUS (continental United States) and proved very capable, particularly in the lower altitudes. We were greatly disappointed not to get a chance to try the plane in combat. During all our sorties in Vietnam we received many SAM warnings but none apparently was fired against the F-5. We ran into ample AAA, but because of our altitude, flight pattern, and speed of approximately 500 knots, we took few hits.

During these activities, as well as those in the South, the evaluation team continued gathering data. The evaluation eventually confirmed that although it suffered the limitations of a small aircraft, the F-5 could do an excellent job in ground attack or air-to-air roles where long-range and all-weather capability were not the primary considerations. It was a tough bird—durable, simple to repair—and provided a lot of capability in a simple package. More important, it is a pilot's airplane and all who flew it liked it.

How do the F-84 and F-5 actually compare? I would say "not very much," if the comparison is based on physical characteristics and performance. However, in concept and employment there is a great deal of resemblance. The F-5, like the F-84, was a simple design, and both answered the need for a func-

tional and comparatively reasonable day fighter. In fact, from a desk in the Pentagon, both are remembered as fantastically good aircraft.

Brig. Gen. William F. Georgi entered the service in 1942 as an aviation cadet and served as a pilot and later Commander of the 352d Bomb Squadron in North Africa. In 1952 he served in Korea as the Commander of the 9th and later the 8th Fighter Bomber Squadrons, flying 148 missions in F-84 aircraft. Varying assignments in both operations and Research and Development followed. During 1965 he served on temporary duty in the Republic of Vietnam as Deputy Commander of Project Skoshi Tiger, test of the F-5 fighter aircraft in Vietnam. He flew 162 in- and out-country missions.General Georgi went to Raimstein Air Base, Germany, in August 1970 as Vice Commander of the 26th Tactical Reconnaissance Wing and became commander of the Wing in March 1971. In February 1973 he assumed command of the 86th Tactical Reconnaissance Wing at Ramstein Air Base. In May 1973, he joined the Organization of Joint Chiefs of Staffs as Chief, International Negotiations Division in the Plans and Policy Directorate.

Opposite page: Another look at the F-84.

F9F-2 Panther

Cecil B. Jones

It was big, blue, and beautiful. As I approached the F9F-2 Panther on the Air Group 11 flight-line at NAS North Island, San Diego, I tingled with anticipation of the greatest natural high a mortal can experience. The pilot, strapped in unity with his aircraft, strains his guts and screams with joy as he flies his bird to the outer limits of its performance envelope. Early in 1950 I did not know that the Panther and I had a rendezvous with war. In two combat tours off a Navy carrier I would become so familiar with the aircraft's instruments of destruction and its response to my control that the cockpit would become a place of security and in flight the aircraft would be my perfect and absolute domain. I need not explain this feeling to any other fighter pilot, and no amount of explanation would be adequate for nonpilots.

The carrier naval aviator naturally thinks about his aircraft in terms of its combat capabilities as well as its shipboard handling characteristics. The carrier, as a vehicle to get the aircraft within combat radius of action, may never be relegated to the status of a mere floating airfield. Aircraft and carrier compatibility is so obviously an imperative that the need to reaffirm it periodically with every "joint" Navy/Air Force fighter development and procurement is nothing less than incredible.

The F9F Panther, an early straight-wing Navy jet fighter, provides a classic example of the technological interrelationship of aircraft and carrier and of some of the associated problems.

The first flight of the XF9F-2 on 24 November 1947 was powered by a British Rolls-Royce Nene. A second prototype was equipped with the Allison J-33 engine. Throughout its service life, the Panther name covered a small

family of differently powered aircraft. The F9F-2 I flew was equipped with the
5,000-pound thrust Pratt & Whitney J-42-P-6 centrifugal-flow jet engine. The
F9F-3, nearly identical with the F9F-2, was powered by the Allison J-33-A-8 with
4,600 pounds thrust. The F9F-4 carried the Allison J-33-A-16, which delivered
5,850 pounds thrust. The F9F-5, which shared the same airframe with the
F9F-4, was powered by the Pratt & Whitney J-48-P-4, delivering 6,250 pounds
thrust. None of the Panther series was equipped with afterburner.

In all, 1,388 Panthers of various dash models were procured. The first
delivery to an operational unit was to VF-51 at NAS North Island, San Diego,
on 5 August 1949. The last delivery by Grumman was in December 1952. From
a numbers viewpoint, the Panther was the most important of a small generation of straight-wing carrier jet fighters. Total production of all the others—the
Chance-Vought F6U Pirate, the North American FJ Fury, the McDonnell FH
Phantom and F2H Banshee—was less than that of the Panther. This meant
that in the opening years of jet carrier aviation, more naval aviators earned
their spurs in the Panther than in any other jet fighter.

The Panther was the first carrier jet to enter combat, and it carried the
brunt of the Navy's Korean jet effort. Panthers from VF-51, flying off the U.S.S.
Valley Forge, shot down two prop-driven YAK 9s on 3 July 1950, seven days after
President Truman ordered the Seventh Fleet to give support to the Republic
of Korea. Later that year, 9 November, a Panther piloted by LCDR Tom Amen
of VF-111 made the first Navy contact with a Soviet-built MIG-15 and downed
it (see LCDR W. T. Amen, "Scratch a MIG," *Flying*, Nov. 1951, Vol. 49, No. 5).

The F9F-2B, so designated because of its bomb carrying capability, was
combat-demonstrated on 2 April 1951, when LCDR Ben Riley and LCDR Ray
Hawkins of VF-191 attacked a railroad bridge. Each aircraft carried four
250-pound and two 100-pound general purpose bombs. This was the first Navy
combat use of a jet fighter in a bomber role, and it marked the end of a period
in which Navy jets had been limited to Combat Air Patrol over the carriers with
only occasional opportunities to engage in air operations over the beach. The
principal missions over land were fighter escort for Navy prop bombers (F4Us
and ADs) and escort for the photographic version of the Panthers. The success
of this first bombing was marginal and suspect. The bridge had previously
been knocked out and rebuilt. To assure hits, the attack was made from very
low altitude. One Panther was severely damaged by its own bomb blast. The
"evidence" was nevertheless accepted as establishing that Navy jets had other
roles to play besides air-to-air combat. And the incident was glorified by James
Michener in *The Bridges of Toko-ri*.

The Navy wasn't being archconservative in its reluctance to use its jets in a
ground-support role. The Panther aboard the Essex class carrier in the early

1950s was operating with very little margin for error. In mid-1947 the Navy announced a carrier improvement program, "Project 27A," to modify the Essex class to handle heavier, faster aircraft. Later, as the result of jet-carrier experience during the Korean War, this project was modified in February 1952, and more powerful arresting gear and higher performance catapults were called for. The margin of safe operations for Panthers from an Essex class carrier may be identified by a practice resorted to for catapult launches with low-wind conditions. Following readings from a hand-held anemometer, the Catapult Officer would direct the off-loading of 100-pound bombs or 5-inch rockets, one at a time, until the aircraft weight came down and the estimated minimum aircraft catapult end-speed could be achieved with maximum catapult launching pressures. Under these conditions it was a common experience to settle off the end of the catapult with the stick-shaker (stall-warning device) delivering its omen of apparent impending disaster. One soon became accustomed to this and, provided the nose was not rapidly rotated, the aircraft quickly accelerated out of this situation. The stick-shaker, mounted on the control stick, was operated by signals from an outside sensing vane, which was designed to detect an approaching stall condition.

If the Korean War had not developed in mid-1950 and thus forced new defense funds to be made available, naval carrier aviation would have faced a crippled future. In 1949 when the 65,000-ton supercarrier U.S.S. *United States* was cancelled by Defense Secretary Louis Johnson and $36 million cut in fiscal 1950 research and development funds for naval aviation, a whole generation of planes designed to use the proposed carrier was scrapped. The mortgage on the future of naval aviation may have been more than the naval service, beset with internal feuding between "black shoes" (nonaviators) and "brown shoes" (aviators), would have been capable of paying off.

As *Aviation Week* (11 July 1949) noted in an editorial entitled "Crises in Naval Aviation—An Analysis," the reduction of R & D funds and the cancellation of the U.S.S. *United States* had the effect of placing an artificial ceiling on the technical development of naval aircraft. A comparable case, it noted, would have occurred if Air Force planes had been limited to runways of a certain length and thickness.

It should be recalled that the F9F Panther was developed at the same time as the F-86, the first American swept-wing jet fighter. Prototypes of the two different aircraft first flew within two months of each other. The same swept-wing and jet technology available to North American engineers from German World War II developments was also available to Grumman engineers. The first experimental flight of a Navy jet was the straight-wing North American FJ Fury. Had there been any chance of developing a swept-wing Navy jet fighter that could have operated off the carriers available, the Navy would not have been a half generation behind the U.S. Air Force and the Soviet Union in operational jet fighters in the early 1950s. The practical importance of this was not lost even to a junior naval aviator as he went into combat in 1950 from a carrier platform that was marginally capable of handling his aircraft under certain operational conditions. That the Soviets built from German World War II jet technology and had purchased the Nene engine from the British were also sobering facts. In the early 1950s, the hackneyed vision of Ivan whipping his tractor for better performance was irreversibly replaced with a new respect for Soviet technological accomplishments.

My introduction to the F9F Panther came after a swift familiarization course to jet aviation. On 19 January 1950, I completed seven carrier landings in the Grumman F6F Hellcat aboard the U.S.S. *Saipan,* cruising in the Gulf of Mexico off Pensacola, Florida. This was the culmination of advanced flight training, and the following day, after being designated a naval aviator, I was ready to report to a fleet fighter squadron as an Aviation Midshipman. With the aid of outstanding instructors, reasonable skill, and breaks in the weather, I had completed the training program ahead of the normal schedule and was destined to serve in the fleet as a Midshipman four months before being commissioned. Although this may have been a poor economic fate, the luck of my availability caused me to be sent to the first formal Navy jet training class at NAS Whiting Field, Florida.

After ten days of ground school, this pioneer class was led to the flight line and each student strapped into his Lockheed TO-1 Shooting Star (the Navy's designation of the F-80 never became common parlance in the aviation community). Sixteen days later, after 24 flights totaling 28 hours, I was certified jet-qualified and sent to the fleet, which was still predominantly prop equipped.

My first squadron, the Sundowners of VF-111, was in the process of transitioning from the Grumman F8F Bearcat to the F9F Panther. In those relatively casual days, the process of new aircraft checkout was simple to the point of being hazardous. The naive assumption was that a set of Navy wings was a golden key that unlocked any box a plane came in. I proved this absurdity several times. The most dramatic occasion was when the squadron, equipped with only a dozen F9Fs, was scheduled to move to NAS El Centro for a week of gunnery practice. The natural scheme of things assured that no Midshipman would be assigned an aircraft to ferry over to El Centro. There were two other options: travel on a bus or vie to fly one of the two F4U Corsairs to be used as tow aircraft during gunnery hops. When the Schedule Officer asked for volunteers for this last assignment, one Midshipman, who had completed advanced flight training in F4Us, eagerly stood up. I was a fraction of a second behind him. My speed was unnecessary; no one else in the ready-room had ever flown the Corsair. All others were willing to suffer the indignity of a bus ride rather than challenge the bent-wing eliminator's reputation on a spur of the moment urge.

My total checkout consisted of the plane captain's shocked response to my question, "How do you start this thing?" Not only did I survive the flight over to El Centro, which was highlighted by an unintentional spin coming out of a poorly executed loop, but my second takeoff, my first with a tow target, took place immediately after landing. I was cautioned not to drag the banner along the runway but to get airborne as quickly as possible. The resulting spectacular launch was a subject of considerable squadron discussion, and I was labeled a number one Corsair driver. My reward was six consecutive F4U hops before I was allowed my first F9F flight.

The Panther was a solid beast built in the tradition of other Grumman fighters which had long survived the punishment of carrier operations. It had a feel of strength and stability that the F-80 lacked, but was limited to Mach .83, which could be achieved only in a dive, and was easily recognized by severe buffeting and almost uncontrollable pitch-up. A more practical limiting Mach number was .79. Beyond this, it was difficult either to fire the guns effectively or to drop bombs or shoot off rockets accurately because of moderate buffeting and lateral wobble and trim changes.

On all missions the standard pilot paraphernalia included a G-suit, whose air-inflatable compartments on the legs and abdomen helped maintain blood pressure to the eyeballs and brain during high positive G loads. In the early 1950s the G-suit was not an integral part of the flight suit, but rather a separate corsetlike garment worn from ankle to stomach under the regular multipocketed flight suit. One issue of the summer flight suit was particularly well received. It was a green, extremely lightweight see-through nylon garment. On low-level summer flights, wearing the required inflatable Mae West, which was festooned with packets of fluorescent dye marker, shark chaser, combination day and night flares and smoke, signaling mirror, whistle, and compass, this suit transmitted a maximum amount of air conditioning. But soon after its issue it was recalled and replaced. In a fire, the nylon welded itself to the body and created a vicious scar on any survivor. Although I was willing to give up this suit for flight, its comfort and status symbolism were too great to part with. Twenty-five years later, I occasionally don its well-worn remains when the car needs washing. This has always seemed a safe utilization of the suit; my only complaint is that each year it seems to shrink a bit more.

An essential flight item was the pilot's knee clipboard. Strapped to the thigh during flight, it contained the shorthand essence of the flight briefing and was used in flight to write down clearances and in combat, if circumstances permitted, to document details that were always required in post-action debriefings.

The pilot in the F9F sat on his parachute, which always remained in the cockpit. Between a seat cushion and the parachute was a compartment that contained a one-man life raft, a chemical desalting kit, a solar still, a radar reflector, and a rubberized poncho. Designed to meet the emergency needs of World War II carrier flight missions, this equipment was of no value to a pilot who survived a parachute descent over land behind enemy lines. During the Korean War, each pilot augmented an issued personal survival kit according to his expectation of the risks ahead. Often this was practically determined by the amount of pocket space in the flight suit and flight jacket. Some squadrons removed the desalting kits from the seat pack and substituted tins of high-energy food such as sardines. Personal two-way mini-radios were not in the Navy inventory at that time. A .38 caliber pistol was issued to each pilot, and it was not uncommon to have a round accidentally fired in the ready-room by a pilot who was professionally qualified to handle 20 mm cannon and 5-inch rockets but failed to give proper attention and respect to the simple single-action revolver.

In combat the pilot's personal gear was limited to what he could wear and stuff in his pockets. On noncombat cross-country flights personal gear could be stowed in the sliding nose compartment which provided normal access to the battery and the four 20 mm cannons. The standard-issue naval aviator's green bag fitted snugly in the bottom quadrant of the nose section, an area first exposed when the sliding nose section was opened. The fit had to be tight because the green bag held itself in position while the nose was open for loading or unloading. With care, a two-suit clothes bag could be draped over the rear of the 20 mm cannons and the sliding nose section closed over it. A mark of the successful cross-country F9F-2 driver was a clothes bag scarred with small cuts from the nose assembly and dabbed with assorted colors of paint used to mark 20 mm ammunition. The void area where the green bag fitted had a combat role. The 20 mm brass shell cases accumulated there when the cannons were fired. Their weight maintained the center of gravity within limits. Back aboard ship, the squadron ordnance crews fitted a large canvas bag under the rear of the nose section and when the nose was opened, the brass was neatly collected.

The roomy cockpit was an early and successful example of careful attention to the physical and psychological needs of the pilot. Because the plane was designed strictly as a daytime fighter, the cockpit was not encumbered with displays and instrumentation required by night and all-weather fighter aircraft. Access to the cockpit was a self-contained sliding step, which recessed flush in the fuselage when stowed, and two higher-up toe indents and one handhold, which were flush in flight. Their half-moon covers were spring-loaded closed.

The starting procedure was simple. External electrical power was required for engine starts. When the cranking switch was hit, the starter quickly brought engine rpm up to 8–10 percent. At that point, the throttle was moved outboard to the "Start" position. This motion opened a high-pressure fuel cock and actuated power to the spark igniter. A normal light-off would take place in less than 30 seconds. The rpm increased to 20 percent and the tailpipe temperature rose to 400 degrees Celsius. At that point, the throttle would be brought "around the horn" into the "idle" position. Idle rpm was set at 28 percent, and the generators cut in at 36 percent. Approximately 51 percent was required to initiate taxiing. Steering at taxi speeds was done by toe brakes. Because each minute on the ground reduced aircraft range 2.5 miles, standard shipboard handling procedures attempted to reduce the deck running time to absolute minimum.

Standard checks of the air-conditioning, electrical, and hydraulic systems were made immediately after start-up, completing the pretakeoff check list, except for placing the flaps in the "take-off" position. The Panther had a water-injection system that provided a one-shot quantity of 22.5 gallons of water-alcohol coolant mixture for takeoff. When this system was to be used, the cabin pressure switch and the air-conditioning were turned off to alleviate the danger of alcohol fumes in the cockpit. When the air-conditioning switch was turned on after the coolant injection had been consumed, it was not unusual for a cloud to form in the cockpit momentarily. Although the experienced pilot would anticipate this, experience was not an adequate substitute for visibility. Many rendezvous immediately after launch were aborted because of this phenomenon.

More spectacular than this transient cockpit IFR condition was a situation involving the F9F-3 pressurization and air-conditioning system. The F9F-2 cockpit was air-conditioned and pressurized via perforated tubes ringing the canopy. The F9F-3 had some of this arrangement, but the main duct was located forward of the gunsight and had a fan-shaped opening approximately 1 inch wide and 8 inches long. With warm outside temperature and maximum cooling selected for inside cockpit temperature, ice would form in the duct until it was obstructed to the point where pressure would launch a small oblong "snow ball" over the gunsight. This missile would strike in the vicinity of the forehead of an average-sized pilot. It was a rule that knowledge of this potential was never divulged to the uninitiated.

A ground launch required steering with brakes until the rudder became effective at approximately 70 knots. Lift-off speed for a nominally loaded aircraft weighing 17,000 pounds was 115 knots. At approximately 105–110 knots, the stick was eased back until the nosewheel was just off the ground. This attitude was easily identified because of the sudden reduction of noise and vibration of the nosewheel on the runway. The aircraft smoothly became airborne in this attitude. Landing gear was immediately retracted and the flaps were raised at 130–150 knots. In this speed regime no sinking occurred, and acceleration was relatively rapid to 330 knots, which produced the best rate of climb. The flap system of the Panther featured a "droop snoot" leading edge, which moved in conjunction with the regular trailing edge flaps. These provided added lift and improved stall characteristics. The F9F with the stick-shaker was very honest about stalls. Practicing stalls at altitude in a landing configuration, the stall warning device would practically mix a cake in the cockpit before the nose fell through. The pilot's handbook warned that without this device there was no natural aerodynamic stall warning. Wing design was outstanding for its generation, and the aircraft performed within its envelope without any abnormalities. It was virtually impossible to overcontrol and stall the wing.

Launch from the carrier was always accomplished via catapult. As the aircraft was brought up from the hangar deck, the wings, which had been folded to allow compact storage, were spread upon signal from a deck plane handler. Weaving toward the catapult, the aircraft became a part of the moving scenery of the flight deck ballet for which carrier aviation is noted. Brown-shirted plane captains were checking and rechecking their aircraft even after start-up. Red-shirted ordnancemen faded wearily into the background to enjoy a short rest until it was time to prepare for the next strike. The green-jerseyed catapult crew tensed to their responsibility—a safe launch with a minimum launch interval. The prima donnas of this ballet corps were the yellow-jerseyed plane directors. Their starring performances were supported by the blue-shirted aircraft handlers and chockmen. This colorful and deadly serious ballet-drama approached a climax for the Panther pilot when his nosewheel eased over the catapult shuttle and the cable bridle was attached to the aircraft's fuselage catapult hook and a hold-back arm and ring were connected to the after underfuselage. With feet off the brakes, tension was taken on the bridle. After final instrument checks at 100 percent power, the pilot's ready-to-launch salute was followed by the catapult officer's sweeping launch signal. The hold-back ring predictably parted and the aircraft accelerated to 115 knots in nearly as many feet. The hydraulic catapults of that era strained at every shot to fling the Panther into safe light.

Immediately after catapult, a clearing turn away from the carrier's launch path was made to assure a turbulent-free launch for following aircraft. In quick sequence the gear was raised, canopy closed, and flaps raised as the rendezvous evolution began.

The Panther carried fuel in two soft, cell-type, self-sealing fuselage tanks located between the cockpit and the engine (a total of 683 gallons) and two fixed aluminum wing-tip tanks (120 gallons each). Full fuel load from tip tanks could be dumped by ram air pressure in approximately one minute at 340 knots. Many photographs have been published of Panthers in formation alongside a carrier, majestically polluting the air and sea with POL products as they came in for a break. The Panther pilot who ended up dumping fuel should not be branded as wasteful and a poor manager of his consumables. Among other considerations was the requirement to be below the maximum arrested landing weight of 12,600 pounds. If he had been on CAP (combat air patrol) over the carrier at high altitude, he probably kept some fuel in his tip tanks to dump in the event of an actual air-to-air encounter with the faster MIG-15. With a 100 mph disadvantage, the Panther pilot would naturally desire the most favorable weight-to-thrust ratio he could get.

The average combat mission for the Panther in 1950 and 1952 was 1.6 hours in length. (This figure is based upon 150 missions flown, the longest being 2 hours, and the shortest being an over-the-beach hop of one-half hour.) Missions were flown at a variety of altitudes, most of them below 5,000 feet on armed reconnaissance. Following the catapult launch, a running rendezvous en route to the target area was commonly made. Once together, the division aircraft would visually check each other's external ordnance for general security and for the status of arming wires. In formation, the 20 mm cannons would be charged and test-fired. Once done, the master arm switch would be secured until the aircraft was in the target area. Previously, immediately after takeoff, the gyro gun sight was turned on. In a short time it was up to speed and ready to function. If the mission was CAP, the division would climb to altitude under radar control. On these missions no external ordnance was carried. The division would be positioned between the fleet formation and the threat area. Primarily, for radar control training, the four-plane division would be broken up into two sections and practice intercepts made on each other for an hour. Return-strike aircraft were often intercepted, again for practice, or occasionally to escort a battle-damaged jet aircraft.

The most challenging over-the-beach mission was flak suppression. This required a high order of coordination and precise timing to obtain maximum results. The Panther, with its high speed and excellent ordnance platform, was cast in the role of preceding the more heavily armed and slower propeller-driven AD Skyraiders and F4U Corsairs on target. The Panther's job was to engage the antiaircraft positions, gun barrel to gun barrel, just before the prop aircraft rolled in for their attacks on the defended target. Ordnance for the Panther on these missions included the 20 mm cannons, VT-fused fragmentation bombs, and 5-inch rockets. Properly executed, the antiaircraft positions would be either damaged or destroyed and their crews forced to take cover while the attack prop aircraft steadied into their dives. Poor timing made life exceedingly unpleasant for the slower more vulnerable prop aircraft. Release of bombs and firing of rockets caused virtually no effect on handling the Panther. This was primarily because the largest weapon carried was the 250-pound general-purpose bomb.

A third mission was armed reconnaissance. On this, a two-plane section would cover a preplanned road or rail route at low altitude looking for targets of opportunity. Occasionally and only after considerable experience, some of the usually superb Korean and Chinese camouflage efforts would be detected and a worthwhile target taken under attack. Normally, nothing but foot and bicycle traffic moved by day—sparse, if not insulting, targets for a sleek jet. The night-attack pilots had a much different story to tell, and often the first early daylight strike would be against a train trapped in the open by the efforts of the night-attack group. A common and frustrating sight during daytime armed reconnaissance flights was engine smoke drifting out of the opening of one of the hundreds of tunnels that marked the North Korean railroad system. All pilots at one time or another attempted to lob a bomb into a tunnel entrance. Many thousands of rounds of 20 mm were shot into these black sanctuaries without any signs of results. The following day's review of such gun-camera film always included at least one hairy pull-up over the rim of the mountain that had been tunnelled through.

The Panther handled extremely well in the air. Maneuverability was excellent and there were no significant restrictions on flight maneuvers, even with external stores and full tip tanks. Only snap rolls and abrupt rudder reversals were prohibited with external stores and tip-tank fuel. Spins were not prohibited but were avoided because of large loss of altitude, 4,000–7,000 feet, associated with recovery from even one turn. Maximum G loads for the Panther were plus 7.5 and minus 3. The envelope for these maximum figures in smooth air was from sea level to 20,000 feet with airspeeds from 315–420 knots indicated. At 40,000 feet, G limits were plus 1.9 to minus 1.7 at 210 knots indicated airspeed.

The Panther was built to battle and acquitted itself well in combat. In 1952, when the Panther was used extensively in flak-suppression missions, it repeatedly proved it could take hits and still perform. The Korean War established that the Panther was not only rugged but was dependable and relatively easy to maintain. For the period April to December 1950, the Navy reported 96 percent combat availability for the F9F-2. This figure is impressive and meant that even though heavy maintenance work was done at night while the pilots rested, the planes were ready for the following day's missions.

Only once, when I flamed out at altitude on instruments over heavy seas, did I seriously have to consider bailing out. The decision was avoided when my third relight attempt was successful at about 7,000 feet. The ejection procedure required a series of independent manual steps that made the probability of a successful low-altitude ejection very poor. A preejection lever jettisoned the canopy, lowered the seat, and released knee braces on the seat sides. A seat-catapult safety pin was pulled when the canopy jettisoned. The pilot slid his feet back into the seat floor stirrups, set his knees outboard against the braces, and pulled nylon rope handles to bring a cover over his face. This action locked the inertia reel of his harness and fired the ejection charge. Later models of the Panther allowed ejection through the canopy. Separation from the seat was manual, requiring disconnection of oxygen, radio leads, and seat belt. The parachute rip-cord was pulled when seat separation was accomplished.

The Panther was equipped with highly effective dive brakes, which caused a nose-down trim change. A split-S from 40,000 feet to sea level was possible with dive brakes out, throttle retarded, and the aircraft riding the maximum Mach line. When the air speed was below 215 knots, the landing gear was extended. Flaps were lowered below 165 knots. Final approach speed for field landing was 115 knots, with wheels and flaps down, dive brakes up. For carrier landings, the hook was extended by manually pulling the cockpit hook handle 3 or 4 times. Final approach was made at 108–110 knots with 1,000 pounds of fuel. For each 200 pounds of fuel over this weight, an additional knot was added. The optimum cut position with a 30-knot wind and steady deck condition was 300 feet out from the number three wire and 18 feet above the deck.

The break-up for landing normally took place from a right echelon formation with the leader at 500 feet and the division flying down the starboard side of the carrier if it was in the wind. With gear, flaps, and hook down and canopy open, the landing circuit was flown in a conventional racetrack pattern. At the 180-degree point you called in with landing checklist complete and gave your fuel state in pounds. Visibility was excellent throughout the pattern and the Landing Signal Officer (LSO) usually picked up his paddles as you flew through the 90-degree position. These were the final years of having the LSO on the port side of the aft end of the carrier personally working each aircraft aboard; the mirror landing system was under development and first installed aboard the U.S.S. *Bennington* in 1955. At the LSO's signal to cut, the throttle was snapped back to the idle position and a landing made. The throttle was not added again until the hook had been disengaged from the wire by the hook-release man and you were being quickly taxied forward of the lowered barriers in order to clear the deck for the next aircraft, which should be less than 30 seconds from touchdown. In the event of a wave-off, full throttle was added and at least 250 more pounds of fuel would be consumed before you could be at the cut position again. The Panther took an easy wave-off, provided the engine was at or above 52 percent rpm and the aircraft not slow and cocked-up. At the cut, the optimum landing attitude was to have the nose wheel and the tail skid equidistant from the deck when the main gear touched.

As previously mentioned, the F9F-2 aboard the Essex class carrier was not always a comfortable relationship. As might be expected, this was particularly so when a squadron with newly acquired F9F-2s operated off a carrier that previously had handled only prop aircraft. The combination of inexperienced personnel plus the press of operational requirements was often a volatile mixture. For example, when the Korean War opened on 25 June 1950, I had 33 flight hours in the Panther. This included 5 hours in a F9F-3 that had been assigned to the squadron primarily so that hours could be put on it as part of an engine-check program. The air group and the squadron were ordered on immediate deployment. Four flight hours later I had completed field carrier landing practice (FCLP) and qualified aboard the carrier with six landings. Mercifully, the squadron cut the two junior-most pilots with the fewest number of hours in type, and I, along with a squadron mate, was transferred to another squadron just receiving their F9F-2s. From bottom man on the pole I suddenly became a top dog. My 37 hours were puny, but they were more than all of my new squadron mates had together. From my recent rejected status I became an instructor pilot and with a trifle more elan than was justified I checked out the rest of the squadron when the new Panthers arrived. This squadron went through a crash training program and in three months qualified aboard a carrier that had never handled jets before, had itself just come out of mothballs, and had a large percentage of reserve personnel as ship's company.

The photographs of an F9F-2 deck crash document the malconjunction of these factors. A major contributing factor to this accident was a hydraulic tail-hook dash-pot that failed to provide adequate stubbing action to keep the tail-hook on the carrier deck as it groped for a cross-deck pendant. The tail-hook of the aircraft involved bounced rhythmically up the deck, avoiding all wires. The final result of this accident was strike damage to three Panthers and minor injuries to one deckhand. The author, who was in aircraft 104 when it was cut into, was highly excited and shaken up but sustained only a minor headache when the canopy squeezed his crash helmet against the side of the cockpit before the canopy was wedged off by the overriding wing of the assaulting aircraft. Three Davis-type barriers were engaged, but they offered no help. The ship, which had never operated jets before, had rigged an incorrect model of the Davis barrier. The model rigged was for the F7F Tomcat, which had a greater distance between the nose gear and the main mounts than the F9F Panther. The result was that the cable designed to engage the main landing gear was thrown up behind it instead of in front.

The Panther operated extensively off straight-deck carriers in every ocean. By the time angle-deck modifications appeared in the fleet, the Panther was giving way to a new generation of swept-wing fighter aircraft.

By a coincidence of fate, when the Panther family was retired from the fleet, I was forced out of carrier aviation by eyesight problems. Land-based antisubmarine warfare aviation, the next step in my naval aviation career, was an incredibly challenging mission, but I look back at my Panther flying days as the zenith of flying joy and adventure. Nearly 600 hours in its cockpit were far too few for the experience and pleasure I gained there. Of these hours, 240 were in combat, and a more dependable aircraft I cannot imagine.

Cdr. C. B. "Scott" Jones (Ret.) entered the Navy in 1946. Completing flight training in 1950 as an Aviation Midshipman, he joined VF-111, a jet fighter squadron at San Diego. Later, after being transferred to VF-191, he made two combat cruises aboard the U.S.S. *Princeton* (CV-37), in 1950 and 1952, flying the F9F Panther. After a tour as instructor in advanced jet training, again in the Panther, he returned to sea, this time assigned as Intelligence Officer on a Carrier Division Staff. He moved from carrier aviation to land-based antisubmarine aviation in the Neptune P2V-7 as Patrol Plane Commander in VP-18. A series of intelligence assignments in Washington and overseas rounded out most of the remainder of his 30-year career. His last "operational" flying was in the ageless Gooney Bird. As Assistant U.S. Naval Attache to India and Nepal, he flew the DC-3 in and out of twenty countries from Spain to Japan. Now retired, he is currently teaching political science at Casper College, Wyoming.

A-7D Crusader

John C. Morrissey

Late on a Friday afternoon in July 1969 six of us finished a one-week A-7D systems and aircraft engineering course at the Ling-Temco-Vought (LTV) facility in Dallas. My boss and I were to stay on for an additional week and receive five hours of flying in the Corsair II before returning to Luke Air Force base to begin the A-7D operational test program. I was scheduled for an early hop on Monday in what was to be my first experience with a "civilian" checkout program. I distinctly remember being asked to show up around 8:00 for a 9:00 takeoff. At this point there were two definite factors working against me: I had never even seen the cockpit of an A-7 and there were no A-7D Dash Ones (pilot handbooks) available.

Not wishing to dent the image of the USAF fighter pilot, I casually accepted the appointment with what was to be my "office" for the next four years. In 1969, LTV was primarily a Navy firm and in retrospect I surmise that they were trying to see what those Air Force types could do.

Facing the A-7 that Monday morning, I had varied feelings. Having come to the A-7 from the F-105, I considered its airframe a step in the wrong direction. A typical F-105 final approach speed was 185 knots, whereas the A-7D was in the 120-knot category. The Thud had taken me through many tough situations over a period of six years; in fact, as I thought about it, I had developed a sort of special affection for my previous steed, an affection that lingers to this day. My F-105 relationship had been forged in and tempered with combat; little did I realize, standing by that A-7D in 1969, that I would finish in it what we had started in the Thud.

Opposite page: Two A-7Ds.

Luck was with me that morning in the form of two excellent assistants—a civilian crew chief who had been with Thuds at Takhli, and Jim Marquis from LTV flight operations, also ex-USAF. When we were about 30 feet from the bird, I stopped and took in the view. It was the first time I had seen one up close, and I remember thinking that aesthetically Navy designs left a bit to be desired. Compared to F-100s, F-104s, and F-105s, this was definitely "Cinderella's older sister."

Jim walked around the bird with me and pointed out the high spots of the preflight inspection. There was very little to check, but two items stood out— the hydraulics tended to seep a bit at quite a few connectors, and absolutely no ground support equipment was required for starting. Regarding the former, I was tempted to buy stock in a "hydraulic mine" until the Air Force corrected most of the inherent seepage problems; as to the latter, the on-board starting capability was a tremendous operational advantage in that no ground power units were required for either electric power or external air. The basic electric power was provided by a NICAD battery, and the engine was started by an onboard, turbine-powered starting unit.

Access to the wheelhouse was gained by a self-contained ladder and two "kick in" steps on the left side of the fuselage. Several distinct impressions remain from that first cockpit entry. I enjoyed its compactness, which reminded me in a way of the F-100C. The instruments were laid out in usable fashion, but they were the old "round" type as opposed to the vertical tapes in the F-105. Almost all the switches were comfortably forward of the elbow line. The stick was small and had full travel in pitch only; in roll it was hinged just below the stick grip to allow lateral deflection without leg interference. The seat, with its internal parachute, was very firm, and its geometry made the pilot feel as though he was being pushed forward from the waist up. Comfort was not the plane's strong suit. The seat was raised or lowered electrically, but the canopy operation was entirely manual.

The starting procedure on my checkout was very straightforward. I asked the crew chief if he knew how to start it. He allowed that he did, so I watched as he turned on the battery, moved the throttle inboard to energize the self-contained starting turbine, placed it outboard to provide magneto-supplied ignition, and then at 15 percent rpm slid it forward to idle. Engine light-off was quick; when rpm stabilized at 52 percent, he moved the throttle back inboard and that was that. The noise level, even with my helmet off, was much lower than I expected.

Jim then filled me in on a few of the remaining essentials, such as takeoff and landing speeds, the air-start technique, emergency gear- and flap-lowering methods, and finally the ejection (heaven forbid) procedure. As there were no sedan (two-chair) versions of the A-7, I was supposed to be chased by a certain Joe Engle of LTV. But we incorrectly estimated the time required for me to get my jet in motion, and consequently, he was still strolling out to his machine as I began to taxi (AF 1, Navy O, bottom of the first).

Because of the very narrow gear, there was a softer lateral feel to the aircraft while taxiing than other "bent wings" I had flown. Directional control was straightforward and was accomplished with nosewheel steering. Visibility was excellent in the forward quadrants and straight ahead. In fact, I was struck by the feeling of sitting on the edge of a cliff; the cockpit is so far forward that no part of the aircraft forward of the cockpit is visible to the pilot— quite a switch from the long snouts of the "Hun" and the "Thud."

Because of the absence of published procedures for the "D," my pretake-off drill was homespun and very straightforward: canopy down and flaps set for takeoff, seat armed, warning light out, controls checked, fuel feeding, trim set, power 90 percent rpm, engine instruments checked, brakes off, and full power. I had been cautioned not to exceed 90 percent rpm with the brakes on lest I slide down the runway. It was pointed out that this would cause a flat spot to appear on the tires, which would rapidly deteriorate to a hole, causing all the air to leak out.

Acceleration during takeoff was brisk, but not as quick as that of after-burning aircraft. At Luke Air Force Base on a cool morning, the A-7D at 28,000 pounds would accelerate from brake release to approximately 280 knots by the time it reached the far end of a 10,000-foot departure runway. Rotation occurred at 130 knots, with takeoff at 136. Current A-7 drivers may doubt these figures but the empty weight of the early A-7Ds was under 18,000 pounds, and takeoff weights were in the 27,500-pound categories.

Climb performance was very good. The schedule called for 350 knots to be held until reaching .76 Mach and holding .76 until cruise altitude. Time to climb to 30,000 feet on this initial flight was approximately five minutes.

I found the A-7 to have excellent maneuverability in all areas but one— excess thrust. Control authority in roll, pitch, and yaw was more than adequate. The relatively low wing loading (66 pounds per square foot) provided more usable G at lower indicated airspeeds than previous "century series" fighters. It was the most aerobatically suitable fighter I have flown. For example, it was possible to enter a loop at 5,000 MSL (mean sea level) and 400 knots and complete the maneuver at 7,000 feet. With the fuel weight down a bit, loops at altitudes as high as 19,000 feet were possible. Although technically limited to 10 seconds, inverted flying characteristics were very straightforward down to 340 knots. Below that speed, the stick felt a bit soft in pitch. I made several ground-attack simulations. The energy required for reattack was more

than ample in the clean configuration, but as I was eventually to find out, reattack at combat weight in warm weather could be interesting. I should point out that a "clean" A-7D has eight nonjettisonable pylons on board. Removing these pylons reduces parasite drag considerably and the weight by 1,280 pounds. I flew the A-7D for more than a month without pylons, and the performance gain was substantial.

On comparison, the F-100D, F-105D, and A-7D have the same wing area—385 square feet. At equal fuel weights, the A-7D had a slightly lower wing loading and approximately the same thrust-to-weight ratio as an F-100C in afterburner. At this thrust level, the fuel flow in the A-7D was one-sixth that of the F-100. This aspect of the bird was very impressive and made unrefueled combat missions of more than three hours an everyday occurrence. In contrast, F-100s and F-105s were logging slightly over 1.5 hours on unrefueled sorties, and the unrefueled F-4 capability was even less.

By the time I returned to the landing pattern, my chase had become airborne and was now available for assistance. Fortunately, none was required. This was the first "no flare" aircraft I had flown. Jim had cautioned me that final approach speeds would be in the neighborhood of 124 knots with 4,500 pounds fuel remaining and that an angle of attack technique was to be used with a 3° approach to a no-flare landing.

There was no problem adapting to this technique, which in my mind was obviously superior to the "century series" flare procedure that was dictated, I believe, by their "stiff" landing gear. The relatively low final approach speed came as a bit of a surprise—it seemed that we were on final approach for a considerable length of time. The A-7D had an antiskid system that was capable of a "brakes on" landing. The requirement for this capability seems to be related to carrier operations and is consistent with the naval origin of the A-7. This was discussed before the flight, and it was agreed that my last landing would be "brakes on."

I approached this unique ground-contact method with apprehension. Only 2,800 feet of concrete were traversed between touchdown and stop, but with no blown tires, no overheated brakes, and 4,000 pounds of fuel remaining. The only drawback the A-7D demonstrated in the landing pattern was its relatively low crosswind tolerance. Twenty knots direct crosswind was the limit, and at that velocity it was an exciting affair to keep that narrow gear going straight down the runway.

Over the next four years, my impressions of the "7" became more defined. Historically, it has been a fine aircraft that provided significant technological and operational breakthroughs like the head-up display (HUD), Doppler-bounded inertial platform, digital nav weapons computer, projected map dis-

---

Opposite page: Three A-7Ds over the Arizona desert.

play system (PMDS), and turbofan fuel specifics. Each of these items is either a first or a near-first in the fighter field. The HUD provided A-7 pilots with every visual item needed to fly and fight without looking in the cockpit. Watching through the front window as the runway materializes out of the murk on an instrument approach has to be done to be appreciated. In the attack mode, dive angle, airspeed, altitude, drift, and aiming reticle/target relationship were all available "in the window." Doppler-damped inertial platform eliminated the requirement for long ground runs to align inertial platforms. The F-4 series aircraft required either a 13-minute ground run in the chocks before taxiing or a similar ground alignment period with external electrical source before starting to complete the alignment of the inertial platform. This was always an operational impediment and used much fuel. The A-7D could taxi with a partial alignment $2\,^1/_2$ minutes after start and complete the fine alignment in the air. The digital computer successfully tied all of the A-7D avionic subsystems together and, coupled with the HUD, produced a combat dive-bombing CEP (circle of error probability) of approximately 60 feet regardless of aircrew experience. The PMDS provided a very reliable pictorial display of actual present position on two different map scales.

The low fuel specifics of the TF-41-A-1 engine greatly expanded the unfueled radius of our fighter forces. For example, the plane was capable of carrying 12 MK-82 500-pound bombs at 430 KTAS at 33,000 feet while burning only 3,350 pounds/hour. On one well-documented test mission we flew two A-7Ds configured with 4 MK-84 2,000-pound bombs and 1,032 rounds of 20 mm ammunition 440 N.M. to Wendover Range, Utah, and returned to Luke Air Force Base without external tanks or air-to-air refueling. The last 60 miles to the target and the first 60 miles outbound were "on the deck" at full power. Seven attack passes were made in the target area. Two years later, we made a few more 440 N.M. attack missions; the only change was that Korat substituted for Luke and Hanoi replaced Wendover. These features summarize the strong points of the bird.

In all candor, it must be mentioned that the takeoff performance at combat weights and warm temperatures made F-84 drivers look down on us, and that the top speed left something to be desired. In tropical climates, a "clean" bird would do well to indicate 530 knots at low altitude, and any bomb load at all, especially on multiple ejector racks, would make 450 a mighty ambitious goal. Although the redline speed was 645 knots, I don't recall ever coming anywhere near the figure. One fellow was heard to relate, "It's not very fast, but it sure is slow!"

The combat record of the A-7D, by any standard, has to be one of the success stories of the Vietnam era. It entered the theater in October 1972 and

Opposite page: Inspecting an A-7D.

was assigned every fighter mission except air-to-air. It was flown in South Vietnam, Cambodia, Laos, and North Vietnam on close air support, search-and-rescue, armed reconnaissance, helicopter escort, and interdiction missions. In late November 1972, a young lieutenant in my flight, Mike Shira, flew a helicopter escort mission on a successful rescue attempt near Than Hoa in North Vietnam. On that particular flight, he was airborne for 10 hours and 40 minutes, air refueled four times, and was in the target area for over 8 hours below 6,500 feet. During operations in the Hanoi area on 28 December 1972, nine of us escorted two helicopters to a survivor 13 miles from the center of the city. We operated over 1.5 hours at low altitude without tanker, Mig Cap, or anti-SAM support in a vain attempt to save a downed F-111 pilot. Although we were engaged by SAMs and AAA, we suffered no losses and were only forced to withdraw when the survivor's ground position became untenable due to enemy search parties. As of June 1973, I was not aware of any A-7D loss definitely shown to be the result of hostile fire. During Linebacker II, in December 1972, the A-7D dropped more ordnance in the Hanoi area than any other aircraft except the B-52. In executing these missions, it applied far more ordnance per sortie, required less air refueling support per flying hour, achieved the most accurate jet dive-bombing CEP, and sustained the lowest loss rate of any United States fighter employed in Indo-China. In this, the ultimate test, it served our country well, and for this reason alone it must be judged a success.

I climbed down the left side for the last time on 11 June 1973. In the time I have had since then to reflect on the subject, I have become convinced that the A-7D deserved more recognition than it received—especially for extending the frontiers in the field of technical avionic excellence.

Maj. John C. Morrissey accumulated over 3,300 hours in single-seat fighters from 1962 until 1973. He was reassigned to the Army Command and General Staff College in 1973 where he was Senior Air Force Representative.

F-89 Scorpion

Wayne C. Gatlin

The best way I can describe seven years of flying the F-89 Scorpion would be to say that what she lacked in beauty, she more than made up for in reliability and mission capability. My first airborne encounter with the F-89 came in May 1955 at the dedication of the Richard I. Bong Memorial at Poplar, Wisconsin. Our part of the flyby was to form the horizontal portion of a cross in four F-94Bs, while the vertical portion of the cross was formed by five USAF F-89Ds. This cross was led over the memorial site by a civilian P-38. I remember my amazement while flying line-abreast off the huge rocket pod-tip tank of an F-89; the air was a bit rough, and the sight of that big black tank bouncing up and down was mighty impressive.

The first production model was flown in 1950. The early models were equipped with six 20 mm cannon, and pilots who flew them then were able to rack up some very fine air-to-air gunnery scores. The F-89 saw many weapons configurations until it arrived as a J model. Gone were the cannon, replaced by a 250-gallon nose tank, and rockets in the tips were replaced by 600-gallon fuel tanks. The F-89H was the first fighter to see armed service with the Falcon missile, and the F-89J (our model) had the distinction of being the first U.S. fighter to carry air-to-air nuclear armament. It was first to fire the weapon in operation "Plumb Bomb" at the Proving Ground, Yucca Flats, Nevada. We had the F-89 over seven years, finally ferrying part of our fleet to the storage depot at Tucson and the rest to the Aberdeen Proving Grounds, Maryland, where they were to become cannon fodder for weapons evaluations.

The F-89J carried 2,365 gallons of fuel (15,372.5 pounds), which gave it tremendous range. During exercises we were able to go far north into Canada

---

Opposite page: The F-89.

373

on Combat Air Patrol and remain on station for extended periods of time. This gave the SAGE (Semi-Automatic Ground Environment) staff a great advantage in air battle planning and execution. Prior to the F-89 we were able to do all of our weapons training right at home station; we had an air-to-air range out over Lake Superior that had been completely adequate for the .50-caliber guns of the F-51 Mustang and the F-94B Starfire and the 2.57 folding fin aerial rockets of the F-94C. The F-89J with its nuclear-tipped missile "Genie" required a much larger range, and we had to deploy to Tyndall Air Force Base, Florida, to fire the training version of the "Genie." My reaction the first time I fired the weapon was that it sounded like a freight train roaring by, and I was surprised at the intense contrail that it left. Tactics dictated an immediate breakaway, but most pilots were prone to hold off for a few seconds to watch the con and the spotting charge burst out near the target.

With a wing span of 59 feet 8 inches, length of 53 feet 10 inches, and height of 17 feet 6 inches, the F-89 covered quite a bit of ramp. It grossed out at almost 45,000 pounds. Power was provided by two Allison J35s rated at 7,400 pounds of thrust each with afterburner. When you initiated the F-89 afterburner there was no big kick in the seat of the pants as with most afterburners; they sort of went "poof," and you could sense slight acceleration. One radar observer described it as "sort of like a barge leaving the dock" when the afterburners were lit.

The F-89 needed no ladder to the cockpits, which were a long way off the ground; kick steps and handgrips were provided to mount the steed. The only trick was to remember to start the climb with the right foot; otherwise you wound up several feet in the air dangling your left foot in space, unable to step onto the wing because your right foot was your only means of support. The first time I climbed into the cockpit, I was delighted with the roominess—not since the P-47 "Jug" had I seen that much elbow room. The fuel control panel quickly drew my attention, for it looked extremely complicated with a myriad of lights and switches; it turned out to be a pretty simple system to operate, with the capability to balance fuel, to cross-feed to one engine, and to dump the fuel from the tip tanks.

Of all the jets I've flown, the F-89 had the simplest starting system. We started the left engine first by just hitting the starter switch momentarily, checked for a rise in oil pressure, and then moved the throttle to "idle" when the engine reached 7.5 percent rpm. The starter disconnected at about 26 percent rpm, and the engine stabilized at about 50 percent rpm. Right-engine start was the same as for the left.

Directional control during taxiing was maintained with a steerable nosewheel. Pre-takeoff check consisted of placing throttles full open and checking

Opposite page: Scorpions in flight over Alaska.

exhaust gas temperatures and rpm. We then lifted the left afterburner finger switch and checked for thrust surge; next the right afterburner; then the check for fuel siphoning, the brake release, and the start of the takeoff roll. Directional control was maintained with the steerable nosewheel until the rudder became effective at about 70 knots indicated airspeed (IAS). We kept the nosewheel on the ground until we reached our predetermined nosewheel liftoff speed (120–138 knots IAS, depending on gross weight); then we eased back on the stick, allowing the aircraft to fly off the ground at its applicable airspeed 124–143 knots IAS).

Gear up when definitely airborne, flaps up at 160 knots IAS minimum, and gear and doors indicating up and locked. We then accelerated to best climb speed. For a max power (afterburner) climb we started out at Mach .69 at sea level, gradually increasing Mach to .79 at best cruise altitude—normally 30,000 feet. We usually climbed out at military power (100 percent rpm and non-afterburner) to conserve fuel, starting out at Mach .48 (315 knots IAS at sea level) and increasing to Mach .66 at 30,000 feet. Takeoff in the F-89 was not one of its finer points. The takeoff roll in summer got especially long, and with a high field elevation such as at Denver, Colorado, you had a real thrill in store. A zero wind takeoff from Denver on a 70-degree day took a good 9,000 feet of runway. The aircraft would barely stagger into the air, the ground seemed to refuse to release the airplane.

The climb to cruise was long and tortuous—almost 30 minutes to 30,000 feet—and once we reached cruise altitude we had to "hump out" or never make our destination. This consisted of climbing a few hundred feet above level-out altitude, keeping power up, and then diving down to altitude, keeping military power until we got indicated cruise airspeed. Then and only then could we reduce power for normal cruise, which was about 90 percent rpm. A good rule of thumb for cruising the F-89 was 4,000 pounds of fuel per hour to get a 400-knot true airspeed. This was 2,000 pounds per hour per engine, and we would only have to add or subtract the winds-aloft effect to get our ground speed. We used 1,000 nautical miles as a good round number for a no-wind, no-alternate-required, cross-country planning factor.

Once airborne, the F-89 proved to be a fine aircraft to fly. One of my first desires was to see how that much mass would handle aerobatically. Much to my delight it was smooth and fully aerobatic, though a bit heavy on the over-the-top maneuvers. In the traffic pattern it could really bend around with those big wings, and the actual landing was a "piece of cake." All flight controls were 100 percent hydraulically actuated. A sideslip stability augmentor provided good dampening of the high-speed Dutch roll, assisted in making coordinated turns, and helped provide a stable firing platform.

Opposite page: Another view of the F-89.

The stall in the airplane was a mild pitch-down, with drop-off usually to the left. Recovery from stalls was made by lowering the nose slightly and adding power. Intentional spins were prohibited; however, the air plane would not spin inadvertently and had no dangerous spin characteristics. Conventional spin recovery techniques were effective.

One of the finest features of the airplane was the split-aileron speed brakes. We could make letdowns up to 30,000 feet per minute without exceeding 350 knots IAS. The brakes were especially effective for controlling airspeed and altitude during approaches and reduced ground roll appreciably when moved to full open *after* touchdown.

We normally flew a standard 360-degree overhead pattern. Entry to initial approach was at 275 knots and 85 percent rpm. At the break we opened the speed brakes and decelerated to 195 knots, closed the speed brakes, put gear down and flaps to takeoff position, and turned onto final approach at 170 knots. Full flaps on final, maintaining 85 percent rpm until landing was assured. Speed brakes had to be used with caution on final to prevent too rapid deceleration and stalling out. Final approach was 132–157 knots IAS depending on gross weight. Throttle to idle when landing was assured, and speed brakes open after touchdown. Main wheels touched at about 116 knots, and nosewheel down before reaching 111 knots. It was a very nice aircraft to land.

We all swore that Northrop must have subcontracted for the F-89 wheels to a farm implement manufacturer, for they looked as though they had just come off a tractor on the north forty. The tires were imbedded with short steel wires that gave the aircraft very good traction on snow and ice. The gear doors were strong and durable—some said they came off the side of a battleship. I know of two instances where the aircraft touched down on the runway with one main gear retracted but the gear door open, and the aircraft was undamaged except for the grinding off of some of the metal on the gear door; in both instances, the door alone had supported the weight of the aircraft.

We lost one F-89 in seven and a half years of flying in one of the most severe weather areas in the United States. The lone accident was caused by fire in both engines, and the pilot (alone on the flight) ejected successfully, although he suffered hand burns from having to reach for the ejection handles with fire coming through the cockpit floor by the handles.

I purposely haven't said much about the fire-control system for lack of space; however, the F-89 with a good aircrew team of pilot and radar observer was a match for any target that could be put up against it. The fact that it had no infrared heat-seeking weapons reduced its capability against low-altitude targets, and its overall lack of a high-speed dash capability hurt if the target

Opposite page: Top view of the F-89.

ever got past the F-89. But more often than not the old bird got everything head on and was perhaps the best all-weather interceptor we had at the time. The twin-engine concept more than paid for itself over the years, for we had a number of aircraft return on one engine. In mid-January 300 miles north of Duluth, Minnesota, one appreciated that capability.

In our eagerness to get operationally ready in the F-89, we jumped at every chance to get a sortie that filled one of the requirements. It so happened that my first night intercept mission was between layers of clouds on a black, moonless night. The intercept phase went fine, but the eventual formation join-up and penetration were hairy; the aircraft's external lighting was not conducive to formation flying, and the vertigo I suffered during the ensuing recovery was monumental!

My first hassle with the F-102 proved to be delightful, for the Deuce jockey fought my kind of dogfight and elected to turn (and the Deuce will turn, as I learned in over four years of flying it after the F-89). I got on his tail without effort and stayed there with ease. Of course he could have left me at any time had he plugged in his burner, but apparently he was low on fuel and just sort of slunk away with his tail hook behind him.

Yes, what the Scorpion lacked in beauty, she more than made up for in reliability. Like the B-36 she never fired a shot in anger, but she took part in the defense of the United States and more than adequately provided her share of deterrence against any possible aggressor.

Col. Wayne C. Gatlin, a World War II veteran, is commander of the 148th Fighter Group, Minnesota Air National Guard, stationed in Duluth. He has logged nearly 6,000 flying hours, mostly in fighters.

F-106 Delta Dart

Jack Gamble and Patrick K. Gamble

To put it simply, the F-106 Delta Dart is a honey. And I emphasize the "is" because after fifteen years in my inventory it is still a fine fighter and a joy to fly. My first association came in 1960 when I was given the opportunity to command an F-106 squadron. My first impression, formed on my first day in the squadron, is the same impression that still comes to me every time I cross the ramp to the "six" I am scheduled to fly.

When you see a "six" sitting on the flight line, you have to be impressed by its sleek beauty. It is the kind of aircraft that seems to be flying even when waiting silently on the ramp. The clean, slim, Coke-bottle fuselage is enhanced by the elegant delta wing and sturdy rakish vertical fin. These features all combine to produce a feeling in the viewer that this machine was meant to fly.

From a distance her sleekness masks her size; only when you are standing by the wing do you realize that this baby is as long as a C-47 and can gross over 40,000 pounds. But the power of her Pratt & Whitney J-75 engine augmented by an afterburner can lift her mass into the air and up to 40,000 feet and more in minutes.

The F-106 was designed as an interceptor, and the air-to-air role has been her mission ever since. Not once has she been called on to sling bombs or rockets from her wings. Instead her punch is safely stored in a missile bay and exposed only at the moment of launch. Originally she was designed to stand ready against the threat of invading bombers. Today that role has been expanded to include air-to-air combat against other fighters. Her inherent good design, improved by air-to-air refueling and the capability to carry the

---

Opposite page: The F-106.

20 mm Gatling gun, make her a worthy air-to-air opponent even now in her venerable years.

When the F-106 came into the inventory it boasted several innovations. Although it bore a family resemblance to the F-102, it was a new aircraft with more sophisticated systems. The area rule fuselage and vertical tape flight instruments were two of the more noticeable. The MA-1 weapon control system is the electronic heart of the airplane, providing digital computer displays to the pilot which solve the intercept or navigation problem related to the tactical mission. Part of this system is contained in the tactical situation display—a rather large circular map located forward of the control stick between the pilot's knees; by using various TACAN station selections, it shows in map form the area surrounding the station. An interceptor bug on the face of the display continuously locates the aircraft visually in relation to its position over the ground. A target bug is also available to assist in displaying the intercept problem to the pilot in the tactical mode or for other functions in the navigational mode. Other features include automatic control of the aircraft via ground-air data link, automatic navigation, and coupled ILS approach. Many other sophisticated features make it a complex aircraft; the pilot must have a thorough knowledge of all of its systems if he is to stay abreast of all the information available to him and fly the airplane to the extent of its capability.

Cockpit entry is conventional, making use of a special ladder which hooks over the cockpit rail. The clamshell, clear-vision canopy is well out of the way in its full open position. The pilot places his back-type parachute in the cockpit first and connects it to the seat survival kit. Next he connects the parachute firing lanyard to its receptacle on the ejection seat, completing an essential step in the sequenced, one-motion ejection system. Once he stows his other gear it is an easy step over the rail, making sure as his feet ease down into the rudder alleys that a careless toe does not come into contact with the secondary canopy jettison lever located on the lower left forward part of the seat. Out of respect for this particular lever, a "six" pilot never puts anything in his lower left flying suit pocket and always keeps the zipper zipped.

After donning the chute and fastening seat belt and shoulder harness, the pilot has completed the links that provide a rapid and effective ejection system. The one-motion system is started with the pilot raising either hand grip. The canopy leaves the aircraft, and seat ejection follows. Seat-man separation occurs, then forced parachute deployment and survival kit deployment. The system is designed to work from zero feet-zero speed up to 450 knots. Certain combinations of critical attitudes and sink rates introduce limitations, but generally the system is highly effective.

Opposite page: F-106s in formation.

Getting ready to start the engine involves a complete cockpit check to make sure that every switch and lever is properly positioned and every instrument is properly set or giving the right indication. Prior to cockpit entry, the pilot and his crew chief have already completed a walk-around inspection of the aircraft to insure that pressure gauges and fluid levels are in order, leaks have not developed, ground safety pins are pulled, and the aircraft by tacit agreement between the two is ready to fly. When the cockpit check is complete and the pilot is ready to go, he watches for the crew chief to signal that the aircraft is clear and he then is ready for the start.

By depressing the start button on the throttle and manipulating the throttle, the combustion starter is activated, with engine light off taking place a few seconds later. The start is normally assisted by an air cart and electrical power cart, although the airplane can start on its own stored high-pressure air and the aircraft battery. Once the start is complete, aircraft power is turned on and another cockpit check brings all systems on the line. Instruments such as the altimeter and engine pressure ratio gauge are set, and you are ready to taxi.

Up to this point you have been busy making sure that everything has been done properly. As you taxi you have a second to appreciate the power you hold in your left hand and the responsiveness of this beautiful machine, even on the ground. Nosewheel steering is available at the touch of a button on the stick. After engagement, control of the nosewheel is obtained by pressure on the left or right rudder pedal. Once rolling, the "six" is inclined to keep going as if anxious to get airborne; as with a spirited horse that needs a tight rein, you have to hold it in check by gentle use of the brakes.

Additional checks completed while taxiing include such things as the radar and the ground-air data link. Final checks before lining up for takeoff include canopy locked, pressurization on, fuel switches on, ejection seat safety pin out, and no warning light on in the cockpit. With clearance from the tower and the airplane lined up on the runway, the throttle is advanced all the way. The primary gauge at this moment is the engine pressure ratio gauge, which indicates whether engine thrust on the ground is suitable for takeoff. One final check that all systems are go, and brakes are released. Immediately the 16,000 pounds of thrust push you back in the seat as the "six" accelerates down the runway. A quick look at the instrument panel tells you all is O.K., and the throttle is moved outboard to light the afterburner. The bang as the burner lights and another push in the back tell you that the additional 8,000 pounds of thrust have taken hold and you are being propelled down the runway at an ever-increasing pace. Nosewheel liftoff speed of about 130 knots is soon reached, and back pressure on the stick smoothly lifts the nose to takeoff attitude. Proper angles of attack are important at this point; either too high or too low will increase the ground roll. Putting the nose on the horizon or 10 degrees up on the attitude indicator allows the aircraft to fly at the best ground roll for the field elevation and surface temperature. Once safely airborne the landing gear must be retracted immediately since the gear-down speed can be exceeded very easily.

The airplane flies in a most conventional fashion despite its delta wing and lack of conventional empennage. It is completely responsive to the controls, and a light touch with the stick is the name of the game. Inattention or ham-handedness can result in being a thousand feet higher than you want or over on your back. When flown within its envelope the "six" has no bad habits. However, like most high-performance aircraft, if you venture outside the envelope, you do so at your own risk. The Mach 2 speed capabilities of the aircraft give it a wide range of options in its combat role, and it is a potent adversary against targets well above 50,000 feet.

With its two 360-gallon external supersonic fuel tanks, the F-106 has a most comfortable range and endurance compared with other fighters of its vintage. When afterburner is used, fuel consumption goes up and range and endurance correspondingly decrease. But all things being equal, it is no problem for the "six" to leave a West Coast base and cross the continent with only one refueling stop. If air refueling is used in a deployment, spanning an ocean becomes quite practical.

Landing an aircraft has always been the most challenging phase of flight to me, and landing the F-106 is no exception. The handling characteristics of this aircraft at pattern speeds and altitudes are excellent. The landing approach can be made from a visual overhead pattern or by use of ground controlled approach (GCA) or instrument landing system (ILS) approach. The landing gear is lowered at 250 knots and checked down by three green lights indicating each wheel. Flaps do not come into play (the "six" is not so equipped), but speed brakes are opened as the descent is started on final if under GCA or ILS. Approach speed varies with the gross weight of the aircraft as affected by remaining fuel and armament on board. Using 180 knots as a good average approach speed, altitude is held at 1,500 feet AGL (above ground level) as you approach the GCA glide path. As speed bleeds off, the delta wing configuration causes the angle of attack to increase continually. Since this subtle change is not particularly discernible unless you watch the attitude indicator and altimeter, it is easy to lose altitude gradually because outside references incline you to undercompensate for the amount of nose-up required to maintain level flight. When the glide slope is reached and the controller tells you to begin your descent, you open the speed brakes, reduce power, and establish your rate of descent. Airspeed to the knot is displayed on

the vertical tape airspeed indicator, which can be cross-checked against the angle of attack tape readout. Airspeed and rate of descent are essentially controlled by power adjustments.

Approaching the end of the runway at 180 knots is a thrill to say the least, and at that speed the margin for error is minimal. Back pressure on the stick is applied and power smoothly reduced as the touchdown is approached. The main gear tires gently kiss the runway as the power hits idle. The drag chute handle is pulled, and a few seconds later a definite tug is felt and deceleration increases. At 90-100 knots the nosewheel is lowered gently to the runway by easing the back pressure on the stick, and the rollout is under way. Nosewheel steering is engaged, and gentle braking slows the aircraft down for the turnoff at the runway end. Dropping the drag chute, cleaning up the cockpit, and a careful taxi back to the ramp completes the mission. At this point any F-106 pilot has a deep sense of satisfaction.

I have flown about 400 hours in this airplane, and if I had to pick a favorite among all the fighters I have flown, the "six" would be it. It is a complex and challenging airplane to fly, but it is honest. I have enjoyed and appreciated each moment I have flown it and look forward to many more hours of association with this fine aircraft.

Maj. Gen. Jack Gamble, commander of the 25th North American Air Defense Command (NORAD) Region, flies with the 318th Fighter Interceptor Squadron at McCord Air Force Base, Washington, as a combat-ready pilot in the F-106.

On Armed Forces Day in 1961 I stood beside the runway mobile unit and watched a "fourship" of F-106s prepare to take off for their flyby. The noise was deafening, and sooty black smoke billowed out behind the aircraft as the pilots ran the engines up. I could see the element leads clearly as they nodded their heads to signal brake release, and then as the afterburners lit on those big J-75s I knew I wanted to be an Air Force fighter pilot. More than that, I wanted someday to fly that very airplane—the F-106. It was quite a few years from that day as a high school sophomore until November 1970 at Tyndall Air Force Base, Florida, when I was once again listening to an F-106 engine run up. But this time I was in the airplane and preparing to fly it for the first time. Now, three years later, I still get the same thrill listening to that engine and flying what I consider to be one of the finest true fighter aircraft in the world.

The technology behind the F-106 was pushing the state of the art in the mid-fifties, and the aircraft was the first Mach 2 production fighter. Its computerized fire control system was a revolution in avionics. Designed as an interceptor against large bomber-type targets, its speed, maneuverability, armament, and the later addition of external fuel tanks for long range were

---

Opposite page: An F-106 in flight.

the fulfillment of the very same requirements that a successful interceptor needs today. Despite the seventeen years since the first models rolled off the assembly lines, the F-106 remains our first line of defense against an aircraft threat to the North American continent.

Many modifications have enhanced the airplane's capabilities. Originally conceived as a point-defense aircraft that would operate out of only one base for its entire life span, the "six" has been retrofitted with such items as an air refueling system, solid-state avionics components, and a clear-topped canopy (the old canopy had an eight-inch-wide steel bar running longitudinally through the apex) and soon will be modified for quick installation of the M-61 Gatling gun and a fantastic new gunsight. The designed 3,000-hour lifespan of the airframe has been more than doubled through a structural integrity evaluation. If future modification proposals are approved, the airplane will virtually have a new lease on life. It currently carries a worldwide deployment capability.

Approaching an F-106 on the ground you can't help but admire the natural beauty of the airframe. The long needle nose is angled slightly downward since the airplane sits a little "downhill." It's not a small airplane (combat weight is 42,000 pounds), and the single cockpit sits high off the ground. But the 70-foot fuselage is gracefully curved by the Coke-bottle waist or "area rule" design—one of the key reasons the airplane is able to go Mach 2. Like its predecessor the F-102, the "six" has delta wings with elevons. These control surfaces replace the aileron/horizontal stabilizer package and are on the trailing edge of the wing acting as elevators and ailerons simultaneously. Lack of flaps or boundary-layer devices dictates a higher final approach airspeed than most fighter aircraft, normally in the 180-knot range. The Delta Dart is powered by the J-75 axial flow engine with an afterburner thrust rated at 24,500 pounds and a military thrust of 16,100 pounds. One of the finest features of the F-106 is this outstanding Pratt & Whitney engine. Being a single-engine fighter, the reliability of that engine is most important, especially on missions several hundred miles out over water or up into the Canadian wilderness. Even with occasional problems of a serious nature, the engine continues to get the pilot home. I once had a main bearing failure 200 miles from the nearest suitable landing field. Despite severe vibrations and noise so loud I couldn't hear my UHF radio turned full up, I flew the 200 miles and landed safely. Upon landing I also had a primary hydraulic failure which was attributed to the hydraulic reservoir cracking from the severity of the engine vibrations. The ruggedness in this incredibly reliable engine is added insurance appreciated by the pilots.

The pilot preflight is really simple for so complex an aircraft. During the walk-around the pilot or crew chief pulls the gear pins and the safety pins for

---

Opposite page: Front view of the F-106.

the external tanks and the tail hook. The pilot checks the engine access panels to make sure they are closed and examines fittings and lines for general condition and leaks. Certain hydraulic reservoir and accumulator gauges as well as the missile bay and the system air pressure are given cursory examination, but these are quick looks and not time-consuming. Although the pilot's checklist itemizes the preflight sequence, each pilot develops a habitual pattern that includes items not listed in the checklist. This results in the pilot preflight becoming a *very personal* action.

Climbing into the cockpit you are aware of the comfortable surroundings and ample leg room. The radarscope sits directly in front of your face. The right and left consoles are crowded with switches and dials, but the cockpit layout is convenient. When strapped in you are snug but not crowded. Engine start requires pressing the ignition button atop the throttle and listening for the familiar pop of the combustion starter; then into idle at 10 percent and disconnect the ground power. Once the generators are switched on the line and the radar is turned on, you are ready to taxi. There is very little to turn on after engine start in an F-106, and this makes a scramble easy. I have seen a flight of two break ground 2 minutes and 43 seconds after a no-notice active air scramble. Nosewheel steering is activated by a button on the stick, and the airplane taxis easily. ADC (Air Defense Command) squadrons perform "last-chance" just prior to takeoff. This last-minute once-over by a ground crew has spotted many aircraft malfunctions that have manifested themselves between the parking area and the runway—mainly in the area of leaks or unsecured panels that would probably come off in flight. I have personally seen a pair of chocks in the gear doors, a small nosewheel-well fire, cut tires, and large air system leaks caught in last-chance. A thumbs-down by the last-chance crew is a mandatory no-go; the pilot must go back to the parking area for a fix or, if that's not possible, a ground abort. In three plus years of flying the F-106 I have been turned back three times; twice I had to abort the mission. It goes without saying that if the additional quality control provided by last-chance has saved even one aircraft, it has been worth the time and effort.

On engine run-up you check the hydraulic pressures, oil pressure, exhaust gas temperature, fuel flow, and EPR (a measure of engine efficiency dependent on temperature) . You also set the attitude indicator to show 5° nose low, and as you rotate for takeoff you raise the nose to indicate 10 degrees nose high. This compensates for gyro acceleration error in the indicator and prevents overrotation. The pilots soon develop outside references for takeoff, such as the "put-the-pilot-boom-on-the-horizon" method. Of course these vary according to the individual's height. The same explanation can be made for landing attitudes. (Check the skid plate under the tail of almost any F-106 and

---

Opposite page: Another view of the F-106.

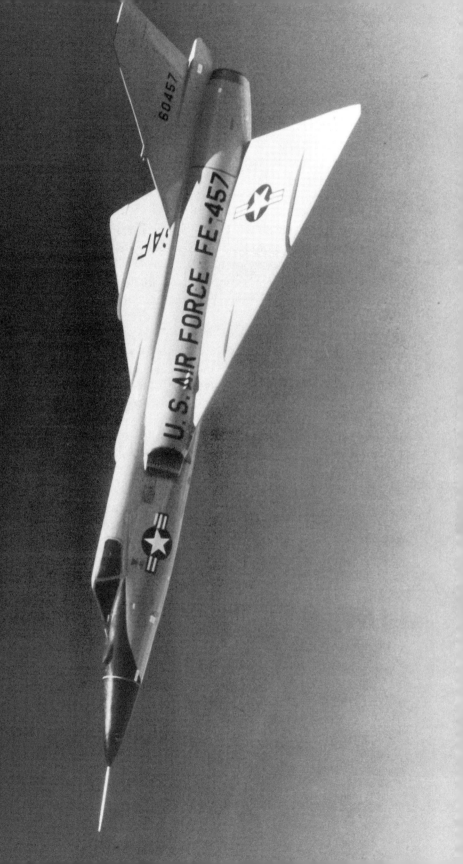

you will see the system isn't foolproof!) One last flight control check and then you release brakes. After insuring that you are rolling straight, you pull firmly on the throttle outboard of the full forward position to light the afterburner (AB). With pressure applied the throttle clicks out to the AB range. It can then be smoothly moved back and forth from min to max AB just as if you were moving it normally; AB is not forward of the military position but alongside of it. Full mil is as far forward as full AB, and min AB is about equal to the 92 percent (normal thrust) position.

There is a very definite kick in the pants, especially noticeable in the winter or in an airplane without the two 360-gallon external tanks, when that AB cuts in. Airspeed increases rapidly to the rotation speed of 120–135 KIAS (knots indicated airspeed). At this speed you pull back smoothly on the stick until the nose is raised 15 degrees. Holding this altitude the airplane becomes airborne at about 184 KIAS. The F-106B, the tandem two-seater, flies at slightly higher airspeeds. Takeoff distance is normally between 3,000 and 4,000 feet, depending on temperature and winds. At 250 KIAS the afterburner is terminated and the airplane is accelerated to 400 knots and climbs at this airspeed until Mach .93. This Mach is held for all further climbs and cruising. If the mission is to be a practice intercept sortie, the armament safety check is completed and the IR (infrared) system is initially tuned. The IR seeker head is recessed in the top of the aircraft nose and is raised at the flick of a switch. This system allows the pilot to acquire a target by homing on the radiation of its engine exhaust and is a great aid when the radar is malfunctioning or during an attempt to track a heavy ECM (electronic countermeasure) emitter.

Soon after takeoff the pilot selects the data link receiver to begin receiving the coded UHF messages that inform the aircraft computer what type of intercept and target information is available. This information is displayed to the pilot on his instruments; the mission is not dependent on voice communications with GCI (ground control indicator) controller.

Once the target appears on the radarscope as a small blip, the pilot must use the left half of the Y-shaped stick and lock onto the target by moving the stick to superimpose a "gate" on the radarscope over the target. Once this is done, the fire control system automatically displays steering information and overtake rate.

The pilot has a choice of weapons—two radar-guided AIM-4F Superfalcons, two AIM-4GIR Superfalcons, or the AIR-2A Genie nuclear-capable rocket (sometimes called the blivet or the bean). This mixed load makes the F-106 a multishot weapon and adds versatility to combat not only against high-speed, high-altitude targets but also against high-speed, low-altitude targets.

Opposite page: An F-102—predecessor of the F-106—in flight near Saigon.

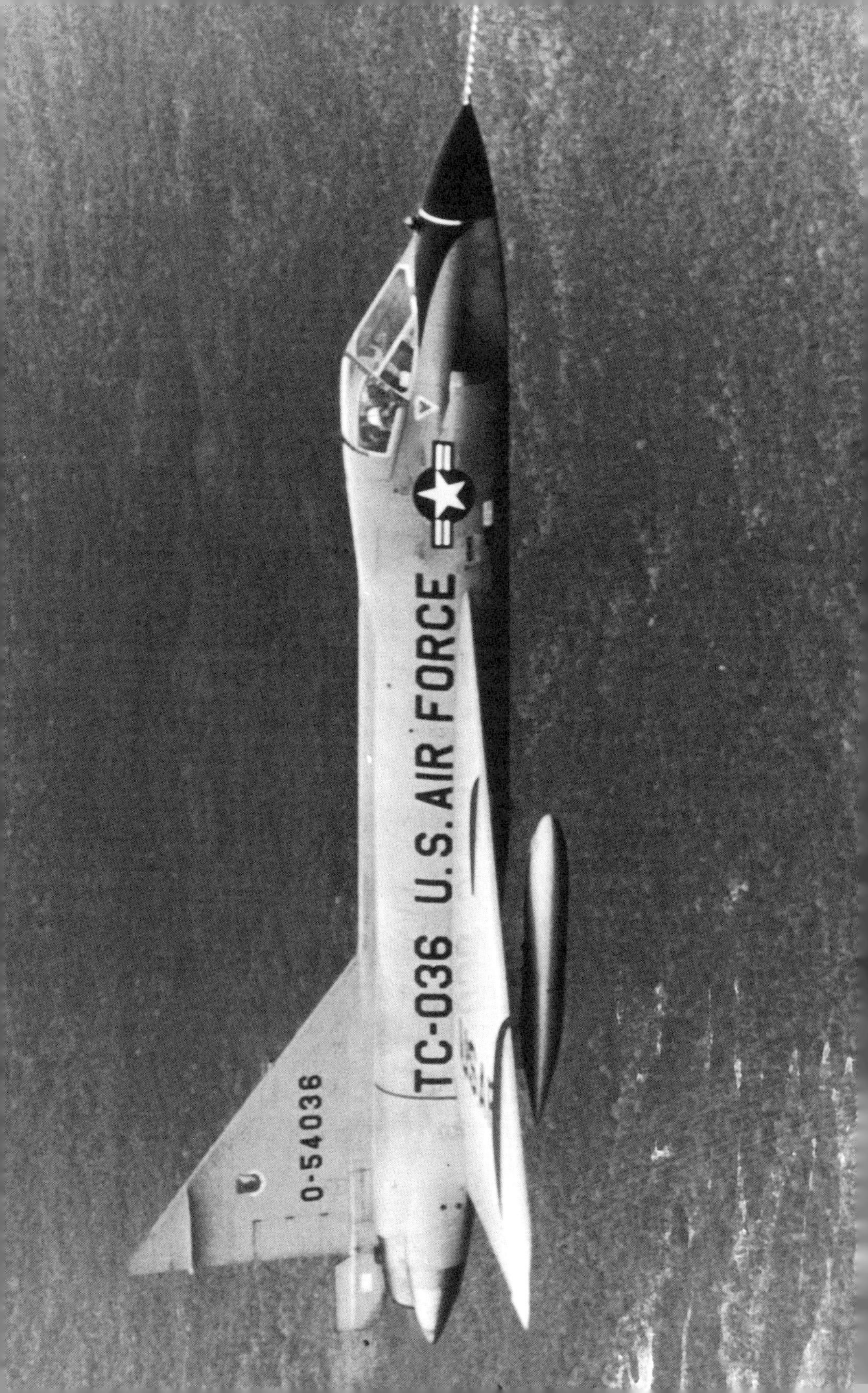
TC-036 U.S. AIR FORCE
0-54036

With the addition of the M-61 20 mm gun, the F-106 will have the close-in kill capability it currently lacks. All weapons are carried internally and cause no performance restrictions.

The average training mission flown by squadron pilots consists of a profile of intercepts and tactics. A formation takeoff and cruise to the intercept area is followed by low-altitude intercepts against a T-33. The venerable T-bird is equipped with chaff and an ECM pod. By varying his use of these countermeasures and varying his heading and airspeed, the target pilot attempts to cause the interceptor to miss its attack. If it is missed because of a mistake made by the interceptor pilot, it is called a "PE" or pilot error. If the attack is successful, the pilot calls "MA"—mission accomplished. Following several low-altitude passes the fighters move to the medium-altitude area where they may "bump heads" or take turns being targets themselves while the other fighters attack. A few high-altitude snap-ups complete the profile. Here the F-106 target is cruised subsonic or supersonic at 49,000 feet while the attackers combat from 34,000. The attacker must lock on, accelerate, and pull sharply up (snap-up) to fire against the high-altitude target. The maneuver is actually a simulation of the type of attack necessary to combat a bomber target in excess of 55,000 feet. Following completion of the intercepts the fighters reach "bingo fuel." This means they have to return to base because they have only a predetermined amount of fuel remaining. The formations rejoin and recover to single-ship or formation landings.

Since 1968 ADC has been training its pilots in air combat tactics (ACT). The Command-initiated idea was soon adopted by the Navy and Marines, and more recently TAC (Tactical Air Command) established a squadron of T-38s used as "aggressors" against the TAC fighter squadrons. Under the supervision and direction of the Interceptor Weapons School (IWS) at Tyndall Air Force Base, Florida, ADC conducts College Dart. This ACT program features the F-106 flying against F-4s, F-8s, and A-4s from Navy, Marine, and TAC squadrons. Pilots get a full week of advanced air-to-air training against an aircraft very different from their own. College Dart has demonstrated the fantastic air-to-air potential of the F-106. Only within the last four years has this most underrated fighter been given some of the recognition it is due. Closely approximating the MIG-21 in overall performance, the F-106 is (in 1974), in the opinion of most fighter pilots who have flown in it or against it, the best production air-to-air machine in the U.S. inventory. Its acceleration enables it to engage and disengage comfortably. The ability of the delta wing to turn at high altitude is used to great advantage. Because it is a single-seat aircraft, ADC has developed the "Six Pac" tactics group to enable the F-106 pilot to best employ the aircraft in a fighter-versus-fighter environment. The tactics

Opposite page: An F-102 in flight.

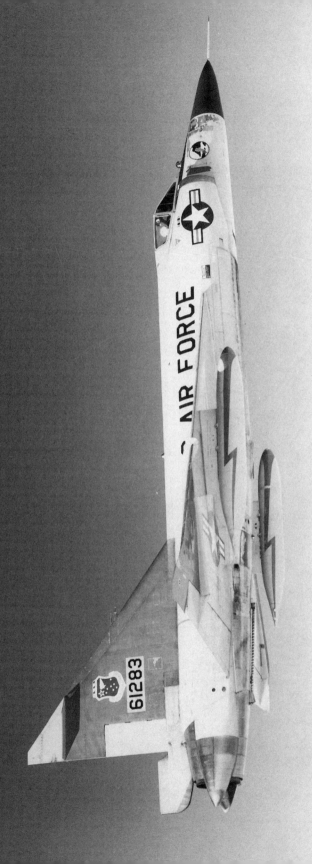

are based on an element of two aircraft both employed as shooters but maintaining close mutual support. Those familiar with the F-104 double-attack system and the Navy's loose-deuce tactics would notice many similarities in Six Pac. Obviously one week at a time does not an ace make, so the squadrons have their own ACT continuation training program. The pilots are required to fly a mandatory number of these missions each year. Because of the excellent support given by headquarters of ADC, the individual fighter squadrons are encouraged to make trips to various Naval fighter bases to participate in more dissimilar combat. The Navy squadrons also fly into the Sixes' home bases on occasion. The flying that results is aggressive, spirited, and educational. The mistakes made by both sides are lessons well learned in peace and won't be forgotten in combat.

I have yet to describe the actual flying characteristics of the airplane itself. In a word they are super. It is feather light in pitch responsiveness compared to the T-38. Without the external fuel tanks it is almost as responsive in roll as a T-38; with full external tanks the roll is slower and restricted to 100 degrees per second. The airplane has 752 KIAS "Q" limit, a Mach 2 restriction, and a skin temperature limit. It will easily go supersonic right on the deck or exceed the Mach 2 at altitude. During a recent TAC exercise two F-106s caught and successfully intercepted an F-111 going supersonic below 1,000 AGL (above ground level). Approach to a stall is very honest with light, medium, and heavy buffeting. Then lateral instability sets in causing the nose to wander in yaw. If the angle of attack is increased further beyond the critical, the adverse yaw induced by any aileron input will trigger a violent roll and pitch-up maneuver known as the post stall. The aircraft will oscillate about all three axes and if not recovered will likely enter a flat spin. Once established, the developed spin can be difficult to break. The rudder in the F-106 is extremely effective and in the high angle of attack regime is used to roll, thus avoiding the adverse yaw caused by aileron. The zero G maneuver to kill drag and prevent the stall is also effective in countering out-of-control flight. The F-106 accelerates beautifully, especially if already flying at a high indicated airspeed. By lighting the afterburner and pushing the nose over to zero G, the airspeed increases almost unbelievably. This airplane will go supersonic in a climb; it will even go super at high altitude in idle power by simply lowering the nose a few degrees. In fact if there is one complaint a "six" pilot has, it is that the airplane is difficult to slow down when you want it to.

Back in the landing pattern you fly initial at about 325 knots. The "break" is in a clean configuration rolling out on the downwind around 1,500 feet AGL, gear down, at about 240 knots. The final turn is flown at 200 knots in moderate buffet with a cross-check on the angle of attack. The pilot may opt

Opposite page: An F-102 launches a salvo of Falcon guided missiles.

to extend the speed brakes anywhere throughout the final turn or on approach. Power is gradually reduced after rolling out on final to transition from the final approach speed to the prior-to-flare speed. Then power is retarded to idle and the aircraft rate of descent is gently killed, causing airspeed to decrease another 10 knots to the touchdown speed. All three speeds are based on fuel remaining during landing. Once the wheels touch, the drag chute handle on the upper left side of the instrument panel is pulled and the drag chute deploys, causing a definite tug in the cockpit. The pilot raises the aircraft nose up to about 16° causing aerodynamic braking, being careful not to scrape the tailpipe. (That could cost him a case of beer to his crew chief.) When approaching 100 knots he lowers the nose to the runway and touches the button to engage the nosewheel steering. After turning off the active runway, he jettisons the drag chute by simply pushing the handle back in, and all the after-landing checks are then completed. The normal mission is two hours long, and unrefueled cross-countries have gone as much as three hours and fifteen minutes, covering over 1,600 N.M. Not bad for a fighter.

After 600 hours in the F-106 I still get a thrill walking up to her side. Airborne she's a thing of beauty to watch and a thrill to fly. Tactically the bulk of North American Air Defense responsibility still rests on her venerable old shoulders, and she always handles the job with style.

Capt. Patrick Gamble, the son of Major General Jack Gamble, is a squadron flight commander and instructor pilot at Grand Forks Air Force Base, North Dakota, with nearly 600 hours in the F-106.

Opposite page: An F-102 takes off in Alaska.

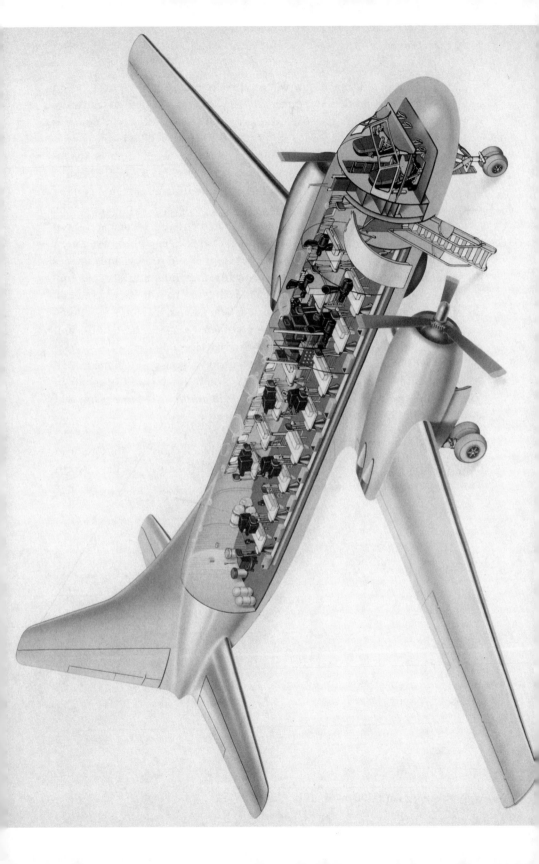

The T-29

John L. Zimmerman

After a year of pilot training I still had not reached a level of expertise that would allow anyone much confidence in my ability to land an airplane successfully. This is not to say that all my landings were disasters, accompanied by flashing red lights and red-faced runway control officers. I had never ground-looped a T-6, but scoring well on the various types of landing stages, which along with the more critical checkrides were the hurdles to be surmounted on the way to graduation, was an accomplishment that always had eluded me. And the situation did not improve with my advancement into the North American TB-25. One afternoon after landing at Vance Air Force Base in Oklahoma with another student in the right seat, I was ordered to park the aircraft as I was taxiing back around for another takeoff. Because my scheduled time for that day had not yet been completed, I did not understand what the problem might have been. As I pulled into the parking slot, the disgusted look on the crew chief's face suggested that all was not well. It turned out that there were a few bushes caught in the landing gear as a result of my landing a wee bit short of the runway.

In other aspects of flying I didn't do too badly at all; I really enjoyed the precision of instrument flying. But the admonition of Lieutenant Parker, our instructor pilot in TB-25s at Vance, when Don Yorgin (now a captain with Delta Airlines) and I departed on our first "solo" cross-country, was probably well founded: "If you get into weather, Zimmerman can fly it; but when you get near the ground, Yorgin, you land it."

It was just that I somehow never had developed that comfortable feeling of knowing where the airplane was in relation to the surface of the runway.

Opposite page: Cutaway view of a T-29C.

403

This all changed, however, when I was assigned to the Convair T-29 at Ellington Air Force Base outside of Houston, Texas, upon my graduation from basic flying school. This same aircraft, when designated as the C-131, was used for administrative flights and air evacuation, but our planes were equipped with four astrodomes along the top, a radar bubble underneath and just forward of the wing roots, and stations for about twenty navigation students. Maybe it wasn't as fancy as the commercial version of this aircraft that was being widely used in the mid-fifties on feeder routes throughout the nation, but it was the lap of luxury compared to the cramped quarters and inoperative heaters of the "Baker-two-bits."

Perhaps it was the shine on my newly minted wings, perhaps not; but my first day of transition in the co-pilot's seat bordered on the miraculous. The instructor pilot pointed out a spot on the runway where I was supposed to land and told me to drive it there. I did. And it worked. With a little practice in throttle control, I even began making smooth landings with astonishing regularity. I finally had been assigned an aircraft that was good enough to make up for the innate lack of ability that my instructor back in primary had recognized and entered in my file, ending his critique with a devastating, "but he tries hard."

The T-29 really was a fine airplane. It had to be, because I'm sure our squadron of largely young and relatively inexperienced pilots imposed a great deal of pilot error on the ship that a more temperamental craft would not have tolerated. So there were very few, even moderately serious, accidents. Mechanical failure also was rare. My only experience in two years was soon after I finally had become qualified as an aircraft commander. Immediately after entering the overcast on my takeoff climb, I lost power on the right engine. The aircraft performed sympathetically, even though fully loaded, and maintained altitude while we were vectored by Houston radar for an instrument approach and an uneventful landing.

Our particular mission at Ellington in 1956 and 1957 was to fly the students in the observers' program and their instructors on their various navigation training flights. There was a set of six or seven routes radiating out of Houston to turn-around points two or three hours away. With an aura of drama akin to "Hamburg" or "Schweinfurt" in all those airplane movies that I had devoured during the way years, the briefing officer would announce, "this evening it's Kingfisher, Oklahoma" or "Bay Minette radio beacon today, gentlemen." Usually we were cleared "on-top" between 8,000 and 10,000 feet as the engines of our A and B models lacked superchargers, even though the cabin was pressurized. This altitude usually was adequate for navigation missions like sun-line, celestial, radar, and grid; but for map-reading and multiple drift, the students had to be able to see the ground at least some of the time.

The student navigators were organized around a "lead," whose job it was to communicate with the pilot as to where we were supposed to be and what heading we were supposed to fly. One of the navigation instructors kept a plot of where we really were as a benchmark against which to evaluate the students' performances. The second navigation instructor in the crew was there to help the students. As you might expect, we were not always on course. In recognition of this reality, our flight clearance usually permitted us to maintain a position somewhere within a 50-mile wide corridor along our intended flight path. With the radio navigation aids available to the pilots, we did not have to depend on just a three-star fix or a map verification through a hole in the undercast to know exactly where we were. As we came to better understand what was going on in the back end of the aircraft, most of us became quite tactful in our hinting to the student "lead" that we were wandering pretty far from where we were legally supposed to be. And even when we received a course correction of over 90 degrees, we smiled grimly and hoped that the student would indeed learn something from the obvious disaster he was perpetrating back there.

There were missions, however, when we did not know where we were. Like when we went on our run out to 25N, 90W in the Gulf of Mexico, north of the Yucatan Peninsula for LORAN practice. Since we were usually out of VHF range after we were 100 miles or so beyond the coast, all the OMNI stations from Brownsville to Mobile were of little help, and so we were grateful for the navigators that, we hoped, did know where we were. Because LORAN reception or station availability—I never really knew which—was better on the East coast, about once a month we TDY-ed to Miami International for flights out over the Bahamas. With the tradewind cumulus, white beaches, and waters varying in color from royal blue to emerald green, these flights were the most aesthetically enjoyable of my short Air Force career. But getting in and out of Miami International was sometimes hectic, even in those days.

Our squadron was divided into two sections that alternated between flying days one week and nights the next. The first morning briefings started at 0600 with two additional sessions at one-hour intervals. Each briefing included about 10 to 15 aircraft. The evening briefings began with the first about 1930 with the two others similarly at one-hour intervals. During most of my time at Ellington, almost the entire squadron was checked out in the left seat so that Operations alternated our daily assignments between aircraft commander and flying co-pilot.

The preflight check began with an interior inspection that included checking the Form 781, not only to see if there was anything seriously wrong with the airplane but also to check that all the navigation equipment required by the students for that particular exercise was installed and working properly. If it was to be an overwater flight, it was also important to see if the 20-man life raft was properly stowed by the rear door of the aircraft. Sometimes it wasn't. Yet there was one incident that made us wonder if it really would matter if it was missing. During one of the periodic water survival demonstrations in which we participated, the raft was thrown into the swimming pool and began to inflate properly, but then slowly sank to the bottom of the pool. Needless to say, those of us witnessing that event did not have a particularly sanguine view of the probability of our survival out there in those shark-infested waters.

The exterior check of the aircraft started at the nose with the removal of the pitot tube covers and proceeded clockwise around the plane. Although there was a detailed list of items that were to be checked, and which were indeed carefully checked, it really was a matter of seeing that all the inspection plates and doors were closed and secured and that oil, gasoline, and hydraulic fluids were staying within the maze of tubes and pipes where they belonged and not trickling down the main landing gear strut or oozing out of the propeller governor. And it was always reassuring to look and see that you would still be able to get one more landing out of the tires. It all seemed quite routine until the day two of our colleagues forgot to remove the landing gear locking pins and suffered an engine failure after takeoff, plowing up a very expensive rice field a few minutes later as they could not retract the landing gear to maintain altitude. Such events did tend to remind us of the importance of what we were doing, yet all I remember now is dulling the shine on my shoes every day when the fuel strainer in each nacelle was drained in the due course of following through the checklist.

By the time the exterior check had been completed, the navigation students and their instructor had arrived. It then was usually the task of the co-pilot for the flight to brief the crew on normal flight operations and emergency procedures. Then everybody climbed on board and the entrance door was folded back into the fuselage with much wailing and thumping by the hydraulic system.

Prior to starting the engines, there was the usual constellation of switches, lights, circuit breakers, levers, and gauges to check. If someone in the ground crew had not already connected the external power, the pilot alerted the crew chief by hollering out the cockpit window. With the battery cart running, further vocal communication was out of the question, but a few appropriate gestures indicating the pilot's intent to start engines usually could get a fire guard posted.

The left engine was started first, and after the prop had turned through eight blades to insure that there was no hydraulic lock, the ignition switch was turned on, the primer activated, and usually the engine would start without torching or backfiring and frightening all the beginning navigators out of their anxious minds. Hopefully, we would be just as lucky with the right engine.

All this time, the navigation students would be going about their various preflight activities, climbing in and out of the astrodomes, lining up drift meters, digging through their satchels for Weems plotters, and crawling around trying to find where they dropped their one and only pencil. Engine start-up and pre-taxi checks were accomplished with little difficulty, but sometimes we had to wait for the students. If it was going to be an instrument departure, we had already been assigned a specific takeoff time and to miss that time slot meant being at the end of the line. Depending on the status of the weather and the takeoff interval, that could be as much as one hour later. So the pilots tended to become a little impatient with the students who for any reason were not ready to go when the aircraft was ready to taxi.

The pilot had a steering wheel by his left knee that hydraulically controlled the nosewheel, so taxiing involved no throttle control for turning; and with the reversible propellers, you could even back up.

It was necessary to taxi with the engines at just below 1,000 rpm in order to keep the generators in operation and to insure radio contact with ground control. This power setting gave a fairly brisk taxi speed, so that even though overuse of the brakes was to be avoided, it was almost necessary. Prolonged ground operation also was to be avoided to prevent spark plug fouling, but a dozen or so aircraft awaiting instrument takeoff clearance was just as much a delay then as it is now at 5:00 P.M. on a snowy Sunday evening at O'Hare. To combat the fouling accumulations in the cylinders, every ten minutes or so the aircraft was turned into the wind and each engine was run up separately to a manifold pressure equal to that of field barometric pressure for about a minute. The ease of steering allowed by the hydraulically controlled nosewheel sometimes led to complacency in this situation. The taxiways at Ellington were bordered by gravel-filled "French" drains to accommodate the runoff from the often torrential rains of the Texas Gulf coast. The steerable nosewheel gave a turning diameter of about 60 feet, which was more than adequate to pull into the wind for run-up and then turn back to proceed farther

down the taxiway as one moved up in the line of aircraft awaiting takeoff. But sometimes an aircraft pulled up too far, and rather than make the error obvious by reversing the propellers and taxiing backwards, a pilot might attempt to make a sharper turn than was actually possible. During my two years at Ellington, more than one landing gear sank into the gravel of the French drain, which required that the aircraft be shut down and towed out.

Engine run-up included the usual check of propeller speed controls, feathering mechanism, electrical system, and magnetos. Each engine was equipped with an autofeathering system that was supposed to feather the engine automatically within about three seconds of a sudden power failure during takeoff. I never had seen this actually work in an emergency, but it was carefully checked during run-up since most of us didn't trust it at all. We were quite relieved when the system was deactivated soon after each takeoff even though I never had heard of an engine being inadvertently feathered due to a malfunction. Elevator trim was then set slightly nose-up, and the flaps were set for the takeoff as computed from the weight and balance and atmospheric conditions. Or, if this had not been done, 20 degrees for the flaps seemed to work best under most conditions.

With clearance from the tower and a call over the loudspeaker to alert the students that we were taking the active runway, we were off on a flight of about five hours that would bring us right back to where we were—that is, if everything worked well and the coastal fog did not creep in earlier than forecast.

One of the tasks to be completed during preflight briefing was the determination of the two airspeeds related to takeoff: that speed at which we were committed to go and that speed at which we would become airborne at the particular weight we were carrying and under the current atmospheric conditions. Usually these two speeds were so close together that their separate consideration produced little concern. But besides backing up the throttles for the pilot, one of the co-pilot's duties during the takeoff roll was to call off these two airspeeds. Up to about 80 knots, the pilot could use the steerable nose-wheel for directional control; but at higher speeds, the rudder surface became effective. At about 10 knots below the approximately 120 knots takeoff speed, the aircraft was put in the nose-high takeoff attitude and it just flew itself off the ground.

Even with a full load, the T-29 had a high rate of climb for those of us whose only other twin-engine experience had been in the TB-25. But seldom were we able to realize this potential because of the restrictions to reach certain check points at predetermined altitudes, even under VFR conditions.

Opposite page: A C-131.

The only time we could approach a maximum performance climb was at the mid-point in the mission when we often used a chandelle to change altitudes for our return back home on the reverse heading. Of course, during our periodic check rides, the prescribed procedural turn was carefully followed.

Once the assigned mission altitude had been reached, the fuel booster pumps were turned off and the engine controls set and adjusted to maintain the desired indicated air speed. Once the aircraft was properly trimmed, the autopilot was engaged and the hardest part of the flight began. It was hard because there was so little to do. Once an hour as a precaution against fouling of the spark plugs, the engines were run at full rich and increased power for about a minute or so. This procedure created problems for the students on certain types of missions if you didn't warn them what was going to happen. For example, for exercises requiring the use of the drift meters, they apparently had such a difficult time using this equipment under the best of conditions that in their concentration they would be completely unaware of a change in airspeed while hunched over the eyepiece, particularly if their airspeed indicator was back to where it was when they returned to their work space. With an erroneous airspeed thrown into their calculations, the correct solution to their problem became even more improbable.

Major in-flight engine failures were rare, but minor emergencies like generator failure or a rough engine occasionally did result in aircraft being forced to land for repairs at bases away from home. If this happened during the week, one aircraft in the next day's mission could be scheduled to drop needed parts or even pick up the crew. One of the least desirable assignments was being scheduled for maintenance stand-by on the weekend. This meant that you were on call to fly support for stranded aircraft and crews from Friday's missions. This was before the days of "beepers" so that it required being home guarding the phone rather than spending the day at the beach.

Chronic oil leaks seemed to plague most of the aircraft we were using, but these problems often looked more serious than they really were. We carried a reserve oil tank in the aft section of the aircraft and the oil could be pumped forward to replenish the oil supplying the engines. Even though the nacelle might be heavily streaked with oil, if the rate of loss was not great enough to predict oil exhaustion before the end of the flight, it seemed most reasonable to us to complete successfully the assigned missions even though we might be receiving some worried looks from the back end.

Another moment of concern for the students occurred during takeoff on their first flight, even though they were looking forward to actually flying rather than doing another paper mission on the ground. With the increase in power at takeoff there was obvious activation of the cabin pressurization system and a decrease in cabin temperature. Given the very humid Gulf coast air, "smoke" poured from all the air vents. If, during the crew briefing, we had inadvertently forgotten to make the students aware of what would happen, some would think that this long-awaited flight would be their last.

Because of the regularity of the flight paths which we took, we all came to know limited strips of the south-central United States rather well. We also got to know the voices on the FAA radios, too, as we were always at about the same place at each reporting interval. I especially remember the feminine voice at Lake Charles who would bid each plane a pleasant "good night" as we reported in during the early morning about one hour from home on the inbound leg. Indeed, the only variation we encountered occurred during the winter when the prevailing north winds would carry the then poorly controlled pollution from the industries along the Houston ship channel directly over Ellington, producing low ceilings and poor visibility in the cool, humid winter air. Then approach-control radar would route us variously, dependent upon the prevailing traffic, usually dropping us off on final approach over the Pearland radio beacon or, if ceilings were quite low, passing us on to the GCA controller. One of the benefits of this duty was that we obtained enough real weather time to maintain a reasonable level of proficiency.

For most missions, flight procedures for the pilot were like every other aspect of the operation—quite routine. So you could pay attention to details, like making very sure that the propeller was properly, thus comfortably, synchronized so that there was no disturbing beat. But also it was necessary to learn the routine of the students. On a celestial navigation mission, this knowledge was critical. In order that the students could work in the astrodomes, there were stands that could be put in place to span the aisle under each dome and on which they stood while taking their readings on Deneb, Dube, and—with a peak earthward—Dallas. The latrine facilities were in the rear of the aircraft, and you could not make it aft very easily when the students were up in the domes. So if one had to use the facilities, you had to plan ahead. This, in turn, determined your coffee-drinking schedule: one cup after level-off at cruising altitude before the students made their first fix, another cup right before turn-around as the students were getting their logs in order after the first leg, and one last cup right before let-down as you then could probably wait until you were back on the ground.

Missions were typically terminated at a check point about 15 minutes away from the base. If time permitted, we might make a practice ILS approach to the nearby Houston airport (now Hobby Field), but usually we just made a practice GCA approach into Ellington. When I first arrived at Ellington, they were flying a combat-style 360-overhead approach for landing, but soon after the landing pattern was changed to the standard, rectangular downwind-base leg-final approach. Maybe this change was made to motivate the pilots to make more practice instrument approaches because a GCA usually got you on the ground more directly than plodding around the pattern for the active runway.

The power-off glide angle of the T-29 was quite steep, so that landings were made with the power on. Indeed, some power was maintained during the landing flare right up until touchdown. As soon as the plane was solidly on the runway, the flaps were retracted and throttles moved to the reverse thrust range for aerodynamic braking. The co-pilot held the control yoke forward to insure good nose-wheel contact, and the pilot used the steerable nose-wheel to drive the aircraft down the runway and to turn off at the first appropriate exit. While taxiing back toward the apron, you tried to remember exactly where that particular aircraft had been parked while the co-pilot tried to remember all the minor malfunctions that needed to be recorded in the Form 781. With the help of some frantic waving by the ground crew, you soon found the proper place, parked the aircraft, ran through the post-flight checklist, shut down the engines, and signed off the 781.

The T-29 did not have the glamour of a high-performance aircraft, nor were the missions that we flew spirited challenges or dramatic encounters, yet the safe and dependable characteristics of the aircraft provided the perfect vehicle for the efficient training of a large number of students in basic navigational techniques. In the score or so years since I last flew the T-29, I have talked with a surprisingly large number of people who either had flown or trained in the aircraft during their Air Force years, and all agree, with a touch of fond remembrance, that it was a good plane. Lieutenant Parker—even Zimmerman—COULD LAND IT. What better reputation could an aircraft desire?

Dr. John L. Zimmerman is an ecologist and professor of Biology at Kansas State University. He spent his entire Air Force career in the Air Training Command, beginning with the Air Force ROTC program at Michigan State University during the Korean War, a year in pilot training at Stallings Air Base in North Carolina and Vance Air Force Base in Oklahoma, and a final two years at Ellington Air Force Base in Texas, where he was a mission pilot in the T-29.

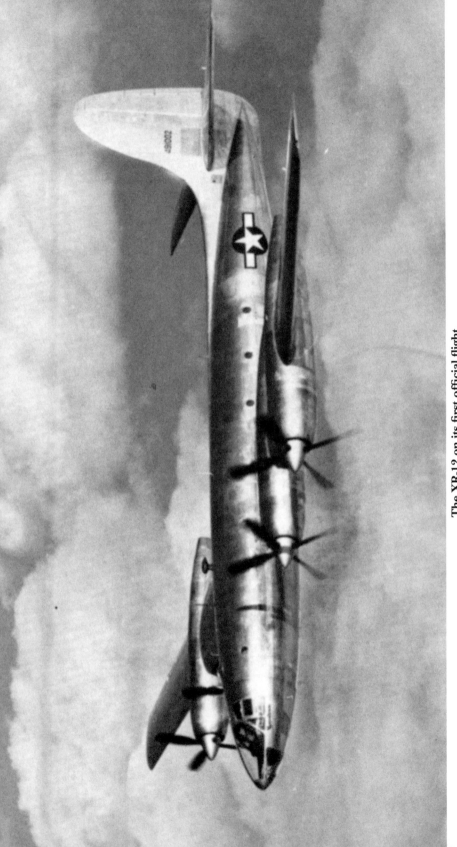

The XR-12 on its first official flight.

XR-12 Rainbow

L. L. Brabham

It was due to no lack of perfection in design but solely to the condition of the economy at the time that the Republic XR-12 was not placed in volume production and only the original order for two aircraft was completed. It is doubtful if any aircraft design has ever had such impact on the aviation community as did the Rainbow. It was the long-awaited solution to the problem facing the photoreconnaissance people and was heralded by airline officials as the ultimate answer to air transportation.

The aircraft was flown for the first time early in 1946, and I had the pleasure of demonstrating it in flight to heads of the world's leading airlines and their engineering pilots. Two of the airlines placed firm orders for the airplane and others placed options, but because of the uncertainty of postwar travel volume predictions one of the major orders was canceled, and this required termination of the other orders. The military was experiencing similar budgetary problems, and after firm orders were placed and then canceled several times the construction program came to an end, when the first airline fuselage was within one month of coming out of the jig. Just imagine, an airliner cruising at 450 mph in 1947! Probably the world's greatest expert in aerial reconnaissance and then head of the photo lab at Wright Field, General George Goddard, said when the program was terminated, "We have hung black crepe on all the doors of the photo lab."

World War II pointed up the paramount importance of aerial intelligence gathering; with the very best efforts of the photorecon units there was never enough photo coverage of potential targets and bomb damage to furnish even the minimum requirements of the commanders in the field. Up to this time the only photo aircraft were fighters or bombers that had been modified to accommodate cameras. From lessons learned the hard way, the Army Air Corps leaders laid out detailed requirements for what was to be the first photorecon aircraft embodying all the capabilities then thought to be necessary: (1) range of 4,000 statute miles; (2) cruise altitude of 40,000 feet; (3) cruise speed of 400 mph; (4) capacity for carrying a very large variety of photorecon equipment, including a 108-inch focal length camera then under development; (5) ability to process film in flight to save time after landing (in this regard we were working on radio transmission of data which would permit analysis by ground commanders before return of the photo mission).

The aircraft that seemed to meet all the requirements—the Rainbow—came out like this: weight 137,000 pounds; span 129 feet, 2 inches; length 98 feet, 9 inches; powered by four Pratt & Whitney R4360 Wasp Majors, each boosted by two large turbosuperchargers. The ideal power plant installation was a very ingenious design and deserves special comment. The engines were very tightly cowled, and air was forced to the front of each engine by a two-speed fan. To control the pressure drop a flush sliding ring was placed at the rear of the engine; the exit area thereby determined the drop in pressure over the engine. Thus the air at the front of the engine was compressed, the heat from the engine was picked up and spouted out the rear, and the result was a thrust gain rather than the usual cooling drag. The air for engine power, oil coolers, and intercoolers was ingested through openings in the leading edge of the wing between No. 1 and No. 2 engines and No. 3 and No. 4 engines. This saved much drag over projecting scoops and radiators.

Another bonus gained from the engine installation came from the unique positioning of the turbosuperchargers. The engine nacelles were quite long and extended well behind the main wing. The two turbos for each engine were installed in a reclining position in the rear of the nacelle with the discharge pointing rearward. The aft end of the nacelle made an ideal jet nozzle, and when the area was dimensionally correct we were provided with the equivalent of about 200 hp per engine in jet thrust—just about for free!

Familiarization with a project such as this presents no problem, since the crew has months or even years to follow engineering data as it is compiled, with results of wind tunnel tests and so on. By the time the first airplane is on the flight line, one's impressions are well formed; it is helpful if those of the flight crew are enthusiastic—as mine were. It is like a close relationship with an old friend which becomes even closer when you go for a ride in the air together.

For the first flight of the Rainbow I selected Oscar P. Hass as copilot and James J. Creamer as flight engineer. It might be interesting to note that Jim

Creamer was a nineteen-year-old usher at Radio City Music Hall just six years before being a flight engineer. At the time of our XR-12 flight he was one of the most skilled aircraftsmen I have known.

After the Rainbow had been in preflight for a short time we were asked for a flight schedule and were able to give a tentative one. It was quite a surprise to read in the company newspaper a few days later that the entire plant would be given time off on that tentative date to see the first flight ever of the Rainbow. And at 10 o'clock sharp! In spite of everything that day arrived with several unsolved mechanical problems; but the excellent training of the ground crews paid off, and with the entire factory watching we taxied out for takeoff at exactly 10 o'clock.

The first takeoff of the Rainbow was easy and smooth, with those 16,000 horses really hurling the lightly loaded airplane into the air. It was obvious that the acceleration was such that gear speed of about 250 mph would be exceeded before the gear was up, so the aircraft was pulled up into a pretty steep climb until the gear was up and locked. The flaps were about half down for takeoff, and when we attempted to raise them there was no response. We decided to try to get as much out of the flight as possible so checked control responses and approaches to stalls and the usual things; then we attempted to get the airplane into landing configuration with gear down and full flaps. When the flap switch was placed in the down position, there was no action from the flaps, but the cabin did fill with dense smoke. About then we felt it was time to get this thing back on the ground, which we did without further delay. With half flaps and light weight I think I made my best landing on that first attempt. We soon learned what our problem had been: the two electric motors activating the flaps had burned up. After replacement we had no more flap trouble.

The best way an old fighter pilot might explain what it is like to fly the Rainbow is to suggest that one take all the best flying fighters and lump the best of the best into one: there you have the Rainbow. This does not mean that there were no bugs; there were, and our job was to eliminate them.

Since the flying done on the XR-12 was totally of an experimental nature, it is a little difficult to follow the same descriptive format as for an established production aircraft. All flights were to obtain certain test in formation—best rate of climb and time to climb; and speed, power, and performance at all altitudes. Changes were made which resulted in better handling qualities; the result was an aircraft that had a well-balanced control force gradient, adequate response, and stability about all axes. Test data showed that best climb, glide, and landing speeds were in the conventional range for aircraft with comparable wing loadings.

During the flight test program a number of novel schemes were employed to get as much data per flight as possible. During the stability tests we placed a large tank in the front of the aircraft and one of equal size in the rear, connected by pipes and a water pump. We filled one tank with water and in flight could study longitudinal stability throughout the range of center of gravity by pumping the water in the quantities required for whatever CG was desired.

Engine and propeller deicing could be checked by a system for spraying water into the front of the engine; icing condition could be created by seeking a flight level where the desired temperature prevailed.

There was early concern that the extended Plexiglas nose would create visibility problems in rain and glare. To study these effects we mounted a nose section mock-up high on a truck; the crew and I spent a great deal of time on rainy nights chasing up and down runways under various types of lights, testing internal as well as external light effects. This proved valuable in pinpointing trouble areas before they came as a surprise under actual flight conditions.

One problem we were aware of was that the entry to the crew quarters was through a door in the rear. From there we had to detour around camera stations and various test installations to get forward. This was of some concern, since egress in an emergency might be difficult—although an Air Corps crew did successfully abandon one of the aircraft sometime later in the vicinity of Eglin Air Force Base, Florida.

The R-4360 Wasp Major engines were reliable and very easy to start. With external power plugged into the aircraft we usually started No. 2 engine first, then No. 1, followed by No. 3 and No. 4. This is standard practice for four-engine aircraft and gives some protection to ground crews. Because of false fire warnings we had to shut down and feather engines a number of times on takeoff. Since the engines were placed so far out on the wing, an outboard engine caused considerable but not objectionable yaw. Flight could be continued on any three engines from any point on the takeoff run on a 5,000-foot runway. Loss of either No. 2 or No. 3 engine was hardly noticeable.

On the early flights it was determined that the double-slotted flaps produced a great deal of drag at maximum deflection, and also that at less deflection the lift was not affected noticeably and the drag was greatly reduced; so we reduced the max flap down setting from about 55 degrees to about 45 degrees. At the 45-degree setting the approach and flare were very comfortable, and excessive power was not required to recover any loss of speed during approach.

Touchdown was smooth, and the adequate landing struts made the entire landing very soft. Aerodynamic calculations indicated a high stick force during the landing due to ground effect, but it was decided that the first flight would

---

Opposite page: The author awaits the all-clear signal.

The underside of a wing. Note the pressure-regulating rings.

be made and the ground effect investigated. The stick force buildup during flare and touchdown was negligible; but if the stick force was monitored continuously, the ground effect did become pronounced as speed was reduced. I have compared this observation with pilots of many different types of aircraft, and there is no question that there is this brief but rapid buildup of stick forces due to ground effect during the deceleration phase of landing. I have personally checked this out in the DC-4 and the B-29 as well as in the Rainbow.

As for control forces, they were adequate for the aircraft. An aircraft of this size has very long distances from control wheel to control surface, and there is a problem in reducing friction and drag around pulleys. This problem was met satisfactorily in the XR-12, and the final configuration was very satisfactory. Later large aircraft had controls that were hydraulically boosted, and any desired feel could be built in.

The XR-12 had one of the early propeller-reversing systems installed as a backup for an experimental magnesium casted brake system. This reversible feature saved the aircraft in a landing at Mitchell Field when the brake castings burst and brakes were lost completely.

The Rainbow had a complete flight engineer panel, and the instruments at the pilot crew stations were kept to a minimum. I developed a system whereby the engineer was used to the fullest possible extent. Most taxi operations were powered by the engineer, who was an indispensable crew member on this aircraft.

Because the Rainbow was so easy to fly, one felt perfectly at home with it after only four or five hours and a couple of landings. I had done the prototype tests of the P-47 Thunderbolt and remembered the early phenomenon of so-called freezing stick at high Mach number. One day we were doing some kind of test in the XR-12 that required stabilizing in level flight with METO (maximum except takeoff) power at 35,000 feet. When the test was almost complete I asked the copilot if he noticed something radically wrong. He checked his panel and consulted with the engineer, then informed me that everything was shipshape. I then pointed to the airspeed indicator; since he was also a Thunderbolt pilot, he immediately realized that we were in this big airplane exceeding in level flight the allowed diving speed of the Thunderbolt at that altitude. This does not mean that the Rainbow had a higher critical Mach number than the Thunderbolt, but with the power we carried to that altitude we could reach a speed in level flight that would be too close to trouble for the Thunderbolt—which would have to be in a dive to achieve the same speed.

It may be confusing that the Rainbow is referred to as both the XF-12 and the XR-12. The former designation was used for early photographic aircraft.

For the more sophisticated weapons systems the designation was changed to XR to indicate the broader concept. Some changes were made to convert the XR-12 to a transport plane, and we were able to guarantee a cruising speed of 450 mph for this version. Also the fact that the Rainbow would operate at 25,000 feet with any one engine out prompted one of the airlines to act to get the aircraft certified as a three-engine transport, so that a flight would not have to be aborted if one engine was feathered early in the flight.

Some of my remarks about the Rainbow may sound as if I were sold on it and just a little prejudiced. If so, I plead guilty as charged.

L. L. Brabham resigned from the Army Air Corps in 1940 to become a test pilot for Republic Aviation Corporation. He retired as vice-president of that organization in 1964 but still flies his Mooney Super 21 about 300 hours a year.

Index

Page numbers in italics indicate photographs.

Stackpole Military History Series

MESSERSCHMITTS OVER SICILY
DIARY OF A LUFTWAFFE FIGHTER COMMANDER
Johannes Steinhoff

Driven from their North African bases, the Luftwaffe
regrouped on Sicily in early summer 1943 as the Allies
prepared to invade the island. Despite crushing odds, the
pilots of the 77th Fighter Wing took to the skies and
attempted to ward off waves of Allied bombers and
fighters. Wing commander Johannes Steinhoff chronicles
those frantic months when the Luftwaffe fought to stay
alive and engaged in fierce aerial combat.

$17.95 • Paperback • 6 x 9 • 288 pages • 17 b/w photos

WWW.STACKPOLEBOOKS.COM
1-800-732-3669